Completed man[illegible]
during the long [illegible]
hours.

E M James JD PhD
Lansing MI

Practical Aspects of Rape Investigation

A Multidisciplinary Approach

PRACTICAL ASPECTS OF CRIMINAL AND FORENSIC INVESTIGATIONS

VERNON J. GEBERTH, BBA, MPS, FBINA *Series Editor*

Practical Homicide Investigation: Tactics, Procedures, and Forensic Techniques, Second Edition Vernon J. Geberth

The Counter-Terrorism Handbook: Tactics, Procedures, and Techniques Frank Bolz, Jr., Kenneth J. Dudonis, and David P. Schulz

Forensic Pathology Dominick J. Di Maio and Vincent J. M. Di Maio

Interpretation of Bloodstain Evidence at Crime Scenes William G. Eckert and Stuart H. James

Tire Imprint Evidence Peter McDonald

Practical Drug Enforcement: Procedures and Administration Michael D. Lyman

Practical Aspects of Rape Investigation: A Multidisciplinary Approach Robert R. Hazelwood and Ann Wolbert Burgess

The Sexual Exploitation of Children: A Practical Guide to Assessment, Investigation, and Intervention Seth L. Goldstein

Gunshot Wounds: Practical Aspects of Firearms, Ballistics, and Forensic Techniques Vincent J. M. Di Maio

Friction Ridge Skin: Comparison and Identification of Fingerprints James F. Cowger

Footwear Impression Evidence William J. Bodziak

Practical Fire and Arson Investigation John J. O'Connor

The Practical Methodology of Forensic Photography David R. Redsicker

Practical Aspects of Rape Investigation

A Multidisciplinary Approach

Edited by

Robert R. Hazelwood
Supervisory Special Agent
Federal Bureau of Investigation
Faculty Member
Behavioral Science Unit, FBI Academy

Ann Wolbert Burgess
van Ameringen Professor of Psychiatric Mental Health Nursing
University of Pennsylvania School of Nursing
Associate Director of Nursing Research
Boston Department of Health and Hospitals

Library of Congress Cataloging-in-Publication Data

Catalog record is available from the Library of Congress.

Direct all inquiries to CRC Press, Inc., 2000 Corporate Blvd., N. W., Boca Raton, Florida, 33431.

International Standard Book Number 0-8493-9509-7

Printed in the United States 7 8 9 0

Printed on acid-free paper

This book is dedicated to
the victims of rape.

Contents

Preface

Sexual crimes have shown a marked increase nationally over the past decade. In terms of reported rape cases, the FBI Uniform Crime Reports cite an increase from over 37,000 in 1970 to 87,340 in 1985. However, only slightly more than half (54%) of the reported rape cases in 1985 resulted in the arrest of a suspect. These figures are even more critical when one considers that less than half of all rapes believed to occur are reported to law enforcement agencies, and that the number of assailants arrested must be reduced even more to arrive at the number who are convicted of rape. Although it is not possible to determine if the apparent increase in rape is due to better reporting methods or to the sex offender who is not arrested or convicted repeating his behavior, the problem is now being addressed by all professions whose work brings them into contact with the victim or the offender.

Concurrent with the increasing numbers of rape victims has been a burgeoning of research into a multitude of factors interwoven with sexual violence and its aftermath. Substantial contributions have been made to advancing the state of knowledge for law enforcement agents, health professionals, and criminal justice staff. Although most people working with the problem of sexual crimes see either the victim or the offender, the investigator and prosecutor frequently encounter *both* victims and offenders. Thus, it becomes crucial that these two groups have the benefit of research results in the fields of victimology, criminology, behavioral sciences, forensic sciences, and criminal justice. Such information has the potential to impact substantially on the effectiveness of the investigative interview, the collection of forensic evidence, and the prosecution of cases.

The aim of this book is to present new and challenging directions for the investigation and prosecution of rape cases. A unique feature of the book is the incorporation of traditional police procedures in rape investigation with new and contemporary techniques developed during the past decade, such as criminal personality profiling.

The book is divided into four sections. Section I includes three chapters that provide a basis for examining some of people's thoughts about and reactions to the problem of rape. Myths and stereotypes surrounding rape are influential because they represent what people believe. In the first chapter, "Public Beliefs and Attitudes Concerning Rape," Ann Wolbert Burgess identifies the wide range of feelings and reactions that people experience when confronted with the topic of rape. These reactions are both immediate and subjective and have their origins in the past on the basis of personal experience or long-held societal beliefs and reactions to the subject of rape. The intent is for the reader to examine his or her subjective responses as a way to increase sensitivity to the nuances of this social problem. The second chapter, "The Victim's Perspective," by Ann Wolbert Burgess and Robert R. Hazelwood, describes a composite case and captures both the thoughts and reactions of the victim going through the assault and its distressing aftermath. Myths about the victim are interspersed with steps in the investigator's approach to interviewing the victim as a means of helping the officer understand the wide range of behaviors that occur when a rape is reported. Such understanding will benefit the victim in his or her recovery and the officer in his or her investigation. Chapter 3, "Police Attitudes and Beliefs Concerning Rape," by John C. LeDoux and Robert R. Hazelwood, reports the results of a national random-sample survey of over 2100 police officers. The survey concerned police officers' attitudes toward rape and how their attitudes affected the effectiveness of their work with rape victims, the suspect, and the criminal justice system in general.

Section II of the book is about the investigation of rape. Chapters 4 and 5, written by Dale M. Moreau, discuss the collection and presentation of physical and trace evidence from the victim, the offender, and the scene of the crime. Chapter 4 addresses concepts of physical evidence in rape investigations, while Chapter 5 sets forth major physical evidence to be sought in such investigations.

Criminal profiling is one of the most promising tools available to the investigator. It involves the gathering of information about offender behavior in a manner designed to focus the investigation and identify a subject quickly. Chapter 6, "Criminal Personality Profiling: An Overview," by Robert R. Hazelwood, Robert K. Ressler, Roger L. Depue, and John E. Douglas, traces the history of criminal personality profiling within the FBI Academy's Behavioral Science Unit and presents criteria both for preparing such profiles and for becoming a profiler. In Chapter

7, "The Behavioral-Oriented Interview of Rape Victims: The Key To Profiling," Robert R. Hazelwood and Ann Wolbert Burgess describe how to interview the victim to determine the verbal, physical, and sexual behavior exhibited by the offender during the commission of the crime. The purpose of such interviews is to elicit information from the victim that can be used in preparing a profile on the unidentified offender. In Chapter 8, "Analyzing the Rape and Profiling the Offender," Robert R. Hazelwood presents an initial categorization of rapists from a profiling standpoint. He then sets forth a detailed case history followed by an analysis of that case and the resultant profile.

Chapter 9, "Child Molesters—A Behavioral Analysis for Law Enforcement," by Kenneth V. Lanning, describes a typology of offenders who assault children. Designed for law enforcement investigators looking at child molesters, this typology includes incest offenders, pedophiles, and psychopathic character-disordered offenders. This carefully designed typology is derived from cases investigated and is presented from the law enforcement perspective.

Chapter 10, "Investigative Assessment," by Richard L. Ault, Jr., and Robert R. Hazelwood, sets forth the value of assessing an individual's strengths and weaknesses prior to interrogating that individual as a rape suspect. A list of questions is presented, as an appendix, to provide guidance for the gathering of information necessary for the assessment of an individual.

One of the thorniest problems in rape investigation is that of false allegations. An inherent conflict arises between the investigator's obligation to accept the victim's complaint as legitimate and his obligation to develop the facts of the case. In Chapter 11, "False Allegations," Charles P. McDowell and Neil S. Hibler present cases designed to assist investigators in distinguishing between legitimate and false rape allegations. A new syndrome is discussed for investigators to consider in identifying people who injure themselves and then report rape. Cases of false allegation span a long continuum from obscene telephone calls to the extreme of self-mutilation and/or amputation to substantiate a claim of rape.

In Chapter 12, "Rape Investigators: Vicarious Victims," James T. Reese places in perspective the stressful aspects of investigative work and recommends strategies for stress management as a means of coping with work.

Section III is on medical aspects of rape investigations. In Chapter 13, "Medical Exam in the Live Sexual Assault Victim,"' Joseph A. Zeccardi and Diane Dickerman orient the rape investigator to the conduct of a medical examination and the manner in which evidence should be collected. The rationale for, as well as the intricacies of, the medical examination is presented.

Section IV is on prosecution of rape cases. In Chapter 14, "Prosecuting Rape Cases: Trial Preparation and Trial Tactic Issues," William Heiman describes the standard processing of rape cases in the criminal justice system. Difficult cases discussed include identification issue cases, consent issue cases, and the unpopular cases. The use of expert testimony is also discussed. In Chapter 15, "Prosecuting Sexual Assault: The Use of Expert Testimony on Rape Trauma Syndrome," Eugene Borgida, Patricia Frazier, and Janet Swim present judicial decisions that highlight key issues in the prosecution of sexual assault cases. They also discuss current rape trauma syndrome cases in terms of the arguments made for and against their admissibility, address some of the particular objections that have been raised, and suggest some responses to those objections.

This book represents a major commitment from its authors to present the most current knowledge for the investigation and prosecution of rape cases. We wish to thank the many people who assisted in this endeavor.

Editorial Note

While it is recognized that males are also victims of rape, the gender descriptor *she* is primarily used in this text.

The male pronouns are also used at times when the female gender would be equally applicable. This is done in the interest of sentence structure and readability.

Acknowledgments

The editors wish to acknowledge the following individuals without whose efforts this book would not have been possible.

For their encouragement and support: Peggy Driver-Hazelwood, Allen Burgess, Assistant Director James D. McKenzie (FBI), Deputy Assistant Director James A. O'Connor (FBI), and Unit Chief Roger L. Depue (FBI).

Others deserving special thanks are Cynthia J. Lent, for her dedication and untiring editorial assistance; Leslie Daubenspeck, Jean Adams, and Sheena J. Hatch, for typing the manuscript; Mr. Charles Stanley, for his invaluable assistance in the preparation of Chapter 3; and Retired Supervisory Special Agent Howard D. Teten (FBI), for his insight and professional advice over the years.

A special word of thanks to Vernon Geberth, without whose assistance this book would not have been included in the Elsevier series.

About the Authors

Robert R. Hazelwood is a Supervisory Special Agent of the Federal Bureau of Investigation. He is a faculty member of the FBI Academy's Behavioral Science Unit and an adjunct faculty member of the University of Virginia. He received his undergraduate degree from Sam Houston State College and earned his master's degree from Nova University. Mr. Hazelwood also attended a one-year fellowship in forensic medicine at the Armed Forces Institute of Pathology. Prior to entering the FBI in 1971, he served 11 years in the U.S. Army's Military Police Corps, attaining the rank of Major. His works have been published by the *Journal of Police Science and Administration, Social Science and Medicine, American Registry of Pathology, Journal of Forensic Sciences, FBI Law Enforcement Bulletin,* and other professional journals. He coauthored the book *Autoerotic Fatalities* and has lectured extensively on criminal sexuality throughout the United States, Europe, Canada, and the Caribbean. He has been consulted by law enforcement officers throughout North America in the investigation of sexual assaults and homicides.

Ann Wolbert Burgess, R.N., D.N.Sc., F.A.A.N., is the van Ameringen Professor of Psychiatric Mental Health Nursing at the University of Pennsylvania School of Nursing and is associate director of nursing research of the Department of Health and Hospitals of Boston. She studied at Boston University and received the Doctor of Nursing Science in psychiatric-mental-health nursing at Boston University. She is co-principal investigator on a joint research project with the Behavioral Science Unit of the FBI Academy studying sexual-homicide crime scenes and patterns of behavior, funded by the National Institute of

Justice. Dr. Burgess has held faculty appointments at Boston College and Boston University. She has written textbooks in the field of nursing and crisis intervention; coauthored articles in the field of victimology; and coauthored the clinical textbook *Sexual Assaults of Children and Adolescents*.

Richard L. Ault, Jr., Ph.D., served four years in the U.S. Marine Corps. He received his B.S. degree in psychology from Huntington College in Montgomery, Alabama; his M.A. in counseling psychology from the University of Alabama; and his Ph.D. in counseling and development from the American University, Washington, D.C. Dr. Ault has also studied at George Washington University, Washington, D.C., and Sophia University, Tokyo, Japan. Prior to joining the FBI, Dr. Ault worked briefly in the federal prison system as a test administrator for prisoner classification. He has been assigned to the FBI Academy at Quantico, Virginia, since 1975. Dr. Ault's assignment at the FBI Academy encompasses the teaching of criminal psychology, applied criminology, hostage negotiation, and research methodology. Dr. Ault is an adjunct faculty member of the University of Virginia.

Eugene Borgida is an Associate Professor of Psychology and Adjunct Professor of Law at the University of Minnesota. Much of his research over the past 10 years has concerned the psychology of legal evidence.

Roger L. Depue, Ph.D., was appointed a Special Agent with the Federal Bureau of Investigation in 1968. He has been assigned to the New Orleans, Louisiana, and the Washington, D.C., Field Offices. In 1974, he was assigned as a Supervisory Special Agent to the Behavioral Science Unit of the FBI Academy at Quantico, Virginia. Since 1980, Dr. Depue has served as Chief of Behavioral Sciences, and in 1984, he was appointed as the administrator of the FBI National Center for the Analysis of Violent Crime (NCAVC). Special Agent Depue holds a bachelor of science degree in psychology from Central Michigan University and a master of science degree in the administration of justice and a Ph.D. in counseling and development from American University. Dr. Depue is an adjunct faculty member in psychology and sociology at the University of Virginia. Prior to entering on duty as a Special Agent with the FBI, Dr. Depue was employed on the local level of the criminal justice system as a county juvenile officer for the Clare County, Michigan, Juvenile Court, and served as a police officer and as Chief of Police in the city of Clare, Michigan.

Diane E. Dickerman, M.D., was born in 1954 in Philadelphia. She received a bachelor of science degree from Temple University School of

Pharmacy, Magna Cum Laude, in 1976, and her M.D. from Hahnemann Medical College in 1983. She completed her residency training in emergency medicine at Thomas Jefferson University Hospital in June 1986 and plans to practice Emergency Medicine in the Philadelphia area.

John E. Douglas entered the FBI in 1970 following four years' service in the U.S. Air Force. He is a graduate of the University of Wisconsin where he earned his master's degree in educational psychology. He is currently working toward a Ph.D. in adult education at Nova University. Mr. Douglas is a Supervisory Special Agent and faculty member of the FBI Academy's Behavioral Science Unit and an adjunct faculty member of the University of Virginia. He manages the FBI Criminal Personality Profiling and Consultation Program and has participated in the crime analysis of hundreds of rapes, homicides, kidnappings, arsons, and bombing matters.

Patricia Frazier is a doctoral student in the Counseling Psychology Program at the University of Minnesota and a psychology intern at the Veterans Administration Hospital in Minneapolis. Her research focuses on the psychological and legal aspects of rape trauma syndrome.

William Heiman, Esq., graduated from the Wharton School of the University of Pennsylvania in 1964 and Temple University School of Law in 1967. He was an assistant district attorney in the Philadelphia District Attorney's Office from 1972 to 1985. He served as Chief of the Rape and Child Abuse Unit from 1978 to 1984. In 1981, he received the Program of Excellence Award from the National Organization of Victim Assistance, recognizing the Philadelphia District Attorney's Rape Unit as the most outstanding unit of its type in the country. Mr. Heiman is author of several articles on rape prosecution issues and is currently a member of the law firm of Sacks, Basch, Brodie and Sacks in Philadelphia.

Neil S. Hibler, Ph.D., is the Command Clinical Psychologist and Chief of the Behavioral Sciences Division, Directorate of Investigation Support, Headquarters, U.S. Air Force Office of Special Investigations, Washington, D.C. Before becoming the first mental health professional to work exclusively with a federal investigative agency, he was a Special Agent with the USAF Office of Special Investigations and later an instructor at the USAF Special Investigations Academy. His professional training includes two master's degrees and a doctorate in clinical and community psychology from the University of South Florida. Dr. Hibler is a Diplomate in Clinical Psychology, American Board of Professional Psychology.

Kenneth V. Lanning is a Supervisory Special Agent assigned to the Behavioral Science Unit at the FBI Academy in Quantico, Virginia. He has made presentations before the National Conference on Sexual Victimization of Children, the National Conference on Child Abuse and Neglect, and the American Orthopsychiatric Association. He has testified before the U.S. Attorney General's Task Force on Family Violence, the President's Task Force on Victims of Crime, and the U.S. Attorney General's Commission on Pornography. He has also testified before the U.S. Senate and the U.S. House of Representatives and as an expert witness in state and federal courts. Mr. Lanning has lectured before and trained thousands of police officers and criminal justice professionals.

John C. LeDoux, Ph.D., was appointed a Special Agent of the Federal Bureau of Investigation in 1971. He is currently assigned as the Program Manager of Computer Based Training for the Training Division of the FBI. He has published research in the areas of higher education for law enforcement, police attitudes toward rape, and computer-based training. He holds a doctorate in adult and vocational education from Auburn University and has been selected for inclusion in the 1986 edition of the Marquis *Who's Who in the South and Southwest.*

Charles P. McDowell, Ph.D., is the Command Crime Advisor and Special Assistant to the Director of Fraud and Criminal Investigations, Headquarters, U.S. Air Force Office of Special Investigations, Washington, D.C. His duties include original research on crime-related issues as well as oversight for all major investigations involving crimes against the person. Prior to becoming a civilian Special Agent, Dr. McDowell held a variety of academic positions. He received his M.P.A. degree from the City University of New York, his M.L.S. from the University of North Carolina at Greensboro, and his Ph.D. from North Texas State University. Dr. McDowell is the author of four books and numerous articles in the professional literature.

Dale M. Moreau, Supervisory Special Agent, entered the Federal Bureau of Investigation in 1971 and served as a Fingerprint Technician and as a Physical Science Technician in the Laboratory Division. He has also served as a field investigator in three FBI field offices. In 1975, he was transferred to the FBI Laboratory as an examiner in the Document Section. In 1979, he was transferred to the Forensic Science Training Unit located at the FBI Academy, Quantico, Virginia. Since then, Mr. Moreau has had the responsibility of providing instruction in physical evidence matters to personnel at all levels of law enforcement. Mr. Moreau has been tasked with providing technical assistance to the FBI and other law enforcement agencies regarding crime-scene searches and physical evidence recovery techniques. In 1985, he was designated to serve as a special advisor on a national advisory committee established to study protocols of investigation in sexual assault cases. This committee was created as a result of a U.S. Department of Justice grant administered by the Illinois Attorney General's Office. Mr. Moreau has a B.A. degree from Louisiana State University, Baton Rouge, Louisiana, and a M.A. degree from George Washington University, Washington, D.C. He maintains membership in professional forensic science organizations and is an adjunct faculty member of the University of Virginia.

James T. Reese, Ph.D., has been a member of the Federal Bureau of Investigation since 1971, and is currently assigned as a Supervisory Special Agent and faculty member of the FBI Academy's Behavioral Science Unit. He holds a B.A. and an M.S. and received his Ph.D. from American University, Washington, D.C. Dr. Reese managed the pilot program for psychological services within the FBI and is responsible for FBI research and training in law enforcement stress. As an adjunct faculty member of the University of Virginia, he teaches advanced and applied criminology, police psychology, and stress management courses. Dr. Reese was an exchange faculty member of the Police Staff College, Bramshill, England, and is on numerous editorial and advisory committees. He is co-editor of a book entitled *Psychological Services for Law Enforcement* and is currently co-editing three other books on police psychology.

Robert K. Ressler has been a Supervisory Special Agent with the Federal Bureau of Investigation for 17 years and has served as an instructor and criminologist in the FBI Academy's Behavioral Science Unit. He also holds adjunct faculty status with the University of Virginia and is a Senior Research Fellow with the University of Pennsylvania. Mr. Ressler earned his M.S. degree in 1968 from Michigan State University. Prior to entering the FBI, he served ten years with the U.S. Army as a Military Police and Criminal Investigation Officer, and currently holds the rank of Colonel in the U.S. Army Reserve. In addition to his faculty status at the FBI Academy, Mr. Ressler is the manager of the Bureau's Violent Criminal Apprehension Program (VICAP). In this capacity, he has directed research in the area of violent crime, serial and sexual murder, and criminal personality profiling. Results of this research have been published in the *American Journal of Psychiatry*, the *FBI Law Enforcement Bulletin*, and other professional journals. He has taught law enforcement officers and served as a consultant to police agencies in the U.S. and abroad.

Janet Swim is a doctoral student in the social psychology program at the University of Minnesota and an instructor on the faculty of Carleton College in Northfield, Minnesota. Her research interests are in applied social psychology, with particular emphasis on women's issues and legal psychology.

Joseph A. Zeccardi, M.D., earned his B.S. degree from Villanova University in 1961 and his M.D. degree from Temple Medical College in 1965. Following a rotating internship at Mount Zion Hospital in San Francisco, he completed pediatric residency training at St. Christopher's Hospital in Philadelphia in 1968. After two years as a Lieutenant Commander in the Navy assigned as a pediatrician in Morocco, he worked as a pediatrician with the Kaiser Permanente Group in Hayward, California. He also served as Director of the Children and Youth Program in Thomas Jefferson University's Pediatric Department and Director of the Emergency Department at Thomas Jefferson University Hospital. Since 1976, Dr. Zeccardi has been the Director of the Sexual Assault Unit at Thomas Jefferson.

I

ATTITUDES AND BELIEFS ABOUT RAPE

1 Public Beliefs and Attitudes Concerning Rape

ANN WOLBERT BURGESS

> I prefer five clean murders to one rape case. The more you investigate and get into it, the stickier it gets. . . . Murder I can understand, but I can't really understand rape.
>
> **—Detective**

Relatively few problems are as emotionally entangling and as scientifically elusive as that of rape. Society's perception of rape is strongly influenced by a puzzling mixture of prejudice, credence, and voyeuristic curiosity. Perhaps reactions stem from acquired attitudes and perhaps reactions stir deep-seated aggressive or defensive impulses in people; perhaps the myths and stereotypes surrounding rape linger because they represent what people believe.

People's reactions to the subject of rape can range from the immediate, intuitive or "gut" response to the distress of victims to subjective reactions that are based on stereotypes and myths.

Both intuitive and subjective reactions impact on the rape victim. She suffers not only from the incident itself—the painful, violent penetration of her body—but also from the reactions of people, especially the negative subjective reactions based on the myths and stereotypes that surround the subject of rape.

Police officers working with rape victims should be aware of these two types of reactions, since they will emerge from the network of people who deal with the victim officially—police officers, detectives, nurses, physicians, lawyers, judges, counselors, and crisis workers. They are found in the police officer who initially investigates the rape case, the staff nurses who first talk with the victim in the emergency ward, the physician who examines the victim, and the district attorney who prosecutes the case. All people who are involved in a rape investigation and want to help the rape victim must come to terms with these reactions and emotions within themselves if they are to function effectively and be most helpful to the victim.

In this chapter, I will describe the themes that were expressed again and again by people I met with as I examined rape cases, counseled rape victims, and accompanied them through the medical and court systems. The remarks were made spontaneously to me, in private or in a public setting, during the course of my work. They came from people of all walks of life. They are presented here in order to help the police officer understand his or her own attitudes, and those of society, that may reflect on the victim. Also these statements may serve as the basis for discussions, where officers, by sharing their feelings with colleagues, might come to terms with their emotions and subjective reactions and thus be better able to provide emotional support for the victim.

Intuitive Reactions to Rape Victims

Distress

1. I have five daughters and I feel it would be better for them to fight a rapist, even if this provoked him to kill them. If you live, you will look back on the rape as a bad memory. If you are dead you have nothing to worry about.

   —Detective

2. NURSE: I'm shaken.
   SERGEANT: God help us.
   NURSE: He [sergeant] needs the Valium as well as the mother.

   —Hospital staff and police

3. Doesn't it just make you sick?

   —Pediatrician

4. There are rape cases that are distressing and it disturbs your mind. You start thinking this could happen to your family—like when you see a young kid raped.

   —Gynecologist

5. I find some cases very depressing.

   —Physician

6. Don't you find this work very depressing?

   —Nurse; police officer; lawyer

7. What a way to have to make a living.

   —Pediatrician

The police and the hospital emergency service staff are two professional groups that see the rape victim within hours of the attack. They routinely see all victims and often their immediate reactions are reactions of distress.

Police must face many unpleasant and difficult situations as part of their daily work. Although they might feel depressed when dealing with a rape victim for many reasons, one of the most common is a feeling of helplessness—of not knowing what to do to relieve the distress of a victim. Knowledge of crisis intervention skills, however, can diminish this feeling considerably. In the first quote (1), the officer believed that death was preferable to living with the memory of the rape. Expressing such an opinion to the victim could only have a negative effect on her recovery. Officers and front-line crisis intervenors have considerable influence on the psychological state of the victim and must use their knowledge and skills to positively assist the recovery process.

Involvement

8. I don't get involved in these cases. I just bring the girl to the hospital, and that's it. You'd go soft if you really thought about the rape cases you see every night.

—Police officer

9. I don't have time to listen to their stories.

—Nurse

10. I am calling about a woman who just came to our clinic and said she was raped. I thought you would know what to do.

—Mental health worker

People who work with rape victims admit they have difficulties thinking about the problem, thus implying that it is overwhelming. Professionals might say they are too busy to think about it or to listen to the victim. Or they may not want to deal with the victim and seek advice from others.

The more aware officers become of their own feelings and the causes for them, the better able they are to control them. For example, what if a victim frustrates the officer working with her? If the officer acts on these feelings, he might terminate the meeting or allow the victim to know his feelings, thus delaying the interview and possibly losing valuable time and information. If the officer can understand his own feelings and reactions, however, he can keep himself from overinvolvement, overreaction, and overcompensation.

Avoidance and Silence

11. Rape cases are closed-mouth affairs. No one likes them. Police develop certain attitudes toward them.
—Police officer

12. There is rape and there is rape. I'd rather have a robbery or murder case than these rape cases.
—Assistant district attorney

13. Most hospitals in this city won't touch a rape case because of the legal implications.
—Social worker

Sexuality is not generally discussed openly in American society. Criminal sexuality is even less openly discussed, and it is apparent that by not addressing the topic, society in general and the criminal justice system in particular deny the extent of the problem and insulate themselves from its realities. Indeed, those who force our attention to the subject are often deemed to be strange or involved in "kinky work."

Rape has been treated through history with silence. People find it difficult to talk about, and the police and legal system find it equally difficult to deal with. Professionals often avoid rape cases because of the inconvenience of the legal process.

Sympathy for the Victim

14. When you see a victim like that who has evidence of trauma and you know she has been emotionally raped and sexually assaulted and all, well, your heart just goes out to her.
—Gynecologist

15. I remember one 60-year-old woman who was stabbed and raped and unnatural acts performed on her. I felt so depressed.
—Gynecologist

16. I'm not a father, but with a minor child, I can understand how upset you [mother] must be.
—Assistant district attorney

The severely bruised (14), the old (15), and the young (16) victims of rape receive considerable sympathy from professionals. Perhaps in such cases the violence and nonsexual aspect of rape may be seen most clearly.

Anger and Revenge

17. Only one thing to do with these guys—cut it off.
—Police officer

18. Thank God, she is OK. If she wasn't, I'd want him castrated.
—Victim's father

19. The man is a degenerate. He should be put away.
—Pharmacist

20. When I'm called on a rape case, I am angry; not at the patient, but at the guy.
—Gynecologist

21. I'd go out and get the bastards myself if anything happened to my daughters.
—Gynecologist

The biblical solution of an "eye for an eye" is offered by some people as a method to compensate the victim for the trauma she had to suffer (17, 18). In fact, the earliest beginnings of social order were based on a primitive system of retaliatory force—*lex talionis*. Other people believe the assailant should be sent to jail, given psychiatric treatment, or sentenced to death. Others state how they personally would deal with the assailant.

Anger at the System

22. I have heard the police treat you terribly. I wouldn't want to be questioned by them.
—College student

23. I had a friend who had to sit and wait for hours at the hospital, and then they just rushed her through.
—College student

24. If guys were hitchhiking and got beaten up by four girls, would they blame the guys? Hell, no. The newspapers play that up.
—Secretary

25. We break our necks to get these guys to court, and then the door just opens and they walk right back on the street.
—Police officer

Many people vent their angry feelings against police and medical and legal personnel, displacing frustration they feel for the victim onto those they believe can influence the system.

Quite often the victim displaces her anger and frustration from the rapist, who is no longer there, to the responding police. In one case, a woman phoned the police to advise them that a man was attempting to enter her residence, she kept her phone off the hook, and the entire rape was recorded. Following the assault, she returned to the phone and hysterically berated the police officer on the line. When an officer arrived at her residence shortly thereafter, the victim profanely attacked him for not getting there in time to protect her.

The police (22) and hospital (23) receive many unfavorable comments about the way they treat victims: The courts do not strive to protect the victim from added psychological insult, and the news media (24) very often present a biased opinion. One part of the system may even blame other parts, as when police express their frustration with the courts (25).

Besides the immediate and intuitive reactions that people express in terms of positive feelings for the victim, they also express ambivalent and negative feelings and reactions.

Voyeurism

26. Oh, goodie, I get to listen.
—Nurse

27. Is that the little girl who. . . .
—Male mental health worker

28. She really has lived! (referring to the victim's age and sexual history)
—Nurse

29. I think it is exhibitionistic to talk about rape.
—Victim's mother

Something about rape seems to fascinate people. Some express their interest by exhibiting curiosity about the victim and the circumstances of the rape. Others may attempt to hide their fascination by indicating disapproval of discussing such a topic or by classifying any such discussion as exhibitionistic.

Even police are not immune to this somewhat discomfiting interest in sexual assaults. Officers investigating such cases will attest to the fact that uninvolved officers may be voyeuristic about rape. While verbally expressing anger, rage, and desire for amputatory revenge, they pore over the victim's statement.

Frustration

30. I wish I had the bruises from the previous victim and the body of the other victim and then this case would really be strong.
—Prosecutor

31. Some women come in with a very defensive position which is almost belligerent. I had to get over that prejudice to be able to help them.

There are two types: the upset ones and the defensive ones.
—Gynecologist

Police, medical, and legal professionals all admit to experiencing frustrations and difficulties in their work with rape victims. A district attorney prepares trial strategies designed to make the case appear "strong." A physician may analyze the different personality styles of victims so he may relate more effectively to them. A police officer attempts to prepare the victim for the forthcoming attack on her reputation.

The Ideal Rape Victim: An Image

Police may have in mind an image of the "ideal" rape victim and the "ideal" rape case, often based on personal beliefs. By recording all comments made by police in a recent study (Holmstrom and Burgess, 1983), four types of criteria were identified by which police officers judge a rape case.

First, police look at the quality and consistency of the information they have obtained. To be strong, the case cannot rest on the victim's statement alone; it must be corroborated by other evidence. Further, all information must be consistent. Describing a strong case, officers will say, "Everything fits together so well." Conversely, describing a weak case, officers say, "She used a fake name. She's a runaway. . . . Everything she said was a bunch of lies." Police also like to have witnesses—especially police witnesses—to the crime. In one case, the officers arrived while the assailant was still at the scene and were so enthusiastic they said, "We'll testify even if the girl doesn't." Police hope the victim can provide a good description of the assailant or of his belongings, such as his car. Officers look for corroborating medical evidence such as clinical evidence of intercourse or physical injuries. Police are most impressed with a consistent and unchanging story.

Second, police officers look at the personality of the victim—her behavior and her moral character. In a strong case, the victim is forced to accompany the assailant; in a weak one, she accompanies him willingly or asks him to accompany her. As one officer said, "She won't have much of a chance in court. She invited him over."

Third, police look at the relationship between victim and offender. In a strong case, the assailant is a stranger. Ages of victim and offender are also important and police pursue a case more enthusiastically if an age difference exists.

Fourth, police look at characteristics of the offender. Nothing makes them more enthusiastic about a case than to find out the assailant has other charges against him or has a prison record.

Subjective Reactions Based on Myths and Stereotypes

Subjective feelings are unique reactions having their origins in past personal experience or long-held societal beliefs and reactions to the subject of rape. For example, a police officer may suspect that every rape victim is making a false accusation because he was warned of "such women" early in his career or has experienced one or more false complaints. One officer reported that he was ridiculed by fellow officers for his sensitivity to the plight of rape victims and accused of being more of a counselor than a police officer. When he accepted and actively pursued a complaint of rape, only to determine it was false, he felt he had been "burned" and vowed it wouldn't happen again. The police officer might then respond to every victim as if she were falsely accusing a man and not rely on his immediate, nonbiased, intuitive reaction. Or a hospital staff nurse may think the victim is lying because she once heard a supervisor state that "half of the rape victims make up their stories." Or a prosecutor may say, "This wasn't like some rapes where I grew up . . . with the women really upset afterwards."

The belief system in our society does not discourage the commission of rape. Victims have difficulty convincing others that they were victimized. Not only are police, hospital personnel, prosecutors, judges, and jurors skeptical, but in some cases, so are husbands, partners, and family members. The general public often has an image of rape that only recognizes scenarios that fit within certain parameters (Holmstrom and Burgess, 1983).

Several studies indicate how stereotypes and beliefs operate in society. Martha Burt's work on "rape culture," for example, examines whether people in the general population believe such myths as "Only bad girls get raped," "Any healthy woman can resist a rapist if she really wants to," and "Rapists are sex-starved, insane, or both." Her data were obtained by interviewing a random sample of 598 adults in Minnesota. The results show that many people do believe many of the rape myths. Moreover, their attitudes toward rape are strongly associated with other attitudes; among these, the person's acceptance of interpersonal violence is found to be the strongest attitudinal predictor of his/her acceptance of rape myths (Burt, 1980).

Another group study (Scully and Marolla, 1982) concentrated on convicted rapists. The investigators divided a sample of convicted rapists into those who admitted the rape and those who denied it. Those who denied the rape described the victim in a way that made their own behavior seem more justified or appropriate. For example, one denier said of his victim, "She semi-struggled but deep down inside I think she felt it was a fantasy come true." The important observation made by Scully and Marolla is that these rapists do not invent their rationalizations. Rather, they draw their vocabulary from cultural or social myths reflecting ideas they have reason to believe others will find acceptable. "Our culture seems in many ways to see forced sex as acceptable" (Holmstrom and Burgess, 1983).

It is no myth that in our society males have more power and status than females, both in the area of interpersonal relations and in our structural systems (e.g., law, politics, education). It has been suggested that men's possession of (and in some cases, desire for) greater power contributes to the rape of women. It is this power differential that prompted Susan Brownmiller, the widely quoted feminist journalist, to say:

> Man's discovery that his genitalia could serve as a weapon to generate fear must rank as one of the most important discoveries of prehistoric times. . . . From prehistoric times to the present, I believe, rape has played a conscious process of intimidation by which all men keep all women in a state of fear. (Brownmiller, 1975, p. 5)

Brownmiller has been criticized for her interpretation, but leaving aside the issue of whether the process is conscious, Holmstrom and Burgess (1983) believe there is considerable insight in the statement and suggest that Brownmiller might have been more accurate had she said instead that rape is one way in many (but not all) societies that men as a class oppress and control women as a class. In our society, for example, statistics on reported rapes versus convictions for rape suggest men as a class wield power over women as a class by the threat and fear of the act of rape. Of course, many individual men do not identify with or sympathize with notions that rape is desirable, just as many individual men do not identify with various other traditionally masculine themes. However, the fact remains that "macho" values have become institutionalized. The criminal justice system, for example, is masculine in structure, ideologically and socially, and rape victims do not fare well in it. This bias is typical of the institutionalized handicaps that women have in our society (Holmstrom and Burgess, 1983). However, as LeDoux and Hazelwood report in Chapter 3, police attitudes about the crime of rape and its victim are much less negative than has been reported in the anecdotal literature.

Much attention has been given to the changing role of women in our society in areas such as equality in employment and in the family. Much less attention has been given to the fundamental way in which the rights of women are violated through sexual assault. As not much progress has been made in changing the social myths that depict women in subservient roles, subjective reactions to all elements of a rape remain current.

Struggle and Force as Elements of Rape

Although force and penetration of the body are key elements in the definition of rape, there is the myth that a woman cannot be raped against her will. The following statements reflect this belief:

> It's not really possible to rape a woman unless she is willing—physiologically possible, I mean—is it?
> **—Psychiatrist**

> You can't put a peg in a moving hole.
> **—Businessman**

Sometimes the comment is made that women provoke rape:

> I don't think rape is a one-way thing; the woman provokes it.
> **—Victim's mother**

> In most of these cases, the woman is just asking for it.
> **—Lawyer**

Rape is not perceived by the public to be the result of a society that defines women as the appropriate objects of male violence. Rather, our society is more likely to believe that the victim provoked the crime. One police officer, learning of my interest in the emotional problems after rape, said, "This girl won't have any problems. . . . It's not right for a girl to go into a stranger's apartment, drink beer, and then be upset when the guy makes advances."

Why should the rape victim be expected to struggle? She has been socialized against aggressiveness and does not know how to fight successfully against a male. In normal relationships she is often expected to be the passive and submissive sexual partner. The irony is that when confronted with a rapist who is physically stronger and may be armed, she is suddenly expected to struggle, fight, and resist.

Reporting the Rape

Societal expectations concerning reporting a rape are contradictory. One view is that if a woman is raped, she should be too upset and ashamed to report it; the other is that if a woman is raped she should be so upset that she *will* report it. Both expectations exist simultaneously, but it is the latter one that is written into law. This legal principle was researched and reported by Brownmiller to have precedent in the 13th century, when (according to Henry of Bratton [Bracton], a 13th-century authority on Saxon times), the procedure a raped virgin was to follow went like this:

> She must go at once and while the deed is newly done, with the hue and cry, to the neighboring townships and show the injury done to her to men of good repute, the blood and her clothing stained with blood and her torn garments. (Brownmiller, 1975, p. 17)

If the accused man protests his innocence, the raped virgin must then have her body examined by four law-abiding women sworn to tell the truth as to whether she was defiled or still a virgin (Brownmiller, 1975). In modern parlance, she had to "make a fresh complaint." The assumption is that if she really has been raped, she will make it known to others immediately. Today the same interest in the state of the hymen remains in place, although a hospital staff conducts the physical examination.

Blaming the Victim

It is well known that the main strategy of defense lawyers is to blame the victim, but society in general is often equally quick to find the victim at fault. According to Bracton, the man accused of rape in the 13th century had several possible defenses.

Prior Sexual Relationship

This defense states that the accused man had the woman as his concubine before the date of the alleged rape. This defense is still viable in court today and is quickly used when such a relationship existed.

The Act Was Not against the Victim's Will

"She was defiled with her consent." Defense lawyers attempt to broach the issue of consent in a variety of ways, using anything they can about the victim's behavior, emotional state, or character that makes her consent seem plausible. Often, the defense trades on current normative expectations about sex roles. They know that anything the female does that deviates from the norm of "appropriate female behavior" can be used to attack her in court. Certain stereotypes can be used against the victim to imply consent.

> But don't a lot of women ask for it, I mean, they take risks going out in certain areas.
>
> **—Secretary**

> She was hitchhiking. She said "Next time I'll know better." She *should* have known better *before*.
>
> **—Nurse**

> Just look how girls are dressed these days.
>
> **—Businessman**

> I didn't want the victim to go home. We had some indecisive doctors on duty that night. No one would take a stand. I got a psychiatric consult. She [the psychiatrist] said, "She sounds like she asked for it. I don't know what you want me to do."
>
> **—Nurse**

> After 6 years on the force, I don't believe any of them.
>
> **—Detective**

> Just had a case of a girl hitchhiking and the guy raped her. Most officers are not sympathetic. Many feel there is more behind the story than the woman tells.
>
> **—Police officer**

Suspicions about women, their motives, and their truthfulness are realities that the victim faces when telling her "story" to the officer or nurse.

Woman as Fickle and Full of Spite

Another stereotype is that the feminine character is especially filled with malice. Women are seen as fickle and as seeking revenge on past lovers. This stereotype is used against the rape victim, and is especially effective when the assailant is known to her, as with a former boyfriend.

> A lot of rape cases are for spite; the woman is just getting back at the guy.
>
> **—Policeman**

Good Girls/Bad Girls

Individual women are seldom thought of as having integrated personalities that encompass both maternal love and erotic desires. Instead, they are categorized into one-dimensional types. They are maternal or they are sexy. They are good or they are bad. They are madonnas or they are whores. The split view of woman has been noted by many writers. The historian Vern Bullough (1974), discussing the formation of Western attitudes, describes the "two faces of woman"—the dutiful housewife and loving mother on one hand; the erotic lover and temptress of man on the other. Chafetz (1974), a sociologist, has reported on a study of the words people think most Americans use to describe masculinity and femininity. "A basic dualism is . . . displayed toward the female, who is simultaneously held to be 'sexually passive, uninterested' (the Virgin Mary image),and 'seductive, flirtatious' (the wicked Eve tempting poor innocent Adam). This theme runs throughout the history of Western civilization and our mores concerning 'good' and 'bad' females have no parallels for males."

A Victorian belief is that good girls don't get raped and bad girls should not complain.

Sometimes people make statements that refer to the game of rape and who wins. Sometimes people infer prostitution rather than victimization and some statements refer to the myth that women secretly wish to be raped.

> They ought to reward the bastard.
>
> **—Defense lawyer**

> Who are you interested in: the victim or the victor?
>
> **—College professor**

> She is very ambivalent since the judge found no probable cause for the rape. She might file a civil suit. If so, she'd end up getting paid after all.
>
> **—Victim's psychiatrist**

> Most men think the women enjoy being raped.
>
> **—Female police officer**

> She is a known prostitute and junkie. She stated she took drugs with her consent prior to the experience. She didn't struggle. She knew the men and the women involved. Her facts kept on changing.
>
> **—Detective**

The Female under Surveillance

Females in our society are more tightly restricted in their sexual activities than are males. Their sexual behavior is more subject to surveillance. Before marriage, they are expected to abstain from sex. After marriage, they are to be the sexual property of their husbands. Even though in practice women have premarital or extramarital sex, the norm still exists that they should not. This norm is used against them in rape cases. It is assumed that the female's sexual behavior, depending on her age, is under the surveillance of her parents or her husband and, more generally, of the community. Thus, the argument may be made that if a women was raped, it must have been because she consented to sex that she was not supposed to have. She got caught and now she wants to get back in the good graces of whoever has her under surveillance. A variation on this theme may be that she was out later than she was supposed to be, got caught, and needed an excuse for her tardiness.

Disputing That Sex Occurred

Another common stereotype is that females fantasize rape, and make up stories that sex occurred when, in fact, nothing happened. In other cases, women are thought to fabricate the sexual activity, not as part of a fantasy life, but out of spite. Thus another way to blame the victim is to say that she invented all the sexual activity. As one attorney said:

> I'm 99% sure my client never committed it. I hear the victim has deep sexual fantasies. What is your professional opinion on that?
>
> **—Public defender**

It is to be noted that while such situations do occur, they are atypical and reflect an emotional problem that needs to be addressed (see Chapter 11).

Emotionality of Females

Females are assumed to be "more emotional" than males. The expectation is that if a women is raped she will get hysterical during the event and she will be visibly upset afterwards. If she is able to "retain her cool," people assume that "nothing happened"—that she was not raped. In actuality, data show that many victims, through a conscious act of will, do retain control over their emotions in order to survive the assault, and that even afterwards, they may present themselves to others in a composed manner.

The concept of the emotional female puts rape victims in a double bind. If women live up to the expectation and become so upset during the rape that they cannot remember details, they are blamed for not being able to testify about the assault, or some other reason is advanced for their being upset. If, however, they retain their cool and remember details, it is assumed that nothing happened.

Rape Is a Way of Life

Some people feel that rape is different to some women, some ethnic groups, or some cultures. The following statements attest to this:

> For this victim, rape is a way of life. I don't think these women react to rape as we would.
>
> **—Social worker**

> There is the South Boston rape. That is where a young girl is a junkie who goes around to bars to gather contacts, and then she gets her head beat in and she comes to the hospital. This rape represents a special kind of case we get here in Roxbury. That's why I object to these lawyers from the public defenders and their arguments. Fear and intimidation were part of the rape.
>
> **—Assistant district attorney**

Insulting the Victim

As if the original rape were not distressing enough, at court the woman again must submit to direct and indirect insults while she must remain silent. In the following statements, a defense lawyer presents his opinion of the victim and a judge explicitly states his opinion of the victim.

> "Your honor, this young lady is obviously a woman of the world."
> The judge interrupted angrily and said, "I don't know what you mean by that phrase."
> The defense lawyer, grinning, said, "Well, your honor, I didn't mean it the way you probably thought I did."
> The judge replied, "What do you know about the way I think?"
> The defense lawyer said, "I apologize, your honor. Strike that from the record."

In some cases the judge takes a firm stand in that such statements are not allowed to be passed over. However, even if the words are stricken from the record, they have registered with the jury. In another case, the judge himself insults the victim.

> The judge, in a matter-of-fact tone of voice which all people in the courtroom could hear, gave his succinct summary of the case. "She is an alcoholic. She is no good. But you have no right to rape a drunk either."

Summary

In summary, perhaps there is a continuum relationship to male sexuality as is being proposed by sociologists. Perhaps there is a relationship between rape and women's role in society. Perhaps research will provide some answers. But most importantly, perhaps the human dimension may be brought into sharper focus for rape victims, and police officers, hospital staff personnel, and court officials will be sensitized to the plight of the victims. In order to accomplish such a goal, police officers need to understand their intuitive and subjective responses to rape and to be aware of how strongly held beliefs and stereotypes influence their responses.

References

Brownmiller, Susan. *Against Our Will: Men, Women and Rape.* New York: Simon and Schuster, 1975.

Bullough, Vern L. "Formation of Western Attitudes," in *The Subordinate Sex: A History of Attitudes Toward Women.* Baltimore: Penguin Books, 1974, p. 49.

Burt, Martha R. "Cultural Myths and Supports for Rape." *Journal of Personality and Social Psychology* 38 (1980): 217.

Chafetz, Janet Saltzman. *Masculine/Feminine or Human? An Overview of the Sociology of Sex Roles.* Itasca, Illinois: F. E. Peacock, 1974, p. 39.

Holmstrom, Lynda Lytle and Burgess, Ann Wolbert. "Introduction to the Transaction Edition," in *The Victim of Rape: Institutional Reactions*, rev. ed. New Brunswick, N.J.: Transaction Books, 1983.

Scully, Diana and Marolla, Joseph. "Convicted Rapists' Construction of Reality: The Denial of Rape," paper presented at the American Sociological Association meetings, San Francisco, September 1982, p. 13.

The Victim's Perspective

2

ANN WOLBERT BURGESS
AND ROBERT R. HAZELWOOD

> For too long we have viewed the victim as evidentiary baggage to be carried to court along with blood samples and latent fingerprints. It is about time that we as police began to view crime victims as our clients, as the aggrieved party in need of representation, reparation, and recognition.
>
> **—Chief Robert P. Owens,**
> *testimony presented to the President's Task Force on Victims of Crime*

If police officers and prosecutors are to take seriously the words of Chief Owens, they first must have an overview of the victim's perspective as she moves through the criminal justice system. The following account is adapted from the final report of the President's Task Force on Victims of Crime and represents a composite of a rape victim in America circa 1982. This victim is every victim; she could be you or related to you.

> You are a 50-year-old woman living alone. You are asleep one night when suddenly you awaken to find a man standing over you with a knife at your throat. As you start to scream, he beats you and cuts you. He then rapes you. While you watch helplessly, he searches the house, taking your jewelry, other valuables and money. He smashes furniture and windows in a display of senseless violence. His rampage ended, he rips out the telephone line, threatens you again, and disappears into the night.
>
> At least you have survived. Terrified, you rush to the first lighted house on the block. While you wait for the police, you pray that your attacker was bluffing when he said he'd return if you called them. Finally, what you expect to be help arrives.
>
> The police ask questions, take notes, dust for fingerprints, make pho-

tographs. When you tell them you were raped, they take you to the hospital. Bleeding from your cuts, your front teeth knocked out, bruised and in pain, you are told that your wounds are superficial, that rape itself is not considered an injury. Awaiting treatment, you sit alone suffering the stares of curious passersby. You feel dirty, bruised, disheveled, and abandoned. When your turn comes for examination, the intern seems irritated because he has been called out to treat you. While he treats you, he says that he hates to get involved in rape cases because he doesn't like going to court. He asks if you "knew the man you had sex with."

The nurse says she wouldn't be out alone at this time of night. It seems pointless to explain that the attacker broke into your house and had a knife. An officer says you must go through this process, then the hospital sends you a bill for the examination that the investigators insisted upon. They give you a box filled with test tubes, swabs and envelopes and tell you to hold onto it.

Finally, you get home somehow, in a cab you paid for and wearing a hospital gown because they took your clothes as evidence. Everything that the attacker touched seems soiled. You're afraid to be in your house alone. The one place where you were always safe, at home, is sanctuary no longer. You are afraid to remain, yet terrified to leave your home unprotected.

You didn't realize when you gave your name and address that it would be given to the press and to the defendant through the police reports. Your friends call to say they saw this information in the paper. You haven't absorbed what's happened to you when you get calls from insurance companies and firms that sell security devices. But these calls pale in comparison to the threats that come from the defendant and his friends.

You're astonished to discover that your attacker has been arrested, yet while in custody he has free and unmonitored access to a phone. He can threaten you from jail. The judge orders him not to annoy you, but when the phone calls are brought to his attention, the judge does nothing.

At least you can be assured that the man who attacked you is in custody, or so you think. No one tells you when he is released on his promise to come to court. No one asks you if you have been threatened. The judge is never told that the defendant said he'd kill you if you told or that he'd get even if he went to jail. Horrified, you ask how he got out after what he did. You're told the judge can't consider whether he'll be dangerous, only whether he'll come back to court. He's been accused and convicted before, but he always comes to court; so he must be released.

You learn only by accident that he's at large; this discovery comes when you turn a corner and confront him. He knows where you live. He's been there. Nowhere are you safe. He watches you from across the street; he follows you on the bus. Will he come back in the night? What do you do? Give up your home? Lose your job? Assume a different name? Get your mail at the post office? Carry a weapon? Even if you wanted to, could you afford to do these things?

You try to return to normal. You don't want to talk about what happened, so you decide not to tell your co-workers about the attack. A few days go by and the police unexpectedly come to your place of work. They show their badges to the receptionist and ask to see you. They want you to look at some photographs, but they don't explain that to co-workers. You try to explain later that you're the victim, not the accused. The phone rings and the police want you to come to a line-up. It may be 1:00 AM or in the middle of your work day, but you have to go; the suspect and his lawyer are waiting. It will not be the last time you are forced to conform your life to their convenience. You appear at the police station and the line-up begins. The suspect's lawyer sits next to you, but he does not watch the stage; he stares at you. It will not be the last time you endure his scrutiny.

You have lived through the crime and made it through the initial investigation. They've caught the man who harmed you, and he's been charged with armed burglary, robbery, and rape. Now he'll be tried. Now you expect justice.

You receive a subpoena for a preliminary hearing. No one tells you what it will involve, how long it will take, or how you should prepare. You assume that this is the only time you will have to appear. But you are only beginning your initiation in a system that will grind away at you for months, disrupt your life, affect your emotional stability, and certainly cost you money; it may cost you your job, and, for the duration, will prevent you from putting the crime behind you and reconstructing your life.

Before the hearing, a defense investigator comes to talk to you. When he contacts you, he says he's "investigating your case," and that he "works for the county." You assume, as he intends for you to, that he's from the police or prosecutor's office. Only after you give him a statement, do you discover that he works for the man who attacked you.

This same investigator may visit your neighbors and co-workers, asking questions about you. He discusses the case with them, always giving the defendant's side. Suddenly, some of the people who know you seem to be taking a different view of what happened to you and why.

It's the day of the hearing. You've never been to a court before, never spoken in public. You're very nervous. You rush to arrive at 8:00 AM to talk to a prosecutor you've never met. You wait in a hallway with a number of other witnesses. It's now 8:45. Court starts at 9:00. No one has spoken to you. Finally, a man sticks his head out the door, calls out your name, and asks, "Are you the one who was raped?" You're aware of the stares as you stand and suddenly realize this is the prosecutor, the person you expect to represent your interests.

You only speak to the prosecutor for a few minutes. You ask to read the statement you gave to the police but he says there isn't time. He asks you some questions that make you wonder if he believes you.

The prosecutor tells you to sit on a bench outside the courtroom. Suddenly you see that man who raped you coming down the hall. No one has told you he would be here. He's there with three friends. They all laugh and jostle you a little as they pass. The defendant and two friends enter the courtroom; one friend sits on the bench across from you and stares.

Suddenly, you feel abandoned, alone, afraid. Is this what it's like to come to court and seek justice?

You sit on the bench for an hour, then two. You don't see the prosecutor, he has disappeared into the courtroom. Finally, at noon, he comes out and says, "Oh, you're still here? We continued that case to next month."

The preliminary hearing was an event for which you were completely unprepared. Questions are asked as to where you live. You have moved since your attack; you are terrified to give the new address in court. You are also compelled to say where you work, how you get there and what your schedule is. Hours later you are released from the stand after reliving your attack in public, in intimate detail. You have been made to feel completely powerless. As you sat facing a smirking defendant and you described his threats, you were accused of lying and "inviting the encounter." You have cried in front of these uncaring strangers. As you leave, no one thanks you. When you arrive back to work they ask what took you so long.

Now the case is scheduled for trial. Again, there are delays. When you call to talk with the prosecutor you are told the case is reassigned. Continuances are granted because the courts are filled. Time passes and you hear nothing. You learn there are dozens of defense motions that can be filed before the trial. If denied, they can be appealed.

Finally the day of trial arrives. It is 18 months since you were attacked. You've been trying for a week to prepare yourself. It is painful to dredge up the terror again, but you know that the outcome depends on you; the prosecutor has told you that the way you behave will make or break the case. You can't get too angry on the stand because the jury might not like you. You can't break down and sob because then you will appear too emotional, possibly unstable. In addition to the tremendous pressure of having to relive the horrible details of the crime, you're expected to be an actress as well.

You expect the trial to be a search for the truth; you find that it is a performance orchestrated by lawyers and the judge, with the jury hearing only half the facts. The defendant was found with your watch in his pocket. The judge has suppressed this evidence because the officer who arrested him didn't have a warrant.

Your character is an open subject of discussion and innuendo. The defense is allowed to question you on incidents going back to your childhood. The jury is never told that the defendant has two prior convictions for the same offense and has been to prison three times for other crimes. You sought help from a counselor to deal with the shattering effect of this crime on your life. You told him about your intimate fears and feelings. Now he has been called by the defense and his notes and records have been subpoenaed.

You are on the stand for hours. The defense does its best to make you appear a liar, a seductress, or both. You know you cannot relax for a moment. Don't answer unless you understand the question. Don't be embarrassed when everyone seems angry because you do not understand. Think ahead. Be responsive. Don't volunteer. Don't get tired.

> Finally you are finished with this part of the nightmare. You would like to sit and listen to the rest of the trial but you cannot. You're a witness and must wait outside. The jury will decide the outcome of one of the major events of your life. You cannot hear the testimony that will guide their judgment.
>
> The verdict is guilty. You now look to the judge to impose a just sentence.
>
> The judge sentences your attacker to three years in prison, less than one year for every hour he kept you in pain and terror. That seems very lenient to you. Only later do you discover that he'll probably serve less than half of his actual sentence in prison because of good-time and work-time credits that are given to him immediately. The man who broke into your house, threatened to slit your throat with a knife and raped, beat and robbed you will be out of custody in less than 18 months.
>
> Having survived all this, you reflect on how you and your victimizer are treated by the system that is called justice. You are aware of the inequities that are more than merely procedural. During trial and after sentencing the defendant had a free lawyer; he was fed and housed; given physical and psychiatric treatment, job training education, support for his family, counsel on appeal. Although you do not oppose any of these safeguards, you realize that you have helped to pay for all these benefits for the criminal. Now, in addition and by yourself, you must try to repair all that his crime has destroyed; and what you cannot repair, you must endure. (President's Task Force On Victims of Crime, 1982)

Victims confront endless new situations as they wind their way through the criminal justice system. The police are often the first on the scene; it is to them, the first course of protection, that the victim first turns. They should be mindful that, in fulfilling their obligations to solve the crime and apprehend the criminal, they must also treat victims with the attention due them. The manner in which police officers treat a victim affects not only an immediate and long-term ability to deal with the event, but also willingness to assist in a prosecution. This chapter addresses the emotional aftermath of rape and is intended to describe the stress response of rape trauma syndrome. Police officers and prosecutors should be aware of the basic response pattern many victims experience and to which is added the effects of trial preparation.

Rape Trauma Syndrome

> It's been 3 years and I still won't get in an elevator alone or go out alone unless it is very necessary. When I enter my apartment, I don't deadbolt it till I get my knife out and check everywhere—under the bed, in the shower, in the closets. Then I deadbolt the door. I do this two or three times a night. I don't enjoy walking anymore. I never had

> these problems before I was raped. . . . I'm scared I will be like this forever.
>
> **—Rape victim**

Burgess and Holmstrom (1979) published a study of reported cases of rape and sexual assault in which 146 victims were interviewed at a hospital emergency ward and followed 4 to 6 years later regarding residual effects of, and problems they experienced from, the attack. The term *rape trauma syndrome* was used to describe an acute phase and long-term reorganization process that occurred as a result of forcible rape or attempted forcible rape. The syndrome of behavioral, physical, psychological, and social reactions was deemed an acute stress reaction to a life-threatening situation.

The above quote by the rape victim captures some of the distressing and repetitive symptoms that a victim continues to experience long after the rape. The symptoms of this victim highlight the fears and phobias that have developed and the terror from which she may not recover.

The intended readers of this book are those who deal with the victim during the immediate, intermediate, and final phases of her journey through the criminal justice system. They include police officers, crisis intervention workers, attorneys, physicians, nurses, and judges. Each of these individuals may have critical impact on the emotional well-being of the victim and her ability to cope with a life-threatening situation. For this reason, we are describing what may be noted in a victim who has undergone a sexual assault.

The Acute Phase: Disorganization

Immediate Impact Reaction

A prevailing myth about rape victims is that they are all hysterical and tearful following a rape. While this may be the fact in certain cases, it is by no means the prevalent form of reaction and should never be used as a criterion for determining whether or not a sexual assault has occurred.

Victims usually describe and indicate an extremely wide range of emotions in the immediate hours following the rape. The physical and emotional impact of the incident may be so intense that the victim feels shock and disbelief. As one victim said, "I did some strange things after he left, such as biting my arm . . . to prove I could feel . . . that I was real." Another victim, assaulted on the street, ran home. She immediately took a bath and said, "Hours later, I suddenly realized the water was very cold. I got out of the tub and went to bed." It took this victim several days to report the rape and only after strong encouragement by her friends and the rape crisis center staff. Unfortunately, this victim received a cool reception by a police officer who believed that "real rape victims" report right away.

In both examples, the victims experienced a "numbing" response following the rape. They were both so shocked by the experience that their normal mechanisms for making decisions were impaired. This response is not uncommon in other types of crisis situations such as car accidents, robberies, or sudden traumatic events. The delay in taking action, such as reporting the crime, is better understood if the officer takes the time to listen to the victim describe her actions following the rape and asks how she made her decision to report the rape. Many victims seek out advice prior to making a decision to report. Various reasons support this action, such as their fear of a negative response by police or of not being believed, as well as the social stigma that still surrounds rape. Police officers might conduct their own informal survey by asking family and friends what they would do should they be the victim of rape and whether they would report the rape or not.

The emotional demeanor of the victim noted during the initial interview may be one of two types: expressive or guarded.

Expressive Style. In the expressive style, the interviewer will be able to observe, either in the face of the victim or through body language, the feelings experienced by the victim. Fear, anger, and anxiety can be visibly noted in the expressions of the victim. Victims will reveal these feelings during the interview by becoming tense when certain questions are asked, or crying or sobbing when describing specific acts of the assailant. Interviewers should be aware that some victims may smile when certain statements are made. Such a reaction is not uncommon and denotes anxiety, not amusement, on the victim's part. Practically everyone associated with the identification, arrest, and prosecution of the rapist is reassured if the victim exhibits the "expressed" demeanor initially. However, this style is not always presented and should not be expected.

Guarded Style. In the guarded style, the feelings of the victim will not be observed directly. The victim may appear very composed and able to discuss the rape calmly. The feelings are controlled, masked, or hidden. The composed victim is not lying, but rather is able to control her true feelings, is in a state of shock, or is physically exhausted. Silence does not usually mean the victim is hiding facts, but rather that she is having trouble talking and thinking about the assault. This victim typically talks in a calm or subdued manner.

Mixed Styles. The interviewer may note a change from one style to the other, which may be related to time, place, and length of interview. For example, one victim who was expressive during the initial interview that took place at the hospital was very guarded the next day when the police officer came to talk to her at work. She did not wish to talk about the rape. Thus, her demeanor was significantly different. The police officer had not telephoned prior to his arrival, and later the victim refused to proceed with charges. In another case, a victim who was guarded during an initial interview later became less anxious when talked to in her home and was able to provide additional information to the police. Clearly, interviewers can influence the amount of cooperation provided by the victim in direct proportion to the respect they show for privacy and communication.

Physical Reactions to Rape Trauma

Rape is forced sexual violence against a person. Therefore, it is not surprising that victims describe a wide range of physical reactions in the days following the assault. Many victims will describe a general feeling of soreness all over their bodies. Others will specify the body area that has been the focus of the assailant's force, such as the face, jaw, throat, chest, arms, or legs. A 29-year-old woman who was attacked in her bed by a 16-year-old male, who hit her on the hand and head with a heavy lamp prior to the rape, later reported the following:

> At the hospital, I had 19 stitches in the back of my head and my hand was so swollen I couldn't move it for a week. I had bad eye problems—lines zagging in my vision. For months I had headaches, and even now, when I'm under stress, a headache starts and I think back to the rape.

Examples of physical reactions include:

Sleep Pattern Disturbances. Victims have difficulty sleeping in the months following the rape. They complain that they cannot fall asleep or, if they do, they wake up during the night and cannot fall back asleep. Victims who have been attacked while sleeping in their own beds may awake at the same time each evening. It is not uncommon for victims to cry or scream out in their sleep, with or without the presence of nightmares.

Eating Pattern Disturbances. The eating pattern of victims may be affected. Some victims report a marked decrease in appetite and complain of stomach pains or nausea. There are some victims who will report an increase in eating and weight gain; however, the eating is often a coping response to stress rather than a genuine appetite increase.

Physical Symptoms. Victims also report physical symptoms specific to the area of the body that has been a focus of attack. Throat and neck symptoms may be reported by victims who have been strangled or forced to have oral sex. Victims forced to have vaginal sex may complain of vaginal discharge, a burning sensation during urination, and generalized pain. Those forced to have anal sex may report rectal bleeding and pain in the days immediately following the rape.

Emotional Reactions

Prevailing stereotypes of rape are that the main reactions of victims of rape are shame and guilt. In reality, the primary feeling reported by the victim during the assault is that of fear—fear of physical injury, mutilation, and death. This primary feeling of fear explains why victims develop the range of symptoms called rape trauma syndrome: their symptoms are an acute stress reaction to the threat of being killed. Most victims feel they had a close encounter with death and are lucky to be alive. As one victim testified at the President's Task Force on Victims of Crime, "He said, 'Move or yell and I'll kill you.' I didn't doubt his word."

Victims express other feelings in conjunction with the fear of dying, ranging from humiliation, degradation, guilt, shame, and embarrassment to self-blame, anger, and revenge. Because of the diverse feelings experienced during the immediate impact phase, victims often have mood swings. The following quote is from a 31-year-old singer who was attacked by an intruder shortly after entering her apartment:

> I moved immediately from the apartment. I was unable to return to work. I felt I was being watched and followed. My panic was unbelievable. I could not sleep at night and had to catnap during the day. I hugged the walls walking down the street. I could not concentrate, would break out crying for no reason. I threw out every reminder of the rape—my bed, mattress, sheets, pillows and clothes. I became a hermit and stayed in and stared at the television set for months.

Many victims realize their feelings are out of proportion to the situation they are in. They will report feeling angry with someone and later realize the anger was unfounded. Many become quite upset over their behavior, which, in turn, produces more stress for them. One young woman reported feeling on the verge of tears constantly. One mother was distressed when she realized she was disciplining her children more severely than prior to the rape. Victims also report feeling irritated with people during the first few weeks, while the symptoms are acute.

Victims are very sensitive to the reactions of people when they learn of the rape. Perceived lack of concern, as well as insensitive remarks, will devastate a victim who already feels on an emotional rollercoaster. As one professional woman said, "My supervisor told me to take time off, but not to come back until I had my feelings about this under control."

Thoughts

A continual stream of thoughts relating to the rape haunts many victims. They usually try to block thoughts of the assault from their mind, but this intrusive imagery continues to break through into consciousness. "It's the first thing I think of when I wake in the morning," said one victim. "Something will trigger in my head, and it all comes back," said another. The victim may feel as though the traumatic event were recurring: "I panicked at work when two people came into the store and acted suspicious."

There is a strong tendency for victims to try to think how they might have escaped from the assailant or how the situation might have been handled differently. Generally, the conclusion drawn from such thinking is that they would have been beaten or killed if they had not complied with the demands of the assailant.

Victims vary as to the amount of time they remain in the acute phase. The immediate symptoms may last a few days to a few weeks. And more often than not, acute symptoms overlap with symptoms of the long-term recovery process.

The Long-Term Process: Reorganization

> I feel embarrassed that I have not gotten over the rape. . . . It has been 3 years and my self-confidence is still shattered. I find it unacceptable in me that an event of 10 minutes could so interfere with my entire life.
>
> **—48-year-old rape victim**

A rape represents a disruption in the lifestyle of the victim, not only during the immediate days and weeks following the incident, but well beyond that for many weeks, months, and years. On the surface the victim will often appear to function well, resuming work and family and social activites. The well-hidden psychological scars may be undetected by anyone who hasn't taken the time to trace the path of reorganization.

Various factors seem to influence the victim's reorganization of her life: personality style, the people available for support, the way she is treated by people who learn of the rape. This section identifies four lifestyle areas most vulnerable to disruption following rape: physical, psychological, social, and sexual.

Physical Lifestyle

As previously discussed, immediately following rape, victims report many physical symptoms related to musculoskeletal pain, genitourinary difficulties, gastrointestinal upset, general distress, as well as eating and sleeping pattern disruption. The health areas that give victims the most difficulty over a long time period include (1) body areas where injury caused interference to functioning, i.e., broken bones, lacerations, or organ trauma; and (2) gynecological and menstrual functioning. Victims with the latter problems report chronic vaginal problems and changes in menstrual cycle functioning.

Psychological Lifestyle

Dreams and nightmares are major symptoms for the rape victim and occur during both the acute phase and the long-term process. The 48-year-old victim quoted above reported three dreams that recurred frequently during the third year of the reorganization process. First, she reports waking up suddenly and feeling someone is in the room. Her fear, in response to such a dream, is that the assailant has come back to kill her. Second, in a dream she is walking down a hallway and a stranger grabs her. She wakes up with the same feeling she experienced when the assailant grabbed her while she was jogging. Third, she dreams that she is being drowned in a boat. This dream triggers her memory of the location where the rape occurred—along a jogging path by a river.

Dreams may be of three types: (1) replication of the state of victimization and helplessness ("I use my Mace and it turns to water"), (2) symbolic dreams which include a theme from the rape ("I am grabbed from behind and raped"), and (3) mastery dreams in which the victim is powerful in assuming control ("I took the knife and stabbed him over and over)". Nonmastery dreams dominate until the victim has recovered.

Social Lifestyle

Rape has the potential to disrupt the victim's normal social routine. In some cases, several areas of social functioning are disrupted.

Many victims are able to resume only a minimal level of functioning even after the acute phase ends. These women go to work or school but are unable to get involved in other than business-type activities. Other victims respond to the rape by staying home, by only venturing out of the house accompanied by a friend, or by being absent from or stopping work or school.

A common response is to turn for support to family members not normally seen on a daily basis. Often this means a trip home to some other city and a brief stay with parents in their home. In most cases, the victim tells the parents what has happened. Occasionally, the victim contacts her parents for support, but she does not tell why she is visiting. The decision to tell or not tell seems based on how the victim predicts the parent would respond to the news ("I didn't tell mother because I knew she would be very upset and worry that I might be raped again").

There is often a strong need to get away ("I thought I'd go stir crazy if I didn't get out of the city"). Victims who are able to move, will move—sometimes to another city, if practical. Victims also tend to change their telephone number, many requesting an unlisted number. The victim may do this as a precautionary measure or after receiving threatening calls. Victims fear the assailant may gain access to them through the telephone. They are also hypersensitive to obscene telephone calls, which may or may not be from the assailant.

Many victims try to become anonymous and move around to protect themselves; they are trying to gain control over a terrorizing experience. Sometimes police officers incorrectly interpret this behavior as a victim's unwillingness to prosecute. The officer should discuss ways to increase her safety environment with such a victim in order to be sure she stays in contact with the office.

Sexual Lifestyle

Many female victims report a fear of sex after the rape. The normal sexual style of the victim becomes disrupted. The rape is especially traumatic if it is the victim's first sexual experience in that there is nothing with which to compare it. For a victim who has been sexually active, the fear increases when a boyfriend or husband confronts her about resuming their sexual pattern.

Phobias

A common psychological defense seen in rape victims is the development of fears and phobias. Fears are normal; they are protective devices that warn people of danger. A phobia is maladaptive as it prevents a person from acting in a certain situation. Victims described fears and phobias in a wide variety of circumstances: fear of indoors if the rape occurred inside; fear of outdoors if the rape occurred outside the home; fear of being alone ("I just can't stand it if no one else is home"); fear of elevators or stairs or people behind them ("I won't go in some buildings because I am terrified of elevators and stairwells"). A wide variety of activities can trigger a flashback ("Violence on television really upsets me").

The victim may develop specific fears related to characteristics noted in the assailant, such as the odor of beer on the assailant's breath. A facial feature, such as a moustache, may trigger a reaction in a victim raped by an assailant with a moustache. Some victims describe a very suspicious, paranoid feeling ("I felt everyone on the bus knew I was a victim").

The occurrence of a second upsetting victimizing situation following a rape can produce additional fearful feelings. One victim was involved in a car accident the day following the rape and re-experienced the fright and fear of dying.

Partner Reactions

Rape can precipitate a crisis not only for the victim, but also for family, friends, and others in her network of social relationships. Police officers and attorneys will probably have to deal with these family members and should try to understand the impact the rape has on their lives. Officials who can be empathetic and sensitive to the victim and family may find them more cooperative.

One crucial dimension to observe is whether male partners see the victim as a victim. In other words, whom do they perceive to be the victim of the rape—the woman herself, her parents, her husband/boyfriend? Do they see her as a person in her own right who has been hurt by the assault, or do they view her more as their possession whose value has diminished? Do they see the rape as an unfortunate incident that was externally inflicted upon her, or do they see it as evidence of her bad character? Whom do they blame—the assailant, the woman, or themselves? Perhaps the most crucial underlying and typically unstated issue is whether the family member sees the rape primarily as sex or primarily as violence.

The rape of a wife or girlfriend has an enormous psychological impact on her male partner. News of the violation brings forth a great surge of emotion on his part, and he often experiences many conflicting feelings. The process of sorting out what the rape means to him has two major components. The first is dealing with his feelings. In this regard, three issues predominate: (*a*) perceptions and feelings about who is hurt, (*b*) the desire to get the guy, and (*c*) the "if only" reaction. The second component is having to cope with his wife/girlfriend—a woman who now is very upset and in a state of crisis—and to cope with the impact that the event has had on their relationship. The second component also involves dealing with three main issues: (*a*) their discussions of the rape, (*b*) the woman's new phobias, and (*c*) the resumption of sexual relations.

In addition, for those cases that go to court, a partner must deal with the court process and with a wife/girlfriend who is as upset by going to court as she was by the rape itself (Holmstrom and Burgess, 1978).

Dealing with His Feelings

Partner's Own Reactions

The first issue is who the victim is. The view that rape is an act with a victim seems to be widely accepted. There is a difference of opinion, however, as to *who* is hurt by the rape. A traditional view would be that the woman's husband is injured because his wife's value is diminished by the rape. The violation makes her worthless or it reflects badly on him that he should have such a wife. She is stigmatized and possibly to blame as well. One husband clearly was wrestling with the issue of whether or not his wife had betrayed him by having sex with another man. Although she was quite bruised, he implied she should have resisted the assailant more:

> I can't understand her reaction at the time. I can't understand why she did what she did. . . . I don't think the whole truth will come out in court. But I haven't had any trouble with her in 15 years of marriage with other men, so I'll stick by her now.

Another husband said he was ashamed and blamed his wife for the incident. She was a cocktail waitress who was raped as she went to her car after work. She stated:

> I am having problems with my husband. He doesn't want me around his family. He told his mother on Sunday he was ashamed of me. He said I shouldn't have been working there, that it was my fault that I had been working there.

And in still another case, a boyfriend was worried that he would be sexually repulsed by his girlfriend now that she had been raped. The girlfriend's account follows:

> That night as soon as we got back to the apartment he wanted to make love. . . . He admitted he wanted to know if he could make love to me, or if he would be repulsed by it and unable to.

A more modern view would be that the woman has been hurt as a human being, but that this in no way diminishes her value as a wife or reflects badly on her character or her husband. In one such case, the woman said:

> My boyfriend has been so wonderful about it. He is the reason I got through it. His concern was for me. He was just glad to have me alive and well.

Getting the Guy

Strong feelings of wanting to "get the guy" are common among male partners. This desire meant the husband/boyfriend wanted to go after the assailant himself and/or that he wanted very much to pursue the assailant legally through the police and the courts. Sometimes the male partner urges the victim not to press charges, or harasses the police officer during the investigation. In such cases, it might be helpful for the officer to talk with the man about his feelings concerning the rape. Such a response may represent a more traditional view of rape where the partner feels "victimized."

Because victims experience a great deal of ambivalence over reporting a rape, it is not uncommon to see the male partner take the initiative. Sometimes this unilateral decision then becomes an issue between the partners. One girlfriend described such a situation as follows:

> As soon as we got to the hospital, he marched up to the police car that was sitting in the emergency yard and said, "Sir, my girlfriend has just been raped." (How do you feel about that?) I was furious. I didn't want to report it, and to have him do it really made me mad.

The "If Only" Reaction

Very often husbands and boyfriends indicate they wish they had done something differently and thus prevented the incident. As one husband said, "If only I hadn't been working that night . . . maybe it wouldn't have happened."

Dealing with the Raped Woman

While dealing with his own emotions, the male partner must also interact with his wife or girlfriend, who is herself in a state of psychological crisis. Often the partner will say, "She is different since the rape." The woman clearly needs some psychological support during this time of crisis and most often looks to family members.

Discussion of the Rape. One important issue is whether the couple feels able to talk about the rape openly. The rationale is that if they can express their feelings, they will be able to identify the issues that are upsetting them and thus gain more control over these feelings. Thus, the memory of the event will not evoke the painful reaction it once did. However, more often than not, avoidance of the topic is the norm.

New Phobias. The second important issue is dealing with new phobias triggered by the rape. Often this area is where the partner is most helpful if he is able to provide protection and safety for the victim and is willing to be more available to her.

Resuming Sexual Relations. Since sex is the means that the rapist used to attack the woman, it is not surprising that she develops a phobia to resuming sex. It is also not surprising that the male partner has difficulty resuming sexual relations with the rape victim. Two possible factors may be at work. The first concerns the maintenance of a double standard of behavior. For example, one husband reported that although he himself had "not been an angel" all his married life, he still felt betrayed when his wife was raped, i.e., "had sex with another man."

A second factor involves mutual sexual-exclusiveness expectations that couples may have—expectations that apply to both partners. One example of this involves a homosexual couple. The victim was raped by a man; her female partner, with whom she had lived for 3 years, was very upset. For this couple, each of the partners was very jealous over any outside relationships that the other partner might have. Further support for this interpretation is found in the case of a *male* victim in which the husband was raped anally and the wife's reaction was to blame him. She questioned why he was out, why a big man such as he could not fend off an assailant. His "unfaithfulness" during the rape was an issue for her.

Many couples have difficulty resuming sexual relations. The main problems from the woman's point of view are her (*a*) temporary aversion to physical contact, (*b*) experience of flashbacks of the rape, (*c*) physical discomfort during sex, (*d*) changes in physical response to sexual stimulation, and (*e*) worry over her partner's reaction.

Dealing with Court

Court is as upsetting to the woman as the original rape. While testifying in court the victim mentally relives the rape. Court has its own set of pressures. There is the embarrassing public setting, the confrontation with the offender, and the difficult cross-examination by the defense lawyer. The victim finds the courtroom to be very stressful; psychologically, it often returns her to a state of crisis. The husband/boyfriend has the task of supporting his partner through this added stressful event.

Counseling Implications

Law enforcement officers are frequently the first professionals with whom the victim interacts after the crime. It is critical to the well-being of the victim and to the criminal investigation that she be able to resolve successfully the emotional turmoil she is experiencing. An emotionally healthy victim will be better able to assist the police in the investigation of the crime. For that reason, officers should be aware of the value of counseling in such matters.

An understanding of the disruptive capacities of a rape attack requires a brief discussion of the concept of homeostatic balance and the relationship of coping behaviors to stable psychological functioning. The principle of homeostasis is that there needs to be a stable balance within the body to manage effectively in the world. When these psychological balances are upset, self-regulatory mechanisms (coping behaviors) are triggered to help return these balances to healthy levels. Crisis theory is based on this principle applied to psychological functioning.

For each individual, there exists a reasonably consistent balance between the way we think and the way we feel. This homeostatic balance varies from person to person, but each individual maintains his or her "normal" stability. However, each and every day, experiences are encountered that disrupt this balance, giving rise to negative and uncomfortable feelings. These experiences may be termed *emotionally hazardous situations*. Such events give rise to stress and motivate the individual to bring into play coping behaviors that help to reestablish the balance. When the individual experiences an emotionally hazardous situation and is unable to effectively utilize previously learned coping behaviors, an emotional crisis may ensue. In rape, a crisis usually develops because the event is so traumatic, unexpected, and uncontrolled that the person is unable to cope effectively.

Rape, a criminal victimization, poses a situational crisis. The victim was unprepared for the hazardous event; she feels out of control and unable to cope.

Crisis intervention is clearly the treatment of choice when a rape is disclosed immediately after it has occurred. The rationale for this type of treatment includes: (1) the rape represents a crisis in that the victim's style of life is disrupted; (2) the victim is regarded as "normal" or functioning adequately prior to the external event; (3) crisis intervention aims to return the victim to his or her previous level of functioning as quickly as possible. The crisis intervention strategy is to provide or mobilize support for the victim during the acute phase of disruption. The speed of intervention is crucial. Other crisis services to offer the victim include advocacy services, especially regarding legal matters; work with the victim's support system, and victim mutual support groups.

Compound Reaction to Rape

Victims who are raped may describe a past or current difficulty with a psychiatric condition, a physical condition, or a behavior pattern that creates difficulty for them. These victims are frequently known to other therapists, physicians, or agencies and need more than crisis counseling because under the stress of rape, the victim becomes vulnerable to prior difficulties. For example, the victim may develop increased physical problems, increased drinking or drug use, become suicidal, or exhibit psychotic behavior. A careful study of the victim's background will help to determine if the previous therapist or physician needs to be identified for referral. The referral suggestion, if appropriate, is made to the victim.

Silent Reaction to Rape

Most police and law officials acknowledge that there are many victims of rape who do not report the assault. This information alerted clinicians to a syndrome called *silent reaction to rape.* This syndrome occurs in the victim who has not reported the rape to anyone, who has not dealt with feelings and reactions to the incident, and who, because of this silence, has further burdened herself or himself psychologically. When this situation is defined, the referral should be for victim therapy.

Police Response to the Rape Victim

Victims of rape are often first seen by a police officer who responds to a call for assistance. The treatment that a victim receives will influence her recovery process. Other than homicide, rape is the most serious possible violation of a person's body; it deprives the victim of both physical and emotional privacy, as well as autonomy. The victim's response to rape primarily reflects her reaction to violation of self; it is an emotional, as well as physical, assault. The officer must remember that the victim is being asked to discuss with a stranger the details of what is probably the most traumatic and personal experience of her life.

Police officers generally see victims and their families immediately following the crime, when they are most in need of help. The officer's response to these victims often has a major effect on how swiftly, and how well, the victim recovers.

Police officers who respond quickly after a report is made, who listen attentively, and who show concern for the victim's plight will greatly reassure the victim and help her overcome a sense of fear and helplessness. Rape victims who comment favorably on their initial exposure to a law enforcement officer seem to feel more comfortable with police officers who project both personal concern and professional objectivity.

Police Interview

Introduction

The initial interaction with the victim, the introduction, is the most critical phase of the interview process. The victim's perception of the interview will determine whether or not she feels comfortable and confident in the ability of the police to assist her. The officer should introduce him/herself in a professional, confident, and sincere manner, using the victim's last name preceded by Ms., Miss, Mrs. or Mr. The interviewer(s) should accomplish three important tasks during this phase: (1) exhibiting an empathetic attitude, and assuring the victim that she is the *victim* of a crime that was not her fault; (2) assuring her of her safety and that everything possible and reasonable will be done to maintain that safety; and (3) convincing her of the competence and experience of the interviewers. A scenario might proceed as follows:

> Good evening, Ms. Roberts. I am Bob Jackson of the Sexual Assault Unit and, if you are feeling up to it at this time, I would like to discuss the crime which occurred. I want you to know how deeply I regret your being the victim of such an assault and that I and the other members of the department will do our very best in your behalf. Other officers have completely checked your residence (where the assault occurred) and have secured it. I've arranged for our patrols to increase their travel through your neighborhood, and I will also provide you with an emergency police number before I leave. I've been an investigating officer for 9 years and am experienced in such matters, so please don't hesitate to ask questions during our time together.

The officer(s) should explain that the interview will be as brief as possible and that while the questions will necessarily be personal, the importance of her answers cannot be overemphasized. The victim should also be advised that the information she provides will greatly aid in identifying the offender.

The Interview

The officer(s) would be well advised to remember that the process involved is an interview and not an interrogation. The victim has agreed to be interviewed, and this strongly suggests that she wants to cooperate and has faith in the abilities of law enforcement. Consequently, it is recommended that the following guidelines be adhered to during the interview phase:

1. Involve the victim in the interview process. Explain the procedures that have taken place and will occur. Provide her with a phone number that she can call to obtain information about the progress of the investigation, or advise her that you will periodically call to keep her informed. Ask for her opinions throughout the interview.

2. Allow the victim as much control as possible. Ask her permission to use her first name; do not presume the right. Inquire if the interview environment is agreeable to her or if she would be more comfortable elsewhere. Ask if she would prefer to describe the crime in her own words or if she would rather you ask questions. Determine if she wants anyone to be notified.

3. Listen and respond to her wishes and requests if at all possible. For example, she may casually comment that she is uncomfortable. Inquire as to whether it is the situation, environment, or chair, and attempt to alleviate the situation, if possible.

4. Pay attention to what she is saying and be alert to expressions of (*a*) guilt ("I shouldn't have gone to the market so late"), (*b*) fear ("He said he would know if I called the police"), (*c*) humiliation ("I didn't want to do that"), and (*d*) unnecessary attempts to convince ("I know this sounds strange, but it really did happen," or "I tried/wanted to stop him"). Upon hearing such phrases, the officer(s) should reassure the victim: (*a*) "You have a right to travel as you wish without becoming a victim." (*b*) "You're safe now inside your home." (*c*) "You had no choice in the matter." (*d*) "It doesn't sound strange, and I'm sure it happened," or "You're not expected or required to be injured or killed."

5. Balance questions having to do with humiliating acts or sexual aspects with ones relating to the victim's feelings. For example, if the victim has been asked about the occurrence of ejaculation (never ask if she "climaxed"), this should be balanced by a question such as "Do you feel safe now?" or "May I get you something to drink?" or "Would you like to stop for a while?"

6. Begin by utilizing professional terminology. One can always lower the level of discussion, but it is very difficult, if not impossible, to raise the level of discussion. An example would be questions pertaining to forced oral sexual acts. The professional interviewer should begin by using the term "fellatio." It is possible that the victim might not be familiar with the term, and the officer would then use the word "oral sex" to describe the act. Should the victim still not understand, the officer could ask, "Did he make you put your mouth on his penis?"

To appreciate the value of such an approach, simply reverse the sequence.

7. Use language that is not judgmental or threatening to the victim. Instead of "Tell me about your rape," say "Please describe the assault." Instead of stating a biased "What were you doing out so late?" provide the opportunity for the victim to tell what happened ("Please describe what was happening leading up to the assault.") Rather than saying, "Why didn't you fight him?" ask, "Was there any opportunity to resist?" A poorly phrased question may reveal the interviewer's personal biases and feelings to the victim and impede the investigation.

8. Throughout the interview, it should be clear to the victim that power, control, anger, and aggression are the central issues in the crime, not sexuality. Sexuality is not the salient feature of the assault. A crime of violence has occurred, and the victim should understand that it is this aspect (force) on which the investigation will focus.

9. Obtain the details of the crime in as factual a manner as possible. The interviewer should take precautions to ensure that the victim does not perceive the process as being voyeuristic in nature. It must be remembered that the victim is most likely the only witness to the crime, and should she perceive the officer as being invasive, she may withhold vital information. The victim has experienced, and is in, a stressful situation. The officer must attempt to decrease stress, not the reverse. Dwelling on sexual activities or rushing through them may precipitate flashbacks to the rape experience. In other words, a very narrow periphery exists for the interviewer to operate within, and common sense must prevail. In general, the best information is gathered by allowing the victim to tell her story in her own words. This method will help relieve some of her emotional tensions. It will also allow the officer to listen carefully to what she is saying and to evaluate her mood, general reactions, and choice of words. When asking direct questions, the officer should be sure the victim understands what is being asked. It is important to talk on her level. Always give the reason for asking the question.

Concluding the Interview

Following the interview, the investigator should continue to include the victim in the investigation; this prevents her from feeling "used" by the system. The rapist has already induced such a feeling in the victim, and she must not be further victimized by the system designed to identify, arrest, and prosecute her attacker. Therefore, it is suggested that the following information be provided to the victim:

1. Advise her of the next step in the investigative process. At this

point, the victim needs stability in her life and to be reassured that she will not simply become a statistic in some file. She is important and should be made to feel that this is recognized and everything possible will be done to ensure justice is served.

2. As previously mentioned, she should be provided with a number to call or be informed that she will be kept apprised of the investigative progress.

3. The victim should be referred to, or preferably introduced to, supportive services, which have advocacy systems designed to assist her through this emotionally traumatic period in her life.

4. Inquire as to whether the victim has any questions and ensure that she fully understands what will occur in the future and her role in those occurrences.

5. Thank the victim! Express your appreciation for the time she has taken to assist in the investigation. The victim should leave feeling safe, guiltless, and confident in what will be accomplished as a result of her cooperation.

In conclusion, the investigator should be aware that initial descriptions and interviews are likely to be colored by the trauma and crisis nature of the assault. Follow-up interviews with the victim are likely to reveal more details as the victim calms down and attempts to resume her life. The investigator should be aware that the victim, in attempting to return to a normal life, may try to forget the assault ever occurred, and subsequently forget who the investigator is or refuse to talk to him or her. The victim should be alerted to the fact that she may want to forget the assault ever occurred, but that submerging the memory will not make it go away. Instead it will reappear in nightmares, phobias, and other symptoms. She needs somebody with whom to talk until the memory can finally fade naturally.

Special Issue—Fresh Complaint

The issue of "fresh complaint" is a legitimate concern of the criminal justice system and arises quite often in matters involving sexual assault. The victim may choose not to divulge the crime to anyone, including law enforcement; or she may delay reporting it for hours, days, or even longer.

When attempting to understand the dynamics involved in reporting a rape, one must look not only at the victim herself, but at her social network and at her community as well. A striking finding in the sociological study of rape victims by Holmstrom and Burgess (1983) was the degree to which people other than the victim were involved in the chain of events leading her to the police. In more than half of the 92 adult rape cases studied, someone other than the victim was involved in reporting the rape to the police; someone other than the victim made the decision to contact the police, acted as intermediary at the request of the victim, or persuaded the victim herself to call.

The hesitation of many victims and the tendency for family and friends to discuss whether or not to report the rape can be discouraging and sometimes bewildering to police. In many ways, there is a similar feeling among health professionals as to why patients do not report their symptoms earlier and receive medical attention. However, police cannot do their work unless the rape is reported. They also know that any delay "looks bad" in court. Some members of the criminal justice system even label victims as "collaborators" when they do not immediately report the crime.

Socially and psychologically, however, the need of many victims to seek out others for support or for advice makes sense. Rape victims typically experience rape as an attack that threatens their very lives. As a result, they are in a state of psychological crisis. They have experienced an overwhelming danger that they could neither escape nor solve with their customary psychological resources. People in crises typically have difficulty making any decisions at all. It is with this understanding that victims often turn to others. It may be added that some victims of rape also are physically incapable of making any decision at all. The assailant may have beaten them so badly, or so terrified them about reporting the rape, that their faculties are not completely available to them—a fact not always appreciated by professionals.

The officer needs to understand the wide range of behaviors that can occur related to reporting a rape. Rather than project a reason onto the victim as to why she delayed, it is a better interviewing strategy to ask the victim to describe how she was finally able to make the decision to report, thus implying that the decision must have been a difficult one for her and to acknowledge this process rather than judge it.

References

Burgess, Ann W. and Holmstrom, Lynda L. *Rape: Crisis and Recovery*. Bowie, Maryland: Brady, 1979.

Holmstrom, Lynda L. and Burgess, Ann W. "Rape: The Husband's and Boyfriend's Initial Reactions," *The Family Coordinator* 3 (1978): 321–330.

Holmstrom, Lynda L. and Burgess, Ann W. *The Victim of Rape: Institutional Reactions*. New York: Wiley, 1979. Published in paperback with new introduction by Transaction (Brunswick, New Jersey: 1983).

President's Task Force on Victims of Crime, Final Report, December 1982.

3

Police Attitudes and Beliefs Concerning Rape

JOHN C. LEDOUX AND
ROBERT R. HAZELWOOD

Rape, unlike many crimes, is seriously underreported (PCLEAJ, 1967). Victims of rape may decide not to report the crime because they fear police attitudes and beliefs concerning rape, the perpetrators of rape, and above all, themselves, the victims of rape. Blumberg and Niederhoffer, in fact, agree that "in practice, the average policeman exercises greater judicial discretion over cases than does a judge" (1973).

Because the public's perception of police beliefs and attitudes concerning various crimes can affect its willingness to report crime, to assist in identification, to convict an offender, and to support new legislation, law enforcement should study its own beliefs and attitudes—and reform, modify, or use them as indicated. The purpose of this chapter is, thus, to describe briefly the prevailing literature on police attitudes toward rape and to present the initial findings of a nationwide survey of county and municipal police officers conducted by the authors of this chapter.

Traditional Views of Police Attitudes

Historically, descriptions of police attitudes toward the crime of rape and its victims have come primarily from two sources. One source is anecdotal literature wherein popular writers examine and express opinions on the issue of rape. Another source, which is not necessarily mutually exclusive, is empirical research wherein persons attempt to question officers about their opinions.

The anecdotal literature finds that rape victims are generally greeted with hostile, callous, and indifferent treatment by police officers. Susan Brownmiller, in *Against Our Will*, states that "despite their knowledge of the law they are supposed to enforce, the male police mentality is often identical to the stereotypic views of rape that are shared by the rest of the male culture. The tragedy for the rape victim is that the police officer is the person who validates her victimization. A police officer who does not believe there is such a crime as rape can arrive at only one destination" (1975). Brownmiller thus generalizes her opinion of the male police officer to include the entire male culture—and she implies that male and female police attitudes are different.

A similarly negative view is presented by Germaine Greer who writes that "bored policemen amusing themselves with girls who come to them to complain of rape often kick off the proceedings by asking if they have enjoyed it" (1975). Hurst, in *The Trouble With Rape* (1977), reserves most of her criticism for the male officers first dispatched to the crime scene. She states "he [the police officer] is there because his was the patrol car nearest to the address given by the victim and speed in answering a rape call is important. . . . it is at this point in the encounter with the police that the insensitivity usually occurs." Hurst, however, concludes that "some policewomen have as little compassion as policemen."

The empirical literature presents a more balanced view, although the data clearly suggests that some officers are influenced by the particular circumstances of the victim, the assailant, and the act itself. Feldman-Summers and Palmer (1980), after examining data from questionnaires provided by 54 criminal justice system (CJS) personnel in the Seattle area, suggest that the frequent complaints of unsympathetic treatment by rape victims can be linked to "beliefs held by the CJS members which tend to place blame and responsibility on the victim." The authors noted that the beliefs of police officers were similar to those of judges and prosecutors with regard to the causes of rape and ways to reduce its frequency. Social service personnel were found to have significantly different beliefs. However, there was no significant difference between the CJS members and the social service personnel in the section of the questionnaire examining what constituted a valid rape.

Gottesman (1977) examines the impact training may have on police attitudes about rape. The subjects were police officers from two departments in the Midwest. She reports that most (95%) of the officers responded positively to training and increased, for example, their understanding of the rape victim. She finds unchanged by training, however, a belief that victims are partly to blame for the assault due to their manner of dress or their behavior.

A study of police investigators in Texas by Galton (1975) examines the criteria by which rape complaints are evaluated. The findings are based on analysis of rape complaints during a 10-week period of time, interviews with investigators and complainants, and questionnaires completed by police officers. Galton concludes that investigators hold rape victims to a higher standard of behavior than the law requires.

Feild (1978) included 254 police officers from an unspecified number of departments in a study examining attitudes toward rape. Also included as subjects were citizens and rape counselors. Based on a principal component factor analysis with varimax rotation, eight factors were extracted. The factors were labeled: (1) Woman's Responsibility in Rape Prevention, (2) Sex as Motivation for Rape, (3) Severe Punishment for Rape, (4) Victim Precipitation of Rape, (5) Normality of Rapists (6) Power as Motivation for Rape, (7) Favorable Perception of a Woman after Rape, and (8) Resistance as Woman's Role during Rape. Feild suggested that future research should seek to refine the content of his instrument and explore additional content areas.

The major difficulty with these studies is that they have generally been restricted to a single agency and are based on relatively small numbers of subjects who were not randomly selected. The Feldman-Summers and Palmer study, for example, was based on the responses of 15 police officers. This represented only 24% of those asked to participate in the study. Twenty-one people participated in the Gottesman study; ten in the Galton study. Consequently, their findings cannot be generalized to the law enforcement community.

The FBI Study

During the early months of 1983 we speculated on the effect a course taught by Hazelwood to officers attending the FBI National Academy would have on students' attitudes toward rape investigations. This discussion spurred a decision to conduct research on the impact of such training on police attitudes. LeDoux, however, held that the study would be invalid if restricted to students who were not representative of the law enforcement community in general. Thus, we decided to conduct a nationwide study on police attitudes toward rape. A review of the literature, as cited above, indicated that police officers were regarded as insensitive to the plight of rape victims. We questioned whether this was generally true, or whether only a small number of officers held unsympathetic attitudes.

Methodology

The study was limited to sworn officers of county and municipal law enforcement agencies because, statistically, they are most frequently involved in rape cases. Respondents were obtained through the Uniform Crime Report list of contributing law enforcement agencies. These agencies are grouped by geographical region and size of agency, and are classified as either a county or municipal agency. We selected a desired total sample of 3,000 participants and determined the percentage of officers in each region/size/type agency cell. Agencies were randomly selected from each cell, and a list of random numbers equal to approximately 10% of the size of the department was drawn until each cell had a sufficient number of potential respondents. We sent the selected agencies the quota for their organization, and they determined the actual respondents. The respondents were given both questionnaires and envelopes in which to seal the questionnaires, to insure the complete anonymity of their responses. Usable returns were received from 2,170 officers, or 72% of those queried. To our knowledge, these returns represent the largest national survey of police attitudes toward rape.

The questionnaires contained demographic data such as age, sex, and number of rape cases investigated, and listed 39 statements on the subject of rape (e.g., "Most charges of rape are unfounded"). Each officer was asked to indicate (1) to what extent he/she agreed with a given statement by circling one of four numbers (1, strongly agree; 2, agree; 3, disagree; 4, strongly disagree), and (2) how this belief affected the amount of effort the officer would devote to a rape investigation (1, much more effort; 2, more effort; 3, same effort; 4, less effort). Many of the statements were adapted from the work of Hubert S. Feild (1978). The reliability and validity of the instrument were established prior to its administration. Reliability of the study data was tested and found to be acceptable.[1]

Description of Respondents

A profile of the respondents is given in Table 3.1. We have determined that the respondents are typical of sworn county and municipal law enforcement officers because a comparison of our results with a recent nationwide study of similar law enforcement officers (Chronister, et al., 1982) reveals that the demographics are practically identical. LeDoux is currently preparing a paper entitled "Description of U.S. County Municipal Law Enforcement Officers" which will report the similarities. At the end of the analysis section, we will discuss specifics of the data as they relate to the respondents' experience in rape investigation and the amount and type of training they have received.

[1] For details of the methodology, see LeDoux and Hazelwood, "Police Attitudes Toward Rape." *Journal of Police Science and Administration* (1985).

Table 3.1. Description of Respondents

Mean age	36
Years of law enforcement experience	11.5
Race (%)[a]	
White	90.2
Black	5.6
Hispanic	2.9
Other	1.4
Marital status (%)[a]	
Single	9.4
Married	79.1
Other	11.6
Ever divorced (%)	
No	69.9
Yes	30.1
Sex (%)	
Female	6.4
Male	93.6
Job category (%)	
Traffic	8.2
Patrol	42.1
Rape investigator	1.3
Vice (including sexual assault)	0.3
Homicide	0.7
General criminal investigator	14.1
Supervisor	10.5
Staff/administrator	6.2
Other	15.4
Education (%)	
Less than high school	0.7
High school	32.2
Some college	41.7
Four-year college degree	15.6
Some graduate study	5.9
Master's degree or more	3.9

[a] Totals do not equal 100 because of rounding error.

Analysis

A technique called factor analysis was employed to determine the underlying sets of attitude (factors) that made up the officers' overall attitude. The 39 statements were reduced mathematically to 10 factors and reduced logically to 3 sets of factors—victims, rapists, and trials (see Table 3.2). Although we will not attempt, in this brief chapter, to describe factor analysis as a statistical technique, we employed extensive analysis to show the relationship among the factors and the factor

Table 3.2. Factors Listed by Factor Set

Victims
Women as victims
Legal responsibility of victim
Victims' innocence
Victim provocation of rape
Rapists
Sexual motivation for rape
Normality of rapists
Masculinity as a motivation for rape
Trial
Punishment
Victim's influence in trial
Prosecution

sets. Even so, we prefer to consider the factor sets as a logical framework rather than a precise statistical statement.

We shall present the statements contained in the various factors, then indicate the average reality assessment (belief of the respondent) given by law enforcement officers. In the case of items 14, 28, 29, and 31 (which were associated with two factors), we will list the statements only under the factor with which the association was the greatest. Four items (1, 2, 9, 36) did not meet the criterion established for inclusion in a factor and were not used. Table 3.2 lists the factors by factor set.

Victims

The first factor set concerned how law enforcement officers view rape victims. The first factor in this set was entitled "Women as Victims." As may be seen in Table 3.3, law enforcement officers, contrary to popular belief, are not insensitive to the plight of rape victims. As a group they disagree vehemently with statements that suggest the raped woman is not truly a victim.

The second factor in the victim set was entitled "Legal Responsibility of Victim." The items in this factor deal with the legal responsibilities of the victim in rape cases. As may be seen in Table 3.4, the officers tend to disagree with statements that suggest women should have to prove they did not precipitate or encourage rape.

The third factor of the victim set was entitled "Victims' Innocence." The statements in this factor examine the innocence of victims. As shown in Table 3.5, police officers did see women as innocent victims.

The final factor dealing with attitudes toward the victim was entitled "Victim Provocation of Rape." This factor is similar to the factor deal-

Table 3.3. Women as Victims

Statement	Average Assessment
10. A raped woman is a less desirable woman.	3.3
11. If a woman is going to be raped she might as well relax and enjoy it.	3.6
13. Most women secretly desire to be raped.	3.4
14. Some women deserve to be raped.	3.4
16. Nice women do not get raped.	3.6
23. In most cases when a woman was raped she was asking for it.	3.4

1 = agree strongly; 2 = agree; 3 = disagree; 4 = disagree strongly.

Table 3.4. Legal Responsibility of Victim

Statement	Average Assessment
6. A charge of rape made 2 days after the event is probably not a rape.	3.1
7. A woman should be responsible for preventing her own rape.	3.0
17. Most charges of rape are unfounded.	3.0
18. In order to protect the male, it should be more difficult to prove rape than other crimes.	3.2
25. Rape of a woman by a man she knows can be defined as a woman who changed her mind.	3.0
28. The degree of a woman's resistance should be the major factor in determining if a rape occurred.	3.3
38. Previous and willing sex with the accused reduces the seriousness of the offense.	2.5

1 = agree strongly; 2 = agree; 3 = disagree; 4 = disagree strongly.

Table 3.5. Victims' Innocence

Statement	Average Assessment
27. A woman should feel guilty following a rape.	3.5
29. A raped woman is a guilty victim, not an innocent one.	3.5
31. Rape serves as a way to keep women in their place.	3.7

1 = agree strongly; 2 = agree; 3 = disagree; 4 = disagree strongly.

Table 3.6. Victim Provocation of Rape

Statement	Average Assessment
4. In forcible rape, the victim never causes the crime.	2.4
15. Women provoke rape by their appearance or behavior.	2.7

1 = agree strongly; 2 = agree; 3 = disagree; 4 = disagree strongly.

ing with the victim's legal responsibility to prove rape. The data in Table 3.6 reveals divided opinions on whether or not women cause or provoke rape. No clear consensus was reached on "victim never causes the crime" and "women provoke rape."

Rapists

The second factor set dealt with law enforcement officers' perception of the rapist. Each of its three factors was related to motivations for rape, but none of the statements was associated with more than one factor. As seen in Table 3.7, the first factor in this set, "Sexual Motivation for Rape," clearly relates to sex as the primary motivation for rape. The responses indicate confusion over the sexual aspect of rape. Many do not agree that rape is an "uncontrollable desire for sex" and that "most rapists commit rape for sex," yet most agree that rape is a "sex crime" and that "rapists are sexually frustrated."

The second factor in this set, "Normality of Rapists," determines the reason for rape in terms of the underlying mental state of the rapists. Table 3.8 reveals that while the officers do not believe that rapists are "normal," they also do not presume rapists are mentally ill.

The final factor in this set, "Masculinity as a Motivation for Rape," reveals that officers do not consider rape as an opportunity for rapists to show their manhood—although they do believe rape is an exercise in power over women. The two items for this factor are listed in Table 3.9.

Table 3.7. Sexual Motivation for Rape

Statement	Average Assessment
19. Rape is the expression of an uncontrollable desire for sex.	2.9
20. Rape is a sex crime.	2.2
22. Rapists are sexually frustrated.	2.4
24. The reason most rapists commit rape is for sex.	3.0

1 = agree strongly; 2 = agree; 3 = disagree; 4 = disagree strongly.

Table 3.8. Normality of Rapists

Statement	Average Assessment
3. Rapists are "normal" men.	3.2
5. All rapists are mentally sick.	2.5

1 = agree strongly; 2 = agree; 3 = disagree; 4 = disagree strongly.

Overall, the Rapist Factor Set, which especially examines beliefs about the rapist's motivations for the crime, reveals that officers do not believe rapists are mentally ill, i.e., not legally responsible for their acts. However, they don't believe them to be "normal" either. The respondents may be saying that they believe rape is outside the normal behavior of men—but, importantly, does not usually tip into the realm of mental illness.

The other two factors in the set ("Masculinity" and "Sexual Motivation") indicate ambivalence on the part of the officers. On the "Masculinity" factor, respondents indicated that rape is an exercise in power over women, but rejected the contention that it is an opportunity for the rapist to show his manhood. Perhaps the male respondents were unable to correlate rape with the assertion of manhood because such an action would be foreign to them personally.

In the "Sexual Motivation" factor, respondents were in doubt as to whether or not rape is a sexual crime. Their confusion is not surprising since experts in sexual assault have only within the recent past recognized the nonsexual motivational factors underlying rape. We are of the opinion that respondent confusion in this area is caused by the fact that sexual assault typically uses sexual parts of the body to express nonsexual motivation.

Trial

The final factor set deals with the judicial process. The three factors in this set are "Punishment," "Victim's Influence in Trial," and "Prosecution." No item is associated with more than one factor.

Table 3.9. Masculinity as a Motivation for Rape

Statement	Average Assessment
12. Rape provides the opportunity for many rapists to show their manhood.	2.8
21. Rape is a male exercise in power over women.	2.2

1 = agree strongly; 2 = agree; 3 = disagree; 4 = disagree strongly.

Table 3.10. Punishment

Statement	Average Assessment
8. A man who has committed rape should be given at least 30 years in prison.	2.3
26. A convicted rapist should be castrated.	2.5
30. Judges are too lenient on convicted rapists.	1.8
39. The laws concerning rape are too lenient.	2.0

1 = agree strongly; 2 = agree; 3 = disagree; 4 = disagree strongly.

The first factor, "Punishment," examines the degree of retribution that should be dealt a convicted rapist. Table 3.10 indicates that officers believe a rapist should be treated with severity. Such a response is hardly surprising. Past studies have long confirmed that law enforcement officers adhere rather closely to traditional values and desire punishment for those who violate these values (see, for example, Balch, 1972). The respondents' evaluation of judicial sentencing (item 30) parallels their belief that punishment should be severe.

The second factor in the prosecution set, "Victims' Influence in Trial," consists of two items. Both, as may be seen in Table 3.11, examine beliefs about how the victim personally may influence a trial. Officers believe the victim's history, age, and appearance influence the outcome of the trial.

The final factor in this set is somewhat difficult to label. Recognizing the trial experience of our respondents, we entitled this factor "Prosecution." As seen in Table 3.12, the officers believe that in practice neither prosecutors, the public (potential jurors), nor the victims are prepared for the rape trial. "Prosecution," as a label for this factor, would not be as appropriate for persons outside of law enforcement because the public would believe the items in this factor describe a "normal" or "fair" trial, whereas experienced officers realize this is not necessarily true.

The Trial Factor Set demonstrates that officers agree rape is a serious crime that deserves severe punishment. The strong influence of the

Table 3.11. Victim's Influence in Trial

Statement	Average Assessment
35. The victim's history often affects the case.	2.1
37. The victim's age or appearance influences the jury.	1.9

1 = agree strongly; 2 = agree; 3 = disagree; 4 = disagree strongly.

Table 3.12. Prosecution

Statement	Average Assessment
32. Prosecutors are not properly prepared for court.	2.3
33. The public is uneducated concerning rape.	1.9
34. The victim often fails to testify.	2.1

1 = agree strongly; 2 = agree; 3 = disagree; 4 = disagree strongly.

victim at a court hearing is clearly seen in this factor set. More importantly, the officers believe that the public, who will ultimately make up the jury at a rape trial, and the prosecutors who will try the case are not adequately prepared to play their roles in court. Finally, the respondents believe when a conviction is obtained, judges are too lenient in the sentences they give to rapists.

Rape Investigators

We thought it important to single out and examine specifically the responses of those officers who are currently investigating rape cases. Approximately 31% of the total respondents stated that they investigate rape cases; only 3.8%, however, said they were assigned to a specialized squad in rape investigations. The data below describes the responses of the 31% currently involved in rape investigations.

Descriptive Data

The "typical" rape investigator is a married, 34-year-old, white, male patrol officer, who has attended college, been in law enforcement for 5 years, and has investigated less than 10 rape cases. Of course, this description is based on the appropriate average responses and is not meant to be taken as a literal description. See Table 3.13 for a complete breakdown by age, sex, race, law enforcement experience, rank, number of cases investigated, marital status, and education.

Training

One of the primary goals of the study was to examine the type and amount of training rape investigators had received. We were looking particularly for two major types of training: sexual assault training and rape victimology training. One could justifiably argue other types of training could be important to rape investigators (e.g., human sexuality), but to restrict the length of the questionnaire, we focused only

Table 3.13. Descriptive Data—Rape Investigators

	Percentage
Age	
21–30	32.9
31–40	47.0
41–50	15.7
51 or more	4.4
Sex	
Female	8.4
Male	91.6
Race	
American Indian	0.9
Black	3.5
Hispanic	3.5
Oriental	0.2
White	91.9
Other	0.2
Law Enforcement Experience (Years)	
Less than 2	17.1
2–5	35.8
6–10	27.3
11–15	12.8
More than 15	7.2
Rank[a]	
Deputy sheriff	10.1
Patrol officer	46.1
Corporal/sergeant	12.9
Lieutenant	2.9
Detective	21.6
Captain or above	4.2
Other	2.1
Number of Cases Investigated	
10 or fewer	54.1
11–50	33.0
51–100	7.2
More than 100	5.7
Marital Status	
Single	10.2
Married	77.6
Separated	1.8
Divorced	9.8
Spouse deceased	0.6

(*continued*)

Table 3.13 (*continued*)

	Percentage
Education[a]	
High school or less	30.9
1 Year of college or less	10.9
More than 1 year of college but no bachelor's degree	32.4
Bachelor's degree	16.9
Graduate work or degree	9.0

[a] Totals do not equal 100% because of rounding error.

on the two areas. We asked the recency and amount of training the officer had received prior to working on a rape case.

Table 3.14 shows that the overwhelming majority (95.5%) of rape investigators had received at least a few hours of training in sexual assault. A smaller, but healthy, percentage (88%) had received some training in rape victimology. The questionnaire was worded in such a way that rape victimology training could have been concurrent with sexual assault training. Though the vast majority of the officers had received training, relatively few had 40 or more hours of training in sexual assault (18.3%) or rape victimology (3.8%). Only 4.5% had received absolutely no training on sexual assault. This statistic is gratifying and confirms that law enforcement recognizes the importance of such investigations. On the other hand 22% had received no victimology training, a statistic that suggests a need for further educa-

Table 3.14. Type and Amount of Training

	Percentage[a]
Sexual Assault Training (Hours)	
None	4.5
1 to <10	36.7
10 to <20	27.5
20 to <40	12.9
40 or more	18.3
Rape Victimology Training (Hours)	
None	22.0
1 to <10	56.3
10 to <20	12.7
20 to <40	5.3
40 or more	3.8

[a] Totals do not equal 100% because of rounding error.

Table 3.15. Time Factor of Investigative Training

	Percentage
Sexual Assault Training Received	
Less than 2 years ago	50.0
2 to <6 years ago	36.6
6 to <10 years ago	9.9
10 or more years ago	3.5
Rape Victimology Training Received	
Less than 2 years ago	52.1
2 to <6 years ago	37.6
6 to <10 years ago	8.0
10 or more years ago	2.3
Prior Training Received	
None	20.4
1 to <6 hours	41.8
6 to <11 hours	22.1
11 to <20 hours	10.1
20 or more hours	5.6

tional efforts since the emotional trauma suffered by the victim can affect her ability to relate facts about the assault and to assist in the prosecution of the offender.

Table 3.15 sets forth the length of time since the officers last received training in the specified areas. Of those trained, approximately one-half (52.1%) had attended courses within the past 2 years. The table also contains data on the amount of training the officers had received prior to first investigating a rape case. One-fifth of the officers (20.4%) had received no training prior to their first rape investigation. Few (5.6%) had received more than 20 hours of training; most (63.8%) had received less than 20 hours of training.

Summary

Ever since rape became an issue in this country, the public has believed that law enforcement officers deal with victims in a hostile and suspicious manner. Several studies have, in fact, suggested that officers do have unsympathetic attitudes. These studies, however, used such extremely small population samples that their conclusions could in no way be extrapolated to include law enforcement generally.

The authors of this chapter, therefore, conducted a national study of 2,170 county and municipal law enforcement officers to examine their attitudes concerning rape. Using logic and statistical techniques, the authors divided the responses of the officers into categories dealing with the victim, the rapist, and the trial.

Analysis of the resulting data revealed that officers are not typically insensitive to the plight of rape victims. They are, however, suspicious of victims who meet certain criteria, such as previous and willing sex with the assailant, or who "provoke" rape through their appearance or behavior. Further, there is a small subset of officers who agree strongly with inappropriate statements such as "Nice women do not get raped" or "Most charges of rape are unfounded." These officers clearly have a prejudiced attitude toward the rape victim. To involve such officers in rape investigations would be a disservice to the victim and, ultimately, to the agency and the public. Responsibility rests with the supervisor to ensure that professional officers are assigned to sexual assault cases.

The respondents' attitudes toward the rapist were ambivalent. While the officers saw rape as an exercise in power, they did not see rape as an opportunity to demonstrate manhood. Also, the officers as a group were confused as to whether or not rape is a sex crime. These attitudes, when linked with their attitudes toward the victim, indicate a need for increased training of officers in the area of rape investigation and victimology.

Although some of the early studies held that police did not view rape as a "real" crime, the results of this study show that most officers view rape as a serious crime that deserves severe punishment. The study also reveals that law enforcement officers believe prosecutors, victims, and potential jurors are not properly prepared to play their assigned roles in a jury trial.

One of the most encouraging aspects of the study concerned the impact of training. The overwhelming majority of rape investigators had received sexual assault and/or victimology training. The fact that most training occurred relatively recently might explain the difference between the historical picture of police attitudes toward rape and the attitudes expressed in this study. Most importantly, however, the law enforcement community continues to provide education and training in matters pertaining to sexual assault. As a consequence, we expect that investigative capabilities will continue to improve, and that a more educated public will increasingly assist the law enforcement community.

References

Balch, Robert W. "The Police Personality: Fact or Fiction?" *Journal of Criminal Law, Criminology, and Police Science* 63 (1972): 106–119.

Blumberg, Abraham S. and Niederhoffer, Arthur. "The Police in Social and Historical

Perspective," *The Ambivalent Force: Perspectives on the Police.* Blumberg, Abraham S. and Niederhoffer, Arthur, eds. San Francisco: Rinehart Press, 1973.

Brownmiller, Susan. *Against Our Will.* New York: Simon and Schuster, 1975, p. 352.

Chronister, Jay L., Gansneder, Bruce M., LeDoux, John C., and Tully, Edward J. *A Study of Factors Influencing the Continuing Education of Law Enforcement Officers.* Washington, D.C.: U.S. Department of Justice, 1982.

Feild, Hubert S. "Attitudes Toward Rape: A Comparative Analysis of Police, Rapists, Crisis Counselors, and Citizens." *Journal of Personality and Social Psychology* 36 (1978): 156–179.

Feldman-Summers, Shirley and Palmer, Gayle C. "Rape as Viewed by Judges, Prosecutors, and Police Officers." *Criminal Justice and Behavior* 7 (1980): 19–40.

Galton, Eric R. "Police Processing of Rape Complaints: A Case History." *American Journal of Criminal Law* 4 (1975): 15–30.

Gottesman, Sharon T. "Police Attitudes Towards Rape Before and After a Training Program." *Journal of Psychiatric Nursing and Mental Health Services* 15 (1977): 4–18.

Greer, Germaine. "Seduction is a Four-Letter Word," in *Rape Victimology.* Schultz, Leroy G., ed. Springfield, Illinois: Charles C Thomas, 1975, p. 382.

Hurst, Carolyn J. *The Trouble with Rape.* Chicago: Nelson-Hall, 1977, p. 116.

President's Commission on Law Enforcement and Administration of Justice (PCLEAJ). Washington, D.C.: Government Printing Office, 1967, p. 23.

II

INVESTIGATION OF RAPE

Concepts of Physical Evidence in Sexual Assault Investigations

4

DALE M. MOREAU

This and the next chapter focus on various aspects of physical evidence in sexual assault cases. The prominent forms of evidence that have established reliability in science and the courtroom are usually available in these investigations. Once the possible evidence is recovered, a lengthy and complicated process is set in motion. The "silent witness" potential of physical evidence can be affected by many persons, including the responding officers, investigators, crime scene search technicians, prosecutors, medical personnel, and forensic laboratory examiners. Evidence integrity is the responsibility of all individuals coming in contact with the physical evidence at each progressive stage of the investigation.

This chapter and the ensuing one do not discuss physical evidence from the viewpoint of the forensic laboratory analyst. Instead, attention is devoted to the philosophy of evidence utilization, as well as the effective recognition, collection, packaging, and preservation of the types of evidence normally of value in sexual assault cases. The information and recommendations in these chapters are generally confined to the more salient aspects of the crime scene, suspect, and living victim.

The two chapters on physical evidence should be read in sequence because, for example, the discussion of sexual assault evidence collection kits in Chapter 4 sets forth the types of evidence collection choices often included in them, whereas Chapter 5 covers specific details and mechanics associated with the actual recovery of the evidence.

Introduction

The very mention of the words *forensic science* tends to conjure images of scientific instruments, exotic techniques, and sophisticated crime laboratories. Most often, physical evidence located at a crime scene is thought to depend on analysis in a forensic laboratory for it to be useful in court. The scientific examination of evidence in a laboratory setting, however, is but one of a series of interrelated tasks that make it possible to use physical evidence toward legal proof of a crime in the courtroom. The admissibility and relevance of tangible evidence can be affected by persons who may know very little about conducting a forensic examination. Consider, for example, the role of the first responding officer to a crime. This individual may lack the training or knowledge required to deal properly with physical evidence. Evidence can be unnecessarily moved, touched, contaminated, or destroyed as a result of improper actions by the first respondent or any subsequent person who enters the scene.

All facets of physical evidence must be given appropriate attention to ensure effective courtroom use. This evidence is often called a "silent witness," offering objective facts regarding the commission of the crime. This statement presupposes the organized and detailed handling of evidence materials from the inception of the crime scene search to the presentation of the evidence in the courtroom. Unless this entire process is efficient and devoid of contamination, the weight of the evidence material is, and should be, subject to serious question.

The contemporary view of forensic science must be expanded to encompass a broad range of functions, disciplines, and techniques. If investigators feel uncomfortable with the intricate nature of dealing with the various forms of physical evidence, they may be reluctant even to collect and submit certain varieties of physical evidence to a crime laboratory. Often the investigators tend to rely solely on nonforensic information derived from participants or witnesses associated with the crime. Forensic laboratory examinations may not be used to their fullest potential because the investigators do not understand the value of certain types of scientific evidence and how that evidence can support or contradict the testimony of participants or witnesses.

Often, the location of such evidence as latent prints is emphasized to the exclusion of other items, such as small or minute samples of hairs, fibers, and soil. In many instances, the officer on the scene may have little or no knowledge of the correct methods of locating, recovering, packaging, and preserving evidence specimens. The problem is compounded when the investigator is not adequately supported by funding and does not have direct access to a crime laboratory.

Even though the forensic evaluation of physical evidence is in its infancy, it has had a major impact on the conduct of criminal investigations and the litigations that result. It is an established fact that evidence is often present after contact between a victim and suspect. Accordingly, there is an increasing awareness of its prominence in the legal determination of guilt or innocence. Court decisions regarding the rights of defendants have made it incumbent on the law enforcement community to constantly improve its ability to make use of physical evidence in court.

Many significant questions raised in the courtroom due to conflicting or confusing statements by witnesses are answered by the use of tangible items that were collected as possible evidence. As evidence admissibility is established in prominent trials where physical evidence is the key, the tendency for attorneys virtually to insist on its use will surely increase. Attorneys also are certain to become more knowledgeable about potential challenges to the integrity of items of evidence. Skillful legal challenges to the admissibility of evidence will likely focus to a greater extent on chain of custody considerations. Seemingly fundamental evidence procedures are frequently neglected or carried out incorrectly, and these problems can surface during the trial.

It is figuratively, and sometimes literally, a long way from the actual scene of a brutal crime to the confines of a modern crime laboratory. There is often a marked tendency to evaluate physical evidence only from the standpoint of technologically advanced forensic tests. One must remember that a crime laboratory cannot properly examine items that were improperly handled, nor can a forensic scientist examine evidence that was not recognized and collected during an investigation.

The Nature of Physical Evidence

Despite the belief that physical evidence represents an impartial source of facts, these facts do not appear mystically. Information derived from evidence is often the result of laborious work beginning at the crime scene. Articles gathered at the scene will be of no value unless efforts are made to interpret them. Numerous kinds of physical evidence are subject to collection and laboratory analysis, and it can be an overwhelming task to study the appropriate procedures for each. Therefore, it is advantageous to establish basic points that permit the investigators, attorneys, and other involved persons to categorize evidence and the factors that have a bearing on its value in court. This categorization can also enable a jury to systematically organize, comprehend, and interpret the evidence as it is introduced during the course of a trial.

The techniques of forensic science and laboratory examinations are becoming more complex. On one hand, science is able to provide greater forensic insight. On the other hand, the increasingly complicated nature of scientific techniques makes it more difficult for the lay person to understand the facts. The attorney must not only present physical evidence in the trial, but make its pertinence in the case clear and unmistakable. Much greater attention should be given to courtroom presentation of information designed to familiarize a jury with the basic nature of physical evidence. This educational approach can assist the jury in comprehending the central issues addressed by pertinent evidence. Incriminating evidence may be presented in a trial, but if the presentation is confusing or unconvincing to the jury, it fails to accomplish the attorney's objective.

The major concepts usually applicable to evidence in sexual assault cases are:

1. Evidence identification
2. Class characteristic evidence
3. Individual characteristic evidence
4. Evidence transfer
5. Evidence environment
6. Evidence contamination

Evidence Identification

The term "identification" as related to the scientific meaning of the many forms of physical evidence is routinely used in forensic science. There are various levels of what actually constitutes a forensic identification. Each discipline of forensic science has a distinct meaning attached to this concept, depending heavily on the type, amount, condition, and source of the evidence in question.

One type of identification is of a single object or substance. In these cases, laboratory results identify the evidence based on its physical and/or chemical properties. For example, a forensic chemist can state that a suspected drug substance has been identified as heroin because it conforms to scientifically established and reliable data related to heroin.

In some identifications, it can be determined that two or more separate articles were once joined together to form a single object. These identifications are positive and unequivocal from the forensic standpoint. Illustrations of this category would be physically matching the edges of several pieces of torn paper or the broken ends of two pieces of wood.

Many identifications are based on the premise that certain objects may leave unique imprints or markings when in contact with other objects. A prime example would be latent prints on glass which can be positively identified with the dermal ridges of a suspect. Another classic illustration would be a shoe print at a crime scene that can be identified with unique wear characteristics on the sole of a suspect's shoe.

Numerous identifications involve the comparison of two or more items of evidence to establish that these items may be of the same source. Scientifically, however, a conclusive statement of unequivocal identification cannot be made. A comparison of hair discovered on the victim's clothing with known hair samples obtained from the suspect is an example in this area.

Official reports of crime laboratory analyses are many times written in the form of a summary. Words such as *association, correspondence, consistent with,* and *classification,* which frequently appear in these reports, may not be fully understood by the investigator or attorney. Such verbiage usually is a product of the synthesis of all raw data developed in the course of the laboratory examination. For this reason, the laboratory examiner should be contacted for a precise explanation of the full ramifications of forensic analyses whenever questions arise as to the interpretation of a report.

A well-recognized approach to distinguishing among varieties of physical evidence is to separate it into two categories: class characteristic evidence and individual characteristic evidence. This conceptual scheme is relatively simple and applies to virtually any type of physical evidence.

Class Characteristic Evidence

Class characteristic evidence is that which cannot be forensically identified with a specific source to the exclusion of all others. Examples include hairs, fibers, blood, saliva, semen, soil, and minute wood particles. Forensic science has no current methods to positively associate such items with a single or unique source. Here, forensic examination of evidence is directed at providing as much information as possible about each feature exhibited by each item and about many different types of this evidence in combination. The more materials of different types can be associated with a suspect, the stronger the association becomes in the minds of the jurors. Class evidence can be presented in such a manner that there is almost a direct inference of positive, or negative, association of the suspect with the victim, particularly when a preponderance of evidence exists.

There are inherent problems with the effective utilization of class characteristic evidence. The major difficulties appear to be caused by the following incorrect notions:

1. The types of evidence in this category do not provide positive identification of a person, in contrast to an identification provided by latent prints, and are, therefore, not worth collecting. Many persons involved in crime scene searches believe the time spent looking for class evidence could be better directed at searching for latent prints.

2. Collection and handling of very small evidence are too difficult to accomplish at a crime scene or too awkward to carry out with a victim or suspect. Some persons feel that because they cannot see certain evidence with the naked eye, it cannot be present.

3. Typical class evidence (especially hairs and fibers) is so common that, even with the best forensic techniques, it is of limited value in the courtroom.

4. The courtroom introduction of only class evidence may actually have a negative impact. For the most part, this is a result of the belief that any detailed scientific testimony will very likely confuse a layperson injury.

5. There are numerous forensic laboratories in the law enforcement community that do not routinely provide examinations of certain forms of class characteristic evidence.

These and other misconceptions should not be used as reasons simply to ignore the presence, or use, of class characteristic evidence. Many recent advances in the field of forensic science have been made regarding this kind of evidence. Perhaps the best reason to pursue class evidence is that it frequently is the only pertinent physical evidence found at a crime scene.

Individual Characteristic Evidence

The other category of physical evidence has individualizing characteristics. This category covers any evidence that can be positively identified with a specific source to the exclusion of all others. Of all possibilities in this category, latent prints of dermal ridge skin are probably the most frequently sought after in evidence recovery.

Individual characteristic evidence is usually less common than the class type. The investigator or attorney who relies solely on evidence that has the potential to be definitely associated with a singular source is hindered from the outset.

Often an item of evidence collected in an investigation has the potential to furnish information on both class and individual levels. An illustration of this possibility would be a section of cloth ripped from the suspect's shirt by the victim during a rape. Because of the transitory nature of debris-type evidence that may be on the cloth and shirt, the laboratory would first remove any debris present. A subsequent laboratory comparison of the shirt with the torn cloth could result in a positive determination that the cloth was once part of the shirt. However, if the torn edges of the cloth were frayed or worn, the laboratory might not be able to positively match the cloth with the shirt.

The next step would be to compare the composition, color, and construction of the shirt with the composition, color, and construction of the torn section of cloth. Such a comparison might result in a determination that the torn cloth corresponded in these features with the shirt, and, therefore, could have originated from it.

A further examination of individual characteristic evidence reveals two basic subdivisions:

1. Associations that identify a specific "person" as a source
2. Associations that identify a specific "thing" as a source

Identification of a person as the immediate source of a piece of evidence is usually the most desirable situation. Placing a suspect at a crime scene by means of a latent print recovered as evidence allows for an unequivocal statement that the individual was at the scene at some time. Naturally, this evidence is diminished if the suspect had frequent and normal access to the scene of the crime before it occurred. Conversely, the weight of the evidence is enhanced if it can be shown that the suspect had no reason or occasion to enter the scene area before the crime, or has denied ever being at the scene. Any type of positive association of evidence should be supported by corroborating investigation, whenever possible, no matter how straightforward the forensic aspects of the evidence appear to be.

In the next chapter, specific kinds of physical evidence will be discussed. Here it is noted only that there are three primary methods routinely used in forensic science to establish beyond doubt that a particular person is the only source of evidence: latent prints, bite marks (forensic odontology comparisons), and handwriting/hand printing. Considering the multitude of specimens that conceivably could be recovered in a case, it is apparent that the avenues for conclusively identifying a person as a source of individual characteristic evidence are relatively few.

Evidence Transfer

The basic premise behind the use of most evidence as an element of proof is that a person often leaves something at a crime scene and takes something away from it. In crimes of violence, this leads to the intensive search for very small pieces of evidence, generically referred to as *trace evidence*. This term covers almost every possibility, from fibers to small deposits of blood and semen. The very fact that this evidence is so varied and so often difficult to see with the naked eye should be considered an asset. The person who commits a crime of violence may think to wipe away latent prints or completely destroy a weapon. It is unlikely, however, that this individual would even consider the minute trace evidence substances that could be transferred to the victim, his/her clothing, or his/her surroundings.

A reasonable idea of the actions and events of a crime can be revealed by the transfer of evidence from one person or place to another. This is best seen by considering the kinds of evidence found in transfer situations. There are two such situations of significance: *direct* and *indirect* transfer (also commonly referred to as *primary* and *secondary* transfer).

When a transfer of trace evidence is considered, an investigator's initial thought is usually of direct transfer. Physical evidence in this instance is a direct result of the contact between suspect, victim, and the crime scene area. Fibers from the victim's clothes may readily transfer to the suspect's clothing, and vice versa, depending on the type of clothing. The suspect may be cut and leave a small bloodstain on the carpet in the scene. In these examples, the transfer of evidence is an immediate result of the contact between the participants and/or the crime scene.

The evaluation for transfer items should not stop at this point. One should consider that evidence can then be carried away from the scene of victim/suspect confrontation to other locations. Among other kinds of physical evidence, fibers, hairs, and soil from a scene can be transferred to the suspect's clothing or person and then deposited in a vehicle. The vehicle will then have received the resulting evidence indirectly from the scene and/or victim. This process is referred to as *indirect* transfer. The distinction between modes of transfer is important due to the necessity of expanding the search for small physical evidence away from the immediate crime scene. The collection of such indirectly transferred evidence will assist in gaining insight as to the movement and actions of those persons involved in a crime.

Evidence that is transferred in the course of a crime ultimately is deposited in a specific location, depending on the physical actions of persons before, during, and after the crime is committed. Whether transfer takes place between persons, between objects, or between persons and things, the presence of trace evidence can serve to corroborate other information in a case. The interrelationship between evidence recovery procedures and forensic examination in placing items of evidence in a specific place is a critical one. For example, if a suspect was kneeling on a carpet while vigorously assaulting the victim, it would be logical to assume that the majority of transfer evidence (carpet fibers) would be on the knees and lower legs of the trousers. The trousers would have to be handled, from time of recovery to the conducting of a crime laboratory examination, in a manner that would protect the fibers and retain them in place. This may seem to be a minor point, but it can become a major issue in a trial when an attorney attempts to use such physical evidence to support testimony of the victim regarding the presence and actions of the suspect.

Evidence Environment

The concept of evidence environment can assist in increasing the preponderance of trace evidence. The term *environment* is used here to denote that any given area has a combination of different types and kinds of materials. The mingling of these materials can result in identifiable combinations, which can represent a relatively unique condition. When a person enters a particular environment, there can be a transfer of combinations of many separate materials, which together could serve as evidence. The amount and variety of items transferred from the environment to the person depend primarily on the number and types of materials present, the actions and movement of the person, and the time span of contact.

The practical value of this approach can be seen in the following hypothetical situation. Fabric articles in a bedroom, such as bedding, throw rugs, curtains, or chair coverings, may be composed of a multitude of different fiber types and colors. Furthermore, it is possible that different types and colors of fibers may appear in each article, such as a blanket having a cotton, polyester, and acetate fiber composition. A suspect entering the room to commit a rape may pick up these numerous fiber variations on his person or clothing. Through forensic examinations, foreign fibers discovered on the clothing of the suspect can be shown to correspond to the varied nature of the scene environment. Thus, a strong association can be made connecting the suspect with the bedroom.

To use the environment concept effectively, a structured foundation must be established to depict the meaning of the evidence in a given investigation. Major points that should be incorporated in order to reach this goal are:

1. Due to the transitory nature of the kinds of physical evidence usually involved, the transferred evidence tends to reflect the nature of the last environment contacted by a person or object.
2. The meaning of the evidence is greatly enhanced by the presence of any materials that can be shown to be peculiar or relatively unique. Conversely, if the evidence is extremely common, less weight, if any, may be attached to it.

3. It is advantageous to demonstrate that multiple types of evidence have been associated between an environment and the object or person in question. Additionally, it should be emphasized that the places from which these materials were recovered as evidence coincide with the known actions and movement of persons or objects associated with the crime.

4. The greater the number of transfers of trace evidence, the more strongly the association is inferred between an environment and person or object. This point is of special importance when the types of evidence are limited. For example, it would be more meaningful to find numerous hairs on the victim's clothing that correspond to those of the suspect than it would be to locate one such hair. The sheer quantity of transferred evidence is suggestive of the nature of the struggle that took place.

Effective use of the environment concept is often limited or even nonexistent. There are many possible reasons for this. Two of these that predominate are:

1. Crime scenes are often searched primarily for evidence that appears to be foreign to the scene itself. "Known" articles that existed in an area prior to and during the time of the crime are not sampled. In terms of the previous bedroom example, this would mean that known fiber samples were not taken from the carpet, bedspread, chairs, and other appropriate items. The fiber evidence from the room on the suspect's clothing would have no probative value without a direct forensic comparison with the fiber content of the scene environment.

2. Transfer evidence is often introduced in the courtroom in a disjointed and piecemeal fashion without any planned and organized attempt to demonstrate interrelationships. This circumstance can result in an inability to portray the evidence in a way that would lead to a conclusion that the victim and the suspect once shared a common environment.

Evidence Contamination

One of the prime responsibilities in processing evidence, whether in the field or in the crime laboratory, is to avoid contaminating it. Physical evidence is frequently subjected to various contaminating influences from environmental or natural sources long before it is discovered in an investigation. When the evidence is discovered, attention should be given to halting or limiting further contamination. Another major area of concern is inadvertent contamination as a direct result of improper handling or packing of the evidence. The four main categories of inadvertent contamination are:

1. Nature of the evidence environment
2. Field personnel
3. Packaging materials
4. Laboratory environment

Physical evidence may exist in any environment, from a crime scene in an apartment to the physical person of a victim or suspect. Some environments have so much inherent potential to contaminate evidence that personnel have to be exceedingly cautious in the most routine collection and movement of the evidence. For example, when a suspect and a victim both have bled in the immediate area of a crime scene, it would be easy to contaminate an item bearing the victim's blood with some of the suspect's blood. Also, an environment containing numerous fabric items may make it difficult to keep extraneous fibers from contaminating items that did not actually come into contact as a result of the crime. Personnel should be fully aware of the potential of a given evidence environment to provide contamination of this sort. The best way to control such contamination is to conduct a preliminary survey of the environment for the purpose of identifying potential contamination hazards. A thorough evaluation of the evidence-gathering conditions peculiar to the given case will assist in devising a strategy to avoid difficulties.

The very presence of law enforcement personnel in an evidence environment tends to promote the possibility of contamination. On a practical level, someone has to be present to assess and collect the evidence. The number of individuals having these duties should be kept to a minimum so that organization will be maintained and contamination minimized. Further, field personnel who collect physical evidence should be cognizant of the fact that they can increase the potential for contamination through excessive handling of the evidence.

When an item is to be recovered, it should be marked for identification and placed in an appropriate, labeled container. The container should be sealed at the scene and not opened until the evidence is subjected to analysis in the crime laboratory.

The evidence should not be placed in one package or container, transported, and then removed for separate packaging and marking in a different location. Not only would this procedure increase chances of contamination, but it would also make it virtually impossible to state with certainty that trace evidence came from a particular item to the exclusion of all others in that one package. This point often becomes a major one at the time of trial.

There is little in forensic literature regarding the clothing worn by law enforcement personnel in evidence recovery circumstances, but the type of their clothing and its fiber composition can influence or contribute to the level of contamination. Clothes not only can add extraneous materials to the evidence environment, but may also collect foreign materials.

Even the specific fiber composition of garments worn by search personnel is important for consideration. Suppose, for example, that blue polyester fibers are found on the skin of a victim during an evidence examination, and subsequently, the clothing of a suspect, including a blue shirt, is obtained via the execution of a search warrant. Forensic laboratory comparison then determines that the shirt could have been the source of the blue fibers recovered from the victim's body. A logical question that could be asked of persons who were near the victim at the scene might be, "What were you wearing at the time of the crime scene investigation?" This question infers that fibers on the victim may have originated from the clothing of law enforcement personnel. This simple argument could be expanded to include other very transitory forms of evidence materials, such as hairs. Also, it could be quite persuasive to a jury, the members of which may not understand the realities that make evidence searches and recoveries difficult.

Personnel can take steps to avoid this problem by wearing clothing that does not easily shed or collect foreign materials. They might also wear the same type of clothing, thereby limiting the types of fibers that might be transferred. Jumpsuits or similar coverall garments having a tight weave pattern are some of the choices to be considered. The emphasis here is that the fiber content of the clothing worn by evidence recovery personnel would be known in case it became a point of contention. An ancillary advantage is that such detailed thinking about potential contamination promotes an awareness of personal responsibility for its control.

Evidence containers are key items in the recovery process, and they should be viewed as tools designed to protect the evidence in its original and uncontaminated form. There are numerous packaging materials that can be used for the different types of physical evidence. Whatever the choice, packaging materials should be treated in the same manner as the evidence itself. Packaging can be contaminated with foreign debris before it is used to store the evidence. Thus, it would be incomplete to discuss extreme care in the collection of physical evidence without considering contamination due to packaging.

There are several potential sources of contamination with regard to containers and packaging, which can be divided into the following major categories:

1. The packaging medium creates an unfavorable environment for preservation. Airtight containers commonly used to pack biological

fluids (e.g., blood, saliva, semen) often foster the growth of microorganisms that can degrade specimens. The evidence may be drastically affected before forensic examinations are even started in the crime laboratory.

2. The packaging medium itself contains substances that can act as contaminants. For example, if empty, open containers or bags are kept in the trunk of a vehicle, debris may accumulate on them. This can be avoided by ensuring that any items used to package the evidence are kept clean and stored in a sealed and uncontaminated manner. Another potential source of contamination has to do with the manufacturing of the packing material. Of particular concern is the utilization of paper bags or wrapping paper for evidence collection. Many previously unused paper bags and rolls of wrapping paper contain small pieces of paper, fibrous debris, and other possible contaminants.

Physical evidence can also be contaminated while in the crime laboratory, although the controlled environment may minimize or eliminate this occurrence, depending on the practices employed in evidence handling and processing. Attempts of the crime laboratory personnel to keep evidence uncontaminated can be supported if the evidence is packaged correctly by field personnel. Proper packaging will allow laboratory personnel to keep evidence separated for storage and examination.

Field individuals who routinely forward evidence to the crime laboratory should discuss the aspects of recovery, preservation, packaging, documentation, and transmittal with appropriate laboratory examiners. Laboratories have varying requirements and suggestions, which will assist the field investigator in avoiding contamination and realizing the potential offered by the evidence. Laboratory examiners and field investigators who fail to communicate with each other are making their work more difficult and less effective.

In summary, there are three significant and unfortunate consequences of contamination:

1. Evidence contamination is misleading to an investigation. Foreign materials not actually associated with the crime under investigation can lead personnel on "wild chases" for information. This situation results in wasted manpower and time.

2. Evidence contamination results in an inability on the part of the crime laboratory to evaluate the true meaning of forensic results. The crime laboratory may get misleading results and make confusing associations.

3. The confusion created by contamination offers an opportunity for the real evidence issues to become obscured in the courtroom. The

credibility of evidence-handling personnel and procedures can then be seriously challenged, making the task of using the evidence effectively much more difficult.

General Considerations Relating to the Victim, Suspect, and Crime Scene

The recovery of physical evidence in a sexual assault investigation is only the initial stage of the overall evidence collection process. In order to analyze the complex nature of this task, it is relevant to keep in mind four points during the discussions which follow:

1. Major sources that provide evidence
2. Kinds of evidence that one can expect to recover
3. Routine procedures necessary to obtain evidence and ensure its integrity and chain of custody
4. Specialized techniques that can enhance the chance of discovering evidence that is present in small amounts or is difficult to detect

The victim, suspect, and crime scene—primary sources of evidence in sexual assault cases—normally each come to the attention of law enforcement at varying points in time after the crime. These three sources require that systematically planned guidelines and methods for evidence recovery be established and followed.

The Victim

The protection of possible evidence should be initiated as soon as the victim contacts medical or law enforcement personnel. Frequently, the first such contact is by telephone. The victim should be counseled, whenever possible, to make no attempts to clean, bathe, change clothing, or take other action that may destroy or contaminate any evidence present. If the immediate crime scene is in the control of the victim, suggestions should be offered to protect that location. All medical, counseling, and law enforcement personnel must be made aware of this responsibility. These preliminary steps in evidence protection may make the difference between successfully and unsuccessfully bringing a case to a logical conclusion. Additionally, certain forms of evidence present immediately after the assault, such as semen and pubic hair, tend to corroborate the sexual contact indicative of the crime. Such evidence can often be lost to the investigator through actions of the victim.

A patrol officer frequently has the first personal contact with a victim after the crime is committed. The actions required of the officer to preserve the scene area and the evidence present in it make this person a major participant in the evidence process. Because caring for the well-being of the victim is the initial and dominant concern, the officer sometimes tends to neglect the need to secure the crime scene and preserve the integrity of the evidence. Evidence potential of the crime scene can be de-emphasized during the rapidly occurring events at the outset of the investigation.

The author has personally discussed these very problems with numerous police officers from throughout the United States who attend classes at the FBI Academy in Quantico, Virginia. These discussions revealed difficulties in the evidence collection process when the victim is first contacted. The ones that are indicated most often and appear to cross agency boundaries are:

1. Most patrol officers have inadequate training in the areas of evidence handling and dealing with the psychology of a person who has been mentally and physically abused during an assault.
2. Rarely does a patrol officer inquire of the victim as to information regarding possible items of physical evidence and their location at the scene.
3. It is common for patrol officers to be sympathetic to the victim who is obviously traumatized by the rape. They sometimes permit such victims to wash or change clothes prior to being taken from the scene to a medical facility for examination.
4. Some patrol officers do not regard physical evidence handling of any kind as within their sphere of responsibility. As a matter of formal or informal policy, many agencies discourage these officers from becoming involved in the evidence process.

It is not appropriate to regard the patrol officer as an uninvolved party in relationship to physical evidence. Certainly, it is not recommended that the officer embark on a major search for evidence, but the first officer does have an opportunity to take basic steps to protect the scene and the evidence contained therein.

The initial contact with the victim often requires that a decision be made about the clothing worn by this person. In some agencies, the victim is requested to undress prior to being transported for the medical examination. If this is done, the victim must undress over a clean, previously unused, section of white cloth or piece of wrapping paper supplied by the officer involved. Otherwise, evidence may become dislodged from the clothing as garments are removed. The cloth or paper is then marked to identify which side faced the victim, and then folded to retain any evidence. The proper containers for each article should be readily available when the victim undresses. The ideal field investigation setting in which to use this approach would be when the victim is in no need of immediate medical attention and is in a controlled environment, such as a residence.

Sometimes during field investigation, items of potential value as evidence might be seen on the clothing of the victim before this individual undresses. If the items are barely clinging to the clothing or person of the victim, they may be dislodged and lost when the articles of clothing are removed. Therefore, when evidence such as hairs, tufts of fibers, yarns, etc., is seen, a recovery effort should be made. Photographs may be taken and a rough sketch can be made to document the relative positioning of the items on the victim. The materials should be removed, immediately packaged, and the appropriate chain-of-custody data recorded. The person who takes the evidence from the victim should wear surgical gloves so that any contaminating substance on his or her hands or fingers will not come into contact with the evidence.

Careful consideration should also be given to the handling of the clothing of the victim when this individual is present at a hospital or other medical examination facility. Photographs should be taken of the victim prior to the removal of clothing, when possible. These pictures can be used to supplement later photographs that will depict specific injuries and possible evidence observed on the victim during the examination. Once again, it is advisable to have the victim undress over a section of cloth or wrapping paper so that evidence that falls away as the clothes are removed is not lost. Each item of clothing removed from the victim should be placed immediately in a separate evidence container, which is then securely sealed.

The clothing of the victim is sometimes cut away in the hospital due to the life-endangering nature of wounds sustained during the crime. These items normally end up in a disheveled pile as they are thrown away from the treatment area. The realities involved in caring for the victim give hospital personnel or law enforcement officers no ideal alternatives here. Steps should be taken in such situations to recover, package, and seal the evidence as soon as is practical. Whenever possible, the table on which the victim was treated as well as the area immediately underneath the pile of garments should be studied for dislodged items. The fact that the clothing was cut from the victim by hospital personnel must be documented. Assailants in sexual assaults sometimes quickly remove the clothing of the victim by cutting it off. The respective damage to the clothing by each party may become an important issue during trial.

The field or hospital recovery of materials directly from the clothing should be confined to situations in which evidence would otherwise be lost. An unsystematic examination of the clothing accomplished on a routine basis will probably destroy, lose, or contaminate more evidence than it obtains. It is more beneficial for the evidence to be acquired directly from the clothing during a complete forensic laboratory examination.

At some point toward the beginning of the investigation, the sexual assault victim is examined in a medical facility. Medical personnel who come into contact with this victim are trained primarily in evaluating his/her physical health and emotional needs. However, there is also a need to expand this education into the evidentiary realm. Many law enforcement agencies have established liaison and training programs regarding physical evidence collection for hospital personnel. As a direct result of these programs, the use of preassembled sexual assault evidence collection kits has increased. Such kits are designed to collect certain forms of physical evidence directly from the body of the victim. These types of evidence are those that can corroborate sexual activity itself (e.g., semen present in the vaginal area) as well as serve to associate a suspect with the victim. The makeup of the kits and the philosophy behind their use will be discussed later in this chapter.

The victim of a sexual assault is usually released from the hospital when this person's physical and emotional condition permits. In cases where the crime was committed in the victim's residence, he/she must be reminded to leave the scene of the assault intact, should he/she return home before the evidence technicians arrive.

The physical evidence recovered from victims in sexual assault cases is of paramount importance. The ideal or perfect evidence-gathering situation is very difficult to attain. Nonetheless, all activity should be directed at coming as close as possible to the "ideal" in recovery of physical evidence. The victim should be considered the focal point of the crime. This frame of mind automatically will lead to effective handling of the evidence, because the search of the victim is then considered, in essence, as a detailed crime scene search.

The Suspect

One of the primary goals of physical evidence collection is to link the suspect and the victim to each other, and the suspect and/or victim to the crime scene. There can be a multitude of problems inherent in actually doing so. While the victim is normally examined for possible evidence as soon as is practical, the suspect may not be identified for some time. This time span permits the suspect to destroy clothing, shower or bathe, or thoroughly clean out a vehicle used in the crime. The longer it takes for a suspect to be developed, the greater the potential for evidence loss. Once again, attention is directed to the fact that minute evidence of the type encountered commonly in sexual assault cases tends to be advantageous to law enforcement. Very large items, like clothing and bedding, may be thrown away or totally destroyed, but it is very likely that some of the small debris may still remain in the general area where the larger articles were handled by the suspect. Although it is somewhat unlikely, hairs, fibers, and other small evidence also can be dislodged and transferred to the new clothing of the suspect. This possibility of indirect transfer should not be excluded when one deals with a suspect.

The approach to the acquisition of evidence involving the suspect will be directly influenced by the time span problem already mentioned. There are three main situations which are normally encountered:

1. The suspect is developed immediately following the commission of the crime.
2. The suspect is developed as a direct result of having sustained injuries which warrant medical treatment.
3. The suspect is developed a lengthy time after the assault has taken place.

The ideal situation, of course, is for the suspect to be identified immediately after the crime. The evidence on the clothing and the person of the suspect most closely resembles the evidence represented by the victim, the victim's clothing, and the crime scene at this point. Often, the clothing worn during the assault can be obtained without any destruction of evidence. Also, the body of the suspect should be scrutinized for possible evidence materials that would be indicative of contact with the victim. The chance of discovering significant evidence items is at its highest level. It is at this stage that the evidence acquired can be so overwhelming that the guilty party eventually confesses to the crime.

Sometimes, a suspect is physically injured during the course of an assault, and may require medical attention, which leads to identification of the suspect by authorities. Records of the pretreatment extent of injuries and the nature of treatment undertaken, and acquisition of clothing and biological samples (e.g., blood, hairs, saliva), are necessities from the physical evidence viewpoint. Photographs should be taken whenever possible while the suspect is in the medical setting as an integral part of the documentation procedure. These photographs can be vivid representations of the truth, which will assist the jury in overcoming possibly conflicting data during a trial. Photographs represent the best opportunity the investigator has to corroborate the statement of the victim regarding the nature of injury to the suspect.

Often, the suspect is not developed until long after the crime is committed. Many evidence materials on the suspect or in the immediate environment have been completely eliminated by deliberate cleaning or as a result of the time span involved. Even so, very small pieces of physical evidence may linger on clothing or in vehicles for a lengthy period of time. A diligent search may locate significant evidence. The investigator commits an error when the assumption is made that evidence could not be present, or would have no meaning later in court, due to the time lapse since the crime occurred. At the very least, appropriate known samples should be obtained from the suspect, and a search conducted for clothing matching that described by the victim.

No matter which of these time spans is involved, physical evidence should be collected from a suspect. Investigators sometimes fail to institute necessary steps to seek out physical evidence when the suspect "confesses" to the crime. This is based on the premise that the confession alone is sufficient to result in a guilty plea or courtroom conviction. This is a high-risk assumption, especially considering the manner in which the courts have dealt with the legal admissibility of confessions. If the suspect retracts the statement of guilt and the physical evidence has not been collected, serious tactical problems will be encountered by the prosecution from the time of the preliminary hearing to the actual trial. Physical evidence is needed to corroborate or dispute verbal statements by the parties involved. In today's courtroom arguments, actions *not* taken by investigators regarding physical evidence can be of greater discussion and pertinence than those that *were* taken.

Sexual Assault Evidence Collection Kits

The role of physical evidence in sexual assault crimes is not only to associate the victim and suspect with one another, but also to establish that sexual contact has, in fact, occurred. The search for physical evidence in this regard is extended from the crime scene itself to the medical examination of the victim and/or suspect. The necessity of establishing a connection between victim and suspect, and the sexual aspects of the criminal act, require that the victim, and suspect whenever possible, be suitably examined for the presence of physical evidence.

In some instances, the victim first becomes known to law enforcement authorities as a result of hospital treatment for injuries suffered in the assault. It is at this point that the benefits of planning and liaison between law enforcment and the medical community can be realized. If medical personnel have been properly advised and educated in the evidentiary aspects and medical features of treating a victim, the task of using evidence in the courtroom will be greatly facilitated. On the other hand, improperly trained medical personnel can so impair the physical evidence that the suspect cannot be brought to trial. Successfully recovering physical evidence in sexual assault cases must be a combined effort of law enforcement and medical personnel.

The direct involvement of police officers in the evidence recovery process in the medical environment differs considerably depending on such factors as locale, funding, personnel availability, and training. In some areas, a law enforcement representative will be present for the entire course of the examination or at least during the collection of evidence. This situation facilitates maintenance of chain of custody and can decrease the number of witnesses necessary to introduce the evidence in the courtroom. There is the added advantage that any questions about the evidence from the medical personnel can be answered immediately.

There are numerous jurisdictions, however, in which law enforcement personnel have virtually no direct involvement with the medical examination of the victim. Any evidence materials obtained by medical personnel are packaged and then provided to a law enforcement representative at a later time. The burden of providing critical testimony in court relating to the recovery of this evidence is sometimes then placed on the medical professionals. This testimony can often go beyond the realm of normal medical procedures to the establishment of chain of custody and evidence integrity.

Considering the vital role physical evidence plays in sexual assault cases, it can be preferable on occasions to have a trained law enforcement officer present during the medical examination of a victim. This can be of special importance when medical personnel have not been provided training and are unfamiliar with evidence recovery procedures. The officer's presence should be professional and unobtrusive, in a manner consistent with concern for the mental and physical condition of the victim.

It is emphasized that the presence of a law enforcement officer during the examination is an extremely controversial issue. Some law enforcement, medical, legal, and counseling personnel feel this presence is abhorrent and unnecessary. Others feel the evidentiary concerns are so important that a reasonable method of having a trained officer present can be developed and is sometimes desirable. Decisions must be made regarding this issue before cooperative protocols are established about dealing with the victim.

Cooperation between law enforcement agencies and the medical profession concerning controlled evidence-gathering procedures is improving. One of the components of ongoing cooperative education and training programs is preassembled evidence-collection kits. The major goal of using these kits is recovery of certain physical evidence materials in strict keeping with proper medical, forensic, and legal requirements. Medical facilities having contact with a sexual assault victim are usually supplied with numerous kits for use on short notice. The contents of these items often are assembled by trained persons, such as crime laboratory employees. The materials supplied in the package are organized so that they are relatively easy to use in a systematic fashion, and designed to recover physical evidence substances associated with sexual assaults.

Even though the kits are designed with ease of use in mind, training of all medical personnel involved in the contact with assault victims is needed. The actions of such personnel will many times determine whether highly transitory evidence will be recovered or whether it will be lost or contaminated. Therefore, law enforcement officials knowledgeable about the kits and their administration should educate appropriate medical personnel in the forensic and legal procedures involved. This is the first step in the construction of a responsible and successful evidence collection program that will survive the rigors of courtroom challenge.

Prior to a discussion of the items that can be used as components of sexual assault evidence-collection kits, it is necessary to review the role of these kits in the framework of the entire medical examination of a victim. This examination normally involves several major areas, each having a potential impact on evidence recovery and the investigation as a whole. These areas are:

1. Acquisition of an extensive medical history of the person examined, as well as documented legal and competent permission for the examination.
2. Inquiry regarding the nature of the assault itself.
3. Physical examination, including identification of trauma or injury attributable to the assault.
4. Evidence recovery procedures.
5. Detailed chain of custody records concerning physical evidence.

Preassembled evidence collection kits can be found in a variety of designs. Directions on proper use typically are included to avoid confusion and error. Also frequently included are forms covering (1) medical examination and interview of the victim, (2) consent/release regarding evidence obtained from the victim, (3) consent/release concerning authority to disseminate victim-related information, and (4) chain-of-custody documentation. Such documents are best formulated by joint discussion and agreement between law enforcement and medical representatives who treat sexual assault victims.

There are many physical evidence recovery methods and procedures that can be incorporated into a sexual assault evidence collection kit. These methods and procedures will usually depend on the age and sex of the person on whom they are used, as well as whether this individual is a victim or suspect. The following is essentially a general description. The reader should refer to the next chapter for the actual mechanics and precautions of evidence recovery.

Clothing. All clothing worn by the victim should be obtained and packaged in a sealed, secure condition. Each item must be packaged separately to avoid transfer of evidence from one item to another. Sections of manila-type wrapping paper or sturdy paper bags can be supplied for packaging purposes.

Head Hair Combing/Brushing. The head hair region of the victim is combed or brushed for evidence substances. This requires the use of an uncontaminated comb or brush specifically for the head area only. The comb or brush and adhering materials are packaged and sealed.

Known Head Hairs. An appropriate amount of hair to represent color, length, and area variation is obtained. Hairs should be pulled whenever possible. Known hairs should be acquired after the head hair combing/brushing procedure is completed. These hairs are packaged and sealed.

Pubic Hair Combing/Brushing. The pubic region of the victim is combed or brushed for evidence materials. This requires the use of an uncontaminated comb or brush specifically for the pubic area only. The comb or brush and adhering materials are packaged and sealed.

Known Pubic Hairs. An appropriate amount of hair to represent color, length, and area variation is obtained. Hairs should be pulled whenever possible. Known hairs should be acquired after the pubic hair combing/brushing procedure is completed. These hairs are packaged and sealed.

Combing/Brushing of Body Hair Regions Other than Head and Pubic. In the event an individual is observed to have excessive body hair, a separate, uncontaminated comb or brush and appropriate packaging material can be utilized to collect trace evidence that may be present.

Vaginal Swabbings. The vaginal cavity is swabbed to detect the presence of spermatozoa and/or seminal fluid. An unstained control sample of the gathering medium is retained and packaged separately.

Oral Swabbings. The oral cavity is swabbed to detect the presence of spermatozoa and/or seminal fluid. An unstained control sample of the gathering medium is retained and packaged separately.

Anal Swabbings. The anal region is swabbed to detect the presence of spermatozoa and/or seminal fluid. An unstained control sample of the gathering medium is retained and packaged separately.

Microscope Slides of Smears Made from Vaginal, Oral, and Anal Swabbings. Any such slides prepared for the examination of spermatozoa should be retained and submitted along with the swabs used to prepare the smears.

Penile Swabbings. The penis is swabbed to detect the presence of blood or other evidence. An unstained control sample of the gathering medium is retained and packaged separately.

Vaginal Aspirate. In addition to vaginal swabbing, aspiration of the vaginal region is accomplished by irrigation with saline solution. Spermatozoa not located through the swabbing procedure may be recovered in this manner. A separate tube or small vial into which the solution is placed should be supplied. A control sample of the irrigation fluid is retained and packaged separately.

Oral Rinse. The mouth of the person examined can be rinsed in order to remove spermatozoa not collected via the swabbing procedure. The rinse is expectorated into a tube or vial. A control sample of the rinse is retained and packaged separately.

Nasal Mucus Sample. This type of sample is acquired by having the individual being examined blow his/her nose on cloth. The mucus may contain spermatozoa that were deposited in the mouth or facial area. An unstained portion of the cloth can function as a control sample.

Fingernail Scrapings. Using appropriate materials, the areas underneath the fingernails are scraped for significant debris such as hairs, fibers, blood, or tissue. The gathering implement is retained. It is suggested that each hand be scraped individually and the resulting debris packaged separately.

Miscellaneous Debris Collection. Evidence substances not included in the previous techniques can often be observed during the examination of a person. At least two individually packaged swabs or sections of cotton cloth should be available to collect such items as blood or semen found on the skin. Additionally, several separate containers should be included to collect debris taken from the clothing or body of the individual.

Known Blood. Blood is drawn into a sterile test tube for blood grouping purposes. A minimum of 5 milliliters is recommended, preferably without the inclusion of a chemical anticoagulant or preservative.

Known Saliva. Saliva is sampled from the person to assist in the determination of secretor status. An unstained control sample of the gathering medium is retained and packaged separately.

"Catch" Paper/Cloth. A section of paper or cloth on which the person can stand while undressing can be supplied. Additionally, a separate piece of paper or cloth can be used to cover the examining table to collect any evidence that is dislodged during the examination.

The foregoing general information on the possible evidence collection methods that can be included in a preassembled kit is set forth in terms of possibilities, not as an unalterable formula. The exigencies of each case, as well as the personnel and agencies involved, will dictate the contents of a potentially successful kit. There are some additional points, however, which are important regarding what is and is not assembled or used in this kit.

1. Head hair combings are sometimes not provided as components of sexual assault evidence collection kits. A great deal of minute evidence could be present in head hair, including such substances as foreign hairs, fibers, and plant material. Also, only one comb is often contained in a kit for combing all body hair areas. A separate comb should be used for each area.
2. The use of oral and anal swabs is recommended on a case-by-case basis in many kits. Since some victims are extremely reluctant to report the facts in cases where oral or anal contact took place, it may be best to perform these procedures simply as a precaution.
3. The inclusion of a section of paper or cloth on which the person can stand while undressing is a critical item that is not often recognized. Evidence can be lost simply by the excessive movement and handling of clothing upon its removal. The examinee's physical condition following the assault may not permit this action to be taken.
4. The acquisition of questioned liquid or wet body fluids should take into account that these specimens are extremely vulnerable to bacterial attack. Such samples should be air-dried and frozen to retard deterioration.
5. Different procedures for collection of evidence have varying de-

grees of success as far as forensic examinations are concerned. For example, FBI Laboratory examiners have noted to the author that fingernail scrapings, penile swabbings, nasal mucus samples, vaginal aspirate, and oral rinse do not usually yield pertinent evidence in their experience. This statement is not meant to imply that such procedures should not be used. It is included here to emphasize that some techniques may be more routinely productive than others.

6. The sequence in which the components of a kit are used is significant. Most preassembled kits include recommendations on the order of using these components. No particular order is set forth in this discussion, because the complexities of each case will often dictate the appropriate sequence of action. The user of a kit should consider that the collection of evidence usually follows a most-transitory to least-transitory progression.

7. The medical examination of the victim or suspect often involves the recovery of specimens used to test for sexually transmitted diseases. These specimens are usually taken during the evidence collection procedures, but will normally not be submitted to the crime laboratory. The testing of specimens for disease is conducted by an appropriate medical facility. As an additional health and safety precaution, the crime laboratory should be notified immediately when disease is detected.

Sexual assault evidence collection kits are primarily designed for evidence recovery from a female victim who has been raped by a male assailant. Nonetheless, the typical kit contains sufficient evidence collection materials to cover an adult male, an adult female, or even a child who has become the victim of an assault. The type of victim and acts committed would determine the various techniques that would be utilized. The forms of physical evidence normally of importance in cases of sexual assault differ very little depending on the sex of the victim, in most instances. Saliva, blood, hairs, and fibers, for example, are at issue in almost any sexual assault matter.

Consideration should be given to extending the use of evidence kits to suspects in sexual assault investigations. The types of evidence materials that may be located on the clothing or person of the suspect are similar to those found on the victim. The acquisition of known biological samples is basically the same for both victim and suspect. The trace evidence existing on the suspect can be collected in the same manner as that on the victim is collected. In fact, the applicable components of a victim-oriented sexual assault evidence collection kit serve as a good guide for kits used on a suspect.

The primary benefit of the sexual assault evidence collection kit is that it emphasizes the inherent significance of the victim or suspect as a source of physical evidence, and what types of potential evidence to pursue. The focus is on treating the victim or suspect as, in fact, a crime scene. This statement is not intended as a crude or insensitive reference to a victim who has suffered through the tragic and brutal events of a sexual assault. It is a fact that must be recognized in the collection of physical evidence pertaining to sexual assault. The rules that necessarily govern proper evidence recognition, collection, and preservation are as applicable in a hospital examination of a sex crime victim as they are at a crime scene.

The Crime Scene

The phrase *crime scene investigation* is in common use by law enforcement personnel. However, there can be an erroneous assumption that conducting a crime scene search involves no more than picking up articles and placing them into evidence containers. Anyone familiar with this topic realizes that what might appear to be an elementary exercise can become a very complicated task.

Crime scene searches generally are conceived only as efforts to methodically locate and gather physical evidence. However, the evidence recovered will be only as effective, under normal circumstances, as the administration, management, documentation, and collection techniques allow. It is simply not enough to collect the evidence. Precise documentation of the scene and the evidence recovered must meet chain-of-custody and procedural challenges in the courtroom. There can be cases in which incriminating physical evidence is discovered, but is poorly used in court or deemed altogether inadmissible because of poor documentation and confusion at the crime scene. When this occurs, all previous efforts are wasted and become moot when the suspect who indeed committed the crime walks away from the trial a free person.

Searches of scenes involving sexual assaults sometimes are not viewed from the same perspective as searches of areas where a homicide has occurred. When a murder is investigated, the body of the victim frequently is in place and, therefore, is a major concern for those gathering physical evidence at the scene, and subsequently at the autopsy. In contrast, the victim in a rape case often survives the attack and is not physically at the scene itself. Thus, the attention given to the victim occurs primarily at the medical examination of this person. There can be a tendency to concentrate on this facet of evidence collection, without serious action being taken to conduct an intensive search of the scene itself. Such a condition can result in the loss of pertinent evidence that could aid in solving the crime.

At this point, it is advantageous to discuss the fundamental steps through which a crime scene search normally progresses. The following material is not a complete study of crime scene searches, but a concise summary on the essential progression of events.

General Stages of the Search

It is of utmost importance that a proper framework of administration and procedures is used on a consistent basis in crime scene searches. Despite the different administrative procedures developed by various agencies, there remains a series of events that should transpire in any search in order to realize the full potential of evidence from the scene. The following sets forth a suggested pattern of crime scene search steps, without advocating the imposition of an inflexible system in conducting crime scene investigations. The person who attempts to operate in an identical manner on each search will soon discover that there is always some eventuality that does not fall into a preplanned scheme. These basic steps are:

1. Approach scene
2. Secure and protect
3. Preliminary survey
4. Narrative description
5. Photograph scene
6. Sketch scene
7. Evaluation of latent fingerprint evidence and other forms of evidence
8. Detailed search for evidence; collection, preservation, and documentation of evidence
9. Final survey
10. Release of scene

The following discussion summarizes these critical stages of a search and includes some important practical suggestions to assist in conducting an efficient search.

Approach Scene. Law enforcement personnel responding to a crime scene should be alert to a variety of items or events that ultimately may be connected with the investigation. People, vehicles, and objects observed by officers may provide details concerning the crime and the person(s) responsible for it. For example, evidence may have been discarded along a route used by a subject, or potential witnesses may be seen along the roadside as officers proceed to the scene. Further, the presence of possible getaway vehicles may be discovered. All personnel in the area of a crime scene should be alert for information sources that may provide a necessary "link" in the successful investigation of the case.

Secure and Protect. To avoid contamination and prevent unnecessary disturbances of the crime scene, all personnel must strive to secure and protect the scene. Such an effort requires continuous attention and cannot be successful if a haphazard approach is used. "Securing the scene" and "protecting the scene" should be thought of as two separate, but interrelated duties. Before a complete crime scene area can be realistically protected, it must first be adequately secured. Securing the scene will necessitate the establishment of its perimeter as soon as possible. After the perimeter has been established, all reasonable efforts can be made to prevent any disturbance of the original conditions at the scene. Thorough control over all persons entering the immediate crime scene area is of extreme significance. Many of the major courtroom difficulties that can surface regarding contamination of evidence and of the scene revolve around the lack of initial steps taken by law enforcement officers to ensure that the scene was adequately protected.

Preliminary Survey. During the preliminary survey of a crime scene search, the foundation for management, organization, and logistics should be developed to suit the needs of a particular crime scene. Examples of the purposes of the survey are:

1. To establish administrative and emotional control
2. To delineate the extent of the search area
3. To organize the methods and procedures needed
4. To determine manpower and equipment needs
5. To develop a general theory of the scene
6. To identify and protect transitory evidence

The preliminary survey begins after the crime scene has been thoroughly secured and protected. An initial walk-through of the scene is undertaken so that the officer in charge has a solid understanding of the scene as a whole, including the existence and location of observable items with possible evidence value. The initial walk-through should be accomplished by as few persons as feasible to ensure that no one is operating in an uncoordinated and unrecorded manner. The preliminary survey may be the most important stage of administration, because it promotes an organized plan of action and prevents uncontrolled physical activity that could destroy pertinent evidence.

Narrative Description. The narrative description is one of the primary means of documenting the original conditions of the scene as found by law enforcement personnel. It can best be described as a general view of the scene, without undue attention to extraneous detail. The narrative description should not be confused with the use of sketches, close-up photographs, and finely detailed evidence notes that later are part of the process of the search. The narrative description usually will not have the preciseness of the specialized evidence search of the crime scene. Instead, it is normally limited to a general view of the scene as it was first observed by law enforcement officers. The ultimate value of this description is to show a jury how the crime scene initially would have appeared to them if they had been actually present at the scene in the role of the law enforcement officer. Also, the narrative description provides a documented means of determining whether any evidence or scene conditions were inadvertently disturbed as a result of a later detailed search.

The three common modes of preparing a narrative are handwritten notes, audiotape recorder, and videotape with sight/sound or sight-only capability. Each of these methods has inherent capabilities and limitations that should be considered prior to use. For example, videotape equipment can record both the sights and sounds at the scene. The system sometimes also will record irrelevant or off-the-cuff statements on the part of personnel who are at the scene. Such advantages and disadvantages should be explored before the mode of preparing the narrative description is selected.

Photograph Scene. The courtroom role of photography in portraying a crime scene cannot be overestimated. Photography is such a common medium in society that its use in the adjudication of criminal cases should be expected. Photographing a crime scene is a continuous process and must include long-range, midrange, and close-up photographs. These will show the immediate focal point of the crime as well as the entire location. Photographs must be prepared so that the pictures can be used to portray all pertinent segments of the scene. Long-range photographs are often neglected during crime scene searches.

Photographic views of the crime scene can usually be categorized as those (1) focusing on the location of the crime, (2) concentrating on the nature of the crime, (3) centering on the results of the crime, (4) featuring the physical evidence at the scene, and (5) illustrating follow-up activity not directly occurring at the immediate scene.

The location photographs should depict the various places that are part of the crime scene area. Aerial photographs are an example of this. The nature and results of the crime should be depicted by the photographs in a manner that will assist the investigation in determining the type of crime, and actions of the persons, involved. For instance, a rape incident may have begun with a house break-in through a kitchen door, continued with vandalism, and culminated with the rape of the victim who confronted the intruder. Therefore, the results of each portion of the crime should be depicted in a sequence that reproduces the events.

Photographs of the physical evidence are of great relevance, including the use of measurement scales when appropriate. The representation of observable evidence in relation to the entire scene ultimately will enable the evidence to be connected in the courtroom with the crime scene, the victim, and the suspect. Also, photographs of physical evidence can be a major component in establishing the chain of custody of items from the scene introduced in the courtroom.

The follow-up photographs are an outgrowth of the crime scene investigation. Photographs of a victim or suspect showing bruises or wounds are examples in this category. Integration of the information recorded photographically at both the actual scene and during follow-up activities will produce a greater depth of understanding of the realities of the crime scene itself.

Sketch Scene. A sketch or diagram is a commonly neglected method that can be used to document certain important conditions at a crime scene. Many persons mistakenly consider the use of sketches to be outmoded by photographs. A photograph reduces to two dimensions a scene that actually consists of three dimensions. Distance relationships can be distorted and incorrectly interpreted in a photograph. A sketch provides true distance relationships that will complement and supplement photographic representations of the crime scene. The locations of all pertinent evidence can be set forth in a sketch for display in court. A sketch can also be made of locations or items that are very difficult to photograph in a manner that shows desired conditions and detail.

Evaluation of Latent Fingerprint Evidence and Other Forms of Evidence. The crime scene search is concentrated on the discovery and collection of physical evidence that can be used in the investigation. There is a series of organizational and planning requirements involved in bringing the crime scene investigation to the point at which a systematic search can be undertaken. The same type of planning applies to the evaluation of the evidence before it is collected. Both latent fingerprints and other forms of physical evidence present at a crime scene must be studied before attempts are made to collect evidence. For example, a careless dusting procedure for possible latent fingerprints may contaminate, or result in complete loss of, transitory evidence such as hairs or fibers. Likewise, in a poorly executed attempt to collect hairs or fibers, valuable latent fingerprints may be destroyed. Each case will dictate the sequence in which evidence is collected. However, in all cases, the possibilities of the types of physical evidence must be explored and the detailed search should proceed based on this evaluation.

Detailed Search for Evidence; Collection, Preservation, and Documentation of Evidence. Once a systematic evaluation of the evidence has been accomplished at the crime scene, a detailed search can proceed. This stage of the crime scene search will produce the bulk of the potential evidence at the scene. However, the success or failure of the efforts during this portion of the investigation is dependent on planning and organization done in the earlier stages. If an organized and methodical approach has been fostered, the search of the scene will have the greatest potential for success.

Specialized methods needed to recover different forms of evidence come into play at this time. These procedures should be designed to preserve the recovered physical evidence in its original form to the greatest extent possible. Photographic and written documentation should record the locations of items of evidence within the scene. Also, necessary chain-of-custody data must be recorded as the evidence recovery operation proceeds. The possible evidence articles and information acquired during this time are, in essence, the real goals of the search.

Final Survey. Following the complete documentation of the crime scene and the collection of physical evidence, a final survey should be conducted. The purpose of this survey is to review the crime scene investigation process from the beginning. All elements must be weighed against one central idea: Has the crime scene investigation effort considered all possibilities for telling the events of the crime? This introspective approach may prevent such oversights as important evidence being missed, critical photographs being neglected, or obvious facts being overlooked. Especially in view of the stress and confusion often accompanying a crime scene search, time should be taken to review all observations made and actions taken.

Release of Scene. Upon completion of the final survey, a decision must be made to relinquish control of the scene. This decision should be formal and official and leave no room for misinterpretation. The authority for this decision should rest with the person who is in charge of the crime scene investigation. If it is common knowledge that a formal declaration of release must be made, then those persons involved will realize that the job remains unfinished until they are otherwise informed. When considering this decision, the officer in charge should accept input from selected persons involved in the crime scene search effort. In this way, formal release of the scene becomes a joint effort to decide whether or not all reasonable actions have been taken.

In some investigations, there are situations in which forensic specialists examine the crime scene. For example, the patterns of blood present at the scene can offer valuable information about what took place. This can require the presence of specialists during and/or after the initial search. Once a scene is released, there can be legal complexities involved in regaining access. Also, the scene may be cleaned or otherwise disturbed after it is released. The crime scene should be protected and not released until any specialists required can observe its conditions and perform their examinations.

A completed crime scene investigation does not end the evidence process. The forensic evidence must still be examined by the crime laboratory. When all forensic analyses are completed and results submitted for use in the investigation, the crime scene once again must be reviewed. The physical evidence from the scene should not simply be stored away in packages. A thorough evaluation of the total information picture offered by the crime scene, laboratory results, and other investigative work is a necessity. Doing so in a diligent manner is the primary difference between "searching" a crime scene and "reconstructing" a crime scene. The search is the evidence documentation and recovery process. The reconstruction is the interpretation of the facts observed and retrieved in that process. It is entirely possible that a search accomplished in the most competent manner would be of no use if no one made the effort of reconstruction. From the viewpoint of the courtroom, crime scene search and crime scene reconstruction are tools to one end: logical portrayal of the facts.

Summary

This chapter has dealt with general concepts of physical evidence relevant to sexual assault investigations. Also, it has provided information pertaining to the primary sources of evidence: the victim, the suspect, and the crime scene. The physical evidence associated with the crime of sexual assault is not unlike that associated with other types of crime. Nonetheless, the direct sexual contact between suspect and victim tends to leave different and predictable kinds of evidence. Generally, the evidence in sexual assault cases is of the class characteristic kind. This makes it more difficult sometimes to establish, beyond reasonable doubt, that the suspect was or was not involved in the crime. For this reason, hairs, semen, and other class evidence must be used in combination to show whether there are strong or weak evidence associations between suspect and victim, which may or may not corroborate the victim's statements. The investigator and attorney must be prepared for a range of arguments designed to destabilize the weight of the physical evidence either for or against the suspect. One aspect of this preparation is the laying of a reasonable and convincing evidentiary foundation for the jury. It is hoped that the discussion of the elements of such a foundation set forth in this chapter assists in that effort.

Major Physical Evidence in Sexual Assault Investigations

5

DALE M. MOREAU

Virtually any form of physical evidence can figure in the successful identification or elimination of a suspect in the crime of sexual assault. Latent fingerprints, shoe print and tire tread impressions, bite marks, fabric impressions, tool marks, paints, cosmetics, glass, soil, tape, cordage, and documents often play major roles in these cases. *All* evidence possibilities should be considered before evidence collection is undertaken. Important items can be overlooked if searches are conducted for only the "expected" evidence.

The types of evidence discussed in this chapter are limited to those crucial in the majority of sexual assault investigations. They are hairs, fibers, blood, semen, and saliva. These materials were selected because they (1) appear with frequency in sexual assault cases, (2) are primary targets of sexual assault evidence collection kits and crime scene searches in sex crime instances, (3) are used in the courtroom to corroborate the testimony of the victim, (4) are illustrative of the close contact and sexual nature of the crimes committed, (5) are often overlooked because they can be difficult to locate and collect at crime scenes, and (6) are within the forensic examination capability of the modern crime laboratory.

The distinction between "questioned" evidence and "known" evidence is used in this chapter. Questioned evidence is physical evidence that typically is of unknown origin when it is found. It is collected to compare with a potential source at some later time. Known evidence is those materials that must be collected as comparison standards against the questioned evidence. For example, questioned hairs found on the floor of an apartment during a crime scene search have extremely limited value until they are compared with known hair samples taken from the suspect and the victim.

There are also limited instances in which the comparison of questioned evidence with other questioned evidence may be pertinent. For instance, questioned debris on the clothing of a victim might be compared with the questioned debris recovered from the carpet of a vehicle in which the victim is suspected of having been assaulted.

Law enforcement today has many technological resources available for evidence location and collection. These tools, when utilized with adequate training, experience, and discretion, can be effective aids in determining whether or not possible evidence is present. Some devices or methods, however, may destroy or contaminate evidence if used incorrectly or unsystematically. All too frequently, devices or methods are used in an effort to save time, when the best way is normally the most difficult and time-consuming alternative.

The distinction is made here between the discovery and the collection of evidence materials. For some forms of evidence, special techniques can be applied to assist in *locating* the evidence before attempts are made to collect it. This situation usually applies to the items that are difficult to see, but can become visible to the naked eye using various methods. Then there are techniques that are used to *collect* the evidence without really knowing if it is present. Such would be the case with minute particles or debris that are virtually impossible to see with the naked eye under most evidentiary search conditions.

Many systems of evidence discovery and collection available in the controlled conditions of a forensic laboratory may not be readily applicable to field work. Generally, it is more advantageous for the crime laboratory actually to remove the pertinent evidence (e.g., hairs, fibers, blood) from items recovered during field investigations. The techniques used in the laboratory permit the collection of evidence materials that are very difficult to see and/or recover at a crime scene.

Some crime laboratories give the field investigator a wide range of options for evidence handling. Other laboratories feel that giving the investigator too many options will result in decisions being made by this person without the proper forensic considerations. In this chapter, the advantages and disadvantages of various techniques are enumerated. The reader must study the issues raised and seek counseling from the crime laboratory to which physical evidence is to be submitted.

Discussions with laboratory personnel should include safety issues and procedures pertaining to the collection of physical evidence. For example, certain diseases can be transmitted through the handling of materials frequently collected as evidence, such as clothing and body fluids. Surgical-type disposable gloves should be worn routinely. Disposable clothing and protection for the eyes, nose, and mouth may also be warranted. Cutting implements (e.g., razor blades, scalpels) should be used with care so as not to damage protective gloves or clothes or to cut the skin.

The evidence discussions that follow assume that, when appropriate, before evidence is moved or recovered, (1) it will be photographed, using scale when necessary, and (2) documentation, such as sketches and evidence logs, will be used to record chain-of-custody data.

Recovery of Questioned Evidence

Hairs and Fibers

Hairs can be differentiated in the crime laboratory as being animal or human. In some cases, the family or genus of animal from which hairs originated may be established. A human hair may be classified as to its racial origin (Mongoloid, Caucasoid, Negroid), color, method of removal from the body, artificial treatment, body area origin, damage, and presence of foreign substances.

It is not possible forensically to positively identify a questioned human or animal hair as having originated from a particular person or animal source to the exclusion of all others. Nonetheless, forensic analysis can determine that the questioned and known hairs could have originated from the same source, which is of great value in indicating an association in the courtroom.

Textile fibers are classified in the crime laboratory, on a basic level, as being of natural or synthetic (man-made) origin. The specific kind of natural or synthetic fiber can be readily determined, and the color and other information pertaining to the manufacturing of fibers can be established. Foreign substances appearing on fibers also may be of significance. Such features can be used to compare questioned fibers with fibers from a known source to show a high probability of association. It is not possible to state on the basis of forensic comparisons that a questioned fiber definitely came from a specific known garment or other fibrous object to the exclusion of all similar ones.

In terms of actually finding and recovering hair and fiber evidence, hairs are normally more visible to the naked eye than minute fibers. The possible exception would be fibers found together in the form of a cluster or tuft. Hairs and fibers are often difficult to locate and collect, and such efforts can be somewhat frustrating, especially when a large crime scene area is involved. The scene may have so many possible sources of evidence that it is difficult to choose the best course of action. The scene should be evaluated to pinpoint those evidence sources that are likely to be most valuable.

When hairs and fibers are located, it is necessary either to remove this evidence or to collect the item on which the samples are observed. It is preferable to collect the items that would retain hairs and fibers, rather than to attempt to remove each minute piece of debris. Removal of such evidence in the field is exceedingly cumbersome and can result in its loss.

Different methods of locating and recovering hairs and fibers have varying levels of success. The major techniques are:

1. General unassisted visual search (naked eye)
2. Oblique light
3. Ultraviolet light
4. Vacuuming
5. Adhesive lifts
6. Combing/brushing
7. Fingernail scrapings and clippings
8. Laser

Naked Eye. It is feasible to locate hairs and fibers through a visual search. However, especially with textile fibers, this is a limited approach. The many colors and backgrounds on which the evidence can be located may make it difficult to see. For example, fine human hairs or fibers resting on a carpet can easily go unnoticed. Unfortunately, there are instances in which this is the sole technique utilized in the search of a person or crime scene.

Oblique Light. In this method, light is shined across a surface to highlight small debris that is present, and this is a good technique for discovering fibers and hairs. It can be accomplished with a flashlight or other light source that has a directed and narrow beam. Floors, walls, windows, furniture, etc., can be searched at crime scenes in this fashion. This procedure can also be effective in locating small items on the clothing or body of a person involved in the crime.

Ultraviolet Light. Although it can definitely be of value, the ultraviolet (UV) light is an instrument not often readily considered as a tool for hairs and fibers evidence. This device produces light in the ultraviolet portion of the electromagnetic light spectrum. This area of the spectrum generally is divided into short-wavelength and long-wavelength designations. The term *nanometer* is used to measure wavelengths of light in the entire spectrum, with short-wavelength UV light generally measured at 200 to 300 nanometers and long-wavelength UV light at 300 to 400 nanometers. To use the ultraviolet light technique effectively, a device having both capabilities is recommended. Short UV irradiation is dangerous to the human eye, and therefore may not be included in some of the commercially available lights. This point is significant because many materials react differentially to long or short UV irradiation. (Care should be taken to avoid exposure of the eyes to the light. Safety glasses are available for eye protection and should be used.) When UV light strikes certain materials, these items have a fluorescent (glowing) appearance, highlighting the specimen against its background.

Many ultraviolet lights have poor-quality filters, which permit a visible purple/violet light to emanate from the device. This emission can further mask out the visible fluorescence of certain materials. Thus, a filter that would permit no visible light to emit from the ultraviolet light source is recommended.

Fibers may react to ultraviolet light due to the chemical additives which are used in the manufacturing process or, for example, as a result of the addition of optical whiteners and brighteners in detergent used to wash clothing. Hairs normally do not react to UV irradiation unless they are contaminated with substances that fluoresce, such as cosmetics.

A major problem with the ultraviolet light method is that the visibility of hairs or fibers is also directly dependent on the substrate that contains the evidence. The substrate may itself fluoresce to the point that one would be unable to separate that effect from the fluorescence of the evidence. For this reason, it is recommended that items such as bedding and clothing be collected intact and submitted to the crime laboratory.

Vacuuming. Sometimes it is impractical to submit extremely large items (e.g., carpets, furniture) to a crime laboratory. Here, vacuum cleaner devices can be effective aids in collecting hair and fiber evidence. However, the area in question should be first visually examined for all forms of evidence materials, so important items are not destroyed or contaminated. For example, small bloodstains in dried, crusted form can be contaminated by intermingling with the debris that is vacuumed. More importantly, the crusted blood could be lost, or the amount present reduced, by vigorous vacuuming.

Special vacuum kits are produced specifically for gathering hair and fiber evidence. Typically, there is a filter attachment at the nozzle end that serves to collect the vacuumed material. Special porous filters are used for debris collection and should be collected intact with the evidence material on them. The filter is small, so it is not feasible to vacuum more than a small area at a time. The entire area to be vacuumed should be divided into segments, and a separate filter used for each segment. The vacuum filter housing and adjacent area of the vacuum, should be cleaned thoroughly before a new segment is vacuumed.

Major disadvantages that should be considered before a vacuum device is used for evidence recovery include:

1. Contamination could be a problem if the vacuum is not cleaned thoroughly. The collection area of the nozzle can retain debris from one area that could contaminate potential evidence taken from another location.

2. Investigators sometimes gather so much possible evidence by vacuuming at a crime scene that it is difficult for crime laboratory personnel to locate and extract the pertinent materials. This can be caused, for example, by vacuuming too large an area without changing filters.

3. Fibers in tufts or clusters can be separated, possibly losing some of their forensic significance.

4. It is often very important to demonstrate that particular hairs or fibers were collected from a specific location. If relatively large areas are vacuumed per sample, it is difficult, if not impossible, to be certain of the exact recovery location of such evidence. This may reduce or dilute its significance in court.

Adhesive Lifts. There are occasions in general evidence recovery when the use of various adhesive lift techniques may be practical. As an example, a suspect has been arrested a short time after the commission of a rape. It is learned by interviewing the victim that the assailant wore a mask, probably of the ski-mask type. The mask was discarded by the suspect in the yard of the victim's residence during his departure from the scene. Minute fibers like those in the mask may be contained in the head hair of the suspect and could be recovered by combing or brushing. There may also be fibers adhering to the beard stubble on the suspect's face, even if he appears to be clean-shaven. The application of an adhesive lift could remove those valuable materials. Tape lifts can function also to collect hairs and fibers from a variety of crime scene sources, such as vinyl upholstery, tile floors, smooth countertops, and sinks. However, it normally would not be reasonable to completely "tape" every item in a large crime scene. A methodical approach of carefully surveying the scene before acting, therefore, is recommended.

The tape used for lifting purposes should be clear and have an adhesive that is strong enough to retain trace evidence. Any such tape must be cautiously protected from contamination prior to its actual use, as adhesive tends to attract and pick up small debris. Once a lift is made, it is essential that the tape not be folded over upon itself. It can be mounted on Plexiglas, plastic sheeting, or a similar transparent and resilient material. Glass is suitable for this purpose, but is subject to breakage, and appropriate measures should be taken. Paper, cardboard, card stock, or similar items should be avoided as mounting substrates. These materials create difficulty in laboratory viewing and removal of the evidence for examination purposes.

The tape used for lifting can be difficult for the laboratory to deal with. The investigator should discuss the use of taping with the crime laboratory to determine its recommendations and precautions.

Combing/Brushing. Questioned hairs and fibers, as well as other small materials, may be transferred to body hair as a result of physical contact. A technique commonly termed "combing" or "brushing" is most often used to extract these materials from the head and pubic regions of an individual. The combing/brushing procedure need not be limited to the head and pubic regions, but may include other locations where body hair is heavily concentrated on the person being examined.

Two variations of this procedure are:

The utilization of a fine-tooth comb or multibristle brush to collect the transferred evidence. This technique involves the relatively simple procedure of combing or brushing through the hair and retaining whatever debris is removed. This is a reasonably reliable method if accomplished in a thorough manner.

The use of a fine-tooth comb and white cotton batting to collect the transferred evidence. This technique involves pushing the teeth of the comb through the cotton, using the cotton as a handle, and then combing so that the cotton is a backing to assist in the collection of hairs and other evidence. Because the white cotton backing increases the probability of picking up debris and the visibility of the hairs and fibers by way of contrast, this method is felt by many persons to be superior to the use of a comb or brush alone. The use of the cotton batting, however, may be a disadvantage, because some debris, such as fibers, can be lost in the cotton.

Each body hair region of concern must be combed or brushed with a previously unused and clean implement, preferably one with fine teeth or bristles. The comb or brush and the evidence adhering to it are packaged intact as recovered. It is critical that combings/brushings obtained from different body regions be collected and packaged separately. Also, since the combing/brushing method is normally accomplished when known hair samples are taken from an individual, it is recommended that the combing/brushing process be completed before the known sampling is begun. To do so will ensure that all foreign hairs are removed from the person, so that they will not be intermingled in the known sample.

If the person being examined has long head hairs, the combing/brushing procedure can be difficult, especially if the person is standing. The person can lie down with a section of clean, white cloth or sturdy paper under his or her head. The hair is gently spread over the section and the combing or brushing taken. The light-colored background helps make foreign debris visible and serves to collect any that may be dislodged from the hair and not retained on the comb or brush. A similar procedure can be used in combing/brushing pubic hair.

Although somewhat unorthodox, the following two other methods of removing foreign hairs and fibers from body hair locations have been brought to the author's attention. They are not recommended as substitutes for the standard combing/brushing procedure.

The application of a tape-style lift to the body hair region in question. This technique has numerous negative aspects, three of which are the possible physical discomfort to the person, the gathering of only loose, surface hairs, and the retention of numerous hairs forcibly removed from the person. Further, a disadvantage from the laboratory viewpoint is that there can be difficulty in removing the hairs intact from the lift without using a solvent.

The use of a small vacuum cleaner device to remove the foreign hairs and fibers from a person. This method basically has most of the decidedly negative features mentioned regarding the tape-style lift.

Fingernail Scrapings and Clippings. Almost any form of transfer evidence can be recovered from under fingernails. Minute fragments or quantities of hairs, fibers, blood, semen, etc., can be removed with any clean, suitable tool that would not cause discomfort to the person. Clean knife blades, toothpicks, thin wood depressor sticks, and other devices can be useful in this regard. Questioned material from each hand should be removed and packaged separately. The implements used to acquire the specimens also should be submitted to the crime laboratory. The end portions of the nails can be removed with a clean fingernail clipper and submitted to the laboratory. Some dried materials will not be removed easily by the scraping method and may be detected on the nail.

Laser. The use of laser technology in forensic science is expanding very rapidly. Lasers have been used primarily in the crime laboratory for the development of latent prints on porous and nonporous articles, but it has been determined that many additional types of evidentiary materials can be detected by laser instruments. Fibers, threads, semen, urine, and saliva potentially can be observed.

In operation, the laser produces a very concentrated and coherent light, which can cause certain materials to luminesce. The specimens must be viewed through special filters that permit the luminescent effect to be observed. Photography to record the evidence involves the same types of filters.

Today, various laser instruments are available, usually at a fairly substantial cost. Due to the size and operating requirements of most lasers used for forensic analysis (such as the argon–ion and copper vapor types), evidence can only be examined in the confines of the laboratory. Smaller lasers, designed to be portable, are available and can be used in field evidence searches. Laser instruments are gaining in popularity, but are often too expensive to suit the budgets of many agencies.

A detailed discussion of laser technology is beyond the scope of this chapter. However, lasers are brought to the reader's attention because they will become more easily available and procured as research and technology progress. Although the lasers are exotic tools to witness in operation in the laboratory or field, they are simply additional mechanisms to increase visibility and detection of potential evidence. They assuredly will not solve all evidence collection problems faced in day-to-day operations. As long as this fact is kept in perspective, lasers are and will continue to be extremely valuable in the discovery of certain physical evidence.

Blood

Depending on the facts in a given case, blood can become a major evidence substance in sexual assault investigation. Many crime laboratories have the ability to establish that an unknown substance definitely is blood and to differentiate between animal and human blood. The family of animal can often be identified when animal blood is encountered. Human blood can be further characterized by many genetically controlled grouping systems. This capability is based on the forensic identification of many complex chemical substances that exist in the cells and serum of blood. These substances include various protein and other genetic marker systems, divided into a limited number of types within each system. For example, in one enzyme system called *esterase D*, the population can be divided into six categories, and each member of the population will fall into one of these categories. Known blood samples can be compared with questioned blood based on these markers.

A great deal of research is being devoted to enhancing the ability of a crime laboratory to detect and interpret the complex substances contained in the blood in order to increase its weight as class evidence. Although blood cannot be identified at this time as having come from one specific source, its components can establish a high degree of probability for the association of a person with a questioned blood sample, depending on the array of types possessed.

Research indicates the possibility that blood, as well as certain other evidence such as semen and hair, may be individualized through the analysis of deoxyribonucleic acid (DNA). DNA is the genetic material inherited from generation to generation and is the code that confers the uniqueness that each person possesses. Thus, the DNA code is different from person to person (except for identical twins). The structure of the DNA molecule is a double helix, which resembles a huge spiral staircase. The billions of steps of the staircase represent the genetic code, yet there are only four "letters" (called *nucleotides*) that make up this code. The arrangement of these four letters is what dictates uniqueness for each individual. The field of modern molecular biology and the study of recombinant DNA recently have produced methods that make it feasible to determine the unique arrangement of the DNA letters in each person. The DNA of an individual can be cut into specific fragments and separated by electrophoresis. The result is a series of bands that can be read much like a bar code on grocery items. It is the hope of forensic serologists that analyses can be developed that produce unique DNA bar codes for each person so that the DNA found in forensic samples can be exploited to identify positively the person who deposited a sample.

There are two main dilemmas facing forensic laboratories in dealing with blood evidence, as well as other body fluid evidence, such as semen and saliva.

1. Blood is frequently mixed with contaminants and other body fluids, making forensic interpretations difficult and limited. In sexual assault cases, serologists often receive testing results indicating that, in fact, genetic markers apparently have been contributed by both victim and suspect. The forensic interpretation of this mixture can be confusing, especially when the laboratory results appear to be inconsistent with the facts of the crime.

It is essential that any recent sexual activity of the victim be noted by the investigator and made known to the crime laboratory. Body fluids on clothing items (especially undergarments) can be transferred and mixed with other body fluids. Therefore, it is not only significant to know the date of last sexual contact, but also important to know whether the clothes worn by the victim after that contact were the same clothes worn after the sexual assault. Investigators often neglect to obtain this type of information, thus possibly hampering the work of the serologist.

2. Most blood evidence received by a laboratory is in a dried form that is subject to degradation. More potentially probative data can be obtained from fresh, dried blood than from dried blood aged for long periods. In time, genetic information imparted by the proteins and other markers contained within the blood is lost.

The recovery of questioned blood evidence usually involves dealing with various sizes and conditions of stains. Additionally, these stains will be located on items of different colors, textures, and composition. The individual collecting the stains has to use good judgment in establishing the most appropriate manner in which to recover the evidence. Collection of questioned wet and dry blood samples is usually accomplished by (1) recovering the entire item bearing the blood, or (2) separate removal of all, or a portion, of the blood exhibited on an object.

Wet blood samples should be recovered only when the evidence can be immediately transmitted to a crime laboratory or frozen under uncontaminated conditions for a short time before being taken to the laboratory. It is usually difficult in the field to collect bulky evidence (e.g., clothing, bedding, carpet, tile, drywall) bearing wet blood. Small items exhibiting this form of blood generally are more suitable. The personnel involved in field recovery of wet blood should determine whether or not the crime laboratory to which evidence will be submitted can accommodate wet evidence. Some forensic laboratories require blood specimens to be submitted in an air-dried condition because of the problems of properly storing massive amounts of damp evidence.

Eye droppers and syringes are convenient tools for removing wet blood, but the sample must be frozen or shipped to the laboratory immediately. It is almost impossible to air-dry blood in such devices, and separate eye droppers or syringes must be used for each sample collection so as to prevent cross-contamination. Because of these and other difficulties, it is best to avoid collecting wet blood in eye droppers, syringes, or similar articles.

Another technique is the use of swabs, cotton cloth, cotton threads, or filter paper to absorb the wet stain. As much blood as possible should be concentrated on the gathering medium so that a dense stain results. Simply obtaining smears or small deposits of blood can hinder detailed forensic testing. Many times most of the blood is left on the source object, and the absorbent material permits only a limited blood examination, or possibly one of no real evidentiary value at all. Most absorbent methods also often collect surface dirt and other extraneous debris, in addition to the blood.

When absorbent cloth is used to collect blood or any other body fluid, residues of detergent and chemical additives (e.g., optical whiteners) should be rinsed from the cloth before it is used. These materials can detrimentally affect serological testing of biological fluids. Some laboratories boil a new sheet (already washed several times) for several hours before drying and cutting it into appropriate sizes to use for collection of stains. Individual threads removed from this cloth can be used when extremely small stains must be absorbed. The thread can be gently maneuvered to concentrate the blood in a dense manner.

In summary, the recovery of wet blood evidence during field investigations has numerous disadvantages. Because of significant timespan and evidence-storage problems, it is recommended that wet bloodstains be collected, air-dried, and forwarded to the laboratory as soon as possible, or frozen until submitted. Drying allows the fixing of stains in a specific location, reduces the opportunity for intragarment and intergarment transfer, and reduces decay possibilities.

Dried bloodstains frequently are encountered as physical evidence in sexual assault investigations. It is advisable to submit the entire item that bears the stain for forensic analysis. Blood in a dried state should be protected from heat, moisture, direct sunlight, and possible contaminants. Airtight containers are not recommended, because they tend to retain moisture.

Dried blood samples can be removed from articles when it is impractical to submit the entire article to the laboratory or when the stained area is large. Methods most frequently used for removing such blood are:

1. Removing the desired sample completely intact
2. Scraping
3. Reconstitution of the stain

Intact Samples. The removal of an intact stain from an object (when the entire object cannot be collected itself as evidence) is the most beneficial alternative. Cutting out the stained area with an appropriate tool is in many ways easier than undertaking other methods, especially when articles are large. The concentrated stained area acquired by this technique can also result in enhanced forensic examination of the blood. Removing various items such as concrete, drywall, and wood can require saws or similar tools, which produce dust and other particulate matter that can contaminate the blood evidence. In such cases, the stained area should be covered with paper, sections of plastic, or other suitable items before removal.

Scraping. Scraping is not the best way to retrieve dried blood from an object. This procedure often results in obtaining dustlike small particles and can also lead to the loss of the sample. The blood becomes separated to a great extent, making it difficult for the laboratory to evaluate. Furthermore, many possible contaminant substances on the surface from which the blood is scraped can be mixed with the stain. When it is absolutely necessary to use the scraping technique, the stain should be disturbed to the least possible extent. It is suggested that a clean razor blade or scalpel blade be used and submitted to the laboratory as a control specimen accompanying the removed stain.

Reconstitution. The method of applying absorbent material (swabs, cotton cloth, etc.) to a dried bloodstain sometimes does not remove a sufficient quantity of sample. Therefore, it becomes necessary to reconstitute the dried stain so it can be retained on the material. A common item used to perform this task is distilled water. The absorbent material is wetted slightly in this liquid and applied to the questioned stain area. The questioned stain is then concentrated on the material to the greatest extent feasible. Probably the most important drawback to this procedure is the dilution of the sample, which will almost always result in loss of probative genetic information. Further, a reconstituted bloodstain that is not analyzed promptly is fertile ground for bacterial growth, which can be harmful to the sample. Also, as with the scraping technique, surface contaminants are obtained and intermingled with the blood evidence. The reconstitution of bloodstains is best avoided except as a last resort.

There will be instances, however, when it is impractical to remove dried blood without using the reconstitution method. For example, in cases of sexual assault involving bleeding of the victim, it may be appropriate to swab the penis of the suspect for blood or other evidence. Dried blood can be sampled by using a swab moistened slightly with distilled water. The swabbing procedure should avoid the penile opening, unless blood is obviously present there. It is recommended penile swabbing not be used routinely. Instead, it should be limited to those instances in which blood is very likely to be present.

A major disadvantage to both the scraping and absorbent-material procedures of recovery is the difficulty of dealing with porous media. Blood deposited on such articles as concrete, unfinished wood, cardboard, and drywall can be absorbed and much of the stain can collect below the surface. Scraping a porous object normally will remove only surface level substances. Swabs, cotton cloth, etc., moistened with distilled water can cause the stain, when reconstituted, to be further absorbed into the porous object. It is best to simply cut out the bloodstains and send them intact to the laboratory.

The subject of "control" samples is relevant to any situation in which blood is removed from an article. Blood is chemically complex, as are the forensic tests applicable to this type of evidence. Many substances common to everyday life (e.g., detergents, deodorants, fruit juices, plant materials) are capable of interfering with certain blood examination tests. It is a great advantage for the laboratory to know whether or not such substances are present in the area where a bloodstain has been deposited. Whenever a stain is recovered from an object or area that will not be sent intact to the laboratory, an unstained control sample adjacent to the questioned stain should be obtained. A prime example would be the removal of a stain from a wall-to-wall carpet. If the stain is approximately the size of a quarter, it would be satisfactory to cut out a 4-inch-square section of carpet bearing the stain. The unstained area surrounding the suspected blood could be tested by the laboratory to determine whether substances that could hinder examination are present. Also, in instances where swabs, cotton cloth, or filter paper are applied to the collection of bloodstains, control samples of these gathering agents from the same source as those used for actual collection should be retained and submitted to the crime laboratory.

One of the problems in the effective recovery of blood evidence is deciding what amount of blood to remove when a large amount is actually present. Bloodstains that appear to be probative in the investigation should be secured as evidence. However, it is impractical to remove all the blood that is present under some circumstances. Violent physical contact may result in both suspect and victim bleeding in the same general area. Bloodstains in the crime scene, for example, may have come from the victim or the suspect, or be a mixture of blood from both persons. It is not possible to distinguish between different blood types simply by looking at stained areas. However, it is possible to see that blood has been deposited at several different points. Each area where the stains appear to be separated should be sampled.

The apparent path of blood as it moved through the air and struck an object can provide valuable clues in reconstructing a crime. In some instances, a determination can be made as to the position of the person who was bleeding. This determination can assist in identifying possible areas from which samples are to be taken. However, the interpretation of bloodstain patterns often involves a detailed examination of the configuration of individual stain areas. Care should be taken not to disturb the stains by sampling until the documentation and analysis appropriate for this interpretation have been completed.

The application of good judgment based on training and experience will almost always be the final determinant regarding collecting questioned blood samples under such situations. Still, one must avoid the tendency to take random samples without any attention to the amount of blood present or indications that the blood deposits are from more than one person. It is important to note that the terminology in forensic science for properly recovering these specimens is "representative," as opposed to "random."

Representative sampling involves collection of the blood evidence that is felt to be probative, based on the facts and circumstances of the case. Samples are taken by evaluating the size and location of stains. In some instances, the location of a stain may be of more significance than its size. Also, consideration should be given to determining how much blood should be taken per sample and how many samples should be recovered.

In contrast, random sampling involves the recovery of blood evidence in an unorganized fashion. Here, there is no attempt to evaluate the relevant sampling areas before collection is accomplished.

Forensic laboratories have long made use of so-called preliminary tests for the presence of blood. These chemical tests react with the hemoglobin present in the blood of animals and humans and are used to determine whether a stain could be blood. Various substances, such as certain plant materials, have the potential to cause false positive reactions to these tests. Therefore, these procedures do not establish that blood is unequivocally present, only that it may be. In the crime laboratory environment, preliminary (also sometimes referred to as "screening" or "presumptive") blood tests are used under controlled conditions and are supplemented with a variety of other procedures to identify a stain as containing blood and to classify it further.

There has been a marked increase in interest in the potential use of preliminary tests for blood at the field investigative level, primarily due to circumstances in which it would be advantageous to distinguish blood from other substances. Dried blood exposed to numerous environmental conditions can take on a variety of shapes and colors and be difficult to recognize. Similarly, minute spots of blood and diluted blood can escape detection if an individual collects only what can be seen by the unaided eye.

There are a number of commercially available test kits that claim to be ultimate solutions to these problems. However, it is probably better to have the chemical testing agents prepared by the crime laboratory for field analysis. This procedure will better ensure the quality and reliability of results. It is incumbent on an individual who is not a serologist to seek training and guidance in effective use of the tests from experienced personnel in a crime laboratory.

Like any other procedure, preliminary blood tests are to be used with care. This is because:

1. It is possible to destroy or contaminate minute samples by overzealous and uneducated administering of a test.

2. When the suspected blood can be seen by the investigator, generally it should not be tested in the field. Instead, it should be protected and submitted to the laboratory for analysis.

3. In instances when the blood cannot be seen but is believed to be present, field testing is appropriate. This situation is common when an area that at one time contained blood has been washed or cleaned. However, if the investigator cannot visually observe the suspected blood, it is very unlikely that the laboratory will be able to do a great deal with the evidence from the forensic standpoint.

4. Chemical components of the preliminary tests are subject to deterioration as a result of storage time and conditions. When deterioration has occurred, the tests will not be functional even when blood is present. Quality control of test materials must be maintained.

5. Many tests are suited for application in small areas at a time, making it time consuming and difficult to cover large areas or surfaces.

6. The tests can differ in their susceptibility to false positive reactions. The investigator must consult a knowledgeable serologist as to the potential for these reactions.

Chemical agents of various types are used for preliminary blood analysis. Some of those encountered are:

1. Ortho-tolidine
2. Phenolphthalein
3. Luminol
4. Tetramethylbenzidine
5. Leuco malachite green
6. Benzidine (Note: used in the past, but currently not to a great extent)

The ortho-tolidine, phenolphthalein, and other tests (except luminol) work fundamentally in the same manner. The area of the suspected stain is swabbed and treated with the test chemical, and the user visually examines the treated swabs for the appearance of a color. The color reaction (bluish green for ortho-tolidine and reddish pink for phenolphthalein) is indicative of the probable existence of blood in the location swabbed.

Luminol is a chemical test that operates somewhat differently. When luminol comes into contact with blood, it has the capacity to undergo chemiluminescence. This means a positive result would cause the stain to give off visible light that can be seen in a darkened setting with the naked eye. The user then recovers the items that so respond for examination in the forensic laboratory. Luminol testing usually involves spraying of large areas suspected of containing blood. It is not recommended, however, that someone enter a crime scene and completely spray the whole location as a routine procedure. Because of the potential destructive effect on substances in blood that are characterized during serological examination, the application of luminol to suspected blood evidence normally is undertaken with caution. Usually, this method is utilized when bloodstains are so minute or washed out (previously cleaned up with a mop, for example) as to be virtually impossible to see with the naked eye. Luminol can also be used in identifying a specific unknown crime scene when there are a number of possible areas in question.

Anyone applying the tests should know that some of them contain harmful chemical substances. For example, benzidine, which was once used widely (but is now used only by a few individuals), is known to be carcinogenic. This fact reinforces the point that the choice of a preliminary test should be made on an educated basis.

When used properly, preliminary blood tests can be effective, especially in locating blood that might otherwise go undetected. However, preliminary tests should not be viewed as shortcuts to substitute for proven evidence collection procedures. These tests can become misused tools for those persons who are not willing to spend the time and energy required to conduct a search in a methodical and quality manner.

One final difficulty with blood evidence regards handling or touching of stains, or even unstained areas, with bare hands. Aside from health and safety considerations, evidence can be inadvertently contaminated by the presence of biological residues (e.g., saliva, perspiration, body oils exuded from the skin) on the hands of the person recovering it. The person collecting the evidence can protect it by wearing gloves. Surgical-type gloves can be suitable for this purpose, but latent or visible prints can be deposited by someone who is wearing this kind of glove. The gloves can conform so tightly to the skin that dermal ridge detail in the form of a print may be left on an area that has been touched. This possibility, although usually very slight, should be taken into consideration to avoid leaving confusing prints.

Semen

The type of physical evidence probably most frequently associated with sexual assault investigations is semen. The very presence of this male reproductive fluid indicates the occurrence of sexual activity and can assist in corroborating the victim's contention of rape.

The forensic laboratory can determine that an unidentified substance recovered as evidence is semen if male reproductive cells (spermatozoa) are present. Depending on the time that has passed since the crime, these cells may be alive and motile (free-moving) or dead. The motile cells indicate relatively recent sexual contact.

A major distinction must be made between the microscopic examination for motile cells, typically conducted immediately following the medical examination of a victim, and the normal analysis for spermatozoa in the crime laboratory. The crime laboratory does not usually encounter motile spermatozoa in its serological analyses. The serologist almost exclusively deals with dried stains and nonmotile cells, if present. Microscopic examination for motile spermatozoa is best accomplished by a physician or medical technician, as soon as possible after evidence recovery is accomplished. Spermatozoa have the capability to remain motile for a few hours or several days depending on the nature of their environment. Discussions between the author and experienced FBI forensic serologists indicate it is reasonable to expect that spermatozoa can normally be present within the vaginal areas for no more than 72 hours. There are numerous variables that can affect whether or not these cells are present, including normal drainage, action of the vaginal environment, and cleansing actions taken by the person involved. Also, the fact that spermatozoa are present does not necessarily mean they are motile or even intact.

There are times when the collected evidence consists of seminal fluid that is devoid of these reproductive cells. This can occur for a variety of reasons, including a vasectomized suspect, low spermatozoa count, and the difficulty of recovering spermatozoa in the laboratory.

Seminal fluid has various chemical constituents, some of which also appear in other fluids and are, in forensic science, controversial as positive identification of the presence of semen. However, it is scientifically recognized that a protein referred to as prostate specific antigen (p30) can be identified and used to conclusively determine that a substance is semen.

Once semen has been identified, it can be analyzed for chemical substances that will indicate the ABO blood type of the donor. Approximately 80% of the population are *secretors* who have detectable amounts of blood group substances present in body fluids other than blood, such as semen and saliva. Known blood samples and known saliva samples from an individual in question normally are required by the forensic laboratory for the purpose of determining secretor status.

Certain enzymes, or genetic markers, that exist in blood can also be identified in semen. The particular type located in an individual's blood will be consistent with that identified in the other body fluids. The types found in the enzyme systems are independent of the donor's ABO type.

Techniques to remove evidence of semen are most commonly directed at collecting spermatozoa, or chemicals known to exist in seminal fluid, in the vaginal or cervical region of a victim. Even when penetration of the vagina by the penis did not occur, there is still the possibility that semen will be present. Furthermore, even when the victim states that only vaginal contact took place with the suspect, consideration should be given to her potential reluctance to admit that oral or anal contact did, in fact, also occur. This situation is often the case due to embarrassment and revulsion at the notion of such sexual violation. Based on the circumstances of an incident, it may be advisable to take oral and anal swabbings along with vaginal samples, to cover just such a possibility. Each area should be swabbed separately. The resulting swabs should be packaged individually and labeled as to

It is very important that the bare hands of the person obtaining the sample does NOT touch the known sample or questioned sample to avoid contamination.

their origin. At least two swabs, but no more than four, should be used for each area. Unstained control swabs should be furnished to the laboratory.

If the swabs used for evidence collection are subsequently used to make smears on microscope slides (to facilitate a microscopic examination for spermatozoa), both swabs and slides should be furnished to the crime laboratory. Additionally, when the slides are examined by the physician or technician, they should not be treated with a fixative if a serological examination is anticipated, because the fixative may interfere with subsequent laboratory testing.

A somewhat unusual and often unproductive method of evidence recovery is to have a victim who has had oral/nasal contact with semen actually blow his/her nose on a clean section of cotton cloth. It is possible that spermatozoa and/or seminal fluid have entered the nasal passages after first entering the mouth or facial region. This method of evidence recovery is easily accomplished and normally would not be as traumatic to the victim as others used to recover evidentiary materials during a clinical examination. A section of cloth approximately 6 inches square can be sufficient to both gather the evidence and serve as a control specimen. As is the case when dealing with any form of body fluid evidence, efforts should be made to ensure that the bare hands of the evidence technician, physician, nurse, etc., do not touch the cloth prior to the necessary forensic analyses. This recommendation obviously also applies to the swabs, already mentioned, for the collection of semen.

Swabbing of the oral region may not extract spermatozoa that is located in places that are difficult to reach, such as between the teeth and under the tongue. Therefore, another possible way to obtain semen evidence is to have the victim's mouth rinsed with distilled water. The solution can be expectorated by this person into a sterile container for submission to the laboratory. It is also possible, but unlikely, that motile spermatozoa could be discovered if a microscopic analysis is performed soon after the rinse is taken. After this analysis is accomplished, such a liquid sample should be frozen and sent to the laboratory. The retention of a control sample of the fluid rinse is advisable, should it be needed later in forensic analyses.

The author's contact with serologists in the FBI Laboratory indicates that semen has a relatively short survival rate in the oral cavity. This means that sampling in the oral cavity should be done as soon as possible after the sexual assault. The examination for motile spermatozoa requires microscopic observation to detect these cells. The analysis of "wet" samples immediately following the medical examination of the victim usually is necessary in this situation. If circumstances do not permit such rapid examination, the obtained specimens of swabs, microscope slide smears, or cloth should not be packaged in a wet condition. To do so can result in deterioration of the evidence from the serological perspective. It is proper to air-dry these materials and then package them in paper or cardboard containers for immediate shipment to the crime laboratory. Once the evidence reaches the crime laboratory, it should be frozen until the time of examination.

There is a tendency to concentrate on the presence of semen on the person of a victim because it is indicative of evidence transfer through sexual contact. Semen is often also found on clothing, bedding, carpets, and car seats, but can be located on almost any other article, depending on the movements of the victim and the suspect. Reasonable efforts should be undertaken to recover the entire item containing a suspected semen stain. With large items (e.g., wall-to-wall carpets), regions on which semen is believed to have been deposited should be cut out. An uncontaminated and unstained area surrounding the semen deposit, large enough to function as a control sample for forensic testing, should be included. Before it is cut, the area in question should be scrutinized for other forms of evidence, such as hairs and fibers, that may inadvertently be lost during the removal process. Also, the area should be covered during removal if a considerable amount of extraneous debris is expected to be generated. No matter whether the entire item or a portion of it is to be retained as evidence, any wet item that cannot be immediately examined in a forensic setting must be air-dried, packaged in a paper or cardboard container, kept free of moisture, and frozen whenever possible.

Despite the best attempts to recover semen evidence in the previously discussed manner, there will be situations in which it is necessary to remove wet or dried semen from a particular kind of surface. Recovery of dry specimens can be accomplished by cutting, chipping, or scraping; and of wet samples, via swabs, sections of cloth, or filter paper. Of particular concern is the collection of dried semen from such materials as glass and painted substrates when entire items cannot be recovered. Semen can be removed from glass by gently scraping it into a paper or cardboard container. As much of the sample as possible should be scraped. As such scrapings are often of small quantity, small containers should be used. A painted surface bearing dried semen should be sampled, if possible, by cutting or chipping out the entire section of paint exhibiting the evidence. In this way, the stain will be preserved in its original state.

One suggestion for the recovery of dried semen is the use of distilled water to reconstitute the stain onto a swab or similar gathering medium. The reconstitution of any dried body fluid is to be regarded as a technique of last resort. The difficulties and disadvantages of this method, previously referred to in the discussion of blood evidence, pertain to semen collection and preservation as well.

Wet stains can be recovered through the use of swabs, sections of cotton cloth, or filter paper. The correct procedure would then be to air-dry the swab, cloth, or filter paper. This wet stain then ends up being handled generally in the same manner as a dry stain.

One of the salient points regarding field recognition of semen evidence is the utilization of lighting techniques and preliminary chemical testing when investigators are attempting to identify the crime scene itself. Often, the exact location of the scene is not known, due to circumstances in the case. As with blood evidence, reliance on lighting techniques or chemicals has the potential of becoming a means to avoid the more detailed and tedious work needed to locate potential evidence.

The ultraviolet light is commonly utilized as a major tool in the location of semen in crime scene investigation. This instrument certainly can function as an aid, but cannot discriminate between stains that are exclusively seminal in origin and those that are not. Semen stains may fluoresce when exposed to ultraviolet light. However, the level of fluorescence visible to the unaided human eye is minimal in many instances. Fluorescence of a stain is sometimes difficult to see, even when semen is located on a nonfluorescent background. If the substrate is highly fluorescent under ultraviolet light, the semen often will appear darker than the surrounding unstained area. If an individual is looking only for the fluorescent effect associated with semen, this darker spot could be overlooked as evidence.

A field technician is likely to discover numerous items that exhibit a high level of visible fluorescence and are not semen. Clothing, bedding, cosmetics, deodorants, laundry detergents, and other common articles can exhibit a high level of visible fluorescence under ultraviolet light, which may obscure the low visible fluorescence normally exhibited by semen. When used without knowledge of this limitation, the ultraviolet light procedure could be extremely misleading and even cause pertinent evidence to be overlooked or disregarded.

Presumptive chemical testing for the presence of semen is in general use in crime laboratories. This analysis is utilized in the attempt to determine whether a specimen could be semen. The application of chemical testing procedures has also been expanded to field investigation. Kits are available in the law enforcement supply market that are designed for field-testing of suspected semen stains. The most common type of such kits is directed at detection of acid phosphatase, a chemical present in relatively high levels in semen.

There are a variety of difficulties inherent in the indiscriminate use of any preliminary chemical tests for semen at the field investigative level. One major difference between field situations necessitating preliminary analysis of blood and of semen is that semen deposits are more likely to be found only in the immediate area of the assault. This circumstance is due simply to the amount of semen usually ejaculated and the time span in which ejaculation takes place. Blood, on the other hand, may appear in areas that are completely separated due to the size of a wound, blood velocity, movement of the person who is bleeding, and other related variables.

Therefore, the items that have a high probability of containing semen (e.g., bedding, clothing, upholstery) can be logically identified in many instances. This is not to imply that the semen will be easily visible to the unaided eye in all cases, but that the articles that could hold it can be discovered with reasonable effort. Correspondingly, the emphasis should be on collection of the items that may contain semen, rather than selective recovery of only the articles that react positively to a chemical field examination. Selective recovery could result in loss of many other forms of physical evidence. For example, a pillowcase exhibiting no positive reaction to the acid phosphatase preliminary analysis may contain hairs, fibers, cosmetics, etc., that are trace in nature and could serve to furnish valuable forensic information.

To realize the worst misapplication of chemical field testing, imagine an investigator who feels that the discovery of semen must occur for prosecution of a sexual assault suspect to be successful in a given case. This person could quickly test the areas where semen should, using common sense, be detected at the crime scene. If no positive results are observed, the collection of evidence might stop at that point. This unfortunate situation has on too many occasions been related to the author by individuals involved in day-to-day field operations.

The discussion thus far has centered primarily on semen evidence when it is recovered as an intact, uncontaminated substance. In realistic terms, there are numerous cases in which semen will be mixed with urine, blood, vaginal fluid, saliva, and other materials. Analytical difficulties can arise in the laboratory when there is a mixture of body fluids from two or more persons. Blood groupings, for example, can be dramatically affected.

Every attempt should be made to ensure that suspected semen deposits do not come into contact with other possible body fluid stains as field technicians or laboratory personnel handle articles of evidence. For instance, a blouse worn by a victim of a sexual assault may bear semen from the suspect on the lower portion and blood from the victim's head wound on the upper area. Folding the blouse, causing direct contact between the semen and blood, could contaminate both evidence substances. Furthermore, an item exhibiting wet stains should be dealt with in a manner designed to eliminate inadvertent transfer of this evidence to a location that was previously unstained. This is of significance regarding semen evidence because the location in which the stain appears can be of great relevance. A wet stain mistakenly transferred by improper handling or packaging may subsequently be placed in an area that is inconsistent with a statement, for example, of a victim.

Saliva

The forensic analysis of saliva involves the detection of its suggested presence and a determination of the possible ABO blood group of the depositor, if that individual is a secretor. At the present level of forensic science, saliva cannot be individualized to the same extent as blood or semen.

Compared to blood and semen, saliva evidence is encountered less frequently in the field and the crime laboratory. Blood and semen have obvious physical appearances, including their color and texture, unlike saliva. Stains of blood and semen, having a crustlike appearance and recognizable color, can be distinguished in both wet and dry forms. Saliva, on the other hand, tends to defy detection by the naked eye once the initial "wet" appearance of the stained area has disappeared. To further complicate matters, saliva evidence tends to be located in places and under conditions which promote contamination. A typical example is cigarette butts in an ashtray filled with debris. Furthermore, the presence of saliva in a given area is sometimes easier to explain than blood or semen. Saliva is readily emitted from the mouth, whereas blood and semen are internal body fluids that appear externally only under certain physiological conditions.

Saliva can be located on both porous and nonporous articles. As with the other biological fluids discussed, each situation will dictate the proper method of retrieval and preservation. Bare wood, wallboard, paper, and like porous items bearing possible saliva deposits should be removed intact without adding contamination to the area of concern. The evidence material should be permitted to air dry, packaged in a paper, cardboard, or other container that will allow the movement of air, and submitted to the crime laboratory as soon as possible. A control sample of the area surrounding the potential saliva stain should be acquired for forensic analysis.

The utilization of swabs, cotton cloth, or filter paper with distilled water as a mechanism to reconstitute dried saliva is definitely not recommended on porous substrates. Such techniques can serve to dissipate the evidence even further by causing it to migrate deeper into the porous material. It is reiterated that stain reconstitution is to be regarded as a last resort in almost any situation relative to body fluids.

Cigarette butts represent examples of porous articles that are often collected for saliva evidence. The environment of ashtrays and similar trash disposal receptacles can be disastrous to the forensic potential of saliva. One of the erroneous recommendations about handling evidence in these cases is to package all of the debris, including the cigarette butts, into one container for preservation as evidence. Doing so only serves to further contaminate the cigarette butts, as cigarette ashes are highly alkaline and can have a harmful effect on any saliva that is present. The cigarettes should be placed in a separate container to minimize contact with potential contaminants.

Cigarette butts, aside from furnishing saliva evidence, can be sources for the recovery of latent prints, but recovering both types of evidence can be a problem. Laboratory methods used for chemical processing of latent prints are detrimental to serological analyses for saliva, and vice versa. Because of this laboratory problem, a choice normally has to be made as to whether the item is to be examined for saliva or prints. Sometimes, it is opted to pursue both, despite the fact that saliva is class evidence and latent prints have the potential of furnishing a positive identification of a specific person.

The decision to recover both types of evidence is dependent on the size and condition of the cigarette butt(s) in question. Saliva is most likely to be present in the end of the butt having direct contact with the mouth. Latent prints are many times located on the portion of the butt nearest the burning segment of the cigarette. It is possible, then, to examine these two areas separately by cutting the butt and conducting appropriate analyses on each section. There are too many variables to preclude the presence of saliva or prints on any given portion of a cigarette butt. The salient consideration is to collect as many intact cigarette butts as reasonable, while limiting contamination to them. The greater the size of the intact cigarette butt, the more specimen the laboratory has with which to make decisions regarding the most advantageous examinations to conduct.

Other items on which saliva may be found can be recovered in the same disposal areas as cigarettes. Chewing gum, small bits of food, toothpicks, paper matches that may have functioned as toothpicks, etc., should also be regarded as possibly containing saliva, but are often realistically of limited value. When such items are observed, they should be segregated from ashes and other particulate debris, which have a tendency to contaminate. Any of these evidence materials discovered in a wet condition should be air-dried and packaged in containers that have the capacity for air movement and will not retain extraneous moisture.

Saliva on occasions will appear on nonporous items, such as painted surfaces, plastics, glass, and metal cans. The high possibility of contamination or inadvertent destruction of the saliva due to its low visibility and ready solubility in water can create inherent difficulties. Dried saliva is extremely difficult to see with the naked eye and can be wiped away with the slightest touch. Also, there is often a minimal amount of saliva on nonporous surfaces because they tend not to collect saliva. The field investigator should be cognizant of the need to avoid abrasion of nonporous items that may bear saliva. This should extend to the handling of these items with unprotected bare hands. There is the slight possibility that residues that could interfere with crime laboratory examinations would be transferred from the hands to the saliva.

As with blood, it is feasible to remove a section of nonporous area bearing the suspected saliva stain. Large and bulky articles or things that cannot be moved for practical reasons can be handled in this manner, if care is taken to protect the area in question from debris generated by the removal process. In sexual assault cases, such instances will usually not be encountered with great frequency. A further point for the field investigator is the need to cover an area exhibiting saliva on a nonporous surface. A section of cardboard or other pliable material can be configured to act as a protective cover over this region to prevent rubbing or abrasion from destroying the evidence. The article can be packaged and subsequently furnished to the forensic laboratory.

Saliva can be removed from a nonporous surface with swabs and distilled water. This technique can serve as a last option when the entire item, or an appropriate portion of it, cannot be removed from the scene and submitted to the laboratory. The same cautions already set forth for other biological fluid evidence apply here regarding the reconstitution of a questioned specimen. Control specimens of swabs and control sampling of the region surrounding the area in consideration are also necessary.

Although a somewhat infrequent occurrence, a wet saliva deposit could be located in the course of field investigation. Swabs, sections of absorbent cotton cloth, or filter paper could be used to effect recovery. This is especially useful when the intact item on which the saliva is located cannot be removed from the scene for some reason.

A great deal of attention has been directed both in crime scene investigations and in forensic pathology to the role and nature of bite mark evidence in sexual assaults. Direct contact between the suspect's mouth and the skin of the victim often results not only in a bite mark, but also in the presence of saliva in the immediate region of the mark. The recovery and forensic analysis of this saliva evidence is of extreme importance, especially in cases where the bite mark itself does not exhibit sufficient clarity of detail for positive identification with the dental configuration of the suspect.

The first stage of utilizing saliva in bite mark cases is the recognition of the mark and immediate protection of that location from contaminating or destructive activity. Care should be given to ensure the area of concern is not touched with the bare hands. After documenting the initial condition and location of the mark photographically, a protective cover (e.g., cardboard) should be placed over the region to prevent abrasion or contamination while the person bitten, if deceased, is removed from the scene. When possible, this should also be done with a living person. This task normally involves advising the individual to refrain from washing or touching the area, as well as taking steps to protect it with a small cover. Liaison between hospital personnel and law enforcement is critical, due to the medical treatment necessitated for victims or suspects. It is possible that hospital officials may have the first contact with a victim or suspect and would be in a position to protect the saliva from contamination or loss. Medical personnel should be made aware of the need to refrain from washing a bite mark unless this is necessary during treatment.

Saliva can be recovered from a bite mark by using swabs and/or cotton threads wetted with distilled water. The area adjacent to, but not part of, the bite mark should be sampled as a control. The bite mark itself is sampled separately. Special attention should be given to ensuring that the mark is not altered by the saliva collection procedure. Additionally, sampling from bloody areas of the mark should be avoided. The collection media used to acquire the control samples should not be packaged with the samples recovered from the bite mark. Unstained swabs and/or cotton threads used for evidence collection should be retained as additional control samples.

Saliva can be deposited on the skin in areas other than bite marks. Sometimes a suspect has licked, sucked, or lightly bitten the victim's skin without leaving a recognizable mark. The statements of the victim concerning the actions of the suspect should be considered as indicating locations from which questioned saliva may be recovered.

In some instances of sexual assault, efforts by the suspect to bite the victim (or vice versa) may not necessarily result in a bite mark directly on the skin, due to intervening articles such as clothing, bed sheets, and pillowcases. Therefore, biting through a fabric article may result in the creation of a mark on the skin and the deposition of saliva on the intervening article. Attention for saliva evidence should be given to an area on a fabric item, particularly clothing, which corresponds to the location of a bite mark on the skin. This potentially valuable source for saliva could be missed as a result of not considering that a bite may have occurred through fabric. This circumstance may occur, for example, when an unconscious victim is found nude with her clothing nearby. An assumption that the bite mark was administered to the naked skin may be incorrect and result in pertinent evidence being overlooked.

Recovery of Known Evidence

The recovery of questioned physical evidence will only have real meaning when comparisons with the known evidence sources are conducted. Crime laboratories continually face the inadequacy or lack of known standards required for comparison purposes. Also, forensic examinations frequently are hindered by the use of poor methods to acquire these standards. The recommended techniques for collection of known samples of appropriate quality, which follow, are set forth with the intent of providing the laboratory with the best chance of reaching optimum results from the evidence.

Known Hair Samples

The quality of known hair samples removed from a victim and suspect will directly affect the quality of forensic results coming from the crime laboratory. For a meaningful comparison to be accomplished between questioned and known hairs, the known hairs must be from the same body area as the questioned hairs and represent the variation range of hairs present in that body area. The crime laboratory examiner can categorize hairs as having originated from various areas, which generally are head, pubic, limb, beard or mustache, chest, axillary (underarm), and eye area. However, there can be situations in which hairs may lack certain features necessary for forensic categorization and/or comparison. Head and pubic hairs are the types most often of intrinsic value in sexual assault cases. The reason is that head and pubic hair characteristics vary more from one person to another within the same racial group and possess a greater number of identifiable characteristics. There are circumstances, however, in which hairs from other parts of the body, such as beard hairs, may be pertinent physical evidence.

There are basically five major regions on the head from which hair samples usually are taken: front, top, back, left side, and right side. Proper sampling of these areas is adequate. In the pubic region, the hairs on the pubic bone area can differ from hairs in the area of the vagina or testicles. Therefore, whenever possible, both these areas should be sampled as comparison standards.

A question frequently asked by investigators regarding the acquisition of known hair evidence is, "How many should be taken?" One or two hairs will be inadequate for reliable comparisons to be conducted. Nonetheless, there are differing opinions among laboratory examiners about the exact number to acquire. For example, 100 head hairs (20 from each of the five regions previously mentioned) and 30 pubic hairs (from varying locations) have been suggested as ideal amounts for laboratory comparisons with questioned hairs. However, these numbers are much higher than the amounts of known samples often submitted for comparison purposes. Twenty-five full-length hairs taken from various areas of the head or pubic area generally are considered adequate to represent an individual's hair characteristics. The investigator should discuss this issue with the laboratory that will be responsible for hair comparisons *before* known hairs are acquired in an investigation.

Known hairs are usually taken by pulling out hairs from the area of concern. Removing hairs by this method ensures that the laboratory examiner has the opportunity to study features along the entire length of each hair.

Circumstances sometimes will not permit hairs to be forcibly pulled from the body. The known hairs should then be cut as close to the skin as possible, preferably at skin level with a razor or scalpel. The forensic laboratory which receives these hairs should be advised that the hairs were cut as close to the body as possible and, thereby, full-length hairs have been submitted. Many known hair samples sent to crime laboratories resemble sweepings from the floor of a barber shop because they have been snipped from near the end of the hair shafts. This method can be detrimental, especially if the hairs have been artificially colored or treated. The sampling would represent only the treated ends of the hairs and not the growing areas near the skin, which would have natural color. Transferred hairs in this instance will have treated and natural regions and will be difficult to compare with the inadequately cut known specimens.

It is also advisable to obtain known hair samples via a "combing" procedure to serve as a supplement to the pulled specimens. Although this procedure is normally associated with the recovery of questioned hairs, fibers, and debris, it also serves as a source for collection of other types of hairs of importance. Human hairs go through a growth process having three stages: anagen (actively growing), catagen (resting), and telogen (dormant and ready to be shed from the body). In fact, there are subtle morphological differences, which can be detected by a trained microscopist, as the stages progress. Those hairs normally transferred from suspect to victim, and vice versa, during an assault tend to be those that are ready to be shed from the body, hence telogen. The hairs present on the victim that are in the same growth cycle stage as those most likely transferred to the suspect represent the best possible known comparison standards. These are the kinds of hairs frequently obtained via the "combing" procedure, although a certain number of those hairs obtained by pulling or cutting will also be in this stage.

It is evident from the preceding discussion of hair evidence that a multitude of factors influence its forensic interpretation and use in the courtroom. One difficulty relates to the time span between the assault and the collection of known specimens. If a suspect and victim come to the attention of authorities shortly after an assault has occurred, their hair features probably have not been altered by natural growing or intentional alteration on the part of either person. Many suspects take steps to bleach or dye hair, shave it off completely, or otherwise hinder the acquisition of reliable known standards for comparison. Therefore, known hairs should be taken from a suspect and victim as soon as their identities become known.

Sometimes it is necessary to acquire known "elimination" hair specimens from persons not involved in the sexual assault. For instance, the victim of a sexual assault may have had consenting intimate contact or sexual relations with someone shortly before the crime was committed. Some of the hairs obtained as evidence, especially those secured by the combing procedures, may have come from that contact, and known hair standards should be obtained from that person. This will assist the crime laboratory in eliminating hairs which would be of no real value as pertinent physical evidence.

On occasion, it becomes necessary to collect hair specimens from animals. A dog or cat, for example, can potentially represent a known source of animal hairs located on clothing or other items recovered in an investigation. There are two primary types of hairs on animals, guard hairs and fur hairs. Guard hairs are long and coarse when compared with the fur hairs, which are typically short and very fine. Both forms of hair should be obtained as known samples by removing them from representative areas. Efforts must be made to collect numerous hairs in these locations that exhibit the color and length variations appearing on the subject animal.

Known Fiber Samples

The first known source of fibers that becomes apparent is clothing worn by persons involved in a crime. Although the clothing of victim and suspect is always considered as potentially containing questioned evidence, the fibers that compose the clothing are also utilized in a forensic laboratory as known comparison standards. The recommendation has been made consistently thus far that clothing and other items be recovered intact, whenever feasible. It is not advisable, in the field, for known samples to be removed from clothing by cutting small swatches of fabric. There are instances in which a tremendous amount of clothing is discovered as evidence. In these situations, it may be beyond reasonable practicality to package all the garments for laboratory submission. Still, there is a serious drawback to cutting off portions of the known materials. If clothing fibers were transferred directly to a suspect or victim, there was some extent of physical contact between garment and person. Therefore, the person may have transferred hairs, blood, etc., to the garment, and they would be missed by only removing a portion of fabric sample and not examining the entire piece of clothing. The investigator faced with this situation may request the assistance of the laboratory in making the best determination when such known sampling in the field is being considered.

Aside from clothing, any other fibrous item recovered as evidence can be used as a source of known fibers. Bedding, small rugs, pillows, and similar articles can be excellent sources of fiber transfer and often become important as reliable evidence sources.

The types of fiber sources mentioned thus far are usually collected simply because field personnel are aware that questioned evidence can be contained on them. Many times these ordinary, expected items represent the only known sources secured from a crime scene. However, all of the fibrous materials at a given place represent the complete environment, not just those limited items often taken to the forensic laboratory. One of the methods of ensuring that adequate fibers standards are removed is to survey a scene, as a separate task, for the collection of realistic known fiber sources. This task can focus the attention of personnel on the known fiber acquisition problem.

The actual recovery of the fiber samples is not a matter of randomly cutting pieces of fabric from various items and pulling a cluster of fibers from others. The following questions should be considered before recovery is initiated:

1. How many fibrous objects are present?
2. What colors are these objects?
3. What are the physical conditions of the objects?
4. What is the best way to remove the samples?

Each fibrous article should be sampled if the known fiber environment is to be correctly represented. The samples should be individually packaged and each container labeled as to its item of origin. All the various colors of fibers are to be obtained from each article sampled. For example, a fabric chair having three separate colors would require sampling of fibers exhibiting all of these colors.

Fibrous articles are subject to wear and tear, as well as the deposition of stains from liquids, soil, and other foreign debris. Simple everyday activity on a carpet, for example, will result in varying degrees of wear in different areas, and stains will give more uniqueness to these areas. Known samples should be obtained to represent fibers from areas that would exhibit these physical wear features and foreign substances.

It is advisable to remove intact sections of fabric to be utilized as comparison standards. The collector should ensure that these sections include a sample of yarn of each color present in the article. Any material to which the fibers adhere, such as the backing in a carpet, should also be included for forensic examination. Any sharp instrument will suffice for sample removal, provided it is clean and does not transmit debris or contaminants to the sample.

Known Blood Samples

Obtaining known comparison specimens of blood is a prime consideration in order that characterization of stains may be attained. There can be the assumption that taking known blood involves simply having a physician, or other medically qualified individual, draw the blood into a test tube, whereupon the resulting specimen is transmitted to the crime laboratory for analysis and comparison. However, there are important variables in terms of materials and handling that should be explored because they have a definite bearing on the quality and reliability of the sample.

Known blood samples must be obtained from suspect and victim and, on many occasions, from persons who could be considered as reasonable sources for elimination. The reasons for acquiring the specimens from suspect and victim are obvious because they are directly associated with the crime. However, collection of known specimens should also include those from recent sexual partners of the victim. Known blood samples should be taken from any other person who could have logically deposited a blood or other body fluid stain in the location in question. For example, the child of a rape victim may have bled on a bedsheet prior to the assault that occurred directly on this bedding article. Known blood should be collected to eliminate or include this person as a possible source.

The materials utilized for known blood sampling typically originate from three major sources:

1. Those prepackaged in a commercially available sexual assault evidence collection kit
2. Those prepared and prepackaged in sexual assault evidence collection kit form by a crime laboratory or police agency for use by law enforcement and medical personnel
3. Those not part of any prepackaged kit and normally consisting of materials available at the hospital or medical institution at the time samples are taken from the individual

For the kinds of serological analyses in sexual assault cases, a liquid whole blood sample usually is necessary and superior to a dried sample on, for example, a piece of cloth or filter paper. The determination of secretor status can be accomplished from whole blood through laboratory testing. Such analysis is not functional and reliable when dry blood is examined. Whole blood samples should be refrigerated as soon as possible after they are taken, but must not be frozen. Freezing whole blood will cause the cells to lyse (cellular rupture), which is not beneficial for serological analysis. Refrigeration retards bacterial activity and growth and serves to protect the genetic factors sought by the serologist.

Many of the commercially available test tubes produced specifically for the collection of blood from a person contain chemical additives designed to either preserve blood or prevent its coagulation. These additives are normally placed in the tubes by the manufacturers before they are sealed and distributed for use in the medical community. A variety of different substances are used, such as heparin, sodium fluoride, sodium oxalate, EDTA (ethylenediamine tetraacetic acid), and ACD (acid citrate dextrose).

Experienced FBI serologists have related to the author that there has been some concern as to whether or not these preservatives or anticoagulants affect forensic analyses. Sodium fluoride has been thought possibly to be detrimental to serological testing methods employing electrophoresis. This point is important, since electrophoresis furnishes much of the advanced blood grouping information at this time in forensic science. The majority opinion was that current methods of analysis make the preservative or anticoagulant almost an irrelevant factor in genetic analysis of whole blood samples. Nonetheless, the crime laboratory that is to be involved in a case should be contacted for its experience and/or requirements. Different laboratories can have varied requirements, depending on the methods of analysis used for serology examinations. (Many of the serologists contacted by the author recommended the use of ACD as an anticoagulant, if one is to be used.)

Although anticoagulants or preservatives are often necessary in whole blood samples, forensic analysis of blood is more easily accommodated when no chemical additive is present. Therefore, the acquisition of whole blood samples without any additive is recommended. It is common for the crime laboratory to receive one tube with and one tube without anticoagulant or preservative.

The foregoing statements in reference to utilization of anticoagulants or preservatives are directed primarily at blood grouping. Sometimes the facts of a case will dictate that forensic analysis of blood also encompass drug and alcohol questions. The guidelines concerning chemical additives are then subject to change.

In addition to a test tube for blood grouping, one test tube each should be taken for alcohol and drug analyses. *No* preservative or anticoagulant should be incorporated in the sample to be used for drugs, and sodium fluoride can be included in the one to be used for alcohol testing. Thus, three separate known samplings may be submitted to the laboratory, each for a different purpose. Five milliliters of blood in a sterile test tube is a minimum recommended satisfactory amount to facilitate crime laboratory analysis for each of these types of examinations.

Known Saliva Samples

Known saliva specimens used for ABO secretor status determinations can be collected through a variety of procedures. In general, collection methods can involve obtaining liquid or, preferably, air-dried samples.

Known saliva samples should not be routinely taken in liquid form due to chemical decay and the harmful activity of bacteria. Storage of liquid saliva, even for hours, is extremely detrimental.

The collection of saliva can be better accomplished by having an individual expectorate on cloth or a section of filter paper. The collecting substrate must be clean and free of detergents and chemicals to prevent interference with forensic testing. The sample should be acquired only after the individual has not smoked or had anything to eat or drink for at least 30 minutes. The saliva stain should be no smaller than the size of a quarter. The entire collection surface should not be treated with saliva; the unstained area can then function as a control sample. It can be of value to obtain another complete and unstained collection substrate as an additional control specimen. The saliva should be allowed to air-dry completely and then be packaged in a paper or cardboard container that allows the exchange of air and will not retain moisture.

The use of gauze pads is to be avoided for saliva sampling. Saliva taken in this manner can be too greatly dispersed and difficult to analyze in the laboratory.

The use of filter paper does have advantages that bear mentioning. When the saliva is acquired on this medium, a circle should be drawn around the perimeter of the stain to isolate it for crime laboratory analysis. This outline should be done with a pencil, as certain inks may diffuse and migrate in the paper through time and subsequently come into contact with the saliva. Additionally, steps should be taken to prevent the pencil marks from being smudged over the saliva deposit. Chain-of-custody data can be placed on the filter paper completely away from the saliva.

Another method of obtaining known saliva is to recover it directly from the mouth in the area between the molar teeth and cheek. One suitable technique is to use a piece of cotton cloth or cotton swab, placing it in the mouth for deposition of saliva and removing it for air-drying. Clean forceps can be utilized to place and remove the cloth for sampling, in order to avoid contamination by the hands of the person responsible for taking it. As with other biological fluid evidence, control samples of the substrate used to gather the evidence are to be packaged separately and submitted to the crime laboratory.

Marking of Evidence for Identification

The admission of evidence in the courtroom is dependent on adherence to guidelines of chain of custody. Essentially, physical evidence is subjected to challenges as to proper collection, storage, transportation, delivery, and documentation of that material. Incriminating evidence that cannot be introduced in a trial is realistically of no practical value. The generally accepted considerations for admittance of items as evidence in a trial are:

1. The item of evidence must be authenticated by a knowledgeable person. This person is typically the one who personally recovered the evidence, or one who actually observed it at the scene and saw it being collected.
2. The item of evidence has not been altered to any appreciable degree. This guideline does take into account the need to alter the evidence in reasonable ways, such as marking an item for identification, or consumption of portions of it during a forensic analysis.
3. The item of evidence must be accounted for at all times, from its collection to its introduction as evidence in a trial. This process is designed to ensure that a similar item has not been substituted, either inadvertently or intentionally.

Physical evidence should be marked for identification whenever feasible. Some forms of evidence, such as debris, cannot be marked, but it is possible to do so with larger items. Two marking methods are commonly used: direct and indirect marking. Direct marking refers to the placement of identification marks on the item of evidence itself. Indirect marking involves placing notations of identification on a container in which the evidence is placed.

It is obvious that the most advantageous method is direct identification. The appearance of markings on the evidence itself leaves no doubt as to its authenticity, and chain of custody is more easily maintained for courtroom purposes. It is recommended that when the evidence is marked, the container into which it is placed also be labeled appropriately. The marks used must be suitable to refresh the memory of the person who collected it or examined it in the laboratory. Depending on the size of the evidence, the date of recovery and initials of the recovering person are adequate for authentication. There is no need to place extensive names, dates, times, and case notations on a piece of evidence. Such data may drastically alter its original condition. These items of information are better documented on an evidence log or similar document.

In contrast, the container housing the evidence normally should be labeled more extensively than the evidence itself. The minimum data recorded should be: location and description of the recovered evidence, a specific number or similar designation, person who recovered the evidence, and date of recovery. This information is essential to conform to the fundamental guidelines in a court of law for the gathering of evidence. Agency experience and administrative criteria may dictate that additional data be recorded.

Field personnel in some agencies use evidence tags to mark evidence or its container. These tags normally are attached to the evidence after appropriate notations are written on them. Many individuals feel that this system is convenient and makes it unnecessary to directly mark the evidence. On the contrary, the excessive use of these tags tends to make evidence handling more cumbersome and difficult. A tag can be accidentally torn off or intentionally removed as the evidence is handled or examined forensically. Worse yet would be a situation in which it is lost completely. This has been known to occur and not be noticed until trial, to the detriment of the entire case. The tagging method, thus, has drawbacks, and it does not alleviate the responsibility of the collector to mark the evidence itself whenever possible.

Experience has revealed that it is advantageous to have at least two people observe evidence in place before recovery. One person can actually recover it, mark it directly, and package it. The second party can witness this process and then initial the container bearing the evidence material. This procedure will ensure there is a second person who can authenticate the evidence in the event the person who recovered it is unavailable for court purposes. This may be somewhat impractical for some agencies, but it is mentioned as one additional mechanism that can be used when deemed feasible.

The marking of physical evidence at the time of its collection should be supplemented with an evidence log. This log serves to document the administrative and substantive information concerning evidence recovery. It should record the sequence in which the evidence is recovered, as well as the standard chain-of-custody information mentioned previously. The log should be prepared entirely at the scene.

This is because more complete observations are made when personnel are actually in the process of gathering the evidence. The logging technique is especially valuable in cases where a vast amount of evidence is involved. When a question arises, it is more convenient to review a succinct, organized log for evidence information than it is to sort through many individual evidence containers.

The concept of maintaining chain of custody should extend beyond the field collection stage of the investigation. Transmittal of items of evidence from person to person must be documented in writing so that responsibility will be fixed for preservation and courtroom demonstration of chain of custody. Records are necessary to document times, dates, identities of personnel with access, and other pertinent information regarding any evidence transactions. Recording such information takes only a small amount of time and effort and frequently counters potential challenges to important pieces of evidence. The lack of proper documentation is a hindrance to effective use of the evidence during field investigation, pretrial conferences, and, ultimately, courtroom proceedings.

Materials Used to Package Physical Evidence

The fragile and transitory nature of some types of evidence in sexual assaults makes packaging methods and procedures of utmost significance. Use of incorrect packaging materials can have a disastrous effect on the ability of the crime laboratory to obtain the maximum information afforded by each piece of evidence.

Packaging problems that most often confront field personnel involve either small/minute evidence or large/bulky evidence. A great variety of packaging containers are available, many offered by commercial suppliers. Each agency should study its own needs and make educated decisions. It is relatively simple to accumulate the necessary materials for most packaging situations without resorting to expensive commercially available evidence collection kits.

Sexual assault evidence often comes in the form of small/minute substances, such as tufts of fibers or several strands of hair. Some practical considerations regarding the preservation of such evidence are:

1. Cardboard "pillbox" type containers are useful. These containers can be taped securely, are sturdy, and have surfaces that facilitate the writing of identification notations. Additionally, these items allow the exchange of air and tend not to retain moisture.

2. Envelopes having glued flaps are not recommended for prolonged storage. There is a chance the glued areas will come apart and result in the loss of some or all of the enclosed evidence. Also, it can be

difficult for laboratory examiners to locate the evidence in the envelopes.

3. The druggist (pharmacist) fold is a useful technique. Bond paper cut in 3″ × 5″, 5″ × 7″, and 8½″ × 11″ sizes will accommodate most small items. Bond paper is recommended because it is resilient and can be taped securely. It also supplies a good medium for evidence identification notations. The druggist fold is probably the best method for collecting scrapings of suspected blood.

4. Plastic zip-lock bags are not considered best for evidence storage. There is too much chance of accidental opening of the bags, resulting in loss of evidence. Locating a small fiber that is "somewhere" in one of these bags can be difficult for the crime laboratory. To increase the problems, static electricity can attract a considerable amount of foreign material on the exterior and interior of the bags. Moisture retention is difficult to eliminate in these containers.

5. Film containers (35 mm) can be of value for small/minute evidence. These items are very sturdy and readily available. The containers should be cleaned thoroughly to ensure no contaminants are present before use. Tape can be applied to seal the lid in place as an additional precaution.

Chain-of-custody markings should be placed on the selected container before the evidence is placed inside. This point is especially important when the druggist fold is used. Writing with a ballpoint pen or other instrument having a hard, resilient tip can damage the small evidence housed in the package.

The collection and packaging of large/bulky evidence materials typically present greater difficulty than dealing with the small/minute items. In sexual assault cases, field investigators are faced with the recovery of bedding, furniture upholstery, car seats, carpets, and other large objects. More often than not, the tendency is to cut out the stained regions or other areas containing possible evidence. Throughout the discussions it has been recommended that the entire item bearing the evidence be collected and submitted for laboratory analysis. This point is appropriate; however, it must be tempered with the exercise of good judgment by both crime scene investigators and laboratory personnel. The best approach in these situations is first to look over the bulky evidence for any evidentiary items that may be easily lost due to their transitory nature (e.g., hairs, fibers, threads). Much evidence can be lost in the attempt to collect and package large items at the crime scene.

The author has frequently heard the comment from crime laboratory examiners that investigators often send in virtually all items found at a scene without determining if this is reasonable and, more importantly, worthwhile. On the other hand, the author has dealt with many investigators who feel it is the responsibility of the crime laboratory to search for evidence on these items that is beyond the vision or skill of the field investigator. Lack of communication and education many times is the real source of such conflicts. It is usually unnecessary to submit all items collected at a scene to the laboratory. Careful evaluation of the evidence will dictate which articles are ultimately submitted.

There are significant recommendations pertaining to the packaging of large/bulky evidence materials. The information that follows constitutes an effort to deal with common errors in handling this kind of physical evidence.

1. Any material that is damp or wet is to be air-dried, preferably away from direct sunlight. Storing moist evidence in an airtight environment promotes bacterial growth and putrefaction of most biological substances. Prolonged exposure of blood, semen, and other biological materials to sunlight will be harmful due to the negative effects of continued exposure to ultraviolet light.

2. Drying of large evidence presents a somewhat burdensome problem. A room or other secure location in which to allow moist evidence to dry should be available. Particular attention must be given to the selection of a location that minimizes the chance for contamination and takes the health and safety of personnel into account. Appropriate steps are to be taken so that it also is secure and has a system of accountability to document chain of custody.

3. Plastic bags or other plastic-type containers are not advisable for the packaging and storage of the large/bulky evidence often encountered in sexual assault investigations. Even when the evidence has been air-dried, sealed plastic bags may promote the accumulation of condensation. There are instances, however, in which plastic packaging materials will make it easier to transport evidence to the laboratory for forensic examination. Most often, this circumstance occurs when it is virtually impossible to air-dry numerous items of evidence at a crime scene. Because moist blood and other wet substances on evidence articles would soak through and destroy paper wrappings, sections of plastic wrap or plastic bags can be used here to advantage. The wrap or bags should be retained when the evidence articles are removed later for the purpose of air-drying, as trace evidence may have been dislodged from the articles while they were housed temporarily. This situation is not to be confused with the requirements for extended storage of physical evidence. In fact, the destructive effect of tightly sealed plastic containers on evidence collected during investigation of violent crimes can be a major difficulty for the forensic laboratory.

4. Sturdy paper of the type commonly used for wrapping packages for mailing is easy to obtain and can accommodate a wide variety of

evidence sizes and shapes. Identification notations relating to the evidence can be written on the outside of the paper before that evidence is wrapped and secured with tape. Paper bags also can be utilized, with double-ply bags being the most resilient to tearing and the demands of constant handling. As mentioned previously, these paper materials are to be checked for possible contaminants produced as a result of the manufacturing process.

5. Steps should be taken to avoid excessive handling of the evidence that is gathered. Each handling of the evidence increases the opportunity for contamination and loss of transitory materials. Once the package containing the evidence is sealed, every effort is to be made not to open it prior to submission to the crime laboratory. This action assists an attorney in courtroom arguments as to the positive and detailed methods used to preserve evidence integrity.

6. Ideally, every item of evidence should be packaged separately and not intermingled with other evidence. This approach is recommended as the first choice for collection and preservation. There will be conditions, nonetheless, that make doing so somewhat impractical. It is not uncommon to recover voluminous amounts of clothing and similar materials that are found together and, therefore, can be conveniently packaged together. One important example in this regard involves the handling of bulky bedding items (sheets, blankets, bedspreads, etc.) appearing on a bed in which the victim was attacked. Rather than remove each pertinent bedding article and package it separately, it can be advantageous to collect those bedding materials that logically could be valuable together in the same order in which they were found on the bed. Doing so could prevent the possible loss of trace evidence. The sequence of bedding items can be appropriately marked for reconstruction should the sequence become an issue at a later date. These circumstances are to be regarded as exceptions rather than standard operations. In general, separate packaging is most conducive to laboratory analysis and can also provide a higher degree of credibility to the evidence in the courtroom.

7. Clothing and other articles of evidence from the victim, suspect, and crime scene must not be allowed to intermingle. Contamination can easily occur if contact takes place to even a small extent. The victim's and suspect's evidence should not be handled in the same area, because of the extremely transitory quality of trace evidence materials. As an added precaution, the packages of evidence are to be well sealed. This approach can overcome evidence integrity challenges on the basis that storing these materials together in a box, even though separately wrapped, could result in contamination by the movement of extremely small debris.

The time to accumulate the necessary materials for evidence storage is before, not after, a crime or similar crisis occurs. The human tendency is to use whatever is at hand in times of stress or crisis-level circumstances. Every effort should be made to have the proper evidence packaging materials available to meet the needs, within reason, of almost any situation that could happen on a moment's notice. Neglecting to accomplish this seemingly basic task probably is responsible for many of the common difficulties in crime scene investigation and other evidence collection situations.

Summary

As reflected in this chapter, handling different types of physical evidence can represent a complex task. Specialized techniques that apply to the five major kinds of evidence covered here have been set forth as suggestions and recommendations. The vast possibilities that cannot adequately be anticipated make it incumbent on the crime scene investigator or other evidence-recovery party to evaluate each problem before action is instituted. The number of available personnel, evidence storage facilities, access to a crime laboratory, and requirements established by the laboratory for receipt of evidence from the field are aspects to be considered. Most of all, planning and cooperation will be the prime elements of success. These words are used routinely to the point that they may seem overly emphasized. Nonetheless, as with all areas of human endeavor, these two factors can make the difference between poor, mediocre, and exceptional performance. Physical evidence utilization is no different.

The information provided in this chapter and the preceding one indicates the methodology that law enforcement and the criminal justice community can apply to utilization and interpretation of physical evidence. Many elements must move cohesively toward the central goal of making correct sense of the evidence in court. One element has been mentioned only in passing, but may actually be the one that truly makes the difference between success or failure. Training, experience, and techniques of evidence work progressing from the victim, suspect, and crime scene to the courtroom can be completely overshadowed by the *attitudes* of all persons involved. Attention to detail and care is the key element relating to the successful use of evidence. The ultimate in funding, technique, administration, and organization cannot outweigh the detrimental effects of poor attitude.

Conscious and subconscious psychological reactions are the most difficult aspects of people to predict and control. Law enforcement personnel are no different in this regard from persons in other professions. Thoughts brought about by witnessing the tragic results of the brutality and violence so characteristic of sexual assault crimes can affect a person to the point that good judgment is transformed into frustration and confusion. If responses to evidence collection situations or legal challenges to evidence are reactive and governed by personal feelings, the resulting turmoil can be reflected in a disorganized evidence effort during the investigation and subsequent trial.

The human side of evidence collection and utilization should be recognized and controlled with the intent of anticipating these kinds of problems. This one issue can transcend all the myriad components of forensic science. It must be given appropriate attention when physical evidence is used to assist in the determination of guilt or innocence in sexual assault cases.

The author would like to express sincere appreciation to the following personnel of the FBI Laboratory for their time and assistance concerning Chapters 4 and 5: Dr. F. Samuel Baechtel; Dr. Bruce Budowle; Supervisory Special Agent Harold A. Deadman, Jr.; Assistant Section Chief James J. Kearney; Supervisory Special Agent Randall S. Murch; Supervisory Special Agent Wayne W. Oakes; Supervisory Special Agent Robert P. Spalding.

Suggested Readings for Chapters 4 and 5

For the purpose of these two chapters and in consideration of the target population, the books that follow will provide relevant information to supplement and expand on the discussions. Additionally, the reader should refer to the suggested references, in particular, for coverage of evidence types beyond the intended scope of the chapters set forth here. The reader must also not neglect to obtain handbooks or similar published guidelines disseminated by the crime laboratory in the jurisdiction to which evidence is usually submitted for analysis. This effort is regarded as imperative by the author because of the varying requirements of evidence procedure from one crime laboratory to another.

Buckwalter, Art. *The Search for Evidence*. Stoneham, Massachusetts: Butterworth Publishers, 1984.

Cunningham, Carl L. and Fox, Richard H. *Crime Scene Search and Physical Evidence Handbook*. Washington, D.C.: United States Government Printing Office, 1973.

Deforest, Peter R., Gaensslen, R. E. and Lee, Henry C. *Forensic Science—An Introduction to Criminalistics*. New York: McGraw-Hill, 1983.

Eckert, William G. *Introduction to Forensic Sciences*. St. Louis, Missouri: C. V. Mosby Company, 1980.

Gaensslen, R. E. *Sourcebook in Forensic Science Serology, Immunology and Biochemistry*. Washington, D.C.: United States Government Printing Office, 1983.

Inbau, Fred E. and Moenssens, Andre A. *Scientific Evidence in Criminal Cases*. Mineola, New York: The Foundation Press, 1978.

Osterburg, James W. *The Crime Laboratory—Case Studies of Scientific Criminal Investigation*. New York: Clark Boardman Company, 1982.

Saferstein, Richard. *Forensic Science Handbook*. Englewood Cliffs, New Jersey: Prentice-Hall, 1982.

The Science of Fingerprints—Classification and Uses. Washington, D.C.: United States Government Printing Office, 1984.

Svensson, Arne, Wendel, Otto, and Fisher, Barry A. J. *Techniques of Crime Scene Investigation*, 3rd ed. New York: Elsevier, 1981.

Wecht, Cyril H. *Forensic Sciences—Law/Science/Civil/Criminal*, (Volumes 1–3). New York: Matthew Bender Company, 1983.

Criminal Personality Profiling: An Overview

6

ROBERT R. HAZELWOOD, ROBERT K. RESSLER,
ROGER L. DEPUE, AND JOHN E. DOUGLAS

> What is to be expected . . . is an understanding not merely of the deeds, but also the doers. (Zilboorg, 1968)

Analyzing a violent crime to determine identifiable characteristics of the unknown offender is not a new technique. However, the work being done by the FBI's Behavioral Science Unit (BSU) represents law enforcement's entry into this area for the first time. In the past this procedure has been practiced primarily by clinical psychologists or psychiatrists who, while trained in matters of the mind, lacked experience in conducting criminal investigations of violent crime. As a result, their profiles were couched in terminology largely alien to the intended audience—the criminal investigator.

A criminal personality profile prepared by the BSU provides the investigative agency with characteristics of the unidentified offender that differentiate him from the general population. These characteristics are set forth in such a manner as to allow those who know and/or associate with the offender to readily recognize him.

Information Provided in a Profile

While the format of the profile may vary with the individual preparing it, the information provided is essentially the same. Some prefer an outline format that allows the reader to identify a specific characteristic quickly without having to read through the entire report. Others prepare the profile in a narrative style. The narrative style provides greater detail and allows the reader to follow the process by which the profiler arrives at conclusions. Regardless of the format, a profile furnished by the BSU will include most, if not all, of the following information: approximate age, sex, race, marital status, occupational level, educational background, military history, socioeconomic level, pastimes or hobbies, approximate year and style of vehicle owned or operated, arrest history, appearance and grooming habits, residential information, and victim–offender relationship, as well as certain personality characteristics such as temperament, intelligence level, emotional adjustment, pathological behavioral characteristics, and ability to interact socially and sexually.

Profiling and the Behavioral Science Unit

Criminal personality profiling was initiated within the BSU on an informal basis in 1972 at the FBI Academy. Faculty members would encourage their students to discuss solved and unsolved cases with which they were familiar, and as a result of such discussions, the instructors would note that in similar crimes, the offenders were a great deal alike. In subsequent classes when a student presented an unsolved crime similar to ones previously discussed, the instructors would provide verbal profiles for the student. The students would utilize the information upon returning to their agencies and would report that the use of the profiles saved many investigative manhours by properly focusing the investigation. In a few instances, a profile was credited with being directly responsible for solving the crime.

As other investigative agencies became aware of this assistance, the number of cases received for profiling rapidly increased. Since the faculty had a primary responsibility of instruction, the cases were analyzed on a time-available basis. The volume of requests grew to unanticipated proportions, and in 1978 the program was formalized and submitted cases were assigned to specific individuals for profiling.

In 1981, 55 Special Agents were selected from various offices within the FBI and given 100 hours of instruction to prepare them as Profile Coordinators within their respective geographic regions. Since that time, agencies desiring this service submit their cases to the Profile Coordinator nearest them, and he in turn ensures that the materials necessary to prepare a profile have been included and that the case lends itself to the profiling process. If all prerequisites are met, the case is forwarded to the BSU and assigned for profiling. When the profile is completed, it is returned to the responsible coordinator for delivery to the requesting agency. All submitted materials are retained by the BSU for future reference.

Eventually, the caseload became overwhelming for the available BSU staff and additional personnel dedicated to profiling were necessary. In

1983, four Special Agents (Investigative Profilers) were selected to understudy the BSU faculty and assume the responsibility of profiling. In 1984, four additional Special Agents were assigned as Investigative Profilers. As a result, the backlog of cases has been reduced and more law enforcement agencies are receiving this assistance. In an effort to make this service even more available to local law enforcement, a one-year fellowship in profiling for police officers has been in place since 1984 (Hazelwood, 1986).

Procedure for Submission of Cases

Agencies desiring a criminal personality profile must submit the necessary documentation (see below) to the Profile Coordinator in the FBI office nearest them. The coordinator in turn forwards the material to the BSU, where it is assigned to an Investigative Profiler. Upon completion, the profile is returned to the submitting agency through the coordinator.

Case Criteria

The criteria for a case to be analyzed for criminal personality profiling are minimal. The case must involve a crime of violence, the offender must be unknown, and all major investigative leads must have been exhausted. While virtually any crime evincing mental, emotional, or personality aberration can be profiled, certain crimes are particularly appropriate for the process. Such crimes include a series of rapes, lust murder (mutilation or displacement of the sexual areas of the body) (Hazelwood and Douglas, 1980), serial murders, child molesting, ritualistic crimes, and serial arsons.

Case Materials

Map. A commercially produced map is preferred to one that has been hand drawn. A commercial map provides vital information about the locale(s) involved—deserted, industrial or residential, schools, hospitals, etc. If a commercial map is unavailable, a hand-drawn map will suffice if it is accompanied by a description of the area(s) involved. The map should be notated to indicate all significant locations—where the victim was approached, where the assault occurred, where the victim was left, etc. If these locations are different, the distance between them should be stated. Any other significant locations and distances should be marked as well. For example, if the offender entered the victim's vehicle at point A, forced her to drive to point B where the assault occurred, left her there, and took her car to point C where it was abandoned, all three locations and the distances between them should appear on the map.

Victim Statement. The interview of the rape victim and its documentation are the most important factors in the rape profiling process. Unfortunately, the person preparing the profile seldom has the opportunity to speak with the victim and obtain those facts crucial to analyzing the behavioral aspects of the rape, and is consequently dependent upon a third party, the investigator, to do so. For this reason, one of the authors (Hazelwood) developed a set of questions designed to help the investigators accomplish this task. The detailed interview of the rape victim is discussed in Chapter 7 and will not be addressed at this point, except to stress its importance.

Victimology. The final documentation needed is a summary of facts known about the victim to assist the profiler in determining why the rapist behaved verbally, physically, and sexually as he did. Essential information about the victim includes age; race; if she was with anyone at the time of, or just before the attack; her educational level; whether she appears to be passive or aggressive in nature (did she say or do something which caused the offender to become more violent?); type of employment, and a description of the socioeconomic characteristics of the area in which she resides. Of course, any other facts the investigator deems important should be included.

Suspects. Agencies submitting cases should not include information that identifies suspects in the matter. If a profiler is reviewing a case and it becomes clear that seasoned investigators strongly believe a particular person committed the crime, it is almost certain to bias objectivity and may result in a profile that strongly resembles the suspect.

Nonprofileable Cases. Not all crimes of violence lend themselves to the profiling process. There are situations or circumstances that may preclude the preparation of a valid profile. Of importance is the fact that the process is dependent not only upon the crime that has occurred and its documentation, but also upon the profiler assigned the case. In other words, what may be a difficult case or set of circumstances for one normally proficient profiler, may be quite simple for another. As an example, one person may find it extremely difficult to profile a rape in which the offender is believed to be under the influence of drugs, whereas this poses no problem for another profiler. A case in which the rapist did not speak, used minimal force, and did not engage in atypical sexual activity is extremely difficult for most profilers.

Such a case would deprive the profiler of sufficient behavior to analyze. Rapes in which the victim was rendered unconscious or, because of other reasons, cannot recall details are also very difficult, if not impossible, to profile. A good rule of thumb seems to be that if factors are missing (excluding offender identification) that the officer normally needs to investigate the case, it is not appropriate for the profiling process. It should be noted that, after conversation with the investigating officers and acquisition of additional facts, cases that had originally been determined to be inappropriate for profiling were, in fact, deemed appropriate. Prior to a case being returned as nonprofileable, it will be studied for a considerable period of time, investigating officers will be consulted, and the matter will be discussed in detail with other investigative profilers. However, the fact remains that there are cases that do not lend themselves to the profiling process.

The Profilers

When discussing criminal personality profiling, we are invariably asked what special attributes or education the profiler must possess. Our answer, quite simply, is that the successful profilers with whom we have worked possessed no particular educational degree, although a background in the behavioral sciences was helpful. The qualities and attributes we have consistently noted in successful profilers include investigative and research experience, common sense, intuitiveness, the ability to isolate emotions, the ability to analyze a situation and arrive at logical conclusions, and the ability to reconstruct the crime utilizing the criminal's reasoning process.

Experience

No amount of education can replace the experience of having investigated violent crimes. As an investigator, one begins to collect and store data that is automatically retrieved when a new case is opened. Experienced investigators accept nothing at face value, but instead question what is observed and go beyond what appears to be the obvious. They do not depend on what others tell them about the crime, but check and verify each piece of information. This is the most significant factor differentiating the investigative profiler from the clinical psychologist or psychiatrist who prepares profiles.

During a recent conference on treatment of sexual offenders, a rapist in the treatment program was presented to the audience. After he had departed, the treating psychologist was asked about the criminal history of the rapist. He had not previously inquired into this area, but promised to do so. Obviously he had not considered such information significant to the offender's treatment. A few minutes later, he informed the audience that the rapist had no history of arrest other than a speeding violation. When asked about the source of this information, he said it was the rapist himself!

Over a period of time, an investigator develops an ability to rise above the shock of violence and to move systematically through the often gruesome, but always necessary procedures. We are aware of individuals (not within the BSU) who refuse to examine photographs depicting homicide victims, yet prepare profiles for police agencies. It is our opinion that this is akin to performing surgery without reviewing the patient's x-rays.

Common Sense

It has been our experience that a surprisingly large number of people do not possess the quality of common sense. There are individuals who, when confronted with a novel situation, find it impossible to plan a strategy unless that situation is exactly like one previously experienced or learned. In law enforcement circles, such a person is often referred to as "one who goes by the book." For example, an overriding fear the authors have is that, regardless of our best efforts, some individuals will treat this text as a "cookbook" and, if faced with a situation not specifically addressed in these pages, will consider the entire profiling process to be of no value. It must be remembered that no two crimes or criminals are exactly alike. When dealing with human behavior, it is impossible to arbitrarily categorize that behavior. The individual who has "common sense" will recognize this and will be able to project techniques from the written page or spoken word onto generally similar situations.

Intuition

Webster defines intuition as "the direct knowing or learning of something without the conscious use of reasoning—the ability to perceive or know things without conscious reasoning" (Webster 1972). Police officers refer to it as a "gut feeling." Like common sense, it is not something that can be learned in a classroom or from a book. Realistically, it is probably not a trait that a person is born with either, but rather an ability born from experienced, but forgotten, occurrences. Regardless of its origins, it is a fact that some individuals possess an intuitive ability that is extremely valuable in the profiling process.

Recently, a prosecutor and a detective traveled to the FBI Academy for consultation with two of the authors (Hazelwood and Douglas). The attorney was about to prosecute a man for the rape/murder of an

18-year-old paraplegic girl. The defendant had been arrested after confessing to the crime, but had refused to discuss what had motivated the murder. The prosecutor was justifiably concerned that unless he had an understanding of why the crime occurred, he would have difficulty in presenting knowledgeable and convincing arguments. After reviewing the case materials and discussing the details with the prosecutor and his associate, we felt confident in reconstructing the manner in which the crime occurred and the motivational factors involved. As he was about to leave, Douglas stated that he had "a feeling" that the date of the murder might have some significance to the killer and suggested that the attorney pursue this possibility. It was later learned that the date of the murder was the anniversary of the day on which the murderer was forced to move back into his mother's home. The mother was a very domineering person who had engaged in incest with the young man over a period of years. The defendant despised her, but was emotionally dependent on her. The prosecutor later reported that this information played a large role in the successful prosecution of the offender.

Isolation of Affect

The successful profiler is one who is able to isolate his personal feelings about the crime, the criminal, and the victim.

> A 16-year-old girl was kidnapped by two young men and, over a 6-hour period of time, was subjected to sexual assault and physical torture. Much of her head and pubic hair had been pulled out or burned and she had been severely beaten. She survived, but underwent extensive hospitalization and therapy.

As presented above, the case is somewhat clinical; however, the materials submitted for study consisted of graphic medical records and photographs and a detailed statement from the victim. As parents, law enforcement officers, and members of society, we are outraged at the injustice of such an attack on a child. As profilers, however, we cannot allow these feelings to interfere with the task at hand.

Personal feelings about the criminal must also be isolated. For instance, in crimes such as the one described above, one not knowledgeable about such matters might assume that the persons responsible are insane, have extensive arrest histories, and are unable to function within society. In fact, there is a very real possibility that none of these assumptions is correct. When preparing a profile, one should attempt to describe the offender as those who know him would describe him. The reader is reminded of recent and infamous serial murderers who were perfectly rational and fully functioning individuals: Kenneth Bianchi (Hillside Strangler), John Wayne Gacy, Theodore Bundy, and Wayne Williams (Atlanta murders), to mention a few.

Finally, the profiler must isolate his feelings about the victim. In many instances, the victims of sexual assault and/or homicide are what we refer to as *high-risk* victims. That is to say, the victims may have been particularly vulnerable because they were prostitutes, involved in drug-related activities, hitchhiking, or runaways. If the profiler allows personal feelings about the victim to enter the evaluation, this will seriously impair the process.

Analytical Logic

The ability to study a situation and arrive at logical conclusions is not one that all individuals possess. In profiling, one must make conclusions based upon what has been observed, heard, or read. A great deal of the mystique surrounding the art of profiling disappears when one realizes that a large amount of the information provided in a profile is arrived at analytically and logically. For example, let us assume a profiler has stated that the age of the offender is between 45 and 50 years. It is then quite reasonable to presume that the offender is a military veteran, inasmuch as most males within that age range served in the armed forces because of the military draft. Another example of the application of logic might involve a rapist who is believed, for one reason or another, to be employed in a white-collar occupation. It is then logical to assume that he will operate a vehicle less than 5 years of age, in that his socioeconomic status would allow him to own one.

View the Crime from the Criminal's Perspective

> In a large metropolitan area, a series of rapes had plagued the police over a period of months. In each instance, the rapist had controlled his victim through threats and intimidation. One evening a hospital orderly went off duty at midnight and happened upon a male beating a nurse in an attempt to rape her. The orderly went to her rescue and subdued the attacker until the police arrived. Predictably, he received much attention from the news media and received a citation for bravery from the city. Shortly thereafter, the orderly was arrested for the series of rapes mentioned earlier. During interrogation, he was asked why he had rescued the nurse when he, in fact, was guilty of similar offenses. He became indignant and advised the officers that they were wrong. He would never "hurt" a woman. (Hazelwood 1983, p. 9)

This offender equated "hurt" with physical trauma. The point is that intent becomes clear only if we attempt to view the crime from the motivational standpoint of the criminal (Hazelwood 1983). The ability to observe the crime from the perspective of the criminal is the result of having dealt with violent crime and criminals over a period of years. It is not something that can be learned in a classroom. The profiler must forget that he or she is a parent, a spouse, or a law enforcement officer, and temporarily assume the role of the criminal. Then he or she must begin to ask questions about the crime: "Why would I continue to beat the victim after all resistance had ended?" "Why wouldn't I react more violently after the victim bit me?" To assume this role is not an easy task in that violence is what we, as law enforcement officers, are charged with preventing and/or investigating.

In a recent murder case, two of the authors (Hazelwood and Douglas) provided on-site consultation. It involved the kidnap and murder of a 12-year-old girl who was found after 5 days. After the profile had been prepared and presented to the officers investigating the matter, a clinical psychologist stated that we were, in effect, describing a paranoid schizophrenic. When Douglas and Hazelwood concurred with that assessment, the psychologist asked how they could be so comfortable with that evaluation after simply studying the crime scene data. It was explained that profilers attempt to reenact the crime, to view it as the murderer did, and to reason as he did. When identified, the subject was diagnosed by psychiatrists as being a paranoid schizophrenic.

The Profiling Process

A criminal personality profile is a series of subjective opinions about the unknown individual(s) responsible for a crime or series of crimes. The process in arriving at these opinions is quite difficult to articulate in that the final product is largely dependent on common sense, intuition, and the experience of the profiler. In that this topic is dealt with at length in Chapter 8, we will merely attempt to acquaint the reader with the process utilized when profiling a rape case.

In preparing a rapist profile, there are three basic steps: (1) to determine from the victim what behavior was exhibited by the rapist, (2) to analyze that behavior in an attempt to ascertain the motivation underlying the assault, and (3) to set forth the characteristics of the individual who would commit the crime in a manner that explains the motivational factor indicated by that behavior (Hazelwood 1983).

In our experience, similar crimes committed for similar reasons generally are perpetrated by similar offenders. Given a rape that occurred in Houston, Texas, we can produce a rape that occurred in Arlington, Virginia, that is so similar in nature one might assume the same individual was responsible for both crimes. The explanation for this is really quite simple. Crimes are similar because the underlying motivation is basically the same; therefore, it is logical to assume that the offenders will be as similar as their crimes.

Determine Offender Behavior

It is the behavior exhibited by the offender during the commission of a crime that is studied by the profiler. In sexual assaults, the victim may be able to provide information on three forms of offender behavior—verbal, sexual, and physical (force). She can advise the investigator as to what the offender said or demanded that she say, the type and sequence of sexual acts that were performed, and the amount of physical force used by the offender. Provided with this information, it is probable that the profiler can determine the underlying motivation for the assault. This step is discussed in detail in Chapter 7.

Analyze the Behavior

It is at this step that one studies and evaluates the verbal, sexual, and physical behavior of the rapist, the purpose being to determine the true motivation for the sexual assault. As Groth points out, "rape is, in fact, serving primarily nonsexual needs" (1979, p. 88). One should examine verbal behavior for indications of hostility; anger; a need for affection; concern; or politeness, among other things. The type and sequence of sexual behavior should be analyzed, to determine whether the offender intended to degrade, involve, or punish the victim. Finally, the amount of physical force used should be studied. At what point did the rapist apply force? Was it to intimidate or punish? Did he continue to use force when resistance had ceased? One must be alert to the fact that the motivation for the crime is exhibited through the rapist's behavior.

Prepare the Profile

Once an assumption has been made as to what motivated the crime, the rapist can then be profiled. "The manner in which an individual behaves within his various environments portrays the type of person he or she is. Opinions are formed about a person's self-esteem, educational level, ability to negotiate interpersonal relationships, and goals in life by the manner in which the individual behaves" (Hazelwood, 1983).

A Word of Caution about Profiling

Lecturers on this subject often begin by advising students that criminal personality profiling is an art, not a science. It is simply another investigative tool to assist in the investigation of violent crime. It is not intended to supplant any other investigative step, and in fact, we prefer not to prepare profiles until all conventional investigative procedures have been accomplished and the case remains unsolved. If an investigator depends solely upon a profile to solve his case, that investigator will have acted irresponsibly and will find this counterproductive to the goal of crime solving.

Profiles have led directly to the solution of a case, but this is the exception rather than the rule, and to expect this will lead to failure in most cases. Rather, a profile will provide assistance to the investigator by focusing the investigation toward suspects possessing the characteristics described.

In an evaluation of the Criminal Personality Profiling Program, the Institutional Research and Development Unit (IRDU) of the FBI Academy surveyed user agencies as to the investigative value of profiles prepared in 192 cases. In its report the IRDU stated: "In the 192 cases examined, . . . profiling helped focus the investigation in 77% of those cases where the perpetrator was identified and actually identified the subject in 15 instances. Even in cases where the suspect has not been identified . . . profiling was helpful . . . in that it insured a complete investigation was conducted. . . . Profiling saved an estimated 594 investigative mandays and all users overwhelmingly agreed that the service should be continued" (1981).

It should be made clear that the profile may describe more than one individual, even within the same neighborhood. In a recent rape/homicide profile that was prepared, the description matched three different individuals residing in close proximity to the victim. When the investigators confronted one of the authors (Hazelwood) about this problem, they were advised that the killer was either one of the three *or* someone like them. They were not particularly pleased with that piece of information, but understood that profiling is intended to identify a personality type, not a person.

As with any other human endeavor, failures will occasionally occur and this should not detract from the process. When being interviewed by Porter, who wrote an article entitled "The Mind Hunters" for the April 1983 issue of *Psychology Today*, one of the authors (Hazelwood) noted that he had prepared a particularly erroneous profile on a crime involving the assault of a mother and the shooting of her 3-month-old baby. After the responsible person had been arrested and confessed, a comparison of the profile with the arrested offender revealed that it was correct in only two areas. Mention was made of that case then, and is now, to ensure that the reader does not misinterpret the value of this very subjective process. Human behavior is much too complex to categorize simplistically. To suggest that we in the Behavioral Science Unit have done so, or are attempting to do so, would not be true.

Profilers are not blessed with a sixth sense, nor do we have a crystal ball that provides us with mystical powers. We are encumbered with the same human frailties as anyone else. We have simply had the opportunity to observe a very large number of violent crimes and to assimilate that experience into our work. No one is more enthusiastic about criminal personality profiling than the members of the Behavioral Science Unit. However, we are also the first to acknowledge that proven investigative procedures, not profiling, solve crimes.

Summary

Criminal personality profiling was initiated in the FBI Academy's Behavioral Science Unit on an informal basis in 1972. The program was formalized in 1978, and in 1983, FBI profilers were specifically assigned the task of assisting law enforcement agencies in nonfederal investigations involving crimes of violence.

The criteria for cases submitted for criminal personality profiling are that they involve a crime or series of crimes of violence that are still unsolved after all investigative leads have been exhausted.

Successful profilers are experienced in criminal investigations and research and possess common sense, intuition, and the ability to isolate their feelings about the crime, the criminal, and the victim. They have the ability to evaluate analytically the behavior exhibited in a crime and to think very much like the criminal responsible.

When analyzing a crime for profiling purposes, it is necessary to evaluate what occurred in order to determine the underlying motivation for the crime. One is then able to construct a profile of the person who would have committed such a crime for such a reason. In sexual assaults, the verbal, sexual, and physical behavior of the offender are evaluated.

Criminal personality profiling should be used as an augmentation to proven investigative techniques and must not be allowed to replace those techniques. To do so would be counterproductive to the goal of identifying the unknown offender.

References

Groth, A. N. *Men Who Rape.* New York: Plenum Press, 1979, p. 88.

Hazelwood, Robert R. "Behavior-Oriented Interview of Rape Victims: The Key to Profiling." *FBI Law Enforcement Bulletin,* September 1983.

Hazelwood, Robert R. "NCAVC Training Program: A Commitment to Law Enforcement." *FBI Law Enforcement Bulletin,* December 1986.

Hazelwood, Robert R. and Douglas, John E. "The Lust Murderer." *FBI Law Enforcement Bulletin,* April 1980.

Institutional Research and Development Unit, FBI Academy, Memorandum, "Evaluation of the Psychological Profiling Program," December 1981.

Porter, Bruce. "Mind Hunters." *Psychology Today,* April 1983.

Webster's New World Dictionary of the American Language. 2nd College Ed. New York: World Publishing Co., 1972.

Zilboorg, G. *The Psychology of the Criminal Act and Punishment.* New York: Greenwood Press, 1968, p. 24.

7 The Behavioral-Oriented Interview of Rape Victims: The Key to Profiling

ROBERT R. HAZELWOOD
AND ANN WOLBERT BURGESS

In October 1981, a police department submitted an investigative report of a rape to one of the authors (Hazelwood) and requested that a criminal personality profile of the unidentified offender be prepared. A synopsis of that report follows:

> On October 5, 1981, Alicia B., a 21-year-old Caucasian, who resided alone, was asleep in her apartment. At approximately 2:30 AM, she was awakened by a male who placed his hand over her mouth and held a knife to her throat. The intruder warned her not to scream or resist and advised her that if she complied with his demands, she would not be harmed. He then forced her to remove her nightgown, kissed and fondled the victim, and then raped her. After warning the victim not to call the police, he left. Ignoring the rapist's warning, she notified the police. The victim said nothing had been stolen and that she could not provide a description of her assailant because he had placed a pillowcase over her head. The rapist was with the victim approximately 1 hour.

Prior to preparing a profile, Hazelwood provided the requesting agency with a set of questions specifically designed to elicit information from the victim as to the rapist's behavior during the assault. Using the questions as a guide, the police reinterviewed the victim. They were then able to obtain a nine-page typewritten statement. Based upon the new statement, a profile was prepared. Subsequently, the rapist was arrested and confessed to a series of rapes. The profile

This chapter was adapted from an article published in the *FBI Law Enforcement Bulletin* (Hazelwood, 1983).

was compared with the offender, and only the marital status was found to be incorrect.

Since 1972, members of the FBI Academy's Behavioral Science Unit (BSU) have been assisting city, county, state, and federal law enforcement agencies in their investigations of violent crimes by analyzing crime or crime scene data. Chapter 6 and previous publications by members of the BSU have addressed the development and use of profiling and related topics (Reese, 1979; Ault and Reese, 1980; Hazelwood and Douglas, 1980; Rider, 1980; Ressler et al., 1980; Hazelwood et al., 1982). This chapter will deal with questioning the rape victim specifically for the purpose of determining the behavior exhibited by the offender.

Motivation

During the past 7 years, the authors have reviewed hundreds of rape victims' statements submitted by police agencies. The statements contained details of the crime as well as a great deal of information about the offender's physical characteristics, but there was a marked absence of information that could provide clues as to the offender's motivation (through his behavior) in carrying out the assault. Over a period of time, one of the authors (Hazelwood) developed a set of questions designed to elicit the behavioral aspects of the crime that may assist in identifying the motivation for the crime. These questions are set forth below.

1. Describe the manner in which the offender approached and gained control over you.
2. How did he maintain control of you and the situation?
3. Specifically describe the physical force he used and when during the attack it occurred.
4. Did you resist either physically, verbally, or passively? If so, describe each instance you can recall.
5. What was his reaction to your resistance?
6. Did he at any time experience a sexual dysfunction? If so, describe what type, whether he was later able to sexually function, and any particular act or behavior he performed or demanded that you perform to overcome the dysfunction.
7. Describe all sexual acts forced upon you or performed by the offender on himself and the sequence in which they occurred, including repetitions.
8. As precisely as possible, try to remember what he said to you, his tone of voice, and his attitude at the time he spoke.
9. Did he demand that you answer questions, repeat phrases, or re-

spond verbally in any manner whatsoever? Attempt to recall specifically what he demanded you say.

10. When, if ever, did his attitude appear to change? In what manner did it change, and what occurred immediately prior to the change?
11. What actions did he take to ensure that you would not be able to identify him? Did he take any precautions to ensure the police would not be able to associate him with the crime?
12. Did he take anything when he left? Have you carefully inventoried your personal belongings (undergarments, photographs, etc.) since the assault?
13. Did you receive any calls or notes from unidentified people prior to or since the assault? Have you had any experience which would indicate that he specifically targeted you for the assault?
14. How do you believe individuals who associate with the rapist on a daily basis would describe him as a person?

As investigators, the authors recognize the need for obtaining the offender's physical description, direction and mode of travel, etc., and would not suggest that any less effort be given to these important details. However, additional attention must be devoted to the behavior exhibited by the offender. In so doing, the underlying purpose of the assault becomes clearer, thereby allowing the officer better insight into the type of person he is seeking.

As addressed in Chapter 6, the profiling process in rape cases involves three basic steps:

1. Determine from the victim what behavior was exhibited by the rapist.
2. Analyze that behavior in an attempt to ascertain the motivation underlying the assault.
3. Set forth the characteristics of an individual who would commit the crime, given the motivational factor indicated by behavior.

Steps 2 and 3 are accomplished by using logic, common sense, and intuition derived from the experience of having reviewed several hundred rape cases submitted for profile. The first step, interviewing the victim, is the most crucial one in the process. It is only through the victim that we are able to elicit the information necessary to complete an analysis of the crime. Therefore, it is essential for the investigator to establish rapport with the victim through a professional and empathetic approach to overcome her feelings of fear, guilt, and anger. The interviewer must also isolate his/her emotions and not allow them to interfere with objectivity. During the interview, the investigator will be dealing with three personalities: the victim's, the criminal's, and the interviewer's. Personal feelings about the offense, the victim, and the criminal must be put aside to allow unbiased opinions about the offender to develop. The investigator who is able to accomplish this will find that a much clearer impression of the offender begins to form.

The point is that intent becomes clear only if we attempt to view the crime from the motivational standpoint of the criminal. Once a reasonably safe assumption is made as to why the rape occurred, it is probable that the rapist can be profiled. The basis for this hypothesis lies in the axiom that behavior reflects personality. The manner in which an individual behaves within his various environments portrays the type of person he or she is. Opinions are formed about a person's self-esteem, educational level, ability to negotiate interpersonal relationships, and goals in life, by the manner in which the individual behaves. In rape cases, the victim's descriptions of the offender's behavior enables the investigator to form an opinion as to the type of person responsible.

Questioning for Behavior

In developing the questions set forth earlier, the authors noted that three forms of behavior were exhibited by most rapists: physical (force), verbal, and sexual. A much clearer and less biased view of the offender emerged when his behavior was categorized into these three areas.

Needless to say, the interview must be conducted in a tactful, professional, yet probative manner. It is imperative that the investigator impress upon the victim that he is concerned not only with the arrest and conviction of the offender, but also with the victim's welfare. She has been involved in a life-threatening situation, and the importance of recognizing this cannot be overemphasized. The investigator should inform the victim that the identification of the offender may be expedited through a criminal personality profile. Her contribution of detailed and personal information regarding the assault is necessary for this profile to be prepared.

Recently an elderly woman was raped by an unknown man. The victim's statement, which was submitted to the BSU for profiling, was found to be substantially lacking in detail and was returned to the requesting agency, along with a reprint of an article dealing with rape victim interviewing. The police gave the victim a copy of the article, and after reading it, she expressed her understanding of the necessity for complete disclosure. She then provided the police with a detailed description of the assault.

Each of the questions set forth earlier is fully discussed in the remainder of this chapter. It is to be noted that a profile is not based on any single response, but rather upon an analysis of all responses.

What Method of Approach Was Utilized by the Offender?

When an individual decides to accomplish something, it is human nature to choose a method or course of action with which he or she feels most comfortable and capable. Therefore, it is logical to assume that the rapist, in choosing a method of approaching and subduing his intended victim, would do likewise. Because each aspect of a sexual assault has the potential for providing information about the person responsible, it is necessary to categorize the styles of approach used by the offender toward his victim. These approaches will be referred to as Con, Blitz, and Surprise.

Con. In the Con style, the offender approaches the victim openly with a subterfuge or a ploy. Frequently, he will offer some sort of assistance or will request directions. He is initially pleasant and friendly and may even be charming. His goal is to gain the victim's confidence until he is in a position to overcome any resistance she might offer. Quite often, and for different reasons, he exhibits a sudden change in attitude toward the victim once she is within his control. In some instances, the rapist alters his behavior to convince the victim he is serious. In other instances, the change is merely a reflection of inner hostility toward the female gender. This style of approach suggests an individual who has confidence in his ability to interact with women.

Blitz. A person employing the Blitz approach uses direct and immediate physical assault (physical injury) in subduing his victim. He allows her no opportunity to cope physically or verbally and will frequently gag, blindfold, or bind his victim. His attack may occur frontally or from the rear, and he may use disabling gases or chemicals. Such an approach suggests hostility toward women, an attitude that may also be reflected in his relationships with females outside the rape environment. The offender's interactions, with women in nonrape relationships are likely to be selfish and one-sided, resulting in numerous but relatively short involvements with women.

Surprise. In the Surprise approach, the rapist may either lie in wait for the victim (back seat of a car, behind a wall, in the woods) or wait until she is sleeping. Typically, this individual uses threats and/or the presence of a weapon to subdue the victim. While certainly not conclusive, this style suggests two possibilities to the authors:

1. The victim has been targeted or preselected
2. The offender does not feel sufficiently confident to approach the victim either physically or through subterfuge tactics

How Did The Offender Maintain Control of the Victim?

The manner in which the offender maintains control of his victim is dependent upon the passivity of his victim, his motivation in committing the assault, or a combination of the two factors. The authors have commonly observed four control methods: mere presence, verbal threats, display of a weapon, and use of physical force.

Mere Presence. Depending upon the passivity and fear of the victim, it is very possible that the offender's mere presence would be sufficient to control the victim. This is very difficult for a person removed from the actual situation and/or having a personality different from the victim's to accept. Quite often the investigator judges a victim's reaction on the basis of what he/she would do (or believes he/she would do), rather than taking into account the victim's personality, the circumstances surrounding the assault, and the fear factor involved. The following case is an example of this attitude:

> A woman left her town house at 10:00 AM and walked 10 feet to her automobile. As she was about to enter the car, a man across the street called her name and said, "I want to see you over here now!" Even though she was only 10 feet from her home, she walked to the location pointed out by the subject. At that point she was placed in a car, driven to another location, and raped. Following the assault, she was returned to within two blocks of her home and released.

Initially, the investigators did not believe the victim. They reasoned that if this occurred, all she had to do was run to her home for safety. They failed to consider the victim's personality and instead judged her report based upon "common sense" and what *they* would have done.

Threats. Many victims are intimidated by threatening remarks promising physical violence if compliance is not forthcoming. Clues to the motivation for the assault often lie in these verbal threats. Investigators should elicit the verbatim (if possible) context of the threats and whether or not they were carried out.

Many rapists display a weapon to obtain or maintain control of their victims. It is important to ascertain not only whether the rapist had a weapon, but also at what point he displayed it or indicated that he had one. Did the victim see it? Was it seemingly a weapon of choice (gun or switchblade) or of opportunity (kitchen knife, screwdriver, etc.)? Did he relinquish control of it (give it to the victim, put it down, or put it away)? Did he inflict any physical injury with the weapon?

Force. The use and amount of physical force in a rape attack is a key determinant of offender motivation. The interviewer should determine the amount of force, when it was employed, and the rapist's attitude prior to, during, and after its employment.

What Amount of Physical Force Was Employed by the Attacker?

The amount of force used by a rapist will provide valuable insight into his motivational need. The interviewer should elicit from the victim a precise description of the physical force involved. The victim may exaggerate when describing the level of force, either because she wants to be believed or because she has never been struck or physically attacked before. For example, a victim who was never slapped or spanked as a child or adult may report her attacker as brutal, when she was slapped twice during the rape. Another victim may not be able to distinguish between the sexual assault and the physical assault. For these reasons, the authors have developed descriptions of four levels of physical assault to assist in arriving at an opinion as to the amounts of force used.

Minimal Force. At this level, there is little or no physical force used. While mild slapping may occur, the force is employed more to intimidate than to punish, and the rapist is typically nonprofane.

Moderate Force. When the rapist employs moderate force, he will repeatedly slap or hit the victim in a painful manner, even in the absence of resistance. He typically uses profanity throughout the attack and is very abusive.

Excessive Force. When excessive force is used, the victim is beaten, possibly on all parts of her body. She will have bruises and lacerations and may require hospitalization. Again, the rapist is very profane and directs personal and derogatory remarks toward the victim.

Brutal Force. At the fourth level of physical assault, brutal force, the victim is subjected to sadistic torture, with instruments or other devices often being employed. Intentional infliction of physical and emotional pain is the primary aim of the offender, and he is extremely profane, abusive, and aggressive. Frequently, the victim dies or requires extensive hospitalization following the attack.

Did the Victim Resist the Attacker, and If So, in What Manner?

The victim, when ordered to act, may either comply or resist. Resistance can be defined as anything the victim did, or did not do, that precluded, delayed, or reduced the effect of the attack. While most interviewers are alert to physical or verbal resistance by victims, they often tend to overlook or disregard passive resistance.

Passive. Passive resistance is evidenced when the victim does not resist physically or verbally but does not comply with the rapist's demands. An example would be a victim who is ordered to disrobe but simply, and without verbal or physical accompaniment, does nothing. Passive resistance is also overlooked quite often during the trial process. Prosecutors would do well to educate judges and juries in this regard and to emphasize that the victim, simply by not obeying the rapist's commands, did resist the attacker.

Verbal. Verbal resistance is offered when the victim screams, pleads, refuses, or attempts to reason or negotiate with her attacker. While crying is a verbal act, it is not considered to be resistance in this context.

Physical. Hitting, kicking, scratching, gouging, and running are examples of this form of resistance. When considering the victim's resistance or lack thereof, the investigator should evaluate the victim's personality. He or she should attempt to determine whether the victim is a passive individual who is easily intimidated and controlled or one who is assertive and confident. Is the victim a person who has been protected and cared for during her adult life, or has she been self-sufficient? Factors such as these will have a great deal of bearing on the amount and type of resistance she offers.

If Resistance Occurred, What Was the Offender's Reaction?

People react to stressful situations in various ways. While rape is certainly stressful to the victim, it also creates stressors for the attacker: fear of being identified or arrested, fear of being injured or ridiculed, and fear of being successfully rebuffed. Therefore, it becomes crucial for the investigator to learn how the rapist reacted to any resistance (passive, verbal, or physical) offered by the victim. The authors have observed five rapist reactions: cessation of the demand, compromise, flight, threats, and force.

Cease Demand. In some instances, a rapist who encounters resistance will not insist or attempt to force compliance, but instead will cease his demand and move to another phase of the attack.

Compromise/Negotiate. In other cases, the subject will compromise or negotiate by suggesting, or allowing the victim to suggest, alternatives. For instance, the rapist may demand or attempt anal sex and, upon encountering resistance, instead demand vaginal sex with no further attempt to assault the victim anally.

Flee. The authors have occasionally examined cases in which the rapist left the scene of the assault when resisted. This fleeing reaction is interesting in that it suggests the offender had no desire to "force" the victim against her will or was unprepared for the victim's reaction and/or the attention it might bring.

Threats. Another reaction of the offender may be to resort to verbal or physical threats in an attempt to gain compliance. If the victim continued to resist, it is important to learn whether the offender followed through on his threatened action or not.

Force. A final reaction of certain rapists is to resort to force if they encounter victim resistance. Again, if such is the case, the interviewer should determine the degree of force used and its duration.

Did the Rapist Experience a Sexual Dysfunction?

Coleman defines the term "sexual dysfunction" as an "impairment either in the desire for sexual gratification or in the ability to achieve it" (Coleman et al., 1980, p. 531). In a study of 170 rapists, Groth and Burgess (1977) determined that 34 percent of the offender population suffered a sexual dysfunction during the assault. The authors frequently encounter cases in which either the victim was not asked whether a dysfunction had occurred or the matter was simply noted without further inquiry.

The occurrence of offender sexual dysfunction and an investigative understanding of the dysfunction may provide valuable information about the unidentified rapist. The investigator should be alert to the possibility that a rape victim may not volunteer such information during the interview because she does not consider it significant, she is embarrassed about the sexual acts demanded to correct the dysfunction, and/or she is ignorant of such facts and did not recognize it as a dysfunction. It behooves the investigator to explain the various sexual dysfunctions affecting males and their meaningfulness and to inquire as to the occurrence of each type.

Erectile Insufficiency. Formally classified as impotence, this type of dysfunction affects the male's ability to obtain or maintain an erection for sexual intercourse. Masters and Johnson (1970) describe two types of erectile insufficiency as *primary* and *secondary*. Males suffering from primary insufficiency have never been able to maintain an erection sufficient for intravaginal ejaculation. While this type is relatively rare and not generally of concern to the investigator, it is described herein in the interest of completeness. In secondary insufficiency, the male is currently unable to obtain or maintain an erection.

Groth and Burgess (1977) identified a third form of insufficiency in their study, which they termed *conditional*. In such cases, the rapist is initially unable to become erect, but does so as a result of forced oral and manual stimulation by the victim. The authors would suggest that the methods of gaining an erection not be limited to the ones aforementioned, but include any act demanded by the offender. The act may be sexual (anal sex, analingus, etc.) or may consist of having the victim verbalize certain words or phrases or dress in certain clothing.

Groth and Burgess (1977) compared erectile insufficiency among rapists with a group of 448 nonrapist patients studied by Masters and Johnson. They found that in both instances it was the most commonly experienced dysfunction.

Premature Ejaculation. "Ejaculation which occurs immediately before or immediately after penetration is termed premature ejaculation" (Groth and Burgess, 1977, p. 164). In their study, Groth and Burgess found that this dysfunction affected 3% of the rapists.

Retarded Ejaculation. This dysfunction is the opposite of premature ejaculation in that the affected rapist experiences difficulty or fails to ejaculate. Contrary to popular belief, the individual experiencing retarded ejaculation is not controlling seminal discharge and prolonging enjoyment, but is unable to ejaculate and is, therefore, denied sexual gratification.

Groth and Burgess (1977) reported 15% of the rapist population suffered retarded ejaculation. Masters and Johnson (1970) found it to be so rare among their patients that they did not rank it with a percentage. "When the possibility of retarded ejaculation is not taken into account, the victim's version of such multiple and extended assaults may be greeted with doubts and skepticism" (Groth, 1979, p. 88).

Conditional Ejaculation. The final type of dysfunction the authors have observed in cases submitted for profile is one on which there has been no research conducted and which is not, to the author's knowledge, reported in the literature. The rapist experiencing conditional ejaculation has no difficulty in obtaining or maintaining an erection, but he can ejaculate only after certain conditions are met. Most often, the conditions involve particular sexual acts, such as in the following case:

> A 21-year-old woman was abducted at knifepoint while walking home late one evening. Over a period of 3 hours, she was forced to engage in vaginal, anal, and oral sex. Unable to ejaculate, the offender used lipstick and drew panties and a bra on the victim. Forcing her to fondle herself, he observed her, masturbated himself, and ejaculated.

This is an excellent example of conditional ejaculation and strongly suggests that the offender will have an extensive collection of pornography and/or a long history of "peeping-Tom" activities for which he may have been arrested. What men desire to observe physically or through imagery (fantasy) is extremely important in the sexual gratification process. This explains why men are the primary purchasers of erotic literature, photographs, or films. It also explains why such a large number of rapes involve voyeuristic activity.

What Type and Sequence of Sexual Acts Occurred during the Assault?

"Documenting the kinds of sex acts that occur during rape helps us to more clearly understand rape" (Holmstrom and Burgess, 1980). In order to determine the motivation behind a rape assault, it is imperative to ascertain the type and sequence of sexual assault (including repetitions) that occurred. This may prove difficult due to the emotional trauma experienced by the victim and/or her reluctance to discuss certain aspects of the crime because of fear, shame, or humiliation. Quite often, however, the investigator can overcome the victim's reluctance through a professional and empathetic approach. While it is common to ask about vaginal, oral, and anal acts, the authors do not frequently review reports that include information pertaining to kissing, fondling, use of foreign objects, digital manipulation of the vagina or anus, fetishism, voyeurism, bondage, or exhibitionism on the part of the offender. The following case involves an act of exhibitionism:

> During the course of the attack, described earlier, on the 21-year-old, the offender kissed and fondled the victim. He also engaged in voyeurism, which enhanced his masturbation and resulted in ejaculation. Prior to that, he forced the victim to walk nude through the streets of her neighborhood while holding his penis.

In a sample of 115 adult, teenage, and child rape victims, Holmstrom and Burgess (1980) reported vaginal sex as the most frequent act, but also reported 18 other sexual acts. Repetitions of acts are infrequently reported. More commonly, the report is likely to state, "The victim was raped," "vaginally assaulted," or "raped repeatedly."

"Various socio-psychological meanings are attached to forced sexual acts" (Holmstrom and Burgess, 1980, p. 437). By analyzing the sequence of the assault, it may be possible to determine whether the offender was acting out a fantasy, experimenting, or committing the sexual acts to punish or degrade the victim. For example, if acts of oral and anal sex are forced on a victim and the anal sex was followed by fellatio, the motivation to punish or degrade would be strongly suggested. Anal assault is an example of a sexual act that often has underlying motivation. When anal sex has taken place in a nonconsensual relationship, the authors consider four possible reasons: acting out a fantasy and/or latent homosexuality; sexual experimentation; to punish, degrade, or humiliate; or the behavior of a former convict.

Fantasy. In acting out a fantasy, the offender normally engages in kissing, fondling, and/or cunnilingus. He utilizes minimal force and engages in nonthreatening verbal behavior (apologetic, complimentary, etc.). If fellatio occurs, it generally precedes the anal sex.

Experimentation. With sexual experimentation, the offender is moderately forceful in his physical contact with the victim and is verbally profane and derogatory toward her. He typically engages in a variety (and repetition) of sexual acts, including the use of foreign objects. In this instance fellatio may either precede or follow anal sex.

Punishment. When the offender's intent is to punish, degrade, or humiliate, the victim reports excessive or brutal levels of force accompanied by threatening, derogatory, and profane verbal activity on the part of the rapist. Almost invariably, the rapist will demand fellatio following the anal assault.

Ex-Convict. Finally, the victim of an anal assault may have been attacked by an individual who was formally institutionalized. When analyzing sexual assaults involving anal sex, profilers will refer to the victim's description of the offender to determine the upper-body build. A muscular upper-body physique, combined with an anal assault, may be indicative of former institutionalization and regular exercise. For further indications of such offender background, the reader is referred to the portion of this chapter dealing with actions taken by the offender to facilitate escape or preclude identification.

What Was the Verbal Activity of the Rapist?

> The stereotype of the male rapist's attack is that he attains power and control over the victim through strategies based on physical force . . . not only do rapists use physically based strategies, but also they use a second set of strategies based on language. (Holmstrom and Burgess 1979)

A rapist reveals a great deal about himself and the motivation behind the assault through verbal activity with the victim. For this reason, it becomes extremely important to elicit from the victim everything the rapist said and the manner (tone, attitude) in which it was said.

In a study of 115 rape victims, Holmstrom and Burgess (1979) reported 11 major themes in rapists' conversation: "threats, orders, confidence lines, personal inquiries of the victim, personal revelations by the rapist, obscene names and racial epitaphs, inquiries about the victim's sexual 'enjoyment,' soft-sell departures, sexual put downs, possession of women, and taking property from another male" (p. 101).

Preciseness is important. For example, a rapist who states, "I'm going to hurt you if you don't do what I say," has, in effect, threatened the victim; whereas the rapist who says, "Do what I say and I won't hurt you," may be reassuring the victim in an attempt to alleviate her fear of physical injury and gain her compliance without force. An offender who states, "I want to make love to you," has utilized a passive and affectionate phrase that is indicative of one who does not want to physically harm the victim. Conversely, a statement such as "I'm going to fuck you" is much more aggressive verbiage with no affection intended.

Compliments directed toward the victim (attractiveness, physical attributes, etc.), politeness, expressions of concern ("Lock your doors," "Am I hurting you"), apologies, and discussion of the offender's personal life (whether fact or fiction) may indicate low self-esteem on the part of the offender. On the other hand, derogatory, profane, threatening, and/or abusive verbiage is suggestive of anger and the utilization of sex to punish or degrade the victim.

When analyzing a rape victim's statement, the investigator is advised to write down an adjective that accurately describes each of the offender's statements ("You're a beautiful person"—complimentary; "Shut up, bitch"—hostile; "Am I hurting you"—concerned). The investigator will then have a better insight into the offender's motivation and a verbal picture of the personality of the individual being sought.

Was the Victim Forced to Say Anything?

The mind dictates what is, or is not, sexually arousing and pleasing to the individual and can control the male's ability to function sexually. The involvement of the human senses is also an integral part of human sexual activity, and while sexual activity is basically a biological function among animals, humans are dependent upon psychosexual involvement for arousal and gratification. When interviewing the rape victim for the purpose of preparing a criminal personality profile, one should be alert for atypical utilization of one or more of the senses.

What a person says to his/her sexual partner during intercourse can be gratifying or harmful to a relationship. A person enjoys hearing those things that are pleasing. In a rape situation, the rapist may demand from the victim certain words or phrases that enhance the act for him. The verbiage can indicate what gratifies the rapist and give the interviewer insight into the needs (motivation) of the offender. For example, a rapist who demands such phrases as "I love you," "Make love to me," or "You're better than my husband" suggests a need for affection or ego-building. One who demands that the victim plead, or forces her to scream, suggests sadism and enjoyment of the total control and domination involved. If the victim is forced to speak in a self-demeaning or derogatory manner, the offender may be motivated by anger and hostility.

Was There a Sudden Change in the Offender's Attitude during the Attack?

The victim should be asked specifically whether she observed any change in the attitude of the rapist during the time he was with her. Did he become angry, contrite, physically abusive, or apologetic, and was this a departure from his previous attitude? If the victim reports an attitudinal change, she should be asked to recall what immediately preceded the change. A sudden and unexpected behavioral change may reflect a weakness or fear on the part of the offender, and it becomes important to determine what precipitated that change.

Factors that may cause such changes include offender sexual dysfunction, external disruption (phone ringing, noise, a knock on the door), victim resistance, a lack of fear on the part of the victim, ridicule or scorn, or even ejaculation and/or completion of the rape.

An attitudinal change may be demonstrated verbally, physically, or sexually. As previously mentioned, the rape is stressful not only for the victim but also for the offender. His behavioral reaction to stress may become important in future interrogations, and knowledge of the factor that precipitated the change is a valuable psychological tool to the investigator.

What Precautionary Actions Were Taken by the Offender?

The answer to this question will be a major factor in determining the experience level of the rapist. It may be possible to conclude from the rapist's actions whether he is a novice or an experienced offender who may have previously been arrested or incarcerated for rape or similar offenses.

While most rapists take at least some action (wearing a mask or telling the victim not to look at them) to mask their identity, some go to great lengths to protect themselves from future prosecution. It is the latter group to which this question is primarily addressed. As in any criminal act, the more rapes a person commits, the more proficient he becomes in eluding detection. If a person is arrested because of a mistake and later repeats the crime, it is not likely that he will repeat the same costly error.

The authors classify the offender as either novice or experienced (and/or previously arrested) based upon what protective actions he takes.

Novice. The novice rapist is unfamiliar with modern medical or police technology and will take minimal or obvious actions to protect his identity. For example, he may wear a ski mask or work or leather gloves, change his voice tone, affect an accent, order the victim not to look at him, or blindfold and/or bind the victim. These are common precautions that a person who is unaware of phosphotate tests or hair and fiber evidence would be expected to take.

Experienced/Previously Arrested. The profiler notes factors in the experienced offender's modus operandi that indicate a more than common knowledge of police and medical abilities. In addition to the actions above, an experienced rapist may walk through the residence or prepare an escape route prior to the sexual assault, disable the victim's telephone prior to entry or departure, order the victim to shower or douche, bring bindings or gags rather than using those available at the scene, wear surgical gloves during the assault, and/or take or force the victim to wash items he touched or ejaculated on (bedding or the victim's clothing).

As in all such subjective analyses, the projected experience level of the rapist is a judgmental decision based on the offender's actions and the investigator's interpretation of those actions.

Was Anything Taken?

Almost without exception, police record the theft of items from rape victims. All too often, however, investigators fail to probe the matter further unless it involves articles of value (pawn shop, entry in NCIC, etc.). The profiler is interested not only in *if* something was taken, but also in *why* it was taken. The stolen item may provide information valuable in determining a characteristic about the criminal and thereby aid the investigative process. In some cases, the victim may not realize anything was taken (one photograph from a group or one pair of panties from a drawer).

The profiler categorizes items taken as evidentiary, valuables, and personal.

Evidentiary. As previously mentioned, the rapist who takes evidentiary items (those he has touched or on which he has ejaculated, etc.) suggests experience or an arrest history for similar offenses.

Valuables. One who takes items of value may be experiencing financial difficulties (unemployed or employed in a job providing little income). The investigator may take this a step further in categorizing the offender. It has been the authors' experience that younger rapists steal items such as stereos, televisions, etc., while the more mature ones tend to take jewelry or items that are more easily concealed and transported.

Personal. Personal items taken include photographs of the victim, lingerie, driver's license, etc. These types of items are of no intrinsic value, but instead serve to remind the offender of the occurrence and the victim. When such an item is taken, the investigator must attempt to determine the motivation behind the theft. Was it taken as a trophy or as a souvenir? A trophy represents a victory or conquest, while a souvenir serves to remind one of a pleasant experience. One must examine the physical, verbal, and sexual behavior of the rapist to determine what the stolen item represents to the offender. The abusive, hostile, and physically assaultive rapist typically takes the item as a trophy and tends to be a "macho" type who has little respect for the female gender and is given to bragging about his sexual exploits. On the other hand, the souvenir-taker is generally the "gentleman" rapist who utilizes minimal force and is verbally reassuring and sexually "gentle." Such an individual uses the item to fantasize later and frequently retains the items in his residence or place of work. The item, therefore, provides the police with a means of connecting him to his crimes.

A final factor to consider in this area is whether the offender later returns the item to the victim. If so, why? The trophy-taker does so to intimidate or frighten the victim, while the souvenir-taker does so to convince the victim he meant no harm or was not really a bad person.

Has the Victim Had Any Experience That Would Suggest She Was a Targeted Victim?

Rapists quite often target or select their victims prior to the commission of the crime. The occurrence of a series of rapes involving victims who were either alone or in the company of small children is a very strong indication that the offender was well aware of his victim's vulnerability, either through peeping or surveillance activities. He may also have entered the residence, or communicated with the victim, prior to the offense. The investigator should determine whether the victim or her neighbors had experienced any of the following prior to the rape: calls or notes from unidentified persons, residential or automobile break-ins, prowlers or peeping Toms, or a feeling that she was being watched or followed. Frequently, rapists who do target or select their victims have prior arrests for breaking and entering, prowling, peeping-Tom activities, and/or theft of feminine clothing.

Belief as to How the Rapist's Friends Would Describe Him

The ability of the rape victim to disassociate the individual who raped her from the way he is observed to be by his friends and associates will amaze even the most experienced investigator. Having the victim so describe her attacker will benefit the investigator and the victim.

The officer conducting the investigation would be well advised to seek the victim's assistance in this manner if she is a reasonably intelligent individual. She should also be asked to list (over a period of days) any facts about the crime that she forgot earlier and that later come to mind. She should be asked to list characteristics about the rapist that she feels would be known to those who associate with the offender, i.e., articulate, a leader, shy, unsure of self, neat, rough, etc. Such information is very useful in the search for the unidentified rapist.

This procedure can also aid in the victim's psychological recovery. The rape experience has divested her of her sense of being in control of her life. Being asked to contribute in a rational, concrete, relevant manner to the investigation returns to her some semblance of control.

A word of caution is necessary at this point. Should the victim's "profile" not describe her attacker, it may prove detrimental to the prosecution of the offender (provided to the defense under "discovery" rules). The investigator should seek guidance from his prosecutor prior to obtaining a "profile" from the rape victim.

Summary

Rape is a deviant sexual activity serving nonsexual needs. Through an analysis of the offender's verbal, sexual, and physical behavior, it may be possible to determine what needs were being served and to project personality characteristics of the individual having such needs. It must be remembered that the only available source of information about such behavior is the victim and, therefore, it is necessary to establish a rapport with the victim through empathy and professionalism. One must isolate personal feelings about the crime and the criminal, and view the crime as the rapist did.

If, in fact, behavior reflects personality, it would seem obvious that a set of questions designed specifically to elicit behavioral information would be the first step in the analysis of a rape. One of the authors (Hazelwood) developed and refined the questions in this article over a period of 4 years and has found them to be of inestimable value in understanding the personality involved in the crime of rape.

References

Ault, R. L. and Reese, J. T. "A Psychological Assessment of Crime: Profiling." *FBI Law Enforcement Bulletin,* March 1980, pp. 22–25.

Coleman, J. C., et al. *Abnormal Psychology and Modern Life,* 6th ed. Glenview, Ill.: Scott, Foresman and Co., 1980.

Groth, A. N. *Men Who Rape.* New York: Plenum Press, 1979, p. 88.

Groth, A. N. and Burgess, A. W. "Sexual Dysfunction during Rape." *New England Journal of Medicine,* Vol. 297, No. 4, 1977, pp. 764–766.

Hazelwood, R. R. "The Behavior-Oriented Interview of Rape Victims: The Key to Profiling." *FBI Law Enforcement Bulletin,* September 1983.

Hazelwood, R. R. and Douglas, J. E. "The Lust Murder." *FBI Law Enforcement Bulletin,* April 1980, pp. 18–22.

Hazelwood, R. R., et al. "Sexual Fatalities: Behavioral Reconstruction in Equivocal Deaths." *Journal of Forensic Science,* Vol. 27, No. 4, October 1982, pp. 764–773.

Holmstrom, L. L. and Burgess, A. W. "Rapist's Talk: Linguistic Strategies to Control the Victim," in *Deviant Behavior,* Vol. 1. Hemisphere Publishing Corp., 1979.

Holmstrom, L. L. and Burgess, A. W. "Sexual Behavior of Assailants during Rape." *Archives of Sexual Behavior,* Vol. 9, No. 5, 1980.

Masters, W. H. and Johnson, V. K. *Human Sexual Inadequacy.* Boston: Little, Brown and Co., 1970.

Reese, J. T. "Obsessive Compulsive Behavior; the Nuisance Offender." *FBI Law Enforcement Bulletin,* August 1979, pp. 6–12.

Ressler, R. K., et al. "Offender Profiles: A Multidisciplinary Approach." *FBI Law Enforcement Bulletin,* September 1980, pp. 16–20.

Rider, A. O. "The Firesetter: A Psychological Profile." *FBI Law Enforcement Bulletin,* June 1980, pp. 6–13.

Analyzing the Rape and Profiling the Offender

8

ROBERT R. HAZELWOOD

Any expertise claimed by an individual is nothing more or less than a combination of one's own experience and what one has learned from the experience of others. The material set forth in this chapter is the result of reading; attendance at seminars, lectures, and courses; exchanges with others in the field; 26 years in law enforcement; and having had the opportunity of consulting on over 1,000 rape cases.

While I recognize the impossibility of categorizing human behavior into specific classifications that will be applicable to all rape situations, I am convinced that it is possible to analyze an offender's behavior during the attack and to be able to describe the type of individual who committed the crime. This description can then be set forth in such a way as to allow his friends and acquaintances to recognize him.

As addressed in Chapter 7, the first step in profiling the unidentified offender is to ascertain from the victim what behavior the rapist exhibited. Having obtained a detailed statement, one may then proceed to the next step—analyzing what is known, to determine the purpose of the assault and to elicit behavioral information that will assist in the preparation of a criminal personality profile. The analysis should be as objective as possible, and personal feelings about the crime, the criminal, and the victim must not be allowed to influence the profiler's judgment. The rapist's behavior is easier to assess if it can be seen as part of a systematic pattern. To accomplish this, a typology must be established, one that the analyst believes to be valid and that is easily understood by others. This poses no small problem.

Selfish vs. Pseudo-Unselfish Behavior

In analyzing the statement of a rape victim, the first objective is to determine whether the *rapist* intended the assault to be "selfish" or "unselfish" in nature. To categorize a rapist as "unselfish" may seem contrary to everything the reader believes about sexual assault. However, the use of the term is not intended to portray the offender in a favorable light. The terms were selected in an attempt to establish an easily definable starting point for the analyst to begin the necessary isolation of his/her personal feelings about the offender. It would be simple to describe the rapist as a "no-good, rotten bastard." Doing so might be quite satisfying, but not very analytical. It is to be remembered that a profile should describe an individual as those who know him would. The reader will note that of the six classifications of rapists later described, only one exhibits "pseudo-unselfish" behavior.

As discussed in Chapter 7, the analyst considers the verbal, sexual, and physical (force) behavior of the rapist in his/her study of the crime. The same procedure will be applied in determining whether the offender intended the crime to be selfish or unselfish.

Pseudo-Unselfish Behavior

To the average individual, the word "unselfish" implies sharing or caring. In the context of rape, it has an entirely different meaning, but one that is important in understanding the crime. "Pseudo-unselfish" behavior indicates a belief on the part of the rapist that his "concern" for the victim's comfort and welfare will win her over and a hope that she will "realize" he is not a bad person at all. Therefore, he attempts to "involve" her in the act, both sexually and verbally. He needs the victim to enjoy (or pretend to enjoy) the activity, as this feeds his need for acceptance and power and fulfills his fantasy of the victim's willing compliance.

Most rapists will not exhibit all of the verbal, sexual, or physical behavior set forth below, but will demonstrate a sufficient amount of it to allow classification.

Verbal Behavior. The "unselfish" rapist will verbalize in a manner that simulates a lover rather than a criminal. He will attempt to reassure the victim that he does not want or intend to harm her if she cooperates. For example, he may state, "If you do as I say, I won't hurt you," "I don't want to hurt you," or "Don't make me hurt you." He is frequently complimentary, with such phrases as, "You're beautiful," "You have nice breasts," "I bet you have a lot of boyfriends," or "You're so attractive, why aren't you married?" He may verbalize in a self-demeaning manner with such comments as "You'd never go out with me" or "I'm ugly, you wouldn't like me." On the other hand, he might engage in verbal activity which would indicate ego-building with such demands as "Tell me you love me," "Tell me I'm better than your husband/boyfriend," or "Tell me you want me to make love to you."

Quite often, the "unselfish" rapist will voice concern for his victim's welfare or comfort with such statements as "Am I hurting you?" "You should lock your doors and windows," or "Are you cold?" He may engage in what appears to be unnecessary, and potentially revealing, conversation of a personal nature. An example of this type of verbiage is present in the following case.

CASE 1

The victim, a 27-year-old white female, reported that her assailant awakened and raped her at approximately 2:00 AM. The sexual attack lasted no more than 10 minutes. Following the assault, the offender lay down beside her and conversed for approximately 45 minutes. While asking her questions about her personal life (job, boyfriend, etc.), he was primarily interested in discussing himself and the events of the evening. He stated that he had left his keys in his car, parked a short distance away, and that he was concerned about it being stolen. He told her that a friend of his, Jack, was outside the residence, but that he wouldn't allow him near the victim because Jack was drunk. He identified himself as "David" and stated that he had never done anything like this before. Prior to leaving, he apologized and asked her not to call the police. After he left, the victim discovered that $400 was missing from her purse.

The victim reported the sexual assault and theft to the police on the same morning. Two days later, she returned home from work and found an envelope in her mail box addressed to her, but bearing no stamp or postmark. Inside the envelope, she found the stolen money and an accompanying note which read:

Fran:

I'm just writing to try to express my deepest apology to you for what I put you through. I know an apology doesn't help the way you must feel right now, but I am truly sorry. I found Jack when I left, sitting on the sidewalk in front of your apartment complex. He was still pretty drunk. He took some money from a purse in your kitchen. He's really an alright guy and doesn't usually steal money. I hope this is all of it. I found my car later. Luckily, it wasn't stolen because my keys were still in it. Anyway, I just want you to know that I have never done anything like this before. I wish I could blame this on Jack, but I can't. You're really a sweet person, and you didn't deserve any of this.

You can tell your boyfriend that he's a lucky guy.

Good bye,
David

Typically, the "pseudo-unselfish" rapist is nonprofane. This is not to say that he won't use profanity, but when he does, it is mild in nature and spoken without much conviction. As mentioned in the case presented above, he may ask questions about the victim's lifestyle, occupation, social life, plans, or residence. Very often the victim will report that the rapist was apologetic and/or asked her forgiveness with verbiage such as "I'm sorry," "Please forgive me," "I wish it didn't have to be you," or "You didn't deserve this."

In summary, the rapist exhibiting "pseudo-unselfish" verbal behavior is most often (1) reassuring, (2) complimentary, (3) self-demeaning, (4) ego-building, (5) concerned, (6) personal, (7) nonprofane, (8) inquisitive, and (9) apologetic.

When analyzing a victim's statement for the offender's verbal behavior, the reader is advised to use adjectives similar to those set forth in this section.

Sexual Behavior. As previously stated, the "pseudo-unselfish" rapist attempts to involve the victim. This is especially true in the sexual aspect of the crime. Interestingly, he will normally do what the victim allows him to do (i.e., she does not physically or verbally resist his acts or demands). His behavior does not indicate a desire to harm the victim physically or to force her to engage in acts when she resists. This may be due to a lack of confidence on his part, or a fantasy that she has become a willing partner, which the use of force would destroy. Should the victim resist, this type of rapist may cease the demand, attempt to negotiate or compromise with the victim, threaten her, or leave. Very seldom will he employ physical force.

He often demands that the victim kiss him "like you mean it." He fondles the sexual parts of her body and may insert his finger in her vagina. Frequently, he performs cunnilingus prior to penetrating the vagina, and as he rapes, he may demand that the victim kiss him back, put her arms around him, or stroke his neck or back.

As stated, he will do whatever the victim "allows" him to do, and if he is confronted with an aggressive or resistant victim, he will spend a brief amount of time with her. He will quickly discern whether his victim is thoroughly intimidated and very passive, and may take advantage of such a woman by acting out all of his sexual fantasies. In that case, the acts may include fellatio, anal sex, and the insertion of foreign objects, in addition to vaginal rape.

It is important to note at this point that it is quite possible for the "pseudo-unselfish" and "selfish" rapists to engage in or demand the same sexual acts; the former does what the victim allows, and the latter does whatever he desires. To differentiate between the two types of rapists, the analyst must closely examine the verbal and physical (force) behaviors, as they are seldom similar. One should also consider the sequence of the sexual acts to determine if there was a desire to degrade the victim (the "pseudo-unselfish" rapist infrequently does so intentionally).

Physical Behavior. The amount of physical force utilized by the "pseudo-unselfish" rapist is usually found to be minimal. The reader will recall from Chapter 7 that at this level, force is used more to intimidate than to punish the victim. While mild slapping may occur, the offender does not desire to physically hurt the victim. Instead, he tends to rely on threats, the presence or threat of a weapon, or the fear and passivity of his victim to obtain her compliance.

From a behavioral standpoint, the fact that a rapist exhibits a weapon or advises the victim that he has one does not constitute physical force unless he *uses* it to inflict bodily injury. From a legal standpoint, of course, the presence or threat of a weapon is very significant and escalates the seriousness of the offense. However, I am aware of many instances in which an armed assailant put the weapon aside after gaining control of the victim. I am also aware of a few instances in which the rapist turned the weapon over to the victim. Interestingly, many victims find themselves incapable of using the weapon and return it to the offender.[1] Most of them report that they either were afraid of the weapon, thought it might be a trick (unloaded gun), or were concerned that they might not be able to incapacitate the assailant and that he would then kill them.

Selfish Behavior

Whereas the "pseudo-unselfish" rapist seeks to involve the victim as an active participant and behaviorally indicates some concern for her welfare, no such actions or behavior can be credited to the "selfish" rapist. He neither desires nor wants the victim to become involved. Instead, he uses the victim in much the same way an actor in a play uses a prop. He is verbally and sexually self-oriented and physically abusive. During the time he is with a victim, it is clear that his pleasure alone matters above all else. He will exhibit no concern for his victim's comfort, welfare, or feelings.

---

[1] Invariably, when I lecture to police audiences on this subject, the attendees express amazement at the fact that the victim would not take advantage of the opportunity and shoot the rapist. This attitude is quickly changed to one of empathy when I inquire as to how many of them have spouses at home who are afraid of their service revolver and demand that it be kept out of sight.

Verbal Behavior. Verbally, this type of rapist will be offensive, abusive, and threatening. He utilizes a great deal of profanity throughout the attack and may refer to the victim in derogatory terms such as "bitch" or "cunt." He will attempt to demean the victim with such statements as "You've got no sex in you" or "No wonder you're not married." Frequently, this type of rapist will demand that the victim verbalize in such a manner as to humiliate herself (e.g., asking for or describing sexual activities). His communications will be consistently threatening in nature and demanding in fact. Almost invariably, his verbiage will be nonpersonal and sexual in orientation. An example of "selfish" verbal behavior is set forth in the following case.

CASE 2

A young female was kidnapped, raped, and murdered. Her killer made a tape recording of portions of the verbal interaction between himself and his young victim. The following is a brief segment of that recording.

RAPIST: What are you doing?
VICTIM: Nothing. I'm doing what you told me to do.
RAPIST: What's that?
VICTIM: I'm sucking on it.
RAPIST: On what?
VICTIM: This.
RAPIST: What's this?
VICTIM: Your dick.
RAPIST: You're sucking on my dick?
VICTIM: That's what you told me to do.
RAPIST: Are you doing it?
VICTIM: Yes.
RAPIST: Tell me what you're doing.
VICTIM: I'm sucking on your dick.

In summary, the "selfish rapist" is verbally (1) offensive, (2) abusive, (3) threatening, (4) profane, (5) demeaning, (6) humiliating, (7) demanding, (8) nonpersonal, and (9) sexually oriented.

Sexual Behavior. Sexually, this type of rapist will do whatever he wants to do. The victim's fear, comfort, or feelings are of no significance to him. Physical, verbal, or passive resistance will not deter him in his desire to sexually dominate, punish, or use his victim. Seldom will he engage in kissing, unless he feels it will further humiliate the woman. He is not likely to fondle or stroke the victim. He is much more likely to pull, pinch, twist, or bite the sexual parts of her body. He may force the victim to perform analingus, fellatio, or self-masturbation. The sequence of the sexual acts is more likely to be anal assault followed by fellatio than the reverse. Should the victim complain of pain or discomfort, he will be unconcerned.

Physical Behavior. The "selfish" rapist may utilize moderate, excessive, or brutal levels of force (see Chapter 7). The amount utilized depends largely on the underlying motivation of the attack and is seldom directly related to the amount of resistance offered by the victim.[2] Case 3 illustrates this point.

CASE 3

A 33-year-old woman and her husband returned home from an evening out and were confronted with a burglar/rapist. After binding the husband, the intruder began sexually assaulting the wife, using no force toward her and engaging in vaginal rape only. During the attack, her husband inquired as to her welfare and she stated, "It's OK, he's being gentle." At that point, the rapist began to pummel her breasts. As a result of the beating, the victim underwent a mastectomy. When later interviewing the rapist, I asked why he had beaten her following the comment, and he replied, "I wanted her to know who was in charge, and she found out. Who is she to say I'm being gentle?"

Categories of Rapists

Once the rapist is broadly categorized as being either "selfish" or "pseudo-unselfish," he may then be further classified in an attempt to learn his motivation for the assault. For this purpose, I have chosen to utilize the categories of rapists developed by Groth, Burgess, and Holmstrom (1977). These classifications were developed through empirical research, and I have found them to be quite accurate when compared with the volume of cases received at the Behavioral Science Unit (BSU). They are (1) Power Reassurance, (2) Power Assertive, (3) Anger Retaliatory, and (4) Anger Excitation. I have taken the liberty of somewhat modifying the "Style of Attack" in each classification

---

[2] What should a woman do if she is confronted by a rapist? I am of the opinion that law enforcement officers should not provide specific recommendations when answering this question. I am not suggesting this as an "easy out," but rather as a means of dealing realistically with an impossible task. To begin with, one who is asked this question is immediately confronted with a situation having three unknown variables: (1) environment of the attack, (2) type of rapist, and (3) victim personality. My advice to an assertive woman confronted with an unselfish-type rapist in a parking lot would be entirely different from the advice I would give to a passive individual who is confronted with a sexual sadist on a little-used roadway after midnight. Lacking the variable information, one must proceed cautiously when giving advice. I have no hesitation in providing advice on preventive measures or recommending self-defense courses, firearms training, police whistles, or disabling gases where legal. However, as law enforcement officers, we must remember that when we speak in an official capacity, we speak not for ourselves but for our organizations. If a person following our advice is brutally beaten and requires long-term hospitalization, we or our organizations could be held liable. I once heard a speaker advise women in the audience to defecate, vomit, or urinate if confronted with a rapist, as this would surely deter him. I would refer the reader to Case 9 of this chapter and simply state that the only person such measures would surely deter is the individual who recommended the tactic. Case 3 illustrates the inability to determine what may or may not diminish the probability of a victim being injured. (Hazelwood and Harpold, 1986)

and, as the reader will note, I have briefly addressed the opportunistic rapist and the gang rape. The terms "pseudo-unselfish" and "selfish" are used when I describe the various styles of attack.

A word of caution is necessary here. Seldom will a rapist commit a crime in a manner that will allow the analyst to classify him clearly or simply as one of the types set forth below. More commonly, the investigator will be confronted with a mixture of types. It is at this point that common sense is to be applied. The case I have chosen to analyze and profile later in this chapter (Case 10) is an excellent example of a "mixture" of rapist types.

Power Reassurance Rapist

Purpose of Attack. This type of rapist assaults to reassure himself of his masculinity by exercising his power over women. I ask my law enforcement students to associate with this sense of power by having them recall their first patrol experience after graduation from the police academy. Entering traffic in the police cruiser, they immediately note a decrease in speed by those vehicles in proximity to them and, while not spoken, a sense of power and authority is felt by the new officer. So it is with the Power Reassurance Rapist—the same feeling of power and control over another, a woman. Finally he's in charge! This individual lacks confidence in his ability to interact socially and sexually with women, and through the use of forced sexual activity, he proves himself to *himself*. While he does degrade and emotionally traumatize his victim, he has no conscious intent to do so. This is the type of rapist I have most commonly observed in stranger assaults.

Style of Attack. The Power Reassurance Rapist exhibits "pseudo-unselfish" verbal and sexual behavior and utilizes minimal to moderate levels of force. In police jargon, he is frequently described as the "gentleman rapist," the "apologist," or the "polite type." He selects his victims in advance of the attack, normally through surveillance or peeping-Tom activities. He often has targeted several victims in advance, thereby explaining why, following an unsuccessful attempted rape, a second attack occurs on the same evening in the same general locale.

His attacks generally occur during the late evening or early morning hours, and the victim is most often alone or in the company of small children. He uses the "surprise" approach and may exhibit (or claim that he has) a weapon. He selects victims within his own age range and typically forces them to remove their clothing, thus fueling his fantasy of the victim's willingness to participate. He generally spends a relatively short period of time with the victim. However, if he encounters a particularly passive victim upon whom he can act out all of his sexual fantasies, he will take advantage of that situation and spend more time with that victim. Following the assault, and consistent with "pseudo-unselfish" behavior, he may apologize and ask the victim for forgiveness. Occasionally, he will take a personal item (undergarment, photograph, etc.) as a souvenir.

He may recontact the victim after the assault by calling or writing her. For this reason, I strongly recommend that a tape recorder be attached to the victim's phone for as long as 15 days after the crime.

Following an unsuccessful rape attempt, he will strike again quickly, possibly in the same evening. A successful attack will reassure him, but this feeling rapidly wears off, and he finds it necessary to attack again for additional reinforcement. Therefore, his pattern of attacks will be fairly consistent and will occur within the same general vicinity or in a similar socioeconomic neighborhood. He will continue to attack until he is arrested, moves, or is incapacitated.

With the exception of the Anger Excitation Rapist, this is the only type that is likely to keep records of his attacks. Such a rapist is depicted in the following case.

CASE 4

A black male raped more than 20 black females within a short period of time. The victims were always alone or with other females who were agemates. The offender never struck his victims but relied instead upon threats or the presence of a weapon. In several instances, he left the scene rather than resort to force to obtain victim compliance. Upon his identification and arrest, the investigators recovered a business ledger containing the victims' names, addresses, telephone numbers, and body measurements and a scoring system for the victims' participation in various sexual acts. The ledger also contained similar information on fantasized victims, including movie stars and popular singers.

Power Assertive Rapist

Purpose of the Attack. In contrast to the Power Reassurance Rapist, this type has no conscious doubts about his masculinity. To the contrary, he is outwardly a "man's man." He is, in his own mind, simply exercising his prerogative as a male to commit rape. This individual uses rape to express his virility and dominance over women and is the second most commonly observed type in the cases received by the Behavioral Science Unit for profiling.

Style of Attack. The Power Assertive Rapist is sexually and verbally selfish in his attacks. He makes no attempt to accommodate his victims and exhibits no concern for their welfare or emotional comfort.

He uses moderate to excessive levels of force in subduing and controlling the victim. This style of rapist most often utilizes the "con" approach, changing demeanor only after the victim is relaxed and at ease. Like the Power Reassurance Rapist, he selects victims who approximate his own age.

His rapes are likely to occur at any location that is convenient and that he considers safe. Frequently, he will rip or tear the victim's clothing from her and discard it. He will subject the victim to repeated sexual assaults, as this is a further expression of his manliness and of his natural dominance over women.

If he has transported her to the assault location, he will most often leave the victim stranded at that point and in a partial or full state of nudity, thereby delaying her ability to report the crime. While he doesn't rape as consistently as the Power Reassurance type, he will assault when he feels he "needs" a woman. Case 5 provides an example of this type of rapist.

CASE 5

A female motorist was stranded with her disabled car, when a white male stopped and offered assistance. He raised the hood of her car, examined it for a few minutes, and advised her that it would have to be repaired by a mechanic. Because he was well dressed and very polite, she accepted his offer to take her to a nearby service station. Once in the car, they chatted in a friendly manner until she noticed that he had passed two exits. She inquired as to how far the station was, and he displayed a gun and told her to shut up. She screamed, and he struck her twice on the head, causing her to lose consciousness. When she awakened, she discovered her clothes had been torn off and he was raping her. When she pleaded for him not to hurt her, he cursed her, struck her again and told her to keep quiet. During the next 2 hours, he raped her three times and forced her to perform fellatio twice. Following the assault, he threw her out of the car, keeping the clothes, and told her, "Show your ass and you may get some help." The victim was treated for severe bruises and lacerations.

Anger Retaliatory Rapist

Purpose of the Attack. This type of rapist is identified with anger and retaliation. As Groth, Burgess, and Holmstrom (1977) have stated, the individuals who fall within this category are getting even with women for real or imagined wrongs. They are angry with women and use sex as a weapon with which to punish and degrade them. They do so intentionally, and when one interviews the victim of such an attack or reads her statement, it becomes quite clear that anger is a key component of the underlying motivation in the sexual assault. This is the third most common type of rapist observed in the BSU files.

Style of Attack. The Anger Retaliatory Rapist is sexually and verbally selfish, and he will utilize excessive levels of force. The analyst must recognize the application of such force as the result of intense rage and an almost frenzied attack process due to the emotional involvement of the offender.

The crime itself is not generally premeditated in the sense that a great deal of time was committed to planning or to the selection of the victim. The attack is an emotional outburst that is predicated on anger and, therefore, is an impulsive action.

This type of rapist uses the "blitz" approach, subduing the victim with the immediate application of direct and physical force, thereby denying her any opportunity to defend herself. The actual sexual assault is relatively short in duration, and the total amount of time spent with the victim is also relatively brief. The pent-up anger is vented against the female sexually and physically, and he leaves the victim following the release of tension.

The Anger Retaliatory Rapist typically attacks women who are age-mates or somewhat older than he is. Frequently, he will assault women who, in one way or another, symbolize someone else. The similarity may be style of dress, grooming, occupation, height, weight, race, or a host of other possibilities.

As with the Power Assertive Rapist, this offender is most likely to tear or rip his victims' clothing off. His assaults are likely to occur anytime during the day or night due to the motivational factor of anger. He tends to use weapons of opportunity, most often his feet or fists, and his attacks are sporadic in nature. That is to say, there is no pattern to his assaults. After an attack, his anger is relieved and he feels less tension. Eventually, however, the anger will rebuild and he will again feel the necessity to vent his anger against the source of his problems—women! The following case provides an example of such a rapist.

CASE 6

The victim, a woman in her late forties, was walking toward her car in a parking lot, when a man spun her around and struck her repeatedly in the face and stomach with his fist. In a semiconscious state, the victim was placed in her automobile and driven to an isolated area, where the rapist ordered her to remove her clothing. As she fumbled with the buttons on her blouse, he cursed her and began tearing her clothes off and throwing them out of the car. As she held her arms up in a defensive posture, he continued to beat her severely and to scream obscenities at her. Forcing her into the rear of the car, he attempted to rape her but was unable to obtain an erection. Blaming the victim for a lack of sexuality, he decided that alcohol would "help" her and he forced her to consume a large amount from a bottle, causing her to gag. Under his control for more than 2 hours, she was repeatedly beaten and otherwise abused. He finally pushed her into a ditch and drove away. Upon being taken to a hospital, she was found to have fractures of facial and other bones, as well as multiple lacerations. She required extended hospitalization and long months of mental therapy.

Anger Excitation Rapist

Purpose of the Attack. This type of rapist is sexually stimulated and/or gratified through the victim's response to the infliction of physical and emotional pain. His primary motivation in the assault is to inflict pain that will bring about the desired response of fear and total submission. In the cases on which I have consulted, I have found this to be the least common type of rapist encountered. However, the rarity is more than compensated for by the viciousness of the attack and the physical and emotional trauma suffered by the victims.

Style of the Attack. Investigators will experience no other sexual crime as well planned and methodically executed as that committed by the Anger Excitation Rapist. Every detail of the crime has been carefully thought out and rehearsed either literally or in the offender's fantasies. Weapons and instruments, transportation, travel routes, recording devices, bindings—virtually every phase has been preplanned, with one notable exception. The victim is typically a stranger. While she will meet certain criteria established by the rapist to fulfill his desires and fantasies, she will generally not be associated with him in any way known to others. This is also part of his plan. He wants no ties that will connect him to the victim.

Needless to say, he is sexually and verbally selfish with his victims and typically utilizes the "brutal" level of force, often resulting in the victim's death. He most often uses the "con" approach to gain access to the victim. After gaining her confidence, he quickly immobilizes her with bindings and takes her to a preselected location that provides him with the privacy such activity requires. He normally keeps the victim for extended periods of time (hours to days) and, during that time, may torture her with instruments and/or devices while psychologically reducing her to depths of fear difficult to imagine.

Victims frequently report that, while they remained bound, the rapist would cut and remove their clothing. Such rapists typically use sexual bondage, and the helplessness of the female is stimulating to them. The cutting of the clothing may also be a symbolic cutting of the victim. As previously mentioned, the offender will practice bondage and may also bite the victim and insert foreign objects into the vagina or rectum.

The Anger Excitation Rapist is the most likely to record activities with the victim. The method of recording is dependent upon the offender's desires, maturity or experience, and/or ability to afford the available technology. I have observed cases in which the rapist recorded his acts with a camera, tape recorder, or video recorder or in sketches or writing.

The sexual acts forced on the victim will be varied and experimental in nature, intended to create pain, humiliation, and degradation for the victim. In some instances, I have noted that very little sexual activity took place that involved the offender. He tends to remain emotionally detached from such acts and is almost instructional in his directions to the victim. He is particularly attuned to the visual and audio aspects of the crime.

The victim's age and race may vary if the rapist continues to attack over a period of time. The investigator will note that there is no apparent pattern to the period of time between assaults. In other words, the rapist attacks when he wants to and when he is convinced that his plan is foolproof. Case 7 provides an example of the Anger Excitation Rapist.

CASE 7

The victim, a 32-year-old housewife, disappeared from a shopping center after having purchased groceries from a store. She was driving a motor home at the time of her disappearance. Her nude body was found in the motor home 5 days later. She was lying on her back on the sofa with her hands bound behind her. An autopsy indicated that she had died within the past 2 days, and her death was attributed to the continued ingestion of small amounts of arsenic accompanied by bourbon. She had been raped several times, and it was the considered opinion of those concerned with the case that she had been forced to drink the arsenic-spiked bourbon to induce convulsions of the body for the pleasure of the rapist.

Opportunistic Rapist

Purpose of the Attack. This may be the only type of rapist whose primary motivation in assaulting a woman is sexual in nature. The Opportunist typically assaults as an afterthought during the commission of another crime. An example would be the burglar who discovers a female alone after he enters the residence. He finds her to be sexually attractive and impulsively assaults her. One must not confuse this offender with the burglar who consistently rapes during other crimes.

Style of Attack. The Opportunist is in the midst of committing another crime (burglary, robbery, kidnapping, etc.) when he decides to assault sexually. He generally uses a minimal level of force and spends a relatively short period of time with the victim, leaving her bound when he departs. He is sexually and verbally selfish and has frequently been drinking or consuming drugs prior to the crime. An example of this type of rapist is set forth in Case 8.

CASE 8
The victim, a 17-year-old, was normally in school at the time a burglar entered her residence. Surprised to find anyone at home, the criminal bound and blindfolded the young girl, and after advising her that he wouldn't harm her, he began ransacking the home. Finding the father's liquor cabinet, he consumed a large amount of alcohol and began thinking of the attractive female who was in the house. He became mildly intoxicated and attempted to vaginally assault her, but was unable to maintain an erection. He told the crying girl to be quiet, that he hadn't hurt her, and he left quickly. Upon his arrest, he expressed regret at what happened and said that he had a daughter the same age as the victim. There was no indication that he had ever attempted such an act previously.

The Gang Rape

When confronted with a rape involving two or more offenders, it is especially important to elicit information from the victim about the apparent leader of the group. In practically all rapes of this type, one person emerges as the leader, and it is this individual upon whom the analyst should concentrate.

It should be noted that there is generally a reluctant personality involved in gang rapes in which three or more persons participate. Frequently, this individual is easy to recognize in that he indicates to the victim that he really doesn't want this to happen, but that he is powerless to stop it. Sometimes the victim identifies this individual as a person who attempted to protect her or helped her to escape from others. This individual is the weak link in the group, and if such a person is evidenced, I would apply the profiling techniques to him as well. In all such matters that I have observed, the assault is totally selfish in nature, but the force levels have varied from minimal to brutal. The following case illustrates such a rape:

CASE 9
A 19-year-old female was abducted from a phone booth as she was hysterically explaining to her parents that a group a four young men were following her in a car and threatening to rape her. Four hours later, she was found and immediately transported to a nearby hospital where she was treated for a fractured jaw, a broken arm, and severe lacerations of the vaginal and rectal regions. She later reported that she had been forcibly taken from the phone booth and placed in the back seat of the car being used by the gang. As a result of her extreme fear, she defecated and one of the youths suggested that she be released, whereupon a second male, who was the obvious leader, negated that suggestion and instead stated

that she needed to be taught a lesson. He then twisted her arm so severely that it broke and forced her to orally clean her soiled clothing. The youth who had objected to the rape again objected and was threatened by the leader. Following this, the leader directed the others to have sex with the young girl, and two complied; the third (the reluctant participant) was sexually unable to perform. The leader then anally assaulted the girl and then forced the victim to perform fellatio on him. Following these acts, he vaginally assaulted her. She was later tied to the rear bumper of the assailants' car and dragged over the roadway.

A Case Study

Now that the procedures and classifications I use have been described, we will examine a rape case that was submitted to the Behavioral Science Unit for analysis. The case will be presented as it was received, but with changes made to protect the identity of the victim. Following the case report, the reader will find my analysis of the crime and the offender's behavior. Finally, the offender's characteristics will be set forth. For the reader's information, the rapist has since been identified, and the profile was found to be accurate in over 90% of the characteristics set forth.

CASE 10

Victimology: The victim, Mary, is a white female, 24 years of age. She currently lives alone but previously lived with her parents in another part of the state. Mary attended a university and graduated two years prior to the offense. She is an active Catholic, attending church regularly and participating in church events. After graduating, she obtained a teaching job in a junior high school. According to Mary, she is popular with the students at the school and attributes her popularity to the fact that she is young, friendly, outgoing, a nice dresser, and "is on their level." Mary is friendly with both black and white students and frequently attends their athletic activities. She stated that students would visit her classroom during their free time even though she was not their teacher. She drives an older-model subcompact car, made noticeable by multi-colored fenders salvaged from other vehicles. Her personal life is fairly routine, but she has a boyfriend who lives a few miles from her residence. She visits the Catholic church almost daily after school. She also attends a Wednesday night "happy hour" at a local bar/restaurant that attracts a respectable clientele. She is active athletically and eats out infrequently. She observes regular sleeping habits and is careful to draw her curtains at night. She knows of no black male fitting the physical description of her assailant.

Attack Environment: Mary resides in an apartment complex. The complex is located in a middle-class neighborhood and is in a well-established area of the city. The complex rents to a variety of people, including elderly, singles, and young couples. Mary's apartment is located at the rear of the complex and is one of 20 apartments. Her residence and the two beside hers are secluded and face a heavily wooded area immediately behind the complex. Her apartment is on the ground floor. A person not familiar with the area would be surprised to find the three apartments in the rear of the complex. The windows of the apartment face the wooded area. The management seems sincere in trying to screen all renters and maintain the quiet environment of the complex. This is evidenced by their success in evicting a recent tenant for creating heavy traffic in and out of the complex because of suspected drug dealing.

Assault: On the evening of Thursday, June 29, 1982, Mary went to bed around midnight. The evening was cool and clear, and she left her windows open to circulate the air. She wore a nightgown and panties to bed. Sometime after 2:00 AM, she became aware of the sensation of something tickling her leg. Thinking it was a bug, she tried to brush it off with her hand. When it continued, she tried to brush it again and felt something she believes was a hand. The room was very dark, but she could see enough to determine that a naked black male was beside her bed. When she sat up, he immediately jumped up and pushed her back down on the bed. He put a hand to her throat and told her to be quiet or he would "blow your head off." Mary began asking him to leave, and he put something, which she thought was metal, to her head and told her he had a gun. He told her he had just gotten out of prison two weeks ago and not to make any trouble since he had killed the other girls he had done this with. Mary asked him how he had gotten into the apartment, and he told her he had climbed in the window. He then grabbed the sheet, but Mary kept asking him to leave. He then said he was going to kill her if she didn't let go of the sheet, because he wasn't in the mood for fooling around. Mary let go of the sheet, and he pulled her underpants off. He then told her to spread her legs, but she refused. He again threatened her, and she held her legs up. He began to perform cunnilingus and continued this for approximately three minutes. During this time, Mary tried to talk to him about his statement about just getting out of prison. She told him that she had worked in a prison and that she didn't think that he had just gotten out. He stated that he was in a prison in another state. She asked him to leave several times, but he told her to be quiet and continued to perform cunnilingus. He then inserted his penis in her vagina. Several times when he hurt her, she cried out, and he quickly put a hand to her throat and warned her not to do it again or he would kill her. Mary told him not to hurt her again, and he responded by telling her to take her top (nightgown) off, which she refused to do. He pushed it up and began licking her nipple. During all this time, he was careful not to raise himself above her so that, in the poor light, she might be able to get a better look at him. He "slid" up her body to lick the nipple. At one point, he bit her nipple, causing Mary to cry out. Mary told him he had hurt her, and he said, "I'll show you how I can hurt you," and inserted his penis again. He told her to "shove your ass" while he was inserting his penis, and she responded by telling him that her working was not part of the deal and that she was not enjoying this. He asked if she was only "half a woman" and she said, "Yes, that's right." At one point, he moved his penis to her anus, but she told him he was in the wrong place and he ceased that activity. Eventually he ejaculated in her vagina, and Mary began asking him to leave again.

During the rape, Mary never saw a weapon, but felt a metal object pressed to her head. He continually threatened her with death, but seemed concerned for her during the rape. When he hurt her and she let him know, he would cease the painful activity. He never struck her during the incident and his threats were not made in an angry, but rather in a stern, voice. Mary did not think he had trouble in obtaining or maintaining an erection, although he told her that he was having trouble and compared his erection with "the other." He did not ask her to do anything to help him, apart from saying "Shove your ass," and Mary said that she did not touch him during the entire incident. She did not think that a premature ejaculation occurred, but could not be certain due to her lack of sexual experience. She felt that the actual intercourse lasted approximately 15 minutes and that he seemed to be in control of his sexual sensations during that time. He did not demand that she talk to him during the assault or that she speak any particular words to him. He was not abusive or profane at any time and, according to Mary, seemed to care about her. His demeanor changed only when he threatened her and then it was a stern tone, something Mary likened to a father correcting a child. After the rape, he leaned over the bed, closed the open window, and told her to get out of bed. She asked why, but he just repeated the order. She got out of bed, and he directed her to the living room. He told her not to turn on any lights and placed his hand on her shoulder blade and pushed her ahead. In the living room, he made her lie face down on the rug near her stereo. Mary continually asked him if he was going to leave, but he didn't say anything and she did not hear him put his clothes on. He asked her what she was going to do after he left, and she told him she would probably call her parents and cry. He asked her if she was going to call the cops, and she said no. He then asked where the phone was, and she directed him to the kitchen. She could hear him feeling against the wall but he couldn't find the phone. During the time she was on the floor, he continually ordered her to "keep that nose pressed to the floor." When he couldn't find the phone, he told her to show him where it was located. He then told her to go back and lie down. She did, and he ripped the phone out, saying he was sorry that she couldn't call her folks. He had her show him how to unlock the door (deadbolt lock, manually operated) and took her to the bathroom, keeping a hand on her shoulder. In the bathroom, he obtained a towel, telling Mary not to turn on any lights. They returned to the living room, and he made her lie down again. He ripped the towel into strips, possibly using a kitchen knife, and began to tie one strip over her eyes as a blindfold. He tied it too tight and it hurt her, so she asked him to loosen it, and he did. At this point, she noticed that he was wearing gloves similar to those used by doctors, and work boots. He tied her hands behind her back and tied one of her ankles. Then, with a wet towel, he began wiping her vagina. He asked her if he had gotten all the "semen"; she answered that she didn't know, and asked when he was going to leave. He kept asking what her name was during this time, but she wouldn't tell him. He then tied her ankles together and asked her if she had any money. She replied that she only had $1. He turned on the stereo and the announcer said it was 2:50 AM, and he told her to give him $20 or he would take her stereo. Mary told him that she didn't have $20, but that she would write him a check. He found her purse, took a dollar and change, and asked, "Is your name Mary?"; she assumed he had found her driver's license. He then told her that he was going to take the stereo, and she told him he was going to look funny carrying a stereo around. He replied, "There are ways." Mary told him that she wanted the cassette tapes. He wanted to know if they were mood music, and she said no, but that they had identification on them that might incriminate him if he took them.

He asked if she had any beer or wine in the refrigerator and she said no, but he went to the refrigerator and found a bottle of wine. She told him it was cooking wine, but he drank it anyway. He then told her that he was going to do it again and that he was going to do an "ass job." She refused, and he said, "Yes we are." She refused again and said it would hurt her too much. He then placed a knife to her throat hard enough to prevent her from speaking and told her he was going to kill her. He told her that he had a knife and was going to slit her throat. She asked him why, and he said that since she didn't want to "make it" with him that there was no point in her living at all. He then asked why he should let her live, and she told him that she needed to love, to love her parents, her husband, her children. He asked if she had a husband or kids and she said no, that she had meant her future husband. He asked if she was afraid, and she said yes. He then told her that they were going to do it again. He directed her onto her back, but it was painful and she kept rolling on her side. He put the knife to her throat and said that he didn't want any fooling around. He asked her which way she wanted it and she told him she didn't want it any way. He pressed the knife to her throat again and asked if she wanted to live, and she replied yes. At this point, he told her that he used to be a good Christian boy with a nine-to-five job until one day he came home and found his wife in bed with another guy. From then on, he just went from one girl to another. Mary told him she was sorry. He told her that if she didn't call the cops, he would be back, and she told him that she would call the police. He then told her that, even in the dark, he could tell that she had "nice features" and a "picturesque ass." Mary told him she didn't think he was from prison, and he laughed and said, "No, this is from your own neighborhood." She said she had some black friends and that she didn't know if she could treat them fairly after this. He asked what friends, and she replied that they were black students. He said, "I don't hang around those punks." Mary felt that he was so strong in his denial that it seemed as if he did hang around them. Mary asked why he had picked her, and he replied that he had heard that she was a "classy chick" and that he had seen her around. She said that didn't mean he had to do this to her, and he replied that if he had asked her to screw around, she would have said no. Mary heard him rip some paper and asked him to leave. He replied that he was and slid the knife down her back and between her hands. She asked him to leave a light on, and he said he had. She then heard the door open and close. She began trying to get the blindfold off, and she felt him tapping her on top of the head. He placed the knife inside the blindfold and told her how lucky she was. She heard a big bang, and the stereo stopped playing. She heard the door slam, waited a few minutes, and then worked the blindfold off. She hopped to the door, locked it, and worked the towel from around her ankles. She opened the door and knocked on a neighbor's apartment door, and help was summoned.

Subsequent examination by a physician revealed a small laceration on her neck and towel burns on her wrists. Police investigation revealed that the rapist had removed a screen covering the point of entry (a window). Mary described the rapist as a medium-to-light-skinned black male, 20 to 30 years old, 5′8″ to 5′10″ in height. He had spoken in soft to normal tones and seemed to be articulate. He had been very concerned about physical evidence being left at the scene. She didn't think he had worn the gloves during the rape. The knife was a kitchen knife from her residence. The paper she heard being ripped was determined to be newspaper he had used to light a bowl candle, which was still burning. He had also smoked a cigarette and had taken the butt with him. The "bang" she had heard was from a blow to the stereo with what is believed to have been a metal pipe.

Case Analysis

The investigators in the matter described above requested, and utilized, the questions set forth in the preceding chapter (question 14 had not yet been developed), as a guide during the interview with Mary. The reader will have noted that she gave an extremely detailed account of what transpired during the assault. A great deal of interaction occurred between Mary and her assailant, and it was thoroughly elicited from her. I will now analyze the assault, following the format discussed in Chapter 7. I will also describe the significance of the behavior exhibited during the crime.

Victimology

When a case is analyzed for profiling purposes, victimology is extremely important. An absence of pertinent information concerning the victim may preclude an accurate analysis of the crime. Victims are categorized as being either *low, moderate*, or *high risk*.

Low Risk. Low-risk victims are those individuals whose personal, professional, and social lives would not normally expose them to crime-threatening situations. Such victims have been sought out by the criminal.

Moderate Risk. Moderate-risk victims are those who, while generally of good reputation, have escalated the possibility of their being crime victims through their employment (working hours, environment, etc.), lifestyle (meeting dates through advertisement or in singles bars, etc.), or personal habits.

High Risk. High-risk victims are those whose life styles or employment consistently expose them to danger from the criminal element (drug dealing, residential location, sexual promiscuousness, prostitution, etc.). If a victim is categorized as high risk, the probability of profiling her offender is greatly diminished because the number of potential offenders is extremely large.

Mary would be categorized as a low-risk victim. Her assailant obviously sought her out.

Method of Approach

The rapist in this case utilized the "surprise" approach. He entered her residence at an hour when he had reason to believe she would be asleep and unprepared for an attack. In my opinion, the victim had been targeted in advance, through either surveillance or peeping-Tom activities. The isolated location of the apartment allowed the rapist to observe the victim undetected. Of interest is the fact that the offender felt sufficiently comfortable in the residence to remove his clothing prior to approaching the victim, and he did not inquire as to whether anyone else was in the apartment or was expected. This would indicate that he was somewhat familiar with Mary's routine and was aware that she lived alone. By undressing prior to the approach, he was able to devote himself to controlling Mary and taking precautions to disallow her seeing him sufficiently to identify him.

Method of Control

Although the rapist told Mary that he had a gun, and she felt a metal object at her head, he relied primarily on threats to control her. Of particular interest is the fact that even though he threatened physical violence if she did not comply with his demands, he did not carry out those threats. This suggests that the intent or desire to *physically* punish the victim was absent.

Amount of Force

The rapist had numerous opportunities to rationalize use of physical force against the victim, and yet he never struck her. The amount of force used consisted of (1) pushing her down on the bed, (2) putting his hand to her throat, (3) biting her nipple, (4) tapping her on the head, and (5) inflicting a small laceration on her neck. Of behavioral interest is the fact that when he hurt her and she told him so, he would cease the activity. The reader will recall that when she complained of the blindfold being too tight, he loosened it.

It is apparent that a battle of wills was taking place and, even though the rapist possessed Mary sexually, he failed to intimidate her emotionally. I believe that he was aware of his failure to "control" her and that, instead of acting out against her in a physical manner, he chose to destroy something belonging to her (the stereo) in a symbolic attack.

Given the circumstances reported, the level of force exhibited in this attack would be minimal. Although the victim's neck was lacerated, it was such a minor wound that she made no mention of it in her statement. Furthermore, she reported that the rapist seemed to care about her welfare.

Victim Resistance

There was an abundance of resistance in this case. Mary resisted the offender verbally by consistently rejecting him, questioning his demands, and asking him to leave. She resisted passively by not complying with his order to remove her nightgown, and she resisted him physically by moving away from him to avoid intercourse.

Reaction to Resistance

A very interesting pattern of resistance-reaction emerges upon analysis of the crime. As in his method of controlling the victim, he relied primarily upon verbal threats to overcome her resistance. At one point, Mary refused to remove an article of clothing, and he did so himself, thereby ceasing the demand. After refusing to "shove your ass," the victim was asked if she was "half a woman." Again and again, the potential for physical violence was there, and yet is was not utilized. As mentioned previously, the offender failed to intimidate Mary, and his lack of violent reaction supports my earlier opinion that the desire or intent to physically harm the victim was absent.

Sexual Dysfunction

Mary was unable to determine if any dysfunction occurred. According to her, the rapist had no difficulty in obtaining or maintaining an erection, and he ejaculated within an average amount of time. The offender verbally indicated some difficulty, but Mary was not aware of any such problem. Her lack of sexual experience may have been a factor in her assessment regarding dysfunction.

Type and Sequence of Sexual Acts

The sexual attack included the following acts in the sequence reported by the victim: (1) cunnilingus, (2) digital manipulation of the vagina, (3) vaginal rape, (4) licked nipple, (5) vaginal rape, (6) attempted anal rape, (7) vaginal rape with ejaculation, (8) threatened anal rape, and (9) attempted vaginal rape.

The acts of cunnilingus and digital manipulation of the vagina preceded the first rape. The activity and sequencing suggests an attempt to stimulate the victim. This behavior is unnecessary in a forcible rape situation, and its presence indicates an attempt to "involve" rather than simply "use" the victim. (The reader is reminded that we examine the crime from the offender's perspective, not our own, and certainly not the victim's.) Mary told the offender that she wasn't enjoying sex, that her "working" was not part of the deal, and that she didn't want sex in any way with him. Following the vaginal rape, he attempted to enter her anally and was told by Mary that he was "in the wrong place" (resisted). Rejected, he ceased the attempt, entered her vaginally, and ejaculated. Even though he ceased his attempt to anally assault her, the desire for this type of sexual act was strong and he later told her he was going to do an "ass job." As stated in the preceding chapter, a sexual assault that includes anal sex is of interest to the analyst. His desire for this activity, combined with Mary's description of his having a muscular upper torso and his talk of prison, suggest strongly that Mary's attacker had been institutionalized. This will be more fully discussed in the criminal personality profile.

Sexually, the offender exhibits a mixture of selfish and pseudo-unselfish behavior.

Offender Verbal Activity

We are very fortunate that the victim in this case is articulate and in control of her emotions. She gave a detailed and comprehensive description of the entire episode and provided an abundance of material from which to draw conclusions. Nowhere is this more evident than in the victim's recollection of what the rapist said and the manner in which he said it. When originally analyzing the statement, I wrote adjectives to describe what the rapist said. In so doing, an interesting picture of the offender began to emerge. Let's examine what he said and objectively describe it using adjectives.

1. He threatened to "blow your head off" and stated that he was "going to kill you." The adjective *threatening* is obvious in this situation.
2. He told her to "get out of bed," "spread your legs," and to "hold your legs up." *Commanding* would be appropriate here.
3. He related that he had just gotten out of prison, that he used to be a good Christian boy, and that he had been a nine-to-five person until he found his wife in bed with another man. I would describe this verbiage as *personal*.
4. He spoke in a *derogatory* manner when he asked if she were "half a woman."
5. He was *nonprofane*, as the victim clearly recalled that he had not used profanity during the course of the crime.
6. He was *apologetic* when he told her he was sorry she couldn't call her folks.
7. He repeatedly asked her name, if she had any kids, and if she had a husband. This would accurately be described as *inquisitive*.
8. He was *complimentary* when he told her she had nice features and a "picturesque ass."
9. He was occasionally *angry* when she wouldn't comply with his demands. In one instance, he told her he would show her how he could hurt her.
10. Finally, he was *self-demeaning* when he said she wouldn't have "screwed around" with him if he had asked her.

After examining the verbal behavior, we find that the offender exhibited a mixture of "selfish" and "pseudo-unselfish" behavior. This mixture of behavior allows us to see him as those who know him see him. I will elaborate more fully on this in the profile.

Attitudinal Change

Mary stated that the rapist's attitude changed only when he threatened her. She described the change as being verbal in nature and said he became stern "like a father correcting a child." We see here that the victim is able to differentiate the sexual assault from the offender's attitude. Her description of his change in attitude is helpful and enlightening. The rapist is in possession of a weapon, is physically larger and stronger than Mary, and has met consistent resistance. Yet his threatening attitude is described as being "stern." Certainly not the stereotypic view of a rapist, yet very typical behavior for one not desiring to hurt his victim physically.

What Preceded the Attitudinal Change

The victim stated that only when the rapist threatened her did she perceive a change in his attitude. In each instance, the factor preceding this change was resistance by Mary. Some rapists will use physical force in such situations, others will compromise or negotiate, and still others will leave. Yet this individual chose to threaten. Why? As has been pointed out earlier, the rapist engaged in a battle of wills with Mary and lost. I believe that he is used to winning in confrontations with women, and this was a situation that should have yielded a submissive woman and didn't. His frustrations are evident in his continued threats and the physical attack on the stereo.

Precautionary Actions

This case is replete with actions taken by the offender to protect his identity, facilitate his escape, and deny investigators physical or trace evidence. These actions include: (1) removing his clothing prior to the attack, thereby ensuring that Mary would be unable to provide police with their description; (2) disabling the phone, which delayed her ability to report the crime; (3) readying his escape route by having the victim show him how to unlock the door; (4) blindfolding the victim prior to turning on a light; (5) binding her ankles and wrists prior to departure; (6) wiping her vaginal area to remove semen; (7) wearing surgical gloves, which he believed would preclude the possibility of fingerprints and yet allow the sense of touch; and (8) taking the cigarette butt with him, which denies police the possibility of determining blood type from the saliva residue.

While a few precautionary measures are to be expected in such matters, the care exhibited by Mary's attacker indicates a knowledge of police forensic capabilities beyond the layman level. This area is further addressed in the "arrest history" of the criminal personality profile.

Items Taken

The rapist told the victim he wanted $20 or he would take her stereo. When advised that she didn't have the money, he took a dollar and some change from her purse. These items would be classified as valuables, but the amount is so small as to be ridiculous. I am of the opinion that he took this small amount, not out of need, but rather because he could! In other words, he was showing Mary who was in control.

The reader will recall that he threatened to take the victim's stereo and she "put him down" by telling him he would look funny carrying it around, and he later destroyed it. I don't believe that he had any intention of taking it. His exhibited behavior indicates a more sophisticated and experienced individual than the petty theft of a stereo would indicate. The offender also took his cigarette butt with him, and this would be classified as evidentiary material. Nothing of a personal nature was taken.

The victim reported that there were no previous calls, notes, or break-ins prior to the offense. Follow-up investigation determined that there had been no attempt by the offender to recontact the victim.

Purpose of the Assault

As previously mentioned, most sexual assaults service nonsexual needs. It is my opinion that the rapist in this instance was attempting to assert his masculinity. That is to say, he was expressing his male dominance over women, which he believes is his "right." Such rapists tend to be basically "selfish" in their attacks. The reader will have noted, however, a vacillation between "selfish" and "psuedo-unselfish" behavior. I am of the opinion that the "unselfish" behavior exhibited by Mary's rapist was simply another means to further exploit her. If he had been successful in having the victim even feign passion or involvement, he would have believed it was due to his ability to arouse, and thereby control, women—a characteristic of the offender that would also be found in his noncriminal associations with women.

Criminal Personality Profile

When training law enforcement personnel in the art of profiling, it has been my experience to find that the most difficult hurdle for them to overcome is their reluctance to put opinions in writing without hard facts to back them up. This is perfectly understandable, inasmuch as we have been trained not to do so. Another problem is their concern that they might be wrong in their assessment, and this is also quite natural. It must be remembered, however, that there are no absolutes in human behavior, and it is indeed rare that a criminal personality profile will perfectly match an offender. As was previously stated in Chapter 6, in some instances the profile may be completely inaccurate, and this is to be expected on occasion. However, in most cases, profiling normally is not requested until all investigative leads have been exhausted and the case is virtually at a standstill.

Some students have voiced concern that if they provide an inaccurate profile, it may mislead the investigators or cause them to overlook or disregard viable suspects who do not match the profile. While I am aware of instances in which the profile provided did not match the identified offender, I am not aware of a single instance in which the profile adversely influenced the investigation of a likely suspect. However, in an attempt to ensure that this does not happen, the following disclaimer precedes each profile prepared by members of the Behavioral Science Unit:

> It should be noted that the attached analysis is not a substitute for a thorough and well-planned investigation and should not be considered all inclusive. The information provided is based upon reviewing, analyzing, and researching criminal cases similar to the case submitted by the requesting agency. The final analysis is based upon probabilities. Note, however, that no two criminal acts or criminal personalities are exactly alike and, therefore, the offender may not always fit the profile in every category.

The following profile was prepared based on the preceding analysis and represented my opinion as to the type of individual who would have committed the crime in the manner described and for the purpose set forth above. The profile is in outline format with an explanation of my reasoning for each characteristic addressed.

Personality Characteristics

As stated, the purpose of the assault was to express or assert masculinity. The rapist is confident and overly proud of his manliness and is dominant in his relationships with the women in his life. His vacillation between "selfish" and "pseudo-unselfish" behavior during the assault in indicative of how he is perceived by those who know him. He presents different images to different people in his life. Some would describe him as a respectful and pleasant individual, while others would say he is often hostile and angry. His fruitless attempts to dominate Mary suggest that he considers himself to be a macho individual and works at projecting this image to those around him.

He is a very self-centered person who is not appreciative of criticism, constructive or otherwise. He is a "now" person who demands instant gratification of his needs and desires and would be described as an impulsive individual. Because of this characteristic, his actions are often self-defeating and he seldom achieves his goals. His failures are noted by his inability to accept responsibility, and he projects the blame for them onto others or onto circumstances beyond his control. The attitudinal changes exhibited during the attack on Mary strongly suggest that he cannot stand losing and, therefore, those who know him would state that he is a sore loser. He dislikes authority. Law enforcement officers with whom he has had contact (see Arrest History) would describe him as being cocky and arrogant to the extent of antagonizing them.

He exudes confidence and thinks of himself as superior to others, yet he associates with individuals he considers to be less than equal to him. These associates would describe him as being cool, sophisticated, and somewhat aloof. Recalling his behavior with Mary, it is obvious that he reacts negatively when his authority is challenged, whether in his imagination or in reality. Consequently, some would describe him as being easily antagonized and short-tempered.

Because of his self-centeredness, few people are allowed to get close to him. While he knows, and is known by, many people, few know very much about him. Socially, he will frequent those areas he considers equal to his station in life, primarily well-known and moderately expensive establishments. He also enjoys discos or similar establishments catering to college-age crowds. The reader will recall that he told Mary he had "seen her around." She is known to frequent locations similar to those described herein.

He is a glib talker and extremely manipulative. As mentioned, he is dominant in his relationships with women. However, if he encounters a woman he cannot dominate and totally possess, he will relentlessly pursue her. Women who have dated him over a period of time will report that he was initially charming and attentive, but eventually became overly possessive and irrationally jealous, demanding that they account for the time they spent away from him.

Race

As described by the victim, the offender is a black male. While some may feel this should be an obvious factor (as in this case), numerous rape cases have been submitted for analysis in which the victim was unsure of or unable to describe the race of her attacker. In such instances, the analyst will consider the racial makeup of the assault area, victimology, racial overtones in the offender's behavior, and/or similar attacks in which one or more victims were able to describe the offender's race.

Age

Age is the most difficult characteristic to provide. Its determination is dependent upon a number of factors, including the victim's estimate, type of items taken, the maturity exhibited in the crime, and the type of rapist believed to have been responsible for the crime.

The offender in this case is between 26 and 30 years of age. Although the victim is an educated and articulate individual, her opinion as to the age of the assailant is too general (20–30); therefore, I narrowed the span to 5 years. Mary's attacker is confident of his abilities with women and, therefore, would have selected a woman who approximates his own age range. He is not the type of personality that would attack helpless or hopeless individuals such as children or the elderly. His ego demands that he attack women he considers to be worthy of his time. With this type of rapist (and in the absence of other information), I will generally place his age range 3 to 4 years on either side of the victim's age. In this case, however, an older individual is indicated. If working on a series of rapes committed by this type of person, I would average the age of the victims and repeat the process.

Arrest History

The precautionary actions taken by the rapist demonstrate sophistication obtained through either repeated offenses or previous arrests for similar crimes. In this instance, the offender exhibits an inordinate amount of forensic knowledge, which leads me to believe he has previously been arrested for rape and/or breaking and entering. His obvious desire to assault Mary anally, coupled with a muscular upper torso suggests that he has also been incarcerated in prison and participated in upper-body exercises.

His lifestyle (see Residence) and low income (see Employment) indicate that he is involved in other criminal ventures. For this reason, I believe he may be involved in the sale of narcotics and has been arrested for this in the past. I don't believe he is an addict, in that he did not steal items of value from Mary's residence. In fact, he destroyed a valuable (and easily fenced) stereo.

Marital Status

The behaviors exhibited by Mary's rapist reveal that he is a macho-type male with a dominant attitude toward women. Such individuals who have come to my attention typically have married while in their late teens or early twenties. His attitude toward women is such that his relationships with them are relatively short-lived. For these reasons, I believe him to be either separated or divorced. While he was living with his wife, the relationship involved a great deal of strife, and friends would have noted this. While not physically abusive toward her, he would have abused her emotionally. Typically, he would leave her stranded following an argument away from home and in the company of others.

Residence

The amount of time the rapist spent with Mary provides two significant pieces of information: (1) he was familiar with her routine, and (2) he felt comfortable in the socioeconomic environment in which the assault occurred. The intelligence (see Education) of the rapist is such that he would not assault within an area where he would be recognized or feel uncomfortable. Therefore, he resides in similar-type property (rental and middle class) in another area of town. He will reside with a black female who is faithful to him but whom he regards as just one in a series of women he uses and discards. The residence is an apartment or town house and is rental property. It is nicely furnished and includes an array of video and audio equipment. It serves as a gathering point for large numbers of people at various times of the day or night, which may have caused suspicious neighbors to alert the police.

Education

The offender is educated beyond the high-school level. His verbiage during the assault, the victim's opinion of him, and his strong denial of "hanging around those punks" (students) led me to this opinion. It is possible that his post–high school education was obtained while he was incarcerated. As a student, he achieved above-average grades and exhibited potential for high academic achievement. Because he dislikes authority, it is improbable that he obtained a 4-year degree or utilized his education in gainful employment. Friends and associates would consider him well above average in intelligence and would often seek his advice and counsel. Because of his intelligence and disdain for having others above him, he is considered a leader rather than a follower.

Military History

In determining whether or not an offender served in the military, I consider the age factor. The draft was eliminated in 1972, and the probability of an offender having served after that time is greatly diminished. Therefore, if he is believed to have been 18 or older in 1972, this fact would suggest a high probability of veteran status. If, however, he was born after 1954, it would be less likely that he served in the armed forces.

The offender's strong dislike for authority and regimentation diminishes the possibility of his having served in the military. If, however, he did serve, it would have been as a member of the enlisted ranks and the likelihood of his having been honorably discharged is minimal. His desire to project a macho image would indicate service in the ground forces.

Employment

If employed, he will be working in a job for which he is overqualified. His work performance will reflect an attitudinal problem, and he will complain of being bored. His supervisors will report frustration with his performance because of his potential for excellence. He is frequently late or absent and takes offense at being chastised. His employment is a front, and his primary source of income is from the sale of narcotics or other illegal activities.

Transportation

In keeping with his lifestyle and image, he will operate a two-door vehicle, 2 to 4 years old. It would be described as being flashy, brightly painted, and well maintained. He spends a great deal of time in his car and loves to "cruise." He is strongly associated with his car, and his friends would describe him and his car as inseparable.

Appearance and Grooming

He is a very neat individual whose normal attire is contemporary, with designer jeans at the lower end of his dress style. He takes a great deal of pride in his personal and physical appearance and is critical of those who don't do the same. He exercises regularly and maintains a high level of physical fitness. The women he associates with must be equally conscious of their appearance. He has an expensive wardrobe that is beyond his known financial means. He has regular appointments to have his hair styled and is meticulous about body cleanliness, often bathing or changing clothes two to three times a day.

The reader will note that the profile set forth above was phrased in common terminology and in such a way that those who know the offender would be able to recognize him from this description.

Summary

The first and most important step in profiling an unidentified rapist is to obtain a detailed statement from the victim. Then I analyze the statement to determine whether the offender's verbal, sexual, and physical behavior exhibits a selfish or pseudo-unselfish intent. The intent exhibited provides information about how the rapist perceives women.

Having formed my opinion as to his intent, I then use the rapist classifications developed by Burgess, Groth, and Holmstrom to attempt to determine the motivation or purpose of the sexual assault.

Finally, I describe the offender as I perceive him to be, in a manner that would enable those who know him to recognize him.

References

Groth, A. N., Burgess, A. W., and Holmstrom, L. L. "Rape: Power, Anger and Sexuality." *American Journal of Psychiatry*, Vol. 134, No. 11, November 1977, pp. 1239–1243.

Hazelwood, R. R., and Harpold, J. "Rape: The Dangers of Providing Confrontational Advice." *FBI Law Enforcement Bulletin*, June 1986, pp. 1–5.

Child Molesters—A Behavioral Analysis for Law Enforcement

9

KENNETH V. LANNING

Introduction

The term *child molester* is fairly common and is known to and used by professionals and nonprofessionals alike, including law enforcement officers. Although *Webster's New World Dictionary* (1968) defines *molest* as "to annoy, interfere with, or meddle with so as to trouble or harm," when combined with the word *child* it has generally come to convey sexual abuse of some type.

In spite of its common usage, it is surprising how many different images and variations of meanings the term *child molester* conveys for different individuals. For many, it brings to mind the image of a dirty old man in a wrinkled raincoat, hanging around a school playground with a bag of candy to lure little children. For some, the child molester is a stranger to his victim, not a father having sex with his daughter. For others, the child molester is one who exposes himself to or fondles children without engaging in vaginal or anal intercourse. Still others believe the child molester is a nonviolent offender. Dr. A. Nicholas Groth (1982), one of the leading experts on sexual victimization of children, differentiates between nonviolent *child molesters* who "essentially coax or pressure the child into sexual activity" (p. 131) and violent *child rapists* who "overpower and/or threaten to harm their victims" (p. 132). For law enforcement officers, the term *child molester* is more likely to conform to a legal definition of sexual molestation set forth in the penal code. Dr. Groth (1980) defines a sexual offender against young people, or child molester, as "a significantly older individual whose conscious sexual desires and responses are directed, either partially or exclusively, toward prepubertal children (pedophilia) and/or pubescent children (hebephilia) to whom he or she may be directly related (incest) or not" (p. 3).

For purposes of this chapter, a child molester will be defined as a significantly older individual who *engages* in any type of sexual activity with individuals legally defined as children. In using the term *child molester* no distinctions will be made between male and female, single and repeat offenses, violent and nonviolent offenders. No distinctions will be made as to whether the child victims are prepubescent or pubescent, known or unknown, related or unrelated to the offender. Finally, no distinctions will be made based on the type of sexual activity engaged in by the offender. Although such distinctions may have important legal and evaluation significance, they have no bearing on whether or not an individual is labeled a child molester. For law enforcement purposes, a child molester is simply an individual who engages in illegal sexual activity with children.

Although use of the term child molester has been, and continues to be, commonplace, recent publicity and awareness concerning sexual abuse of children has led to more frequent use of the term *pedophile*. At one time, this term was almost exclusively used by psychologists and psychiatrists. Dr. Groth's definition of a child molester refers to sexual attraction toward prepubertal children as "pedophilia" and sexual attraction toward pubertal children as "hebephilia." Although use of the term *hebephile* is still rare, television, radio, and the print media frequently refer to those who sexually abuse children as "pedophiles." The term is also being used more and more by law enforcement personnel. It has even entered their slang, with some officers talking about investigating a "pedo case" or being assigned to a "pedo squad."

The *Diagnostic and Statistical Manual of Mental Disorders* (*DSM III*) of the American Psychiatric Association (1980) defines pedophilia as "the act or fantasy of engaging in sexual activity with prepubertal children as a repeatedly preferred or exclusive method of achieving sexual excitement" (p. 271). There are several criteria in this definition that must be emphasized. First, it mentions both the *act* and the *fantasy* of engaging in sexual activity. Second, it refers to this sexual activity as being with *prepubertal* children. And third, it states that this activity is the *preferred* or *exclusive* method of achieving sexual excitement. In *DSM III* pedophilia is classified as a paraphilia, one of the psychosexual disorders. Technically, pedophilia is a psychiatric diagnosis, which can only be made by qualified psychologists or psychiatrists. The word *pedophile* is a diagnostic term, not a legal one.

However, its increasing use has, to some degree, brought this term outside the exclusive purview of psychiatric diagnosis. Just as anyone can refer to another as being "paranoid" without implying a psychiatric diagnosis or psychiatric expertise, a social worker, prosecutor, or law enforcement officer can refer to an individual who has sexually victimized a child as a pedophile. When the term is used by criminal justice personnel, the *DSM III* criterion for pedophilia (attraction to only prepubertal children) usually is not intended. *Webster's New Collegiate Dictionary* (1979) gives a layman's definition for *pedophilia*, which defines it simply as a "sexual perversion in which children are the preferred sexual object" (p. 838). For purposes of this chapter, a pedophile will be defined as a significantly older individual who *prefers* to have sex with individuals legally considered children. The pedophile is one whose sexual fantasies and erotic imagery focus on children.

It is important to realize that to refer to someone as a pedophile is to say only that the individual has a sexual preference for children. It says little or nothing about the other aspects of the person's character and personality. The idea that someone is not a pedophile simply because he is nice, goes to church, works hard, is kind to animals, etc., is absurd. Pedophiles span the full spectrum, from saints to monsters and those in between. In spite of this fact, over and over again pedophiles are believed, not charged, or acquitted simply because they are "nice guys."

It is also important to recognize that pedophiles *prefer* to have sex with children. They can and do have sex with adults. Adult sexual relationships are more difficult for some pedophiles than for others. Some pedophiles have sex with adults as part of their efforts to gain or continue their access to preferred children. For example, they might have occasional sex with a single mother to ensure continued access to her children.

What then, if any, is the difference between a child molester and a pedophile? For many the terms have become synonymous. The media frequently make no distinction and use the terms interchangeably. In many instances, there may be no valid reason to differentiate between the terms, as long as the intended audience understands their intended meaning. However, it is the author's opinion that labeling all child molesters as pedophiles is, on balance, unfortunate and confusing. Even the non–mental health professional needs to understand that there are differences between the types of individuals who sexually abuse children. However, the focus of this chapter will be restricted to law enforcement considerations for making such distinctions.

Are all pedophiles child molesters? To a certain degree, this is a matter of semantics. By the definitions set forth in this chapter, the answer is no. A child molester is an individual who sexually molests children. An individual might have a sexual preference for children and might fantasize about having sex with them and, thus, would be a pedophile. But if he (or she) doesn't act out, then he is not a child molester. Some pedophiles might act out their fantasies in legal ways by engaging in sexual activity with adults who look (small stature, flat chested, no body or pubic hair, etc.) and/or act (immature, childlike dress, baby talk, etc.) like children. Others may act out in child fantasy "games" with adult prostitutes. It is almost impossible to estimate how many pedophiles exist who have never molested a child. What society can or should do with regard to such individuals is an interesting area for discussion, but beyond the role of law enforcement. People cannot be arrested for their fantasies.

Are all child molesters pedophiles? Again by the definitions set forth, the answer is no. A pedophile is an individual who prefers to have sex with children. However, an individual might prefer to have sex with an adult partner, but for any number of reasons might decide to have sex with a child. Such reasons might include simple availability, curiosity, or a need to hurt a loved one of the molested child. The sexual fantasies of such individuals do not necessarily focus on children.

Many child molesters are, in fact, pedophiles, and many (maybe most) pedophiles are child molesters. But they are not necessarily one and the same. The law enforcement officer might argue that it is his job to put individuals who violate the law in jail, and that whether or not that offender is a pedophile is of no importance to him. However, distinctions between types of child molesters can have important and valuable implications for the law enforcement investigation of child sexual abuse. This chapter will set forth a model for law enforcement that divides child molesters into two broad categories and several patterns of behavior. These categories are not intended for use by mental health professionals or clinicians. They are intended for use by law enforcement officers in developing the evidence needed to identify, arrest, and convict child molesters. If the investigating officer already has enough evidence to convict a child molester, then it is of small importance whether the molester is a pedophile or not. But if the investigator is still attempting to develop such evidence, the distinction can be invaluable.

Other Typologies

Probably the most commonly used typology for child molesters today is the one developed by Dr. Groth (1980). He classifies sexual offenders against underage people into two groups on the basis of whether this involvement "constitutes a persistent pattern (a fixation) or a new activity or change (a regression) in their sexual orientations or lifestyles" (p. 6). Dr. Groth (1982) further explains that the Fixated Child Molester is one "whose primary sexual orientation is towards children" (p. 133), and the Regressed Child Molester is one "whose sexual involvement with a child is a clear departure, under stress, from a primary sexual orientation towards agemates" (p. 133). In essence, Dr. Groth's Fixated Child Molester is a pedophile in the *DSM III* sense. He prefers children for sexual partners and identifies closely with them. The Regressed Child Molester really does not fit the *DSM III* criteria for pedophilia. He prefers agemates for sexual partners, but because of some stress in his life, he substitutes a child for an adult relationship.

In another typology, Dr. Park Elliott Dietz (1983), a noted forensic psychiatrist, divides all sex offenders, including child molesters, into two broad categories: Situational or Preferential. Dr. Dietz explains that the Situational Sex Offender suffers from no identifiable psychosexual mental disorder, but engages in sex offenses as a result of a wide variety of situational factors such as "intoxication, social stressors, mood and mental conditions" (p. 1489). Such offenders might be "reasonably well adjusted and nonparaphiliac men who committed first offenses while drinking heavily, after being fired, during their wives' pregnancies, following divorce, or during a depressive, manic, or schizophrenic episode" (p. 1489). The Preferential Sex Offender is the individual "whose preferred or exclusive method of achieving sexual arousal involves unconventional mental imagery or acts" (p. 1489) and who is "regarded by contemporary psychiatry as suffering from a diagnosable psychosexual disorder" (p. 1489). Dr. Dietz clearly points out that "many, probably most, individuals with deviant patterns of sexual arousal do not commit crimes in the service of these impulses" (p. 1490). A person can have a paraphilia without being a sex offender. Dr. Dietz also points out that the same offense can be committed by either a preferential or situational sex offender. "For example, babysitters who molest the children in their care include individuals who will have a lifelong preference for sexual contact with children (pedophilia) and those who, with no particular interest in such activity, exploit the opportunity to do something different and forbidden" (p. 1490).

Need for Law Enforcement Typology

It is the author's observation that more and more often the terms *child molester* and *pedophile* are being used interchangeably by individuals, including police officers, who are learning about child sexual abuse. The concepts and typologies of Drs. Groth and Dietz are the foundation for the author's strong belief that not all child molesters are pedophiles. Their work provides the basis for the law enforcement typology set forth in this chapter.

Is there any value for law enforcement in categorizing child molesters? The author believes there is. Mental health professionals and therapists categorize offenders primarily for therapeutic purposes. Although it is important that the various disciplines involved in dealing with the sexual victimization of children communicate with one another, each must also develop the knowledge and skills necessary to fulfill its individual responsibilities. Law enforcement frequently has accepted offender categories and characteristics developed by therapists and criminologists. Often these typologies primarily serve the needs of mental health professionals and have limited application to those of law enforcement. They usually are developed from data collected *from* offenders *after* arrest or conviction and often reflect unsubstantiated information about prearrest behavior. It is the prearrest or preidentification behavior of child molesters that is of most value to law enforcement.

The typology set forth in this chapter is based on the concepts of mental health professionals (Dr. Groth, Dr. Dietz, and others) but modified and adapted from a law enforcement perspective as a result of the observations, experience, and analysis of the author. Psychological terms and characteristics are deliberately avoided. The sole purpose of this typology is to be of practical use to law enforcement. Although others concerned with the sexual abuse of children may be interested in the dynamics of this typology, any value or benefit to them is an unplanned bonus. The purpose of this typology is not to gain insight or understanding about *why* child molesters have sex with children, in order to help or treat them, but to recognize and evaluate *how* child molesters have sex with children, in order to identify, arrest, and convict them. Treatment—which generally follows arrest and conviction—is an issue outside the responsibility of law enforcement.

The author is frequently asked by police officers and FBI agents for advice or guidance about dealing with "a child molester." The assistance frequently is requested as if there were only one kind of child molester. What evidence to look for, whether there are additional victims, how to interview a suspect, etc., all depend on the type of child molester involved.

Child sexual abuse cases can be difficult to prove. Frequently, there is only the word of a child against that of an adult. In addition, many factors combine to make it difficult and possibly traumatic for children to testify in court. In spite of some recent advances that make testimony easier for the child victim or witness, it is the author's belief that a primary objective of every investigation of child sexual abuse should be to prove the case without needing the courtroom testimony of the child.

The child victim should be carefully interviewed, the information obtained should be evaluated and assessed, and appropriate investigative action should be taken. However, the investigator should proceed as though he had information about a crime from a reliable source whose identity cannot be revealed. He knows what happened; now he must prove it without the testimony of the child. This may not always be possible, but it should be the investigative goal. Many children can testify in court if necessary.

One way to avoid child victim testimony is to be knowledgeable about other evidence that might be available to prove the case. Frequently, there is more evidence available than the investigator realizes. Much of this evidence can be identified and located only if the investigator has a solid understanding of the offender behavior patterns involved and knows what to look for.

Law Enforcement Typology

For investigative purposes, individuals who sexually molest children can be divided into two broad categories: Situational and Preferential.

Situational

The Situational Child Molester does not have a true sexual preference for children, but engages in sex with children for varied and sometimes complex reasons. For such a child molester, sexuality with children may range from a once-in-a-lifetime act to a long-term pattern of behavior, sometimes approaching that of the Preferential Child Molester. The Situational Child Molester usually has fewer different child victims. Other vulnerable individuals, such as the old, sick, disabled, handicapped, etc., may also be at risk of sexual victimization by him or her. In fact, most of the day-care center child sexual abuse cases studied by the author do not appear to involve typical pedophile (preferential molester) behavior. Such activity with children often goes far beyond mere sexual preference for children. Other motivational needs and dynamics seem to be involved. The Situational Child Molester who sexually abuses children in a day care center might leave that job and begin to sexually abuse, for example, elderly people in a nursing home at a new job. It is the author's undocumented opinion that the number of Situational Child Molesters is larger and increasing more quickly than that of Preferential Child Molesters. Within this category, at least four major patterns of behavior emerge (see Table 9.1):

Regressed. This pattern of behavior is essentially as described by Dr. Groth in his typology. Such an offender usually has low self-esteem and poor coping skills. He is a reasonably "normal" individual who turns to children as a sexual substitute for the preferred peer sex partner. His main criterion for victims seems to be availability, which is

Table 9.1. Situational Child Molester

	Regressed	Morally Indiscriminate	Sexually Indiscriminate	Inadequate
Basic characteristic	Poor coping skills	User of people	Sexual experimentation	Social misfit
Motivation	Substitution	Why not?	Boredom	Insecurity and curiosity
Victim criteria	Availability	Vulnerability and opportunity	New and different	Nonthreatening
Method of operation	Coercion	Lure, force, or manipulation	Involve in existing activity	Exploits size advantage
Pornography collection	Possible	Sadomasochistic; detective magazines	Highly likely; varied nature	Likely

why many of these offenders molest their own children. His principal method of operations is to coerce the child into having sex. The author has seen few cases involving these "regular," "normal," "good" offenders who molest because they are under stress, although such child molesters probably exist in relatively large numbers. This may be attributed to the fact that the cases seen by the author tend to be the more extreme ones. This type of situational molester may or may not *collect* child or adult pornography.

Morally Indiscriminate. This pattern of behavior seems to be the one most frequently overlooked when the dynamics of child molesters are discussed. Yet, it is the author's observation that this is a growing category of child molesters. More and more cases seen by the author seem to involve this pattern of behavior. For this individual, the sexual abuse of children is simply part of a general pattern of abuse in his life. He is a user and abuser of people. He abuses his wife, friends, employer, co-workers, etc. He lies, cheats, steals, abuses, etc., anytime he thinks he can get away with it. He molests children for a simple reason—"Why not?" His primary victim criteria are vulnerability and opportunity. He has the urge, a child is there, and so he acts. He typically uses force, lures, or manipulation to obtain his victims. Although his victims frequently are strangers or acquaintances, it is important for the investigator to realize that the victims can also be the offender's own children. The incestuous father or mother might be this morally indiscriminate offender. He frequently collects adult pornography of a sadomasochistic nature or detective magazines. He may have some child pornography, especially that which depicts pubescent children.

Sexually Indiscriminate. This pattern of behavior is the most difficult to define. Although the previously described morally indiscriminate offender often is a sexual experimenter, this individual differs in that he (or she) appears to be discriminating in his behavior, except when it comes to sex. He is the "try-sexual," i.e., he is willing to try anything sexual. Much of his behavior is similar to the Preferential Child Molester's. However, while he may have clearly defined paraphilic or sexual preferences (bondage, sadomasochism, etc.), he has no real sexual preference for children. His basic characteristic is sexual experimentation, and he is motivated toward sex with children out of boredom. His main criteria for such children are that they are new and different. He typically involves children in previously existing sexual activity. Again, it is important to realize these children may be his own. Such an individual may also provide his children to other adults as part of some group sex, spouse-swapping activity, or even as part of some bizarre or satanic ritual. Of all Situational Molesters he is by far the most likely to collect pornography. However, child pornography will only be a small portion of his potentially large and varied collection.

Inadequate. This pattern of behavior is also difficult to define. It includes those suffering from psychoses, eccentric personality disorders (schizoid, schizotypal, etc.), mental retardation, and senility. In layman's terms, this type of molester is the social misfit, the withdrawn, the individual who marches to the beat of his own drummer. It might be the shy teenager who has no friends his own age or the eccentric loner who still lives with his parents. Although most such individuals are harmless and not criminals, some can be child molesters and, in a few cases, even child killers. This pattern of behavior was previously almost the stereotype of a child molester (dirty old man in wrinkled raincoat), but in recent years it has been ignored by many. Although not a common type of molester, such offenders do exist. They seem to become sexually involved with children out of insecurity or curiosity. They find children to be nonthreatening *objects* with whom they can explore their sexual fantasies. Often their sexual activity with children is the result of built-up impulses. Some of these individuals find it difficult to express anger and hostility, which then builds until it explodes, possibly against the child victim. Because of mental or emotional problems, some might take out their frustration in cruel sexual torture of children. However, the victim could just as easily be a 79-year-old woman as a 9-year-old girl. Each represents a nonthreatening vagina. This type of offender might collect pornography, but probably it will be of an adult nature.

Almost any child molester is capable of violence or even murder to avoid identification. However, in spite of a few notable exceptions (e.g., Theodore Frank in California, Gary Arthur Bishop in Utah), most of the sexually motivated child murders profiled and assessed by the FBI Behavioral Science Unit have involved Situational Child Molesters, expecially those exhibiting the morally indiscriminate and inadequate patterns of behavior. Sadistic and morally indiscriminate preferential molesters (pedophiles) who kill will be discussed later in this chapter.

Preferential

The Preferential Child Molester has a definite sexual preference for children. All things being equal, given a choice between a child and an adult sex partner, the Preferential Child Molester would choose the child. This chapter will not attempt to explain why these offenders would choose a child. Whatever the reason, such individuals do exist. Their sexual fantasies and erotic imagery focus on children. They have sex with children, not because of some situational stress or insecurity, but because they are sexually attracted to and prefer children. They can possess a wide variety of character traits, but engage in highly predictable sexual behavior. Although they may be smaller in number than the Situational Child Molester, they each have the potential to molest large numbers of victims. For many of them, their problem is not only the quality of their sex drive (attraction to children), but also the quantity of their sex drive (need for frequent and repeated sex with children). Within this category at least three major patterns of behavior emerge (see Table 9.2.).

Table 9.2. Preferential Child Molester

	Seduction	Introverted	Sadistic
Common characteristics	1. Sexual preference for children 2. Collect child pornography and/or erotica		
Motivation	Identification	Fear of communication	Need to inflict pain
Victim criteria	Age and gender preferences	Strangers or very young	Age and gender preferences
Method of operation	Seduction process	Nonverbal sexual contact	Lure or force

Seduction. This pattern characterizes the offender who engages children in sexual activity by seducing them. He seduces children the same way that men seduce women and women seduce men—with attention, affection, and gifts. He seduces children over a period of time by gradually lowering their sexual inhibitions. Frequently his victims arrive at the point where they are willing to trade sex for the attention, affection, and other benefits they receive from the offender. Many of these offenders are simultaneously involved with multiple victims, operating what has come to be called a *child sex ring*. This may include a group of children in the same class at a school, in the same scout troop, or in the same neighborhood. The characteristic that seems to make this individual the master seducer of children, is his ability to identify with children. He knows how to talk to children—but more importantly, he knows how to listen to children. His adult status and authority are also an important part of this seduction process. In addition, he frequently selects as targets children who are victims of emotional or physical neglect.

Introverted. This pattern of behavior characterizes the offender who has a preference for children but lacks the interpersonal skills necessary to seduce them. Therefore, he typically engages in nonpersonal sexual contact with children. Simply stated, he engages in a minimal amount of verbal communication with his victims and usually molests strangers or very young children. He is like the old child molester stereotype in that he is more likely to hang around playgrounds and other areas where children congregate and watch them or engage them in brief sexual encounters. He may expose himself to children or make obscene phone calls to children. He may utilize the services of a child prostitute. Unable to figure out any other way to gain access to a child, he might even marry a woman and molest his own children. He is very likely to molest his children sexually from the time they are infants. He can be similar to the previously described Inadequate Situational Molester, except that he has a definite sexual preference for children and therefore his selection of only them as victims is more predictable.

Sadistic. This pattern of behavior characterizes the offender who has a sexual preference for children, but who, in order to be aroused or gratified, must inflict pain or suffering on the child victim. Although it is extremely unpleasant to think about such offenders, they do exist. They typically use lures or force to gain access to their victims. They are more likely than other Preferential Child Molesters to abduct and even murder their victims. There have been some cases in which seduction-type molesters have become sadistic molesters. It is not known whether the sadistic needs develop later in life or were always there and just surfaced for some reason. In either case, it is fortunate that sadistic child molesters do not appear to be large in number.

It should be fairly obvious that the individual described in this typology as the Preferential Child Molester is the previously described pedophile. Why then refer to such an individual by this new term and not simply continue the term *pedophile*? The author believes there are two valid reasons for the new term. First, not all pedophiles are in fact child molesters. Second, as previously mentioned, there are potential conflicts when law enforcement personnel label an offender with psychiatric terminology. Can a police officer state or testify that a certain offender is a pedophile? The term Preferential Child Molester may be a compromise between the two professions. This does not alter the fact that the term pedophile is being used and will continue to be used more and more often by a wide variety of non–mental health professionals, including police officers. In this typology the term Preferential Child Molester is being used to refer to the pedophile who sexually molests or exploits children.

Since there are federal, state, or local laws that deal with crimes such as the possession and distribution of child pornography, law enforcement officers will sometimes become involved in the investigation of pedophiles and others who have not technically sexually molested children but have sexually *exploited* them. Therefore, pedophiles who do not physically or legally molest children sexually might become of investigative interest to local or federal law enforcement. It is the author's opinion that any individual who collects and/or distributes child pornography actually perpetuates the sexual abuse of the child portrayed. It is no different from the circulation of sexually explicit pictures taken by a rapist of his victim during the rape. Such collectors and distributors of child pornography are in essence child molesters.

Application of Typology

In applying this typology, the law enforcement officer must recognize the difficulty of attempting to put complex human behavior into a small number of neat and concise categories. There will always be exceptions and difficulties. This typology involves two broad categories of child molesters (Situational and Preferential) and seven subcategories or patterns of behavior. These patterns of behavior are not necessarily mutually exclusive.

Combinations

A preferential child molester (pedophile) might have other psychosexual disorders, personality disorders, or even psychoses and/or be involved in other types of criminal activity. A pedophile's sexual interest in children might be combined with other sexual deviations (paraphilias) to include activity with children involving indecent exposure (exhibitionism), obscene phone calls (scatophilia), animals (zoophilia), urination (urophilia), defecation (coprophilia), binding (bondage), infliction of pain (sadism, masochism), real or simulated death (necrophilia), and other behaviors. The preferential child molester is interested in sex with children that might, in some cases, involve other sexual deviations. The morally or sexually indiscriminate child molester is interested in a variety of sexual deviations that might, in some cases, involve children.

The author is aware of cases in which pedophiles were also psychopathic con artists, paranoid survivalists, or even killers. One particularly difficult offender to deal with is the morally indiscriminate, preferential child molester. If an offender has a sexual preference for children and at the same time has no conscience, there is no limit as to how or how often he might sexually victimize children. Such an offender is also likely to abduct and/or murder children. However, while his preferential sexual interest in children affects his selection of victims, most of his behavior is determined by his more pervasive lack of conscience, and he is best viewed as a morally indiscriminate offender or, in some cases, a serial killer. He should be investigated and interviewed as such.

Sex Rings

When investigating cases involving multiple offenders, such as a day-care center or other type of sex ring, the investigator must recognize that the subjects involved could include any combination of molester types. The staff at a day-care center where children are being molested might include a seduction molester, a few morally indiscriminate molesters, or any other combination of the previously discussed types of molesters. A satanic cult involved in sexually abusing children might include morally indiscriminate, sexually indiscriminate, inadequate, and sadistic patterns of behavior. The behavior of the individuals involved must be carefully evaluated in order to develop appropriate investigative and interview strategies.

An important application of this typology is the simple recognition that not all child molesters are the same. Not all child molesters are pedophiles. Not all child molesters are passive, nonaggressive people. Child molesters come in all shapes, sizes, races, sexes, and ages and are motivated by a wide variety of influences. There is no single investigative or interview technique to deal with all of them.

Incest Cases

As an example, let's look at the investigation of incest. It has become commonly accepted that incestuous fathers are typically regressed child molesters who molest only their own children, do not collect child pornography, and are best dealt with in noncriminal treatment programs. However, the author has seen cases in which the incestuous father appears to be a seduction or introverted preferential child molester (pedophile) who married simply to gain access to children. In many cases, the father has molested children outside the marriage or children in previous marriages.

Such individuals frequently look for women who already have children who meet their age and gender preferences. Their marriages usually last only as long as there are children in the victim preference range. In today's more liberal society, such an offender frequently no longer marries the woman, but simply moves in with her and her children. On some occasions, offenders merely befriend the mother and do not even pretend romantic interest in her but only express a desire to be a "father figure" for her children and/or help with expenses. Another technique is to marry a woman and adopt children or take in foster children. The last and least desirable technique for the preferential child molester who uses marriage to gain access to children is to have his own children. This is the least desirable method because it requires the offender to have sex with his wife and because there are few guarantees that his offspring will be of the preferred sex. In order to engage in sexual relations with his wife, the pedophile must create a fantasy. To aid in this fantasy some pedophiles have their wives dress, talk, and/or behave like children. In some cases wives are asked to shave their pubic hair. After the birth of a baby of the preferred sex, such pedophiles may terminate or greatly reduce sexual relations with their wives. Of course, these facts are difficult for the police investigator to learn. Most wives or even ex-wives would be embarrassed to admit such sexual activity or lack of it. They usually blame themselves for their husband's sexual problems.

Other incestuous fathers are morally indiscriminate individuals whose sexual abuse of children is only a small part of the problem. They are cunning, manipulative individuals who can convincingly deny the allegations against them or, if the evidence is overwhelming, claim they need "help with their problem." Their personality disorder is more pervasive and serious than even pedophilia and probably more difficult to treat.

Female Offenders

Where do female child molesters fit into this typology? The answer is unknown at this time. The author is not aware of a sufficient number of cases involving female offenders to include them in this typology. However, it is the author's opinion that sexual abuse of children by females is far more prevalent than most people believe.

Many people believe that sex between an older woman and an adolescent boy is not molestation but a "rite of passage." The boy should feel lucky, not victimized. Sexual activity between women and young children is difficult to identify. Females are the primary child caretakers in our society and therefore dress, bathe, change, examine, and touch children with little suspicion. The author is aware of several cases in which women openly admitted putting their mouths on the genitals of children but claimed this was a family technique to calm the child. There are frequently stories that this and/or similar acts are part of a certain culture or custom. This may or may not be true. However, the mere fact that it is a custom does not preclude its being abuse. In some cultures it is the custom to mutilate the genitalia (female circumcision) of young girls or to kill females who have publicly embarrassed the family. Is this not abuse?

Many of the recent cases involving sexual abuse in day-care centers involve female offenders. There are many cases in which females actively participate in the sexual abuse of children with an adult male accomplice. However, the author has not yet seen a case in which a female offender fits the dynamics of the preferential child molester. This is a new area that needs additional research and study.

Adolescent Offenders

Another area that has recently received increased attention involves adolescent offenders. In past years, adolescent child molesters were usually dismissed with "Boys will be boys" or "He's just going through a stage." Adolescent child molesters can fit into either broad category and any of the patterns of behavior described in this chapter. It is frightening to consider that many of the cases seen by the author involving adolescent child molesters seem to fit the morally indiscriminate pattern of behavior. The adolescent felt like doing it, did it, and can't understand what all the fuss is about. However, the biggest mistake would be to assume that all adolescent child molesters are either good boys just sexually experimenting or evil boys who need to be locked up forever. They must be carefully evaluated for proper intervention and treatment whenever possible. In addition, adolescent (and even younger) sex offenders should *always* be viewed as possible past or current victims of sexual abuse. Recognizing and then investigating this victimization can lead to the identification of additional offenders and victims. The sexual abuse of younger children by an older child should always be viewed as an indication that the older child was sexually abused.

Situational vs. Preferential

For many people, especially social welfare personnel, the term child sexual abuse is synonymous with incest, which is synonymous with a father having sex with his daughter. However, a child can be sexually molested by a relative, by an acquaintance, or by a stranger. Any of these three can be either a situational or a preferential child molester.

Sexual exploitation of children is a term used by the author to describe sexual victimization of children involving child pornography, child sex rings, and child prostitution. Offenders utilizing the services of a child prostitute may be either situational or preferential child molesters. If necessary for law enforcement purposes, they may be evaluated using the criteria set forth below. However, offenders involved in child pornography and child sex rings are predominantly preferential child molesters. Although a variety of individuals sexually abuse children, preferential child molesters (pedophiles) are the *primary* sexual exploiters of children.

An important application of this typology is found in recognizing the highly predictable sexual behavior patterns of preferential child molesters or pedophiles. For this reason, the author feels it is important for the law enforcement investigator to at least attempt to determine whether an offender is a situational or a preferential molester.

It is the author's opinion that there probably are more situational than preferential molesters. However, each situational molester is likely to abuse only a small number of children in a lifetime. A preferential molester might molest 10, 50, 100, or even 1,000 children in a lifetime. To say that someone has a sexual preference for children says little or nothing about his character and personality. However, it appears to say a great deal about his sexual behavior patterns. Although pedophiles vary greatly, their sexual behavior is repetitive and highly predictable. Occasionally it seems as if they are being produced in a factory somewhere. Knowledge of these sexual behavior patterns or characteristics is extremely valuable to the law enforcement investigator.

It is these highly predictable and repetitive behavior patterns that make cases involving preferential child molesters far easier to investigate than those involving situational child molesters. If enough of these characteristics can be identified through investigation, the majority of the remaining ones can be assumed to be present. Most of these indicators mean little by themselves. However, as they are identified and accumulated through investigation, they can constitute reason to believe a certain offender is a preferential child molester as set forth in this typology. The investigator then has sufficient reason to believe the offender has many of the other characteristics not yet known or learned through investigation. You do not have proof beyond a reasonable doubt, but probable cause to believe he possesses these traits.

Preferential Child Molester Characteristics

The four major characteristics of the preferential child molester (pedophile) are (1) long-term and persistent pattern of behavior, (2) children as preferred sexual objects, (3) well-developed techniques in obtaining victims, and (4) sexual fantasies that focus on children. These characteristics, together with the listed indicators, will assist the investigator in identifying the preferential child molester and collecting the evidence necessary to arrest and convict him. At the outset, it must be stated and emphasized that *the indicators alone mean little.* Their significance and weight comes as they are accumulated and come to form a pattern of behavior. If the investigator determines the existence of enough of these indicators, probable cause to believe that the offender is a preferential offender can be developed.

1. Long-Term and Persistent Pattern of Behavior: Indicators of Characteristic

Sexual Abuse in Background. Although most victims of child sexual abuse do not become offenders, research seems to indicate that most offenders are former victims. If a suspect is developed, it would be well worth the investigator's time and effort to determine if he had ever been the victim of sexual abuse and what the nature of the abuse was (age at which it occurred, relationship with offender, acts performed, etc.).

Limited Social Contacts as Teenagers. The pedophile's sexual preference for children usually begins in early adolescence. Therefore, during his teenage years he is likely to have exhibited little interest in opposite sex agemates. Since most teenage social life revolves around dating, his contacts will be or have been limited. As with several of these indicators, this fact *alone* means little. Many teenagers have limited dating experiences.

Premature Separation from Military. If an individual is dishonorably discharged for molesting children, there is not much doubt about the indicator's value. However, it has been far more common for this type of individual to be separated from the military with no specific reason given or available. The military, like most organizations, is frequently interested only in getting rid of such individuals and not necessarily in prosecuting them. Fortunately, this attitude seems to be changing.

Frequent and Unexpected Moves. When they are identified, pedophiles are frequently "asked" to leave town. This may be done by someone in authority, by the parent of one of the victims, or by an employer. This was, and still is, a common way to deal with the problem. Don't prosecute him, just get rid of the guy. The end result is that pedophiles frequently show a pattern of living someplace for several years with a good job, and then suddenly and for no apparent good reason, pulling up stakes, moving and changing jobs. If you conduct an investigation in the place they moved from, chances are you will find no official record of what happened. The pedophile will usually have an "explanation" for the move, but it probably will not reflect the true circumstances.

Prior Arrests. In some cases, pedophiles have previously been arrested for child molestation or sexual abuse. Certainly such an arrest record is a major indicator, particularly if the arrest goes back many years or is repeated. However, investigators must also be alert for the fact that pedophiles may have arrest records for things that do not appear to involve sexual abuse. This might include impersonating a police officer, passing bad checks, violating child labor laws, or other violations that may indicate a need to check further. The investigator should attempt to get copies of the reports concerning the arrests in order properly to evaluate their significance.

Multiple Victims. If investigation reveals that an individual molested multiple victims, that is a very strong indicator that the offender is a pedophile. But more important, if other factors indicate the offender is a pedophile, then a concerted effort should be made to identify the multiple victims. This clearly illustrates the value of these indicators. When you have documented enough of the indicators to allow a reasonable belief that an offender is a pedophile, then you have probable cause to believe many of the remaining indicators are present. If you know of only one victim, but have reason to believe the offender is a pedophile, then begin looking for the other victims. If a teacher who is a suspected pedophile molests one child in his class, the chances are high that he has molested or attempted to molest other children in the class as well as children in all the other classes he has taught down through the years. It is possible there are no other victims, but not probable. This is also true of incest offenders suspected of being preferential child molesters. An active pedophile could molest dozens, hundreds, or even thousands of children in a lifetime.

Planned, Repeated, Often High-Risk Attempts. Bold and repeated attempts to obtain children that have been carried out in a cunning and skillful manner are a strong indication that the offender is a pedophile. For example, what kind of person attempts to seduce a child right in front of its parents? The answer is, a pedophile.

2. Children as Preferred Sexual Objects: Indicators of Characteristic

Over 25, Single, Never Married. By itself this indicator means nothing. It has significance only when combined with several other indicators. Because they have a sexual preference for children, pedophiles usually have some degree of difficulty in sexually performing with adults. Therefore, they typically do not get married. However, some pedophiles do enter into marriage for specific reasons, and this will be further discussed below.

Lives Alone or with Parents. This indicator is closely related to the one above. Again, by itself it has little meaning. The fact that a man lives alone does not mean he is a pedophile. The fact that an individual who possesses many of the other traits discussed here also lives alone might be significant.

Limited Dating Relationships if Not Married. This is more significant than the two indicators above, but still has limited value by itself. However, a man who lives alone, has never been married, and doesn't date should arouse suspicion if he possesses other characteristics discussed here.

If Married, "Special" Relationship with Spouse. When they do marry, pedophiles seem to marry either a strong, domineering woman or a weak, passive woman-child. In any case, they must marry a woman who does not have high sexual expectations or needs, a woman for whom sex is not important. Such women do exist. A woman married to a pedophile may not realize that her husband is a pedophile, but she does know he has a "problem"—a sexual performance problem. Because she may blame herself for this problem and because of the private nature of people's sex lives, most wives will usually not reveal this information to an investigator. However, a wife, ex-wife, or girlfriend should always be considered as a possible source of information concerning the sexual preferences of an offender. Pedophiles sometimes marry for convenience or cover. Pedophiles marrying to gain access to children are discussed elsewhere in this chapter.

Excessive Interest in Children. How much interest is excessive? This is a difficult question. The answer is a warning used by U.S. Postal Inspectors to help protect people from fraud schemes: "If it sounds too good to be true, maybe it is." If someone's interest in children seems too good to be true, maybe it is. This is not proof that someone is a pedophile, but only reason to be suspicious. It becomes more significant when this excessive interest is combined with other indicators discussed here.

Associates and Circle of Friends Are Young. In addition to sexual activity, pedophiles frequently hang around and socialize with children. They may hang around school yards, arcades, shopping centers—any place where children are. Their "friends" may be male, female, or both sexes; very young or teenagers, all depending on the age and gender preferences of the pedophile.

Limited Peer Relationships. Because they cannot share the most important part of their lives (their sexual interest in children) with most adults, pedophiles may have a limited number of close adult friends. Only other pedophiles will validate their sexual behavior. If a suspected pedophile has a close adult friend, the possibility that the friend is also a pedophile must be considered.

Age and Gender Preference. Most pedophiles prefer children of a certain sex in a certain age bracket. The older the age preference of the pedophile, the more exclusive the gender preference. Pedophiles attracted to toddlers are more likely to molest boys and girls indiscriminately. A pedophile attracted to teenagers is more likely to prefer boys or girls exclusively. The preferred age bracket for the child can also vary. One pedophile might prefer boys 8 to 10, while another might prefer boys 6 to 12. Puberty seems to be an important dividing line for many pedophiles. This is only an age and gender preference, not an exclusive limitation. Any individual expressing a strong desire to care for or adopt only a child of a very specific sex and age (other than an infant) should be viewed with some suspicion.

Refers to Children as "Clean," "Pure," "Innocent," "Impish," Etc., or as Objects. Pedophiles sometimes have an idealistic view of children, which is expressed in their language and writing. Others sometimes refer to children as if they were objects, projects, or possessions. "This kid has low mileage" and "I've been working on this project for 6 months" are some typical comments.

3. Well-Developed Techniques in Obtaining Victims: Indicators of Characteristic

Skilled at Identifying Vulnerable Victims. Some pedophiles can watch a group of children for a brief period of time and then select a potential target. More often than not the selected child turns out to be from a broken home, to be the victim of emotional neglect, or to have some other need the pedophile will fill. Evidence of this ability is an indication the offender might be a pedophile, because the skill is developed through practice and experience.

Identifies with Children Better than with Adults. Pedophiles usually have the ability to identify with children. Although this indicator seems somewhat abstract, it is the trait that makes most pedophiles master seducers of children. They seem to know how to relate to children on many levels. They especially know how to *listen* to children. Typical of the pedophile is the ability to identify with children without a corresponding ability to identify with adults. They seem to blossom when they are around children, but are considerably different around adults. Many pedophiles are described as "pied pipers" who attract children.

Access to Children. This is one of the most important indicators of a pedophile. The pedophile *will* have a method of gaining access to children. Other than simply hanging around any place children congregate (schools, playgrounds, shopping centers, etc.), this is done primarily in three ways.

1. *Marriage.* Pedophiles sometimes marry women simply to gain access to children. This technique has previously been discussed.
2. *Neighborhood.* Pedophiles are frequently the nice guys in the neighborhood who like to entertain the children after school or take them on day or weekend trips.
3. *Occupation.* This includes also hobbies and vocations and is the most common method of access to children. A pedophile may seek employment where he will necessarily be in contact with children (teacher, camp counselor, babysitter, school bus driver, etc.) or where

he can eventually specialize in dealing with children (physician, dentist, minister, photographer, social worker, police officer, etc.). The pedophile may also become a Scout leader, Big Brother, foster parent, Little League coach, etc. The pedophile may operate a business that hires adolescents. The pedophile can also use any combination of these methods of access. In one case known to the author, a pedophile married, had a daughter, and molested her. He was the nice guy in the neighborhood who had the neighborhood girls over to his house for parties, at which he molested them. He was a coach for a girl's softball team, and he molested the players. He was a dentist who specialized in child patients, and he molested them.

Activities with Children Often Exclude Other Adults. The pedophile is always trying to get children into situations where there are no other adults present. On a Boy Scout hike he might suggest the fathers go into town for a beer. He will "sacrifice" and stay behind with the boys.

Seduces with Attention, Affection, and Gifts. This is the most common technique pedophiles use to have sex with children. They literally seduce the children by befriending them, talking to them, listening to them, paying attention to them, spending time with them, and buying gifts for them. If you understand the seduction process, it should not be difficult to understand why some child victims develop positive feelings for the offender. Many people can understand why an incest victim might not report his or her father, but they can't understand why a victim not related to the offender does not immediately report molestation by a neighbor, camp counselor, teacher, etc. There are many reasons for a victim not immediately reporting molestation (fear, blackmail, embarrassment, confusion), but the results of the seduction process are often ignored or not understood as such a reason.

Skilled at Manipulating Children. In order to operate a child sex ring involving simultaneous sexual relations with multiple victims, a pedophile must know how to manipulate children. This is not an easy juggling act. It requires the ability to seduce and control children. The pedophile uses seduction techniques, competition, peer pressure, child and group psychology, motivation techniques, threats, and blackmail. The pedophile must continuously recruit children into and move children out of the ring without his activity being disclosed. Part of the manipulation process is lowering the inhibitions of the children. A skilled pedophile who can get children into a situation where they must change clothing or stay with him overnight will almost always succeed in seducing them. Not all pedophiles possess these skills. The introverted preferential child molester is an example of a pedophile who typically lacks these abilities.

Has Hobbies and Interests Appealing to Children. This is another indication that must be considered for evaluation only in connection with other indicators, inasmuch as many ordinary persons might also have such interests. Pedophiles might collect toys or dolls, build model planes or boats, or perform as clowns or magicians to attract children. A pedophile interested in older children might have a "hobby" involving alcohol, drugs, or pornography.

Shows Sexually Explicit Material to Children. Any adult who shows sexually explicit material to children of any age should be viewed with suspicion. This is generally part of the seduction process in order to lower inhibitions. A pedophile might also encourage or allow children to call a dial-a-porn service as part of this process.

4. Sexual Fantasies Focus on Children: Indicators of Characteristic

Youth-Oriented Decorations in House or Room. Pedophiles attracted to teenage boys might have their homes decorated the way a teenage boy would. This might include toys, games, stereos, rock posters, etc. The homes of some pedophiles have been described as shrines to children or as miniature amusement parks.

Frequent Photographing of Children. This includes photography of children fully dressed. One pedophile bragged that he went to rock concerts with 30 or 40 roles of film in order to photograph young boys. After developing the pictures, he fantasized about having sex with them. Such a pedophile might frequent playgrounds, youth athletic matches, child beauty pageants, parades, child exercise classes, etc., with his camera or video equipment.

Collect Child Pornography and/or Child Erotica. This is one of the most significant characteristics of pedophiles and will therefore be discussed in detail in another section of this chapter.

If after evaluating these indicators, the law enforcement investigator has reason to suspect that a particular subject or suspect is a preferential child molester, the investigator should utilize the two most important pedophile indicators to his or her investigative advantage. These two indicators are: multiple victims and collection of child pornography or erotica. The investigator must attempt to identify additional victims to strengthen the case against the offender. The more victims identified, the less likely it is that any of them will have to testify in court. There is strength in numbers. But even more important, *as soon as legally possible*, the investigator must obtain a warrant to search for child pornography or erotica, which is invaluable as evidence. There is a certain urgency in this because the more investigation and interviews conducted to obtain the needed probable cause for a search warrant, the greater the chance the pedophile will learn of the investigation and move or hide his collection. Child pornography, especially that produced by the offender, is the *single* most valuable piece of evidence of child sexual abuse that any investigator can have. The effect on a jury of viewing seized child pornography is devastating to the defendant's case.

Collection of Child Pornography and Erotica

Law enforcement investigations have verified that pedophiles almost always *collect* child pornography and/or child erotica. *Collection* is a key word. It does not mean that pedophiles merely view pornography. It means that they save it. It comes to represent their most secret sexual fantasies. They typically collect books, magazines, articles, newspapers, photographs, negatives, slides, movies, albums, drawings, audio tapes, video tapes and equipment, personal letters, diaries, clothing, sexual aids, souvenirs, toys, games, lists, paintings, ledgers, photographic equipment, etc.—all relating to children in either a sexual, a scientific, or a social way. Not all pedophiles collect all of these items. Their collections vary in size and scope. Factors that seem to influence the size of a pedophile's collection include (*a*) socioeconomic status, (*b*) living arrangements, and (*c*) age. More intelligent, better educated, and more affluent pedophiles tend to have larger collections. Pedophiles whose living or work arrangements give them a higher degree of privacy and security tend to have larger collections. Because collections are accumulated over a period of time, older pedophiles tend to have larger collections.

Pedophiles with the economic means are converting more and more to video tape systems. They are even converting their books, magazines, photographs, and movies to video tape. For less than $1,500, a pedophile can have his own video camera and two video recorders, which give him the capability to produce and duplicate child pornography and erotica with little fear of discovery.

Situational child molesters might also collect pornography, but not with the high degree of predictability of the preferential child molester. In addition, child pornography will comprise a small percentage of the total collection of the situational child molester. In the child pornography collected by situational molesters the children might be dressed up (stockings, high heels, makeup, etc.) to look like adults. The morally indiscriminate child molester might collect pornography or erotica of a predominantly sadomasochistic theme but probably not save the same material for year after year. The sexually indiscriminate individual is the situational child molester most likely to have an extensive collection. However, the majority of it will not be child oriented. His material might display a wide variety of sexual activity and perversions, with child pornography being only one small portion. The law enforcement investigator should always consider the possibility that any child molester might collect child pornography or erotica. However, it is almost a certainty with the preferential type. Because true child pornography is not easy to obtain, some pedophiles have only child erotica in their collections. Because it represents his sexual fantasies (age and gender preferences, desired sexual acts, etc.), the collection of any child molester should be carefully examined and evaluated.

What Is Collected

What the pedophile collects can be divided into two categories: child pornography and child erotica. *Child pornography* can be behaviorally (although not necessarily legally) defined as the sexually explicit reproduction of a child's image, voice, or handwriting. In essence, it is the permanent record of the sexual abuse of a child. The only way you can produce child pornography is to sexually molest a child. Child pornography exists primarily for the consumption of pedophiles. If there were no pedophiles, there would be little child pornography other than that involving adolescent children. It includes sexually explicit photographs, negatives, slides, magazines, movies, video tapes, audio tapes, and handwritten notes.

Child pornography can be divided into two subcategories: *commercial* and *homemade*. *Commercial* child pornography is that which is produced and intended for commercial sale. Because of strict federal and state laws today, there is no place in the United States where commercial child pornography is knowingly, openly sold. The commercial child pornography still being distributed in the United States is imported or smuggled in from foreign countries, primarily by pedophiles. The risks are usually too high for the strictly commercial dealer. But because of his sexual and personal interests, pedophiles are more willing to take those risks. Their motive is more than just profit.

This leads to the other subcategory of *homemade* child pornography. This term in no way implies that this material is of poor quality. The quality of homemade child pornography can be as good as, if not better than, the quality of any commercial pornography. The pedopile has a personal interest in the product. *Homemade* simply means it was not originally produced primarily for commercial sale. Although commercial child pornography is not openly sold anywhere in this country, homemade child pornography is continually produced and traded in almost every community in America. Sometimes homemade child pornography is sold or winds up in commercial child pornography magazines, movies, or videos. Most of the children in prepubescent child pornography were not abducted into sexual slavery. They were seduced into posing for these pictures or videos by a pedophile they probably knew. They were never missing children. In some cases their own parents took the pictures or made them available for others to take the pictures. Children in pubescent or technical child pornography are more likely to be missing children, especially teenage runaways or throwaways being exploited by morally indiscriminate pimps and profiteers.

In understanding the nature of child pornography, the law enforcement officer must recognize the distinction between *technical* and *simulated* child pornography. The federal statute (Child Protection Act of 1984) defines a child as anyone under the age of 18. Therefore, a sexually explicit photograph of a 15-, 16-, or 17-year-old girl or boy is *technical* child pornography. However, such a photograph might be of sexual interest to many who are not pedophiles.

The production, distribution, and, in some cases, possession of such child pornography could and should be investigated under appropriate child pornography statutes. However, the investigator should understand that the consumers of such material are not *necessarily* pedophiles.

On the other hand, sexually explicit photographs of 19-year-old or older males or females are not legally child pornography. But if the person portrayed in such material is young looking, dressed young, or made up to look young (hair in pigtails, shaved vagina, etc.), the material could be of interest to pedophiles. This then is *simulated* child pornography. It is designed to appeal to the pedophile, but it is not legally child pornography, because the individuals portrayed are over 18. This illustrates the importance and, sometimes, the difficulty in proving the age of the child in the photographs or video tapes.

Child erotica, on the other hand, is a broader and more encompassing term. It can be defined as any material, relating to children, that serves a sexual purpose for a given individual. It is in a sense a subjective term, as almost anything could potentially serve a sexual purpose. However, some of the more common types of child erotica include toys, games, drawings, fantasy writings, diaries, souvenirs, sexual aids, manuals, letters, books about children, psychological books on pedophilia, and nonsexually-explicit photographs of children. Child erotica might also be referred to as *pedophile paraphernalia*.

Generally, possession and distribution of these items do not constitute violation of the law. However, besides possible legality, there is another important distinction between child pornography and child erotica. Although both may be used in similar ways by the pedophile, child pornography has the added and more important dimension of its effect on the child portrayed. Discussions and research on pornography often focus on the effects on the viewer, rather than on the effects on the child subject. The latter is particularly crucial in evaluating the harm of child pornography.

Children used in pornography are desensitized and conditioned to respond as sexual objects. They are frequently ashamed of and/or embarrassed about their portrayal in such material. They must deal with the permanency, longevity, and circulation of such a record of their sexual abuse. Some types of sexual activity can be repressed and hidden from public knowledge; child victims can fantasize that someday the activity will be over and they can make a fresh start. Many children, especially adolescent boys, vehemently deny their involvement with a pedophile. But there is no denying or hiding from a sexually explicit photograph or video tape. The child in a photograph or video tape is young forever, and therefore the material can be used over and over for years. Some children have even committed crimes in attempts to retrieve or destroy the permanent records of their molestation.

Whatever the reasons that pedophiles collect child pornography and erotica, their existence is undeniable and widespread. During any intervention or investigation of child sexual abuse, the possible presence of such material must be explored. For law enforcement officers, the existence and discovery of a child erotica or child pornography collection can be of invaluable assistance to the investigation of any child sexual abuse case. Obviously, child pornography itself is usually evidence of criminal violations. However, the ledgers, diaries, letters, books, and souvenirs that are often part of a child erotica collection can also be used as supportive evidence to prove intent and for additional lead information. Names, addresses, and pictures of additional victims; dates and descriptions of sexual activity; names, addresses, phone numbers, and admissions of accomplices and other pedophiles; as well as descriptions of sexual fantasies, background information, and admissions of the subject, are frequently part of a child erotica collection. Child erotica must be viewed in the context in which it is found. Although many people might have some similar items in their home, it is only the pedophile who collects such material for sexual purposes as part of his seduction of, and fantasies about, children. Many people have a Sears catalog in their home, but only a pedophile has albums full of children's underwear ads from past catalogs.

Child erotica must always be evaluated in the context in which it is found. The law enforcement investigator must use good judgment and common sense. Possession of an album filled with pictures of the suspect's own fully dressed children probably has no significance. Possession of 15 albums filled with pictures of fully dressed children unrelated to the suspect probably has significance. Possession of his own children's underwear in their dresser probably is normal. Possession of a suitcase full of little girls' underwear when the suspect has no children or only sons probably is suspicious. Possession of a few books about child development or sex education on a bookshelf probably has no significance. Possession of dozens of such books together in a box probably is significant.

Most people have photographs of children someplace in their homes, and many people also possess photographs of naked children. Under most state statutes and the current federal law, pictures of children portraying simple nudity are not generally considered sexually explicit or obscene. The federal law requires at least "lascivious exhibition of the genitals or pubic area" for a picture of a child to be considered sexually explicit and therefore to constitute child pornography. How then can an investigator evaluate the possible significance of nude and other nonsexually explicit photographs of children found, during a search, in the possession of a suspected offender?

The following criteria are offered for the evaluation of such photographs. As used here, the term *photograph* includes any visual depiction (negatives, prints, slides, movies, video tapes, etc.).

How They Were Produced. Pedophiles are more likely to use trickery, bribery, or seduction to take their photographs of children. They sometimes photograph children under false pretenses such as leading them or their parents to believe that modeling or acting jobs might result. Some offenders surreptitiously photograph children. One pedophile hid above the ceiling of a boys' locker room and photographed boys through a moved ceiling tile. Some pedophiles collect photographs of children who are complete strangers to them. They take these pictures at swimming meets, wrestling matches, child beauty pageants, parks, parades, rock concerts, etc., which are open to the public. These photographs are usually of children of a certain age and gender.

Pedophiles are also more likely to take and possess photographs that focus on specific parts of a child's anatomy. These are most likely to be the private parts of a child such as the genitals or the buttocks, but could include any parts (feet, hands, hair, etc.) of particular sexual interest to a certain offender. In some photographs, the children may be involved in strange or bizarre behavior, such as pretending to be dead or simulating unusual sex acts. In one case, a pedophile photographed young boys in their bathing suits and nude, but first painted bondagelike markings on their bodies using tinted antiseptic spray. Such pictures might be graphic enough to be considered child pornography.

Investigators should make every effort to determine the circumstances under which recovered photographs were taken in order to evaluate their investigative significance as child erotica.

How They Were Saved. Volume is a significant factor. Pedophiles are more likely to have large numbers of photographs of children. One pedophile had 27 large photo albums filled with pictures of children partially or fully dressed. They are more likely to have their photographs carefully organized and catalogued. The photographs are often carefully mounted in binders or albums. These may be photographs they have cut out of magazines, catalogues, or newspapers. Sometimes sexually explicit, written captions are added above, below, or on the pictures.

Photographs are frequently marked with the children's names and ages and the dates taken. Sometimes they are also marked with the children's addresses, physical descriptions, and even the sexual acts they performed. Most people who have photographs of their naked children or grandchildren save them as a small subset of many photographs of these same children as they grow up. The pedophile who collects photographs of children is more likely to have many such photographs together, and all the children portrayed will be of the same general age. There will be few, if any, photographs of these same children when they are younger or older. The pedophile offender is also more likely to have enlargements or carefully arranged groupings of these photographs. They might even be arranged on the wall as a kind of shrine to children.

Investigators should carefully document the context in which such recovered photographs were maintained by the offender. Prosecutors must ensure that jurors understand that the pedophile's collection of photographs of naked children has nothing to do with parents or grandparents possessing a few photographs of their naked young children.

How They Were Used. Pedophiles often use these photographs to help seduce and lower the inhibitions of children. If other children pose for such photographs, it must be okay or fun. Pictures of naked children could be used to convince children to remove their clothing. Children whom the pedophile hopes eventually to photograph in sexually explicit acts can be started and conditioned by copying the behavior of children in nonsexually explicit photographs.

Investigators should attempt to determine how the offender used such material in his interaction with children.

Few police officers would ignore or fail to seize sexually explicit child pornography found during a search. But over and over again, officers ignore and leave behind the child erotica. Although not as significant or damaging as child pornography, child erotica is valuable evidence of intent and a source of valuable intelligence information.

The investigative experience of many law enforcement officers in dealing with pornography is often limited to commercial pornography distributed by individuals motivated by monetary profit. The direct connection between the pornography and sex crimes is rarely a factor in cases of this type. In an investigation narrowly focused only on the pornography or obscenity violations, officers might have legal problems justifying the seizure of child erotica (pedophile paraphernalia) found when executing a search warrant. However, in an investigation more broadly focused on child pornography and its role in the sexual exploitation of children by child molesters, officers should recognize the evidentiary value of child erotica. If the facts of the case justify it, this relationship between child pornography and sexual exploitation of children should always be set forth in the affidavit for a search warrant. Both the child pornography and child erotica should be seized as evidence when found in such cases. The photograph of a fully dressed child may not be evidence of an obscenity violation, but it could be evidence of an offender's sexual involvement with children.

Every effort should be made to attempt to identify the children—even those fully dressed—in photographs or video tapes found in the possession of a pedophile. This is especially true if these items appear to have been produced by the offender himself. Each of these children is a potential victim of sexual abuse. However, this identification must be done discreetly in order to avoid potential public embarrassment to the children, whether or not they were victimized. Sometimes the pedophile makes the identification unbelievably easy by labeling his photographs with names, descriptions, addresses, dates, and even sex acts performed.

Possession of numerous books, magazines, articles, newspaper clippings, etc. (no matter how legitimate or academic) about the sexual development and abuse of children or about pedophilia in general can be used as evidence of intent at a subsequent trial. It is very difficult to disprove the claim of a wrestling coach that his touching was legitimate athletic training or the claim of a teacher that his touching was normal healthy affection. This difficult task can be made easier if police have seized a child erotica collection that includes such items as a diary or fantasy writings describing the sexual stimulation experienced when touching a child to demonstrate a wrestling hold or when fondling a student sitting on one's lap.

For investigative purposes, *child erotica* can be divided into the following categories:

Published Material Relating to Children. Examples include books, magazines, articles, video tapes, etc., dealing with any of the following areas:

Child development
Sex education
Child pornography
Sexual abuse of children
Incest
Child prostitution
Missing children
Investigative techniques
Legal aspects
Access to children
Sexual disorders
Pedophilia
Man–boy love
Personal ads
Detective magazines
"Men's" magazines
Nudism
Erotic novels
Catalogues
Brochures

Examples of access-to-children publications might include listings of foreign sex tours, guides to nude beaches, and material on sponsoring orphans or needy children. Detective magazines saved by pedophiles usually are those containing stories about crimes against children. The "men's" magazines collected are sometimes those that have articles about sexual abuse of children. The use of adult pornography to lower inhibitions is discussed elsewhere in this chapter. Although the possession of information (articles, posters, pictures, flyers, etc.) on missing children should be carefully investigated to determine possible involvement in abduction, most pedophiles collect this material to help rationalize their behavior. They are good because they "love" children. Child molesters are bad because they abduct children. Personal ads might include those published in swinger magazines, video magazines, and even newspapers. Personal ads are usually discreetly worded and often mention terms such as "family fun," "family activity," "European material," "youth training," etc. Erotic novels contain stories about sex with children, but without sexually explicit photographs. They may contain sketches or drawings. Material concerning current or proposed laws dealing with sex abuse; arrested, convicted or acquitted child molesters; and investigative techniques used by law enforcement is common. There is little doubt that someday this chapter will be found in the possession of pedophiles.

Unpublished Material Relating to Children. Examples include items such as:

Personal letters
Audio tapes
Diaries
Fantasy writings
Manuscripts
Ledgers and financial records
Telephone and address books
Pedophile manuals
Newsletters and bulletins
Directories
Adult pornography

Directories usually contain information on where to locate children or other pedophiles. Newsletters and bulletins are distributed by pedophile support groups, such as the North American Man-Boy Love Association (NAMBLA), the Lewis Carroll Collector's Guild, and other similar groups that have emerged or will emerge. Manuscripts are writings of the pedophile in formats suitable for real or imagined publication. Ledgers and financial records might include cancelled checks used to pay victims or purchase pornography or erotica.

Pictures, Photographs, and Video Tapes of Children. Examples include children found in:

Photography, art, or sex education books
Photograph albums and displays

Candid shots
Photocopies of photographs or pictures
Drawings and tracings
Posters and paintings
Advertisements
Children's television programs
Cut-and-paste pictures

Cut and paste involves creating pictures by cutting and pasting together parts of pictures of children or adults, such as pasting the head of an adult on the body of a child or vice versa. Video tapes of children's television programs might include episodes of shows such as "Leave it to Beaver," "Romper Room," "Silver Spoons," or "Family Affair." Seized video tapes should always be viewed in their entirety because a variety of material, including hard-core child pornography and television shows on child sexual abuse, could be together on any one tape. Some pedophiles cut out pictures of children from magazines and put them in albums as if they were photographs. This can be positively determined by laboratory examination.

Souvenirs and Trophies. Examples include items to remember children, such as:

Photographs
Articles of clothing
Jewelry and personal items
Audio tapes
Letters and notes
Charts and records

Photographs collected by pedophiles are often labeled or marked. Charts and records might include astrology or biorhythm charts. Audio tapes, letters, and notes collected for souvenir purposes usually are from past child victims and discuss what the two did together and sometimes how much the victims like the offender. Personal items collected may even include fingernails, teeth, hair, and semen.

Miscellaneous. Examples include items used in gaining access to and seducing children such as:

Computers and peripheral equipment
Sexual aids

Toys, games, and dolls
Costumes
Child- or youth-oriented decorations
Video and photography equipment
Alcohol and drugs

Sexual aids include such items as vibrators and dildos. Offenders involved with adolescent victims frequently use alcohol and drugs to lower inhibitions. Costumes include those worn by the offender and by the children. Computers and related materials, such as access to electronic bulletin boards, can be valuable evidence.

Motivation for Collection

It is difficult to know with certainty why pedophiles collect child pornography and erotica. There may be as many reasons as there are pedophiles. Collecting this material may help pedophiles satisfy, deal with, or reinforce compulsive, persistent sexual fantasies about children.

Collecting may also fulfill needs for validation. Many pedophiles collect academic and scientific books and articles on the nature of pedophilia in an effort to understand and justify their behavior. For example, Adams and Tollison (1979) state that research shows that children often participate willingly in sexual behavior with adults (p. 326). One pedophile arrested by the police had in his possession an article entitled "Children, Sex, and Society" (Haeberle, 1978), stating that children's sexual rights and freedom should include access to pornographic materials and choice of sexual partners, including adults. The article went on to say that child molestation and incest would be criminal acts only if unwilling children were involved. For the same reasons, pedophiles also frequently collect and sometimes distribute articles and manuals written by pedophiles that attempt to justify and rationalize their behavior as not being blameworthy. In this material, pedophiles often share techniques for finding and seducing children and for avoiding or dealing with the criminal justice system.

Commercial child pornography magazines also sometimes contain articles to help pedophiles rationalize and justify their behavior. For example, one such magazine, entitled *Schoolgirls*, is filled with sexually explicit photographs of prepubescent children and has an article in it entitled "The Subteen Bisexgirl." The article states:

> In the past two decades, however, the legal profession, and society as a whole, has taken a closer look at these young sexpots, and has been shocked awake at the avarice and the viciousness of the aggressive young

> "Lolitas." Much psychiatric investigation has gone into determining the motivators behind the acts of the "dirty old men," but it is only recently that psychiatry and medicine, as well as sociology and behavioral researchers, have turned their searchlights on the motivations and the patterns of conduct that now strongly pervade the very young of America. There are no easy answers simply because there is no "normal" behavior for subteenagers. Each young girl who engages in sex for profit, for kicks, or because she cannot help her inner compulsions, is entirely different.

Collecting child erotica and pornography also appears to meet needs for camaraderie and additional behavior validation. Pedophiles swap pornographic photographs the way boys swap baseball cards. As they try to improve and upgrade their collections, they get strong reinforcement from each other for their behavior. This reinforces the belief that because others are doing the same thing, it is not wrong. Collecting and trading becomes a common bond. Only other pedophiles will understand, validate, and reward such behavior.

The need for validation may also partially explain why some pedophiles compulsively and systematically save their collected material. It is almost as though each communication and photograph is evidence of the value and legitimacy of their behavior. For example, one pedophile sends another pedophile a letter, enclosing photographs and describing his sexual activities with children. At the letter's conclusion, he tells his fellow pedophile to destroy the letter because it could be damaging evidence against him. Six months later police find the letter while serving a search warrant. Not only has the letter not been destroyed, it has been carefully filed as part of the second pedophile's organized collection.

Pedophiles frequently collect and maintain lists of names, addresses, and phone numbers of others with similar sexual interests, screening the names carefully and developing the lists over a long time. The typical pedophile constantly seeks to expand his correspondence. Names are obtained from advertisements in "swinger" magazines and pornography magazines and even from legitimate newspapers. Correspondence usually begins carefully to avoid communicating with police. In many cases, however, the need to continually validate behavior and to share experiences overcomes concerns for safety. If mistakes lead to identification and arrest, the pedophile network often quickly alerts its members.

Another important motivation for collecting child pornography and erotica appears to stem from the fact that no matter how attractive any one child sexual partner is, there can be no long-term sexual relationship. All child victims will grow up and become sexually unattractive to the pedophile. However, in a photograph, a 9-year-old boy stays young forever.

a photograph does not change

* It would seem this would make the pedophile very vulnerable to a sting operation.

Pedophiles frequently maintain souvenirs of their victims. The author is aware of several cases in which the pedophile maintained astrology charts on his victims and one case in which the pedophile maintained complete bio-rhythm charts on his victims. A pedophile might keep an article of clothing or any other memento of a relationship. However, the most common souvenirs are photographs or video tapes. Some souvenir photographs may be sexually explicit, in others the child is nude or in varying states of undress, and in still others the child is fully clothed. Although photographs of fully clothed children may not legally be considered child pornography, to the pedophile they are not much different from sexually explicit photographs.

When photos are seized in a police raid, the pedophile may argue that photographs of fully dressed children are not part of the collection. The pedophile often keeps such photographs in his wallet. Many pedophiles even keep two sets of photographs of their victims. One set contains sexually explicit photographs; the other contains nonexplicit photographs. Although this distinction may be important for criminal prosecution, to the pedophile each set might be equally stimulating and arousing. The victim photographs are like souvenirs or trophies of sexual relationships.

Uses of Collection

Although the reasons why pedophiles collect child pornography and erotica are a matter of conjecture, we can be more certain as to how this material is used. Study and police investigations have identified certain uses of the material.

Child pornography and child erotica are used for the sexual arousal and gratification of pedophiles. They use child pornography the same way other people use adult pornography—to feed sexual fantasies. Some pedophiles only collect and fantasize about the material without acting out these fantasies. In most cases coming to the attention of law enforcement, however, the arousal and fantasy fueled by the pornography is only a prelude to actual sexual activity with children.

A second use of child pornography and erotica is to lower children's inhibitions. A child who is reluctant to engage in sexual activity with an adult or to pose for sexually explicit photos can sometimes be convinced by viewing other children having "fun" participating in the activity. Peer pressure has a tremendous effect on children; if other children are involved, the child might be led to believe that maybe it is all right. In the pornography used to lower inhibitions, the children portrayed will usually appear to be having a good time.

Books on human sexuality, sex education, and sex manuals are also used to lower inhibitions. Children are impressed by books, and they often believe that if something is in a book it must be acceptable. The controversial sex education book *Show Me* (1975) has been used by many pedophiles for this purpose. Adult pornography is also used, particularly with adolescent boy victims, to arouse and/or to lower inhibitions. Dial-a-porn phone calls can also be used in this way. If Madonna poses nude in *Playboy* or *Penthouse*, how can it be wrong?

A third major use of child pornography collections is blackmail. If a pedophile already has a relationship with a child, seducing the child into sexual activity is only part of the plan. The pedophile must also ensure that the child maintains the "secret" and tells no one else of the activity. Pedophiles use many techniques to do so; one of them is through photographs taken of the child. If the child threatens to tell his or her parents or the authorities, the existence of sexually explicit photographs can be an effective silencer. The pedophile threatens to show the pictures to parents, friends, or teachers if the child reveals their secret. Children seem to be particularly concerned about these pictures being shown to their peers.

A fourth use of child pornography and erotica is as a medium of exchange. Many pedophiles want additional child pornography and erotica, not money, in return for material in their collection. The object is to "improve" the collection and not necessarily to make money. Some pedophiles exchange photographs of children for access to, or phone numbers of, other children. The quality and theme of the material determines its value as an exchange medium. One Willie Mays baseball card may be worth two or three lesser cards, and the same principle applies to child pornography. Rather than paying cash for access to a child, the pedophile may exchange a small part (usually duplicates) of his collection. The younger the child and the more bizarre the acts, the greater the value of the pornography.

A fifth use of the collected material is for profit. Some people involved in the sale and distribution of child pornography are not pedophiles; they are involved to make money. In contrast, most pedophiles seem to collect child erotica and pornography for reasons other than profit. Others combine their pedophilic interests with the desire to make money. Often they begin nonprofit trading, which they pursue until they accumulate certain amounts or types of photographs, which then are sold to commercial dealers for reproduction in commercial child pornography magazines. Some collectors even have their own photographic reproduction equipment. Thus, the photograph of a child taken with or without parental knowledge by a neighborhood pedophile in any American community could wind up in a commercial child pornography magazine with worldwide distribution.

Characteristics of Collection

The pedophile's collection usually has the following characteristics:

Important. The pedophile's collection is usually one of the most important things in his life. He is willing to spend considerable time and money on it. Most pedophiles make no profit from their collections. After release from prison, many pedophiles attempt to get their collections back from the police.

Constant. No matter how much the pedophile has, he never has enough, and he rarely throws anything away. If police have evidence that a pedophile had a collection 5, 10, or more years ago, chances are he still has the collection, only it is larger. This is a very significant characteristic to consider when evaluating the staleness of information used to obtain a search warrant.

Organized. The pedophile usually maintains detailed, neat, orderly records. There certainly are exceptions, but the collections of most pedophiles are carefully organized and maintained. As will be discussed, some pedophiles now use computers for this purpose.

Permanent. The pedophile might move, hide, or give his collection to another pedophile if he believes the police are investigating him. However, the least likely thing he will do is destroy the collection. It is his life's work. In some cases he might even prefer that the police seize it and keep it "intact" in an evidence room where he might retrieve at least some of it when released from prison. One offender is known to have willed his collection to a fellow pedophile. The will, which was found, also gave the exact location of the collection.

Concealed. Because of the hidden or illegal nature of the pedophile's activity, he is concerned with the security of his collection. But this must always be weighed against his access to the collection. It does him no good if he can't get to it. Where pedophiles hide their collections often depends on their living arrangements. If the pedophile is living alone or with someone aware of his preference for children, the collection will be less well concealed. It might be in a trunk, box, cabinet, or bookcase or out in the open. The child pornography might be better hidden than the erotica. If he is living with family members or others not aware of his activity, it will be better concealed. The collection might be found behind a false panel, in the duct work, under insulation, etc. The collection is usually in the pedophile's home, but it could be in an automobile or camper, at his place of business, in a safety deposit box, or in a rented storage locker. The most difficult location to find is a secret place in a remote rural area. A good rule of thumb is to look in any area that is under the control of the offender.

Shared. The pedophile frequently has a need or desire to show and tell others about his collection. He is seeking validation for all his efforts. The investigator can use this need to his advantage by showing interest in the collection during any interview of a pedophile. The offender might appreciate the opportunity to "brag" about how much time, effort, and skill went into his collection.

Computers

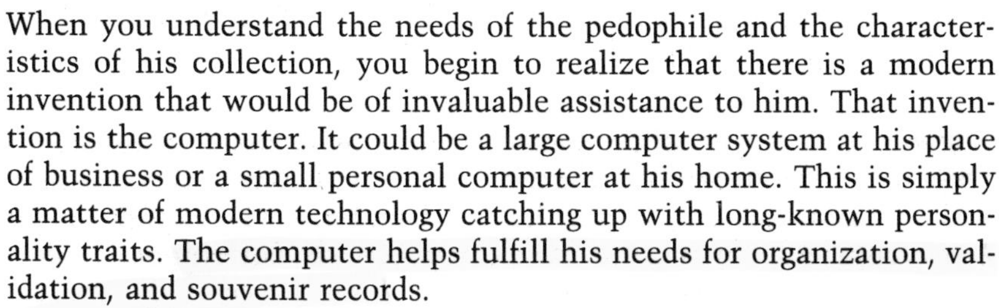

When you understand the needs of the pedophile and the characteristics of his collection, you begin to realize that there is a modern invention that would be of invaluable assistance to him. That invention is the computer. It could be a large computer system at his place of business or a small personal computer at his home. This is simply a matter of modern technology catching up with long-known personality traits. The computer helps fulfill his needs for organization, validation, and souvenir records.

Law enforcement investigation has determined the pedophiles use computers in four major ways:

1. *Storage and retrieval of information.* Many pedophiles seem to be compulsive record keepers. A computer makes it much easier to store and retrieve names and addresses of victims and other pedophiles. Innumerable characteristics of victims and sexual acts can be easily recorded and analyzed. An extensive pornography collection can be catalogued by subject matter. Even fantasy writings and other narrative descriptions can be stored and retrieved for future use.
2. *Communication.* Many pedophiles communicate with other pedophiles. Now, instead of putting a stamp on a letter or package, they can use their computer and some necessary peripheral equipment to exchange information. The amount and type of information that can be exchanged is limited only by the equipment available.
3. *Electronic bulletin board.* Pedophiles can use their computers to locate individuals with similar interests. Like advertisements in "swinger magazines," electronic bulletin boards are used to identify individuals with mutual interests concerning age, gender, and sexual preference. This use of the computer is not limited to pedophiles. In the December 1983 issue of the North American Man-Boy Love Association (NAMBLA) bulletin, a member from Michigan pro-

posed that NAMBLA establish its own electronic bulletin board (p. 9). Private communications firms offer messaging services that allow computer users to have their messages duplicated and routed to designated receivers on the network. The pedophile may use an electronic bulletin board to which he has authorized access, or he may illegally enter a system. The pedophile can also set up his own or participate in other surreptitious or underground bulletin boards. It must be noted that the electronic bulletin board concept is a common and valuable use of the home computer. The pedophile merely uses this concept for his own needs.

4. *Business records.* Pedophiles who have turned their sexual interest in children and/or child pornography into a profit-making business use computers the same way any business uses them. Lists of customers, dollar amounts of transactions, descriptions of inventory, etc., can all be kept track of by computer.

Pedophiles, as well as others involved in sex crimes, can and do use computers. Law enforcement officers must be alert for this valuable source of evidence and intelligence. In one recent case the author is aware of, a teenage "hacker" helped police break a pedophile's computer codes and thereby gain access to his records. Police must be alert to the fact that any pedophile with the intelligence, economic means, or employment access might be using a computer in any or all of the described ways.

Reaction to Identification

When a child molestation case is uncovered and an offender is identified, there are certain fairly predictable reactions by the child molester. This is especially true of the preferential child molester (pedophile). Knowledge and anticipation of these reactions should be beneficial to the investigation and prosecution of such cases. The intensity of these reactions may depend on how much the offender has to lose by identification and conviction.

Denial

Usually the first reaction of a child molester to discovery will be complete denial. The offender may act shocked, surprised, or even indignant about an allegation of sexual activity with children. He will claim to know nothing about the alleged activity. He might possibly claim he does not remember. He might admit to an act, but deny the intent was sexual gratification. ("Is it a crime to hug a child?") His actions were misunderstood. A mistake has been made. His denial may be aided by relatives, friends, neighbors, and co-workers, who will insist he is such a wonderful person there is no way he could have done what is alleged. These associates may be uncooperative and may even hinder police investigation of the offender. They may believe that they are doing the offender a favor. However, sometimes their support, conditioned on the offender maintaining his innocence, actually prevents the offender from admitting guilt and seeking help. In any case, the investigator should anticipate and not be thrown off by strong initial denial by a suspect.

Minimization

If the evidence against him rules out total denial, the offender may switch to a slightly different reaction. He will attempt to minimize what he has done in both quantity and quality. He might claim that it happened on one or two isolated occasions or that he only touched or caressed the victim. He will be knowledgeable about the law and might possibly admit to acts he knows are lesser offenses or misdemeanors (he touched the child only on the outside of the clothing). It is important to recognize that even seemingly cooperative *victims* may also minimize the quantity and quality of acts. If a certain act was performed 30 times, the victim might claim it happened only 5 times, and the offender might claim it happened only once or twice. A victim may admit to having sex but not to having received money for sex, or may admit to receiving oral sex but not to giving oral sex. Victims sometimes deny certain sexual acts in spite of photographs showing otherwise. Adolescent boys especially deny or minimize their victimization.

Justification

Either as part of their efforts to minimize or as a separate reaction, child molesters typically attempt to justify their behavior. They might claim that they care for the children more than the children's parents do and that what they do is beneficial to the child. If the child molester is the father of the victim, he might claim the child is better off learning about sex from him. In other cases, he might claim he has been under tremendous stress or has a drinking problem. He might claim he did not know how old a certain victim was. A large part of his efforts to justify his behavior usually centers around blaming the victim. This is the single most common rationalization of all pedophiles. They have sex with children because children want it. The offender will claim he was seduced by the victim, that the victim initiated the sexual activity, or that the victim is promiscuous or even a prostitute. In a few cases, his claim might even be true, but such justification has no meaning. The offender is an adult, the victim is a child. You don't jump off a 20-story building because a child asked you to. However, in most cases these claims are just rationalizations and wishful thinking on the part of the offender.

Fabrication

Some of the more clever child molesters come up with ingenious stories to explain their behavior. These stories are limited only by the imagination of the offender. One offender, a doctor, claimed he was doing research on male youth prostitution. A professor claimed he was doing research on pedophilia and was collecting and distributing child pornography for scientific research. Another offender claimed he was trying to teach his victims to stop sucking their thumbs. A psychologist claimed he was doing research on the size of boys' penises. A teacher said his students had such a desperate need for attention and affection they practically threw themselves at him and misunderstood his affectionate response as sexual advances. Many incest offenders claim to be providing sex education for their children. In another case, a nursery school operator, who had taken and collected thousands of nude and seminude photographs of young children in his care, claimed they were not for sexual purposes; he simply admired the anatomy of children. Another offender claimed his sadomasochistic photos of children were part of a child discipline program. A choirmaster claimed he was tapping out the rhythm of the music with his hand between the boys' legs. His stroking their genitalia was only part of his effort to emphasize that they bring the notes up from deep inside. One offender claimed the children made a sexually explicit video tape without his knowledge and that he had kept it only to show their parents. Some offenders even claim they are following the word of God. One claimed he was merely keeping the child warm in his bed on a cold night. Depending on the offender and his situation, these stories are sometimes very effective. For example, a wrestling coach might get away with a considerable amount of touching under the guise of legitimately teaching wrestling techniques. These stories work particularly well for professionals such as teachers, doctors, and therapists. The investigator and prosecutor must be prepared to confront them and attempt to disprove them. Finding child pornography or erotica in the possession of the offender is one effective way to do this.

Mental Illness

When other tactics do not result in the termination of an investigation or prosecution, the child molester may then try the "sick game." This tactic involves claiming he is sick and cannot control what he is doing.

Pedophile manuals advocate this tactic when all else fails. It is interesting to note that few child molesters admit this sickness until after they are identified or arrested or until other tactics fail. They first plead not guilty, then when found guilty, they claim they are sick. Of course, if the child molester is "sick" he needs treatment, not a jail term. This chapter will not attempt to debate whether or not pedophilia is a mental disorder that legally alters criminal responsibility for behavior or whether child molesters are mentally sick at all. However, if the behavior of a child molester is considered the result of a mental illness, then it must of necessity be treated as a highly contagious illness that is, at best, difficult to treat.

Sympathy

Another effective tactic for the child molester at any stage of an investigation or prosecution is the "sympathy game." This is designed to make as many people as possible, but especially judges, jurors, and the community, feel sorry for him. This is best illustrated by the "nice guy defense." In this defense, the offender says he is sorry or sick and then presents evidence to show he is a pillar of the community, a devoted family man, a military veteran, a church leader, nonviolent, without prior arrests, and a victim of circumstances with many personal problems. In view of the fact that many people still believe in some variation of the myth that child molesters are totally repulsive, evil, dirty old men in wrinkled rain coats, the "sympathy game" combined with the "sick game" is the most effective tactic to escape responsibility and punishment for their criminal behavior.

Attack

It is important not to overlook another reaction of the identified child molester. It can be used many times and at any time during the investigation or prosecution. This reaction consists of attacking or going on the offensive. It involves such things as harassing, threatening, and/or bribing victims and witnesses; attacking the reputation and personal lives of the investigating officers; attacking the motives of the prosecutor; claiming the case is selective prosecution; raising issues such as gay rights if the child victim is the same sex as the offender; and enlisting the active support of peer groups and organizations (doctors or medical associations, if he is a doctor; teachers or the teachers' union, if he is a teacher, etc.). The offender will call due any political favors or friendships to avoid conviction. In one case, a wealthy pedophile under investigation hired a private detective agency that specialized in digging up dirt about police officers. The police investigator also must consider the possibility of physical violence. It would be a terrible mistake for any police investigator or prosecutor to think all child molesters are passive, inadequate people who are easily intimidated. The author is aware of at least two cases in which the arrested child molester was a survivalist with a massive arsenal of weapons and explosives. In addition, the author is aware of cases in which child molesters murdered their victims, including their own children, to keep them from disclosing the sexual abuse.

Guilty, but Not Guilty

When all of the above reactions, as well as legal tactics (suppression of evidence, etc.) not discussed in this chapter, fail to prevent prosecution, the offender will usually try to make a deal in order to avoid a public trial. Although this results in the highly desirable objective of avoiding child victim testimony, the unfortunate aspect of this is that the offender is often allowed to plead, in essence, "guilty, but not guilty." This sometimes involves a plea of nolo contendere to avoid civil liability. However, the average citizen reading this in the newspaper still doesn't know whether or not the offender did it. In another variation, the offender makes public statements that he is pleading guilty because he "doesn't want to put the children through the trauma of having to testify," or because he "has no more money to defend himself," or for any reason imaginable other than the only important one—because he *is* guilty. This problem is compounded by the fact that it is possible, under the provisions of a U.S. Supreme Court decision (*North Carolina vs. Alford*, 400 U.S. 25, 1970) to plead guilty to a charge while at the same time not acknowledging that you committed the crime. In one case, the offender said he was pleading guilty because he knew a jury would convict him after viewing his evidence, but he wasn't admitting he did it because he just couldn't remember. Although it is understandable why a prosecutor might accept such a plea in some cases, its use prevents the offender from having to accept public responsibility for his behavior. He is once again able to plead "guilty, but not guilty." Another variation of this, which may have increasing popularity in upcoming years, is the child molester pleading not guilty by reason of insanity. If state insanity criteria allow it, he will claim he knew his acts were wrong, but he lacked the ability to conform his behavior to the law and was driven by an irresistible impulse. The fact that he performed his acts only in private and never in front of authorities will be minimized. The judge and jury will then be given the difficult task of differentiating between an irresistible impulse and an impulse not resisted.

A wide variety of criminals may react in similar ways when their activity is discovered or investigated. However, the above-described reactions have been so consistently and repeatedly seen in child molesters, particularly preferential child molesters, that their occurrence is highly predictable and should be anticipated.

Postconviction

After being convicted and if they are sentenced to incarceration, some pedophiles come up with another reaction. This involves asking to speak to law enforcement investigators and claiming to have important information about more serious offenses against children. They might claim to know about organized child sex rings, child pornography, child prostitution, abduction of children, and/or child murders. Although this reaction is not as common as the others discussed here, the author knows of numerous cases in which this has happened. In most of these cases, the information furnished has turned out to be essentially exaggerated, distorted, or false. Investigators have no choice but to investigate and check out such allegations because they might be partially or totally true. However, investigators must be skeptical and cautious in their response. Convicted pedophiles are often motivated to invent such stories in order to delay their incarceration in a penitentiary, where they will not be highly regarded by other inmates, or simply to break up the boredom and routine of prison life. Others are motivated by the continuing need to justify and rationalize their acts with children by talking about the more horrible acts of others, especially child abductors and killers. Such stories should be carefully evaluated and assessed, and early use of the polygraph by an examiner experienced in interviewing child molesters should be considered.

Suicide

One other reaction should also be anticipated in certain cases. An offender—especially from a middle-class-or-above background—who has no prior arrest or one prior arrest should be considered a high suicide risk at any time after arrest or conviction. The law enforcement investigator should be prepared to be blamed for the offender's death.

Investigative Difficulties

The author has observed four major dynamics that make the investigation of child sexual abuse and exploitation difficult for the law enforcement officer and the criminal justice system. There are no magical solutions to these problems. However, recognition and awareness help in dealing with them. Some of these investigative difficulties are not unique to child sexual abuse cases, but only their impact on and relevance to such cases will be discussed here. These four major investigative difficulties are (1) the fact that a child is an ideal victim; (2) isolation of affect; (3) the question what constitutes sexual activity; and (4) societal attitudes.

A Child Is an Ideal Victim

Children in general have certain characteristics that make them ideal victims from the *offender's* point of view. Some of these characteristics are:

Naturally Curious. Children have a natural curiosity about the world around them. As they grow older, one of the things they become curious about is sex. This curiosity is fueled by the fact that for most children, sex is a taboo subject about which they receive little accurate information, especially from their parents. Children quickly begin to recognize that there is "something" going on in the world around them (parental behavior, television, advertisements, magazines, overheard conversations, etc.), from which they are generally excluded and about which they are formally told very little. This natural curiosity and the lack of information to fulfill it can be easily exploited by a clever child molester to lower children's inhibitions and gradually seduce them into sexual activity.

Easily Led by Adults. Many parents specifically tell their children to respect and obey adults. But even when that specific message isn't given, children soon realize that adults hold the power in the world around them and that their very survival depends on these "powerful" adults. In addition to fulfilling physical and emotional needs of children, adults are powerful to a small child simply because of their physical size. Most adults might be highly motivated to follow almost any instructions from a 12-foot-tall, 700-pound giant. Many adults in a child's life (parents, teachers, clergy, police officers, etc.) are extra-powerful adults with even greater influence over children. Any adult child molester can simply exploit his (or her) size and adult status to influence and control a child's behavior. But if he is one of these extra-powerful adults, he has even more influence and control. Parents, priests, ministers, teachers, police officers, etc., do molest children. Some child molesters exploit their status as stepfathers, guardians, Big Brothers, Scout leaders, etc., to entice children into sexual activity. Child molesters who don't actually have this added adult authority sometimes impersonate such individuals. Many child molesters claim to be police officers, ministers, etc., when they are not.

Need for Attention and Affection. This is by far the most significant characteristic of children that makes them ideal victims, especially for the seduction-type child molester. Just observe parents who go to a public pool and play with their child in the water. Usually within minutes, dozens of other children flock around asking the adult "stranger" to "do me next!" Even when they are getting attention and affection at home, children still crave and need it from significant others in their lives. Although all children are at risk from such seduction techniques, it seems that the child who is from a broken home, who is the victim of emotional neglect, or who has strong feelings of alienation is most vulnerable. This vulnerability says nothing about the socioeconomic status of the child victim. Children from middle-class, upper-middle-class, and wealthy families can be starved for attention and affection. Many victims get to the point where they are willing to trade sex for the attention and affection they get from the child molester.

It is sad but true that some child molesters treat their victims better in many ways than the victims' own parents do. The seduction child molester exploits the child's need for attention and affection to his advantage. However, it must be understood that the child molester is usually willing to supply all this attention and affection only as long as the child meets his age preferences. When the child gets too "old," the attention and affection usually turn to neglect and indifference.

Recently reported statistics concerning the large numbers of children being raised in single-parent families and/or with both parents or their only parent working would seem to indicate that our country is almost a utopia for the seduction child molester. Many parents are not only *not* suspicious of adults who want to spend excessive amounts of time with their children, they welcome them with open arms. They are often glad when the nice man down the street wants to play with their child every day after school or take their child away for the weekend. Parents should at least be suspicious of individuals who want to be with their children more than they do.

Need to Defy Parents. This is the least significant characteristic of children that makes them ideal victims. However, many children, especially when they reach adolescence, go through a period when they seem to have a need to do whatever their parents told them not to do. Maybe it is a normal part of growing up and becoming independent. However, this can be exploited by the child molester to his advantage. Any child who gets victimized as a result of disobeying some parental guideline or instruction is going to be very reluctant to tell anyone about it. This is especially true of adolescent boys, who feel they will lose some of their freedom if they reveal their victimization.

Children Are Poor Witnesses. This is the most controversial of the characteristics that make children ideal victims. Are children poor witnesses? Ten or more years ago this was widely accepted and believed. People thought children lived in a fantasy world and couldn't distinguish fantasy from reality. Few believed them when they reported being sexually abused. If some people believed them, they were then allowed to be confused and harassed when they tried to testify in court. Gradually the criminal justice system began to learn more about the dynamics of child sexual abuse. More and more people believed child victims of sexual abuse. Gradually the party line in the child sexual abuse movement became that children *never* lie about sexual abuse. "Children lie to get out of trouble, not to get in trouble" and "If the child has details, it must have happened" became the accepted attitude of many. For some, children came to be viewed as ideal or perfect witnesses. Talking to a child victim was almost like talking to God. Maybe this was almost as big a mistake as the old belief that children can't be believed.

Children are not poor witnesses. They are not ideal witnesses. They are different witnesses. Although child witnesses have many of the same traits as adult witnesses, they are not simply adults in little bodies to be treated by the criminal justice system as if they were adults. The criminal justice system must make special allowances for the developmental stages of children. However, children are not ideal perfect human beings who are incapable of being confused or deceived or, in some cases, of lying or distorting. Information furnished by children must be evaluated and assessed like the information furnished by any victim or witness. It must not be ignored, but it must not be blindly believed in every detail. If possible, as an early step in this assessment, consideration should be given to having a young child victim or witness evaluated by a mental health professional in order to determine the child's developmental progress. This information can be of assistance in evaluating the information and details furnished by the child. However, this is not always possible or practical.

It has been the author's experience that children rarely deliberately lie about sexual abuse, but they do sometimes misperceive events. Children can be confused, tricked, or even drugged by offenders. In today's modern society, even very young children can learn about sex, including bizarre and unusual sex, from peers, television, video tapes, magazines, observation of adults around them, and even from well-meaning sexual abuse or missing children prevention programs. Children can be easily influenced by untrained or overzealous interviewers including parents, therapists, social workers, and police.

However, the bottom line is the fact that the criminal justice system, in the United States, is still struggling with the issues concerning children as witnesses. Therefore, the net result is still that from the offenders' point of view, children, especially very young children, are almost ideal victims.

Isolation of Affect

Almost anyone employed in an occupation that puts him in regular contact with the many undesirable aspects of human life soon begins to unconsciously employ the defense mechanism of isolation of affect. An emotional barrier or wall is built around these undesirable aspects. Law enforcement certainly falls into this category of occupations. Police officers usually learn quickly to bottle their emotions. This is why friends and relatives who knew them before their law enforcement career soon begin to say things like "You've changed, you're so cold and uncaring." Although isolation of affect can be counterproductive if taken to the extreme, it is an important and effective coping mechanism for police officers. Without it, many would become basket cases in a short time.

Over the years, the author has spoken to many police officers about this phenomenon. They repeatedly say that they can usually employ this defense mechanism in almost all cases, *except* child victim crimes—and especially child sexual abuse cases. For reasons unknown to the author, male police officers seem to have a bigger problem with this than female police officers. Male police officers are typically repulsed by, and strongly condemn, child sexual abuse. They believe such cases should be aggressively investigated and prosecuted, but they personally don't want to do it.

Any police officer assigned to the investigation of child sexual abuse should be a volunteer who has been carefully selected and trained in this highly specialized work. This kind of work is not for everyone. Officers must decide for themselves whether or not they can deal with this type of work. Just as important, every officer working these cases must continually monitor himself. The fact that you are effectively coping with it now doesn't mean you will be effectively coping with it 2 or 5 years from now. This is "toxic" work, and each individual has a tolerance level.

It is important for officers working child abuse and exploitation cases to have outside interests and hobbies. One officer assigned to the investigation of child abuse was asked by the author if he had seen a recent television show about sexual abuse of children. He responded that after working this stuff 8 hours a day, the last thing he would watch on television when he got home was a show on child abuse. This is probably a healthy attitude. The fight against sexual abuse should not become a 24-hour-a-day, one-man (or -woman) crusade. If the investigator comes to feel he can't take a moment's rest while children everywhere are being molested, maybe it is time for him to look for another investigative assignment.

Police officers investigating child sexual abuse and exploitation must also learn to cope with the stigma within law enforcement attached to sex crime and vice investigation. Because there is so much ignorance about sex in general and deviant sexual behavior specifically, fellow officers frequently ridicule, tease, and joke about sex crime and vice investigators. They are labeled as department weirdos or perverts. How could anyone normal work that kind of stuff? For officers working child sexual abuse, especially in medium or small departments, it is even worse. They frequently become isolated from their peer group because their fellow officers don't want to hear about child molesters and child pornography. Police officers frequently socialize with each other and talk "shop." However, when an officer working child sexual abuse starts to talk about a child molestation case, someone tries to change the subject or, if that fails, suddenly everyone has to go home. This problem is not as bad for officers assigned to specialized child abuse units in larger departments or to specialized task forces. They can share and ventilate with each other. However, officers in medium and small departments frequently have no one to talk to about their work. Many officers also can't talk about this work to spouses, family members, loved ones, or friends. The author has received numerous phone calls from police officers who have no specific questions but merely want to talk about a case. This is a problem that supervisors, as well as individual officers, must recognize and deal with. One investigator wrote the author that trying to talk to his superiors about the nature and scope of this problem (sexual exploitation of children) was like trying to convince the Air Force of the existence of UFOs.

When a police officer can't isolate some of the emotion of these cases, his emotion/reason scale gets out of balance. As emotion goes up, reason goes down. An officer who gets too emotionally involved in a case is more likely to make mistakes and errors in judgment. He may wind up losing a case and allowing a child molester to go free because he "violated his (the offender's) rights" in some way. The officer also is less likely to interview and assess a child victim objectively.

What Constitutes Sexual Activity?

This appears to be an easy question to answer, but any officer who has investigated child sexual abuse cases knows it is not. Is hugging a child a sexual act? Is kissing a child a sexual act? Is appearing naked in front of a child a sexual act? The answer to all these questions is that it depends. Depends on what? Depends on the intent of the individual performing these acts. Intent is an important concept in any criminal investigation.

Very often the child victim is the most valuable source of information concerning intent. The victim knows or can "feel" the difference between hugging and fondling, affectionate kissing and passionate kissing, simple or accidental nudity and indecent exposure. Proving it in court can still be difficult. Especially in incest cases, many offenders will attempt to claim such acts are an acceptable, and even desirable, interaction with children.

Even seemingly obvious sexual acts such as oral–genital contact or oral–breast contact can be confusing, especially when the offender is a female. The author is aware of several cases in which women have openly admitted to sucking and licking the genitals of a child, but claimed it was part of normal mothering or child care. When a child is crying and upset and other techniques fail, the woman claims it is acceptable to lick the child's genitals. In another case, a female babysitter claimed that having the child suck on her breasts was only part of her efforts to quiet and soothe the child. If a male offender claimed any of this, most police investigators would double over in laughter. But when a woman claims it, people aren't so sure. Usually there is someone who comes forward and claims to have "heard" of such a custom. It is usually a custom or part of a culture in some far Pacific island or wilderness jungle or remote mountain area. Nobody has any first-hand information, they only heard about it. In two cases recently brought to the attention of the author, two female Filipino nannies caring for children in the United States claimed that their fondling and masturbating of the children in their care was part of their nanny training and an acceptable practice in the Philippines. The author is aware of no specific evidence that such acts are or are not part of certain customs or cultures. However, even if they are customs or part of a culture, this does not mean they are not abuse.

Is it a sexual act for a mother to have her 6-month-old baby suck on her breasts? Of course not, most people would respond. How about having her 2-year-old child suck on her breasts? Probably not? How about having her 5-year-old or 8-year-old or 10-year-old, etc., suck on her breasts? At what age does this become unacceptable or possibly a sexual act?

Child molesters frequently engage in acts that are behaviorally, if not legally, sexual acts. Seemingly normal acts such as photographing children, touching children, wrestling with children, or even looking at children can be sexual acts for some individuals. More bizarre acts, such as sucking on toes, urinating, defecating, inserting pins or needles, inflicting physical pain, and many others, could all be sexual acts, whether performed by the adult on the child or by the child on the adult. In one case, an offender got sexual gratification from tape-recording the sound of little boys belching after they drank the carbonated beverages he gave them. When confronted by the police, he turned over hundreds of feet of such audio recordings. What do you charge such an individual with? In another case, an offender got sexual gratification from photographing children pretending they were dead after a make-believe game of cops and robbers or cowboys and Indians. One offender admitted "molesting" about 60 children but stated that that figure did not include the thousands of children he merely "touched" for sexual gratification.

Societal Attitudes

What is society's attitude about the sexual abuse of children? Most would probably quickly respond that it is one of universal condemnation, that American society views child molesting as a serious, horrible crime. Some even point out that even other criminals don't like child molesters. When sent to prison, they must frequently be put in protective custody because other inmates may assault them. There is some degree of truth to these responses, but the total truth requires closer examination.

There are several organizations in this country and around the world that openly voice a far different attitude about adult sex with children. The Rene Guyon Society, the North American Man-Boy Love Association (NAMBLA), the Pedophile Information Exchange (PIE), the Child Sensuality Circle, the Pedo-Alert Network (PAN), and the Lewis Carroll Collector's Guild are all examples of groups that openly advocate adult–child sex and the changing of laws that make it a crime. These groups usually restrict their advocacy to "consenting" sexual activity with children. They usually claim to be opposed to forced sex with children; however, if the child agrees to or originates the activity, it should not be a crime, they say.

In an interview in *Hustler* magazine, Tim O'Hara of the Rene Guyon Society is quoted as saying, "In about 90 percent of the cases, where people get arrested the child pleads for sexual gratification, and the adults cannot stand the child's pleading anymore. Their resistance collapses. But the law says the child should not be gratified, even when the desire to be sexually gratified originated with the child. That law should be changed" (Pesta, date unknown, p. 38). Many people are tempted to laugh at this crudely and bluntly stated attitude. However, as society's attitude about adult sex with children is explored, this attitude will be heard over and over again in much more academic and subtle ways from many others.

In spite of the attention many of these organizations have gotten in the past years from the media and concerned citizen groups, it is doubtful they have had any significant impact on American public opinion in general. Their greatest harm to society is as a source of support and validation for child molesters and pedophiles. These groups and the material they publish help child molesters justify their behavior and feel better about themselves. Many pedophiles are openly proud of their behavior. In a letter to *The Baltimore Gay Paper* published in the July 1984 edition, a convicted child molester writes that to accept that he is one of the sick is "like asking Martin Luther King to brag of white blood in his veins or asking a Jew in Nazi Germany to pass as a Christian. I am not ashamed, but proud that I have been blessed with the love of many fine, beautiful boys in my life. I thank God for making me a boy-lover" (Latham, 1984, p. 2).

Believe it or not, in addition to the previously mentioned groups, some academics, mental health professionals, and sexologists express very similar views. These so-called experts on human sexual behavior sometimes equate the existing laws prohibiting sex with children with old laws that once prohibited masturbation, fornication, and homosexuality. They claim sex with children is not immoral and illegal, it is simply politically incorrect at this time. They advocate changing laws so that children can choose their sexual partners freely, but under the guise of children's rights and freedom. These "enlightened" intellectuals often ridicule the attitude of the common citizen as religious fanaticism driven by repressed sexuality. Investigators need to be aware that these "experts" frequently appear at the trials of child molesters and pornographers to testify either that the defendant's behavior isn't harmful or that the defendant is so "sick" he is not responsible for his acts. Society and the courts often hold these individuals in awe because of their academic credentials and turn to them for answers they don't have.

In addition, there are some psychologists and psychiatrists who accept the highly debated and controversial Freudian view that many females fantasize about their sexual victimization because they secretly love their fathers and hate their mothers. According to a related concept, commonly known as the "Lolita complex," sexual relations between adults and children are somtimes the result of children, especially girls, seducing adults. This is a kind of academic version of what Tim O'Hara of the Rene Guyon Society says.

The attitude that adults have sex with children because children want and initiate the activity, and that therefore adults should not be blamed or punished for such activity, is far more common and pervasive than most people realize. Such attitudes are widespread in the criminal justice system. In one widely reported case, a judge put a convicted offender on probation because the 5-year-old victim was sexually promiscuous. Many people were outraged by this act, but for the wrong reason. They were outraged because they did not think it was possible for a 5-year-old to be sexually promiscuous. It is possible, but this is the result of sexual abuse and not the cause of it. The public should have been outraged, because it makes no difference whether or not the child was sexually promiscuous.

This attitude toward victims is especially prevalent with adolescent victims. Sympathy for victims is inversely proportional to their age. An appeals court in one state overturned the felony conviction of an adult for having sexual relations with a 12-year-old, because the girl was not a virgin. The court felt that the law did not intend to punish consensual intercourse with chaste and unchaste children equally. This attitude is especially common in cases of adolescent prostitution. Do the courts really deal harshly with men who utilize the services of child prostitutes? In another case involving adolescent boys, a prosecutor announced to the press on the day the subject was arrested that the victims were as guilty as the subject. Again we hear the voice of Tim O'Hara.

These may be the attitudes of some child molesters, pedophiles, sexologists, psychologists, judges, or lawyers, but certainly they are not the attitudes of "regular" people? To examine these attitudes, let's examine a true story.

A new chief of police takes over in a medium-sized New England city. Within a few months of assuming his duties, he initiates an investigation that succeeds in identifying and arresting a child molester who had been operating in this community for 30 years. Does the community give him an award? Do they hold a parade in his honor? Do they give him a raise? The answer is none of the above. The community is outraged. They protest his actions and come to the defense of the subject. The chief of police is told to drop the case or go look for another job. What happened in this case? What happened was that the child molester identified and arrested was not a sleazy monster, but a prominent member of the community who was a popular schoolteacher for over 30 years. The community refused to accept this reality. This community's response is not a rare isolated occurrence, but a fairly common reaction. People want to believe that child molesters are evil monsters who are easily identified and not likable neighbors, teachers, clergyman, etc. The most common societal attitude toward sexual abuse of children is denial.

Police investigators must be prepared to deal with the fact that the identification, investigation, and prosecution of many child molesters may not be welcomed by their communities. Citizens may protest, picket, and write angry letters to the local newspaper. Community organizations (professional groups, school boards, employers, unions, etc.) may rally to the support of the offender and even attack the victims. City officials may apply pressure to halt or cover up the investigation.

The final frustration for the police officer often comes in the sentencing of a convicted child molester. If a man lured 20 children into his home over a 2-year period of time, tied them down, and smashed each of their knees with a hammer so that the children were physical cripples for the rest of their lives, society would demand that such an offender be locked up forever or even executed. Society does not want to hear that he goes to church on Sunday, is kind to his neighbors, works hard, or is "sick." The crippled children are there for the court and the world to see. But if a man lured 20 children into his home over a 2-year period of time, seduced them, lowered their inhibitions, and had sex with them so that the children were emotional cripples for the rest of their lives, it's a different story. Character witnesses come into court to testify that the defendant is a nice man who goes to church every Sunday, is kind to his neighbors, and works hard. Psychologists or psychiatrists testify that he is sick. The child victims may be in the courtroom, but who can see their injuries and scars? The result is that such offenders are sentenced to little or no jail time. They are not criminals, they are poor unfortunate sick people. Why the difference in society's response?

There are serious sex offenses, such as lust murder, torture, and sadistic rape, that are generally dealt with severely by the criminal justice system. There are nuisance sex offenses, such as indecent exposure and window peeping, that are generally dealt with lightly by the criminal justice system. The problem is that the non–physically violent sexual abuse of children is more often dealt with as a nuisance offense than as a serious sex offense. Risks, diversion programs, and outpatient treatment that would never be considered for "serious" sex offenders are repeatedly given to child molesters. The only explanation seems to be that sexual abuse of children is not considered to be a serious sex offense, but a nuisance sex offense.

The bottom line is that society often condemns child molestation in the abstract, but responds to individual cases differently, depending on the particular circumstances and who the molester is. Sometimes it is easier to deny what happened or to blame the child victim.

Summary

When investigating child sexual abuse or exploitation, the law enforcement investigator must recognize that not all child molesters are the same. Old *and* new stereotypes must be avoided. Child molesters can be "nice guys." Not all child molesters or child abductors are pedophiles (preferential child molesters). Incest offenders sometimes collect child pornography and molest children other than their own. Child molesters date and marry women to gain access to children. Preferential child molesters almost always collect child pornography and/or erotica, which is invaluable evidence.

Understanding and recognizing different types of offenders and their patterns of behavior can play a large role in enabling the law enforcement investigator to develop the evidence necessary to arrest and convict a child molester *without* the child victims having to testify in court.

The investigation of child sexual abuse or exploitation can be difficult. Investigators assigned to these cases should be carefully selected and trained. In spite of recent public outrage and concern, investigators must recognize that the investigation of these cases is not always welcomed by society and their efforts will not always be rewarded with praise. There may be limits to how long any investigator should be assigned to such cases. Supervisors must recognize the special aspects of these cases and should provide monitoring and support for investigators.

References

Adams, Henry E. and Tollison, C. David. *Sexual Disorders*. New York: Gardner Press, 1979.

Dietz, Park Elliott. "Sex Offenses: Behavior Aspects," in *Encyclopedia of Crime and Justice*, edited by Kadish, S. H., et al. New York: Free Press, 1983.

Diagnostic and Statistical Manual of Mental Disorders, third edition. Washington, D.C.: American Psychiatric Association, 1980.

Groth, A. Nicholas. "Patterns of Sexual Assault Against Children and Adolescents," in *Sexual Assault of Children and Adolescents*, by Burgess, Ann Wolbert, et al. Lexington, Massachusetts: Lexington Books, 1980.

Groth, A. Nicholas, et al. "The Child Molester: Clinical Observations," in *Social Work and Child Sexual Abuse*, edited by Conte, Jon R. and Shore, David A. New York: Hawthorne Press, 1982.

Haeberle, Erwin J. "Children, Sex and Society," in *Hustler* (date unknown). Reprinted from *The Sex Atlas: A New Illustrated Guide*, by Haeberle, Erwin J. New York: The Seabury Press, 1978.

Latham, Ray. "Not Ashamed of Being a Boy-Lover," in *The Baltimore Gay Paper*, Volume VI, Number 7. Baltimore, Maryland: Gay Community Center of Baltimore, 1984.

McBride, Will and Fleischhauer-Hardt, Helga. *Show Me*. New York: St. Martin's Press, 1975.

Pesta, Ben. "Tim O'Hara—Our Slogan is Sex by Eight or Else It's Too Late." *Hustler*, August (year unknown).

Personality Assessment 10

RICHARD L. AULT, JR., PH.D.,
AND ROBERT R. HAZELWOOD

A 19-year-old female was abducted, raped, and murdered, and her body found in a shallow creek. An investigation resulted in the development of a suspect who lived near the site where the body was found. The principal investigator in the case decided to interview the suspect immediately and, needing a partner, took the first detective available. Determining that the suspect was at work in a restaurant, they went to that location and conducted the interview in the establishment's kitchen. The suspect was hostile and shouted at the detectives that he was a homosexual. Very shortly, the principal investigator regretted his choice of partners, who was well-known as an individual who detested homosexuality. Predictably, the partner became increasingly angry and began shouting and menacing the suspect. Needless to say, the interview was a dismal failure and an opportunity to solve the case quickly had passed.

In the above example, several obvious mistakes were made: (1) not knowing the suspect was homosexual, (2) insufficient care in the selection of the partner, and (3) interviewing the suspect at his place of employment. There were many factors that should have been considered prior to conducting the interview, such as: (1) What environment would have been best suited for the interview? (2) What time of day (or night) should the interview have taken place? (3) What sex, race, age, and size of interviewer would have had the most success with the suspect? These are but a few of the significant questions that might have been answered, had an assessment of the suspect's personality been done prior to conducting the interview.

Every investigator has experienced failure in interviewing suspects, subjects, or even witnesses. In many cases, this failure is caused by inadequate preparation on the part of the interviewer. The propensity to interview an identified suspect without proper preparation is a critical mistake. Admittedly, the rush to interview is frequently attributable to external sources, such as case load, administrative pressures, or interference from superiors. All too often, however, the investigator doesn't take the time to obtain the behavioral and psychologically based information about the suspect that may make the difference between success and failure in an interview or trial situation.

The goal of this chapter is to provide the investigator with information on the application of personality assessment—a behavioral science technique—in the investigation of rape. The reader will also be provided with an assessment protocol that may assist in gathering information necessary for the application of this technique. The intent is not to teach the reader how to prepare an assessment, but rather to familiarize him/her with its applications, the type of information that must be collected, and what the best sources of information will be.

It should be noted at the outset that a great deal of time and effort is involved in gathering information and preparing an assessment. Therefore, the decision to have an assessment prepared should be a judicious one. Because of the investment of time and effort, it is recommended that this technique be considered for use in major investigations only. Remember, too, that while information gathering is performed by the investigators and others, the assessment should be prepared by individuals trained in the behavioral sciences who are not directly involved in the case being investigated.

Behavioral Science and Law Enforcement

Traditionally, law enforcement has not trusted the behavioral sciences. One has only to hear five mental health professionals testify in a court of law to see that behavioral scientists do not often agree among themselves. Time and again, investigators have heard contradictory or unrealistic testimony from those who purport to be experts in mental health. Nevertheless, investigators can and should make use of advances in the behavioral sciences for the benefit of the law enforcement profession.

An excellent example of the successful union of behavioral science and law enforcement is profiling, or assessment of crime scenes (Ault and Reese, 1980; Porter, 1983). Criminal personality profiling has become widely used through the Federal Bureau of Investigation's Behavioral Science Unit (BSU), located at the FBI Academy, Quantico, Virginia. BSU profiles are usually quite accurate and become increasingly so as its data improves.

A profile is the end result of a behavioral assessment of a crime scene or, in the case of rape, the interaction between the offender and his victim. The profiler interprets the evidence to produce a vivid outline of the salient characteristics of the offender. In a rape case, for example, the behavioral evidence left by the rapist allows the investigative profiler to determine a variety of information about the unknown assailant. As he demonstrates in Chapter 7 of this book, Hazelwood encourages rape investigators to solicit information about the offender's behavior that may give "the officer better insight into the [psychological and social aspects of] the type of person he is seeking" (p. 153). While Hazelwood's statement concerns criminal personality profiling, it is also applicable to personality assessment. If the investigator's experience in the field is informed by behavioral principles, he will be able to eliminate unlikely suspects and limit the scope of his investigation.

It has been stated that criminal personality profiling is now a widely used technique in rape and other crimes of violence. A lesser-known, but equally valuable, behavioral science technique is the assessment of a suspect or offender's personality for investigative or trial purposes.

What Is Assessment?

Although definitions of assessment abound, most behavioral scientists agree that it is a variable process, not something that can be reduced to a "cookbook" technique. Maloney and Ward (1976) describe assessment as "a variable process, depending on the questions asked, the person involved, time commitments, and myriad other factors. As such, it cannot be reduced to a finite set of specific rules or steps" (p. 5). Sundberg, in his book *Assessment of Persons* (1977), states that "knowing others and ourselves is still largely an art, though certainly it is aided by an emerging science" (p. 2).

There is no simple answer to the question "What is assessment?" Assessment has always been an integral process of human existence. All of us are involved, in one way or another, in assessing others. We select close friends from our acquaintances, we trust our money to one bank or another, and we have our car repaired by one mechanic or another. In these selections, we involve ourselves in an assessment. The friend may have been selected because of his or her attitudes, appearance, humor, or for many other reasons. The bank may have been chosen because of its location, convenient hours of operation, and monetary reserves. The mechanic may have been selected because of his reputation for good work at a reasonable price. In each case, the evaluation process required information about the individual or firm involved.

Assessment is also the term used by mental health professionals when they attempt to determine the mental state of individuals charged with a crime or when screening applicants for employment in law enforcement.

For law enforcement purposes, personality assessment may be defined as an evaluation of behavioral information about a particular individual in an attempt to determine areas of personality that are susceptible to investigative techniques.

The purpose of all assessment processes is to determine what makes people "tick"—what type of person the individual is. Law enforcement assessments do not serve the same goals as those of mental health. Law enforcement assessors are attempting to determine areas of vulnerability in the personality, while mental health professionals are attempting to diagnose and treat. While the goals are different, law enforcement can use the tools of the clinician in identifying those components of the suspect's personality that will be susceptible to the knowledgeable investigator.

Assessment Techniques

There are three basic techniques used by mental health professionals to assess individuals: objective, projective, and behavioral. The following descriptions are necessarily brief. Readers interested in a more detailed discussion are referred to the recommended readings following this chapter.

Objective techniques seek to evaluate aspects of the personality that can be measured by tests usually given by psychologists. The technique is called *objective* because it asks the individual to respond to specific questions, the answers to which do not require much interpretation. The term "cookbook" is often applied to this technique because the final product, the analysis, is a direct result of the ingredients—or answers—that went into it.

There are a number of problems that limit the use of objective techniques in law enforcement, the most obvious being the difficulty of asking a suspect to take a test. Another problem is that the validity of all objective tests requires the respondent to be truthful and not to sway the test in one direction or another. Law enforcement officials would not want to depend solely on such a test to determine personality factors of a suspected rapist for interview purposes.

The objective techniques, therefore, are not often applicable in the assessment of suspects or offenders. However, investigators should never rule out the possibility of obtaining the results of tests suspects or offenders have previously taken while others were gathering background information about them.

Projective techniques are based in part on the theory that an individual, faced with an unstructured situation or stimulus, will reveal some unconscious thoughts and/or emotions as he attempts to make sense of the stimulus (Maloney and Ward, 1976; Sundberg, 1977). The most widely known projective technique is the Rorschach ink blot test, which, like the objective tests, is usually administered by a psychologist.

Projective techniques are controversial. Enthusiasm for their use depends on the examiner's particular school of thought and the use to which the test will be put. One problem with projective tests is that people respond to ambiguous situations with much more than unconscious impulses and needs.

However, law enforcement officers can effectively apply the projective hypothesis to practical situations. When they gather information about a suspect, they must be aware that the quality of that information may depend upon the source from which it was obtained. For example, information received from a suspect's ex-girlfriend or wife may be more valuable than the same type of information obtained from his employer. The suspect, because of his emotional relationship, will relax his defenses and show more (or less) of his thought structure to his girlfriend than to his employer. These principles may help in evaluating contradictory information from several sources.

Behavioral techniques are the types most used by investigative profilers in the preparation of personality assessments. They are based on reported or actual observations of what a person does and what he or she says. They do not rely on self-reported material other than to note how it may contrast with how the individual behaves. Personality assessments for law enforcement purposes are based on observations of behavior accompanied by such questions as: "When was the behavior first observed?" "How frequently did it occur?" "How long did it last?" and "What was going on in the individual's life at the time?"

Observation of behavior is not a new concept to law enforcement, but determining baselines of behavior is. An individual preparing an assessment is concerned not only with *what* behavior is occurring but *how long* it has been occurring. For example, if an officer determined during a rape investigation that a suspect was reported to have increased his consumption of alcohol, the officer should attempt to learn when the increased consumption began. Significant events can cause an individual to alter his behavior to such an extent that the alterations in behavior would be noticed by those around him. The increase in alcohol intake may be indicative of additional stress on the part of the suspect. If the behavior change was noticed shortly after the rapes occurred, it would be of significance to the investigator and the assessor.

The Assessment Process

Often, the assessment process will yield information about a suspect that the investigator is already aware of. This is not necessarily wasted or useless information, in that it is external confirmation and will serve to reinforce the direction of the investigation. Occasionally the assessor's conclusions will clash with those of the investigator, and this may also have positive results. The reasoning by which the investigative profiler arrived at his/her conclusions should always be included so the investigator can observe the suspect from a different perspective. The decision to accept the assessor's evaluation and recommendations is left entirely up to the principal investigator in the case, and the assessment should never be allowed to replace the investigative process or overrule the investigator's decisions.

For purposes of this chapter, the assessor is a person with an advanced degree in behavioral sciences (i.e., social worker, psychologist, clinical psychologist, psychiatrist, etc.), experienced in criminal investigations, who studies the behavior of an individual to determine where he or she may be vulnerable to diverse investigative techniques.

In order to facilitate the process, the investigator must keep in mind certain fundamentals.

First, the investigator must determine the specific purpose of the assessment. Assessments are done with the understanding that a specific problem exists that must be addressed. Each assessment is unique because each is designed to achieve a specific goal or series of goals (e.g., how to best approach a subject for interview, what type of interview conditions would be best for this subject, and what type of interviewer should be used). Some of the ways in which assessments may help the investigator will be discussed in the section "Uses of Personality Assessments."

Second, the most time-consuming and critical step in the process is the collection of information. The appendix to this chapter sets forth a suggested protocol for the gathering of information. While it may not be necessary for all the information listed in the protocol to be collected, it is imperative that the officer, or whoever assists him, collect the behavioral information in a structured manner to assure quality results. The following suggestions will assist in providing the necessary structure for quality results:

1. *Ask the same question of many sources.* For example, if a question concerning fears of the suspect is asked (i.e., "Do you know of anything that scares John?"), then the question should be identically stated to all who are questioned. This is necessary in that once an officer has learned something about a person, he tends to file it away as a fact unless someone contradicts it later on. However, if the

same question is repeatedly asked, the reliability issue is resolved rather quickly.

2. *Determine how the source knows the information.* Information about an individual gains value when the investigator determines how the source became aware of the information provided. For example, if the source reports that he or she observed the behavior (subject drinking himself into a stupor), it would certainly be much more significant than if the source had heard about the behavior.
3. *Determine when the information was obtained by the source.* A "baseline" for the subject's behavior can be established if the assessor is aware of when, and if, behavior has changed over a period of time. Therefore, the investigator should attempt to pinpoint behavioral time factors. One method of doing so is to determine when the source acquired the information that is being reported.
4. *Determine how long the subject has exhibited the behavior.* To further assist the assessor in determining a behavioral baseline, the officer should inquire as to whether the reported behavior (e.g., compulsive gambling) is a recent activity of the subject or one that has been noted over a period of time, and, if so, over what period of time. To learn that a suspect in a rape and torture case reads bondage magazines is very significant if he has been doing so for 2 years prior to the offense. It becomes much less significant, however, if he was observed looking through such a magazine on only one occasion.

Uses of Personality Assessments

Generally speaking, investigators are not aware of what a personality assessment can provide. Typically, they will ask, "What can I expect?" The answer to that question depends on what the investigator intends to do with the assessment and the quality of information that can be collected and provided to the assessor. For example, an assessment may be requested in anticipation of an interview, and the investigator may want to know what type of approach should be made, how questions should be phrased to the subject, what areas should be emphasized or avoided, or what environment would be most beneficial to the investigator; or he may request that all of the aforementioned areas be addressed. Depending on the quantity and quality of information available, the assessor will advise the requesting officer as to whether or not the stated goals can be met. Hopefully, the assessor will suggest additional uses of the assessment that will further assist the investigation.

While the potential for assessment used by law enforcement is virtually unlimited, in rape cases assessments have proven most helpful in the following ways: (1) preparing for the initial interview of a suspect or offender, (2) assisting in the planning of prosecutive strategy, and (3) reducing the number of suspects.

Preparing for the Initial Interview

It is extremely important to note that this investigative technique is most useful in the *initial* interview of a suspect or an offender. It is much less helpful in subsequent interviews. The reason is that the psychological advantage lies with the investigator in the first confrontation with the subject. The individual being interviewed is uneasy and unaware of the extent of the investigative effort, how much is known (or remains unknown), and how long he has been a suspect in the matter. The initial interview may also be crucial to the case if direct evidence linking the suspect to the crime is not available.

CASE 1

A 12-year-old girl had been reported missing, and several days of searching failed to locate her. Her body was found 3 weeks later in a deserted shack within several miles of her home. Evidence indicated that she had been killed elsewhere and her body transported to the shack. Investigators identified one suspect during the period the victim was missing. The suspect, convicted previously on charges dealing with abduction and rape of minors, had served time in prison prior to returning to the area in which the victim resided. The investigators were fairly certain that the suspect had killed the victim, and were about to conduct their initial interview. Realizing they had little evidence to link the suspect to the crime, they wanted to assure that, if he had committed the crime, he would confess. They requested an assessment of the subject.

Collecting the necessary information, the officers learned that the subject was not well educated, but was of average intelligence. They discovered that although he was a loner, he had worked as a security guard for a short time. His employment, and his previous exposure to police, made the suspect well-versed in police methods. The investigators were gratified that they had not rushed into the interview with little preparation. It was obvious to them that a routine interview would have been unsuccessful.

The personality assessment provided them with suggestions for preinterview and interview techniques. The suggestions included interview environment (lighting, seating arrangements, and location); a specific time for the interview to commence; composition of the interview team (age, sex, race, height, attire, and educational level); method of introduction; topical areas to avoid or emphasize; and props to be present and in view of the suspect. The interview was successful, and the offender was later convicted.

Reducing the Number of Suspects

In some cases, more than one person may emerge as a suspect in a rape or series of rapes. Once the investigation has narrowed the number of possibilities to two or three, the assessment technique may prove of value to the investigation.

CASE 2

A series of 20 rapes occurred in an 11-month period; all took place within a large housing complex. Police became convinced, correctly, that at least 18 of the rapes were committed by one individual, and they requested a criminal personality profile. The profile was prepared, and five suspects were subsequently developed. The investigation eliminated all but two of the suspects and, at this point, a personality assessment of these two suspects was requested. Data on the two were collected, and an evaluation of this information showed that significant behavioral changes should have been evidenced by one of the suspects during the series of rapes. The investigators had noticed this fact during the information-gathering stage of assessment, and had begun to concentrate their investigative efforts on the individual prior to receipt of the assessment. This case clearly illustrates the value of gathering such information, whether an assessment is requested or not, since the police would not have noticed the behavior change without the background information.

Planning Prosecutive Strategy

The value of personality assessment in the trial situation has been proven repeatedly. It has proven useful in the development of opening and closing remarks to the jury, as well as the development of questions for use in cross examination.

CASE 3

A 28-year-old man brutally raped and murdered a 21-year-old female. After the murder, he hid the body and left the area. When the body was discovered and the young man became the prime suspect, he was arrested. He told police that the victim was raped and killed by intruders, who then threatened to kill him if he talked to the police. According to investigators, the evidence linking the suspect to the crime was very strong circumstantial evidence, and indicated that the young man had committed the murder. The prosecutor requested an assessment in order to comprehend the motives behind the criminal and the crime so that he might make a strong and logical argument to the jury in the event the suspect took the stand. Two assessors first analyzed the crime behavior, then compared that behavior to the information available about the subject's personality. A logical and comprehensive assessment was prepared that provided the prosecutor with an opinion on the murderer's reasons for the attack and on the victim's behavior that triggered the crime. The assessment also designed specific questions to exploit the offender's weaknesses should he elect to take the witness stand. Following a successful trial, the prosecutor expressed his appreciation for the usefulness of the assessment technique for trial purposes.

Information Required for an Assessment

As mentioned, the appendix to this chapter contains a protocol to be used by investigators desiring a personality assessment. Information generally of interest to an assessor includes: (1) demographic data, (2) religion, (3) education, (4) hobbies or pastimes, (5) physical characteristics, (6) marriage(s), (7) employment, (8) specific types of behavior, and (9) mental and physical health. While the protocol is quite comprehensive, much of the information may not be required. It therefore behooves the investigator to ascertain from the assessor what he/she will require for the process. It is also obvious that it may not be possible to obtain some of the information desired, a limitation that will be understood by the assessor.

In some instances, investigators may be legally or administratively prohibited from obtaining such information or providing it to outside consultants. It is recommended, therefore, that prior to requesting a personality assessment, the officer consult with his superiors and the responsible prosecutor, explaining the time and effort required and the intended use of the assessment. Ideally, the investigator who is most knowledgeable about the suspect/offender should be personally involved in the information gathering. It is imperative that he prepare the information summary that is to be submitted to the assessor.

Sources of Information

The information necessary for the preparation of personality assessment may be viable from many sources. The following have proven to be valuable in past assessments:

Records. Written documentation often provides insight into an individual's personality. For example, a poor credit record might indicate that a sense of responsibility is lacking or that the subject is inclined to impulsiveness. Employment records reflecting disciplinary problems may indicate a dislike for authority. Medical records that reflect numerous, but undiagnosed, ailments may indicate a need for attention. Arrest records and incident reports may provide information about the suspect's attitudes toward women. The type of documentation that may prove helpful is limited only by the imagination of the one seeking the information. Officers should not restrict their search for information only to their geographical area of responsibility, but should consider possible sources that may be found in areas where the individual previously resided.

Suspect's Friends and Associates. This source of information, while potentially rich in nature, should be approached cautiously, unless the investigator is intent on letting the subject know of the investigative interest in him (which may be an investigative suggestion of the assessor). If this is not the intent, the associates having least contact with the subject should be questioned first, followed by those slightly closer to him, and so on.

Former Spouse or Girlfriend. Experience has proven that this source is potentially the most valuable to an investigator desiring to become more knowledgeable about a subject. In many situations, the termination of the relationship was not pleasant, and feelings of anger or a desire for revenge may motivate such a source to divulge information of immense value for an assessment. A word of caution is necessary at this point. Anger or a desire for revenge may cause the source to exaggerate or lie about the subject. The investigator should be alert to this fact and prepare to deal with this possibility. Regardless, the former spouse or girlfriend often has knowledge about the subject that no one else possesses. Specifically, she should be able to advise the investigator about the subject's strengths, weaknesses and fears, sexual habits, what makes him happy or sad, and at what time of day or night he is most alert. This is by no means all-inclusive of the information she may possess.

Criminal Behavior. The behavior exhibited by the offender during the commission of previous sexual crimes should also be provided to the individual preparing the assessment. As addressed in Chapter 7, a carefully conducted interview of the rape victim can yield invaluable information about the offender's personality, motivation, and attitudes toward women.

Summary

For law enforcement purposes, a personality assessment is the evaluation of behavioral information about a particular individual in an attempt to determine his strengths and weaknesses as well as other areas of personality that may be susceptible to investigative techniques. Assessments may be used in preparing for the initial interview of suspects or subjects, to reduce the number of suspects, and in the preparation of trial strategy.

The appendix to this chapter contains a protocol useful in gathering information necessary for the preparation of a personality assessment. Since all of the information may not be required, the investigator should consult with the assessor prior to collecting the information. Sources of information about the suspect/subject may include records and other documentation, friends and associates, former spouses and/or girlfriends, and the behavior exhibited by the subject during the commission of previous or current sexual crimes.

Assessment is a useful tool in rape and other cases. A great part of the usefulness of assessment is that information on the suspect must be gathered that might not normally be collected. While this helps the behavioral scientist to assess the individual, it—more importantly—provides information directly to the investigator about the person being assessed. Thus, while assessment itself may be another tool in the investigative repertoire, the use of it enhances the chance for successful conclusion of the case.

APPENDIX

Principles

1. Ask the same questions of many sources.
2. Determine how the source knows the information.
3. Determine when the information was obtained by the source.
4. Determine how long the subject has exhibited the particular behavior being reported.

Assessment Information

GENERAL

Date of birth

Place of birth

Race

FAMILY

Socioeconomic status of family (upper, middle, lower)

Number of brothers

Number of sisters

Subject's place in birth order (oldest, youngest, middle, etc.)

Parents still living? If no, when did each die? If yes, where are they living?

Religion of family?

To what degree was (is) family involved in its religion?

What is (was) subject's relationship with parents?

a. Was it always like this?
b. When did it change?

SUBJECT

Is subject currently religious? What faith?

To what degree?

Is this involvement recent?

How do high school associates describe subject?

Are school records available for review by assessors?

EDUCATION LEVEL

What is the highest level of schooling subject obtained?

Why did subject leave school?

HOBBIES

What are subject's former hobbies?

What are subject's current hobbies?

What are subject's current special interests?

What are subject's former special interests?

What type of movies does subject enjoy?

What type of reading material does subject enjoy (i.e., spy novels, pornography, adventure stories, etc.)?

Where does subject currently live (rental apartment, trailer, house, etc.)?

Type of neighborhood (middle class, upper class, ghetto, etc.)?

Does subject live alone? If not alone, with whom?

Does subject have any friends?

How do they compare to him (higher/lower class, more/less educated, more/less money, more/less intelligent, any other comparison that is striking)?

Has the subject ever belonged to any groups or organizations (motorcycle clubs, volunteer police, special deputy, volunteer fireman, Explorer Scout, etc.)?

What is the subject's general mode of transportation (walking, bicycling, public transportation, own vehicle, etc.)?

Are there any unusual circumstances connected with subject's selection of mode of transportation?

If subject has his or her own vehicle, how well is it maintained?

PHYSICAL CHARACTERISTICS

What is subject's dress style compared with others in the subject's group (neater, sloppier, uncaring about appearance, stylish, etc.)?

What are your overall impressions of subject's personal appearance?

Has subject had this appearance as long as you have known him/her?

How is the subject's physical health and well-being? If subject has had any major illnesses or injuries, what were they?

Does subject have any unusual physical features (limp, hairlip, cast in eye, stutter, lisp, etc.)?

Does subject wear a beard and/or moustache? How long has the subject had it? Did subject say why he grew it?

Does subject smoke? What does subject smoke? For how long has subject smoked? How often?

Does subject drink alcoholic beverages? What does subject drink? How often? Does subject drink to excess?

How would you describe subject's overall physical appearance (handsome, pretty, fat, skinny, a "hunk," ugly, etc.)?

Does the subject have any mannerisms or gestures that stand out (i.e., places hand over mouth when nervous, talks loudly when scared, face turns red when angry, etc.)?

Does subject have any distinguishing scars, marks, or tattoos?

MARRIAGE

Is subject currently married? How long? How many times?

Was there anything unusual in any of the subject's marriages (i.e., divorced because of "extreme cruelty," marriage lasted very short time, etc.)?

What are subject's sexual preferences?

What are subject's perversions? (Be specific.)

What extramarital activity did subject engage in? Was subject blatant, or a braggart, about extramarital affairs? Please interview former spouses and mistresses, if possible.

EMPLOYMENT

Is subject employed? Where?

Is subject skilled in any area (welder, auto mechanic, electrician, machinist, professional, typist, etc.)?

How does subject relate to co-workers (leader, loner, agitator, etc.)?

How does subject relate to superiors (subservient, defiant, angry, unconcerned, etc.)?

How does subject relate to subordinates?

How many jobs has the subject held in the past 5 years? What type of jobs?

BEHAVIOR

What makes the subject angry?

What makes the subject happy?

Whom does subject turn to for advice?

What sorts of things seem important to subject?

How does subject relax?

How does subject spend free time?

How does subject react to the loss (by death, separation, alienation, etc.) of people important to him/her?

What events seem to shake subject's self-confidence?

HEALTH

Has subject had any major illnesses in past 5 years? If so, what?

Has subject sustained any injuries in past 5 years? If so, what?

Does subject have any history of mental illness?

What are subject's sleep patterns (early riser, up all night, sleep all day, etc.)?

Does subject use drugs? What type? How often?

References

Ault, R. L., Jr. and Reese, J. T. "A Psychological Assessment of Crime: Profiling." *FBI Law Enforcement Bulletin*, March 1980, pp. 22–25.

Maloney, M. P., and Ward, P. *Psychological Assessment: A Conceptual Approach.* New York: Oxford University Press, 1976.

Porter, B. "Mind Hunters: Tracking Down Killers with the FBI's Psychological Profiling Team." *Psychology Today*, April 1983, pp. 44–52.

Sundberg, N. B. *Assessment of Persons.* Englewood Cliffs, N.J.: Prentice-Hall, 1977.

Suggested Readings

Bristow, A. P. *Field Interrogation*, 2nd ed. Springfield, Illinois: Charles C. Thomas, 1964.

Bull, R., Bustin, B., Evans, P., and Gahagan, D. *Psychology for Police Officers.* Bath, England: John Wiley & Sons, 1983.

Duncan, S., Jr. and Fiske, D. W. *Truth and Deception.* Baltimore, Maryland: The Williams & Wilkins Co., 1977.

Eysenck, H. J. *The Structure of Human Personality.* Great Britain: John Dickens & Co., Ltd., 1970.

Groth, A. N. *Men Who Rape.* New York: Plenum Press, 1979.

Hazelwood, R. R. "The Behavior-Oriented Interview of Rape Victims: The Key to Profiling." *FBI Law Enforcement Bulletin*, September 1983, pp. 8–15.

Holt, R. R. *Assessing Personality.* New York: Harcourt Brace Jovanovich, Inc., 1971.

Johnson, W. C., Snibbe, J. R., and Evans, L. A. *Basic Psycholopathology: A Programmed Text.* New York: Spectrum Publications, Inc., 1975.

Knapp, M. L. *Nonverbal Communication in Human Interaction.* New York: Holt, Rinehart and Winston, 1978.

Lanyon, R. I. and Goodstein, L. D. *Personality Assessment.* New York: John Wiley and Sons, 1971.

Maloney, M. P. and Ward, P. *Psychological Assessment: A Conceptual Approach.* New York: Oxford University Press, 1976.

Neirenberg, G. I. and Calero, H. H. *How to Read a Person Like a Book.* New York: Hawthorn Books, Inc., 1971.

Rada, R. T. (Ed.). *Clinical Aspects of the Rapist.* New York: Grune and Stratton, Inc., 1978.

Rider, A. O. "The Firesetter: A Psychological Profile." *FBI Law Enforcement Bulletin,* June 1980, pp. 6–13.

Reed, J. E. and Inbau, F. E. *Truth and Deception.* Baltimore, Maryland: The Williams & Wilkins Co., 1977.

Samenow, S. E. *Inside the Criminal Mind.* New York: The New York Times Book Co., Inc., 1984.

Simpson, K. *Police: The Investigation of Violence.* London, England: MacDonald & Evans Ltd., 1978.

Sundberg, N. B. *Assessment of Persons.* Englewood Cliffs, New Jersey: Prentice-Hall, 1977.

Wiggins, S. *Personality and Prediction: Principles of Personality Assessment.* Menlo Park, California: Addison-Wesley Publishing Co., 1970.

False Allegations

11

CHARLES P. MCDOWELL, PH.D.,
AND NEIL S. HIBLER, PH.D.

The fact that a rape allegation may actually be false provides a major test of any investigator's ability. The knowledge of this possibility can easily foster a tendency to question the information furnished by the victim before obtaining all the necessary facts and evidence. This reaction can in turn make the victim feel defensive even though she is the one who has been wronged—a feeling that results in reduced cooperation. This, of course, causes the investigator to become even more suspicious. The result is a never-ending spiral of suspicion and pain for both.

In many ways, the criminal justice system already imposes an unfair burden on rape victims simply because rape is easier to claim than to prove (MacDonald, 1971). The situation is compounded by the fact that virtually all experienced investigators have taken false crime reports of one type or another in the past and are thus always sensitive to the possibility. Surprisingly, even though this phenomenon of the false rape report is well recognized, there has been little careful research into the problem and more is urgently needed.

This chapter will attempt to examine some of the few known dynamics associated with false reports and the characteristics of the people who make them. In this way, it is the hope of the authors that greater attention and consideration will be focused on this topic. As such, this chapter will not deal with actual rape victims, but rather with those individuals who utilize the criminal justice system to satisfy their own conscious or unconscious needs and desires. That such desperate actions are considered necessary is, in itself, tragic, but the greatest tragedy of all is the fact that it is the real rape victim and the investigator who will ultimately pay the price.

The Importance of Understanding False Rape Allegations

It is important to understand the dynamics of false rape allegations, because these deceptions impact on all who are involved. The foremost consequence of a false complaint is obviously the monstrous problem it creates for legitimate victims. The rape victim has suffered great pain, shock, humiliation, and the fear of death. This, plus the very real possibility of pregnancy or venereal disease, combined with her shattered sense of personal well-being, adds up to an enormous emotional burden. She is then confronted with the unbelievable problem of literally having to prove she was not a willing participant or worse.

As in all reports of violent crimes, investigative, prosecutorial, and medical personnel must, at some point, make a determination as to the veracity of the complaint. These professionals are usually busy and typically depend on "shorthand" cues to help them assess the complaints made to them. The cues are based on experience and conventional wisdom and usually function quite well. However, in the case of a rape report this technique can easily create a tendency to evaluate prematurely. This, of course, significantly reduces the level of rapport and understanding so necessary both to maintain the mental health of the victim and, eventually, to convict the perpetrator.

Second, those who make false allegations may have legitimate problems worthy of attention in their own right. Yet if their false allegations are accepted at face value (rather than as symptoms of other needs), the actual problems may go untreated, and can result in future difficulties. Finally, it goes without saying that a false allegation, especially when it is based on malice, can result in a grievous injustice. Only by understanding the inner motivations of those making false allegations can investigators hope to increase the possibility of convicting rapists, while at the same time providing needed assistance and protection for everyone involved.

On Being a Victim

To be the victim of a rape can be one of life's most traumatic experiences. As Bard and Sangrey (1979) have noted, rape "forces victims to question themselves and their world because it destroys two essential beliefs: their sense of trust and their sense of control over their lives." Rape victims typically require unqualified support, understanding, and the willingness of others to aid in a potentially long period of adjustment. The criminal justice system, health care organizations, and private groups have devised a variety of approaches such as rape crisis counselors and victim advocate groups in an effort to address these needs. The assistance is provided as circumstances and availability dictate, and is oriented toward restoring the victim to "normalcy" or as close to it as possible. On occasion, this attentive support and understanding can also be attractive to those who have not, in fact, been the victim of the crime of rape.

While there are several reasons for a woman to falsely claim to have been raped, one of the most difficult motives to understand is a simple but extremely exaggerated need for attention. Persons making false complaints for this reason usually have overwhelming feelings of inadequacy. They desperately want and need attention, usually in the form of concern and support. In their suffering, a claim of rape may seem a likely method to force a favorable response from friends and relatives as well as the authorities. Besides, they have probably tried a number of lesser methods of getting attention, and these have failed. Although false reports for this reason are relatively rare, it is important for the investigator to be aware of the possibility. The most significant fact in these cases is their reaction to the concern and support exhibited by friends, relatives, and the criminal justice community. In most rapes, even the most compassionate and supportive response from all concerned cannot fully alleviate the horror experienced by the victim. However, for the individual desperately seeking attention this solicitude may very well fill their needs.

Self-Esteem and the Need to Cope: The Framework of False Allegation

Perhaps the central feature of human personality is the concept of self-image. How one views oneself colors one's vision of the rest of the world. As Schlenker (1980) has noted, "One's self-concept and social identity are composed of numerous interrelated images of oneself; each image is discrete yet part of the whole."

Since a positive self-image is desirable, people strive for a sense of self-esteem, a belief in their own worthiness. As a developmental process, self-esteem in an individual must first be created and then maintained. A set of values, beliefs, and expectations becomes internalized and is then reinforced through the approval and acceptance the individual gains from others by living up to those values and expectations. The "others" from whom the individual seeks external approval consist of his or her parents, friends, co-workers, and others whom the individual respects and admires (and whose respect and admiration he or she values).

Self-esteem is maintained by behaving in ways that earn the approval of both the individual's "external audience" and his own conscience. Unfortunately, life is not always fair or easy, nor are people perfect. People occasionally violate their own values as well as those of their role models, and in so doing threaten their sense of self-esteem. When this happens, the need to reestablish a satisfactory level of self-esteem results in one or more of a variety of corrective responses. Thus, when people do something that is in conflict with their values, either they can maturely accept responsibility for their act, or they can protect their self-image by offering excuses to others (or themselves), or they can deny the act ever occurred. For people with highly internalized value systems, the reality of an act such as a casual sexual encounter can be so disturbing that the person may not be able to accept responsibility for it. When this happens the mind activates one or more of a number of possible defense mechanisms (Snyder, Higgins, and Stucky, 1983).

Protecting Self-Esteem: The Use of Defense Mechanisms

Defense mechanisms are the methods the mind uses to protect its self-esteem. They do so by allowing the mind to selectively "forget" what happened, deny responsibility, project blame to someone (or something) else, overcompensate, or seek escape in a world of fantasy. These reactions most often occur spontaneously and are not usually a matter of conscious desire or awareness. Through their use the mind is provided with a way of not having to face a sense of failure or feelings of inadequacy, and thus they assist in maintaining a positive sense of personal worth. Defense mechanisms naturally change the individual's perception of reality and encourage self-deception. Unfortunately, when used too often, the defense mechanisms not only do not solve the problem, they add another dimension to the original one. On rare occasions, activation of the right combination of defense mechanisms can result in a false claim of rape.

When a person utilizing this system falsely claims to be the victim of a rape, the mind has literally created an alternative reality with the crime itself as the focal point. This effectively changes one's role from participant to innocent. In this way the false claim enables individuals to recover, at least in the short term, their self-esteem and, at the same time, avoid responsibility for their own unacceptable conduct. When a false allegation is made in an effort to preserve the individual's self-esteem, the following defense mechanisms are usually involved:

Denial

At the very core of the false allegation is the denial of responsibility. A key to understanding false allegations therefore lies in understanding what really threatens the victim. This usually evolves around the person's internalized beliefs about his or her own courage, integrity, honesty, competence, loyalty, decency, and so on. When a person engages in acts that are so much in violation of his values that they threaten to destroy his entire system of beliefs about himself, the mind can choose to protect itself by denying the person's consensual participation.

Projection

Denial works best if it is accompanied by projection. If the mind chooses to deny responsibility for some act or failure, blame must be placed elsewhere. Through the use of a false allegation of rape, the responsibility and control is shifted to another person, someone whose actions were beyond the victim's ability to control. Thus, responsibility is "projected" or displaced to the criminal.

Escape

Denial is closely associated with escape. By denying responsibility, the mind seeks to escape accountability for actions that are unacceptable to it. By claiming to be the victim of rape, one shifts corrective responsibility to the police. Furthermore, if the "crime" cannot be solved, then the ultimate responsibility for failure lies with the police rather than the victim. The result is that the false claim allows the mind to "escape" the responsibility for the behavior and thus to maintain a positive self-image.

Rationalization

For a false allegation to be credible, it must be logical and believable. This requires the construction of a story that "explains" the crime. Rationalization is the mind's ability to find justification for something the individual has done or plans to do. It provides the superego with a logical reason that absolves the actor of blame and makes the action appear reasonable under the circumstances. The vulnerability of this manipulation lies in the fact that an individual who falsely claims to have been raped may have no understanding of what it really means to be a victim of rape. As a result, the report is based on what she believes happens in a rape situation. Imperfect understanding of rape is often transparent and thus provides valuable clues to experienced investigators who are seeking to provide effective support for the individual while taking the complaint.

Self-Handicapping (Secondary Gain)

In self-handicapping, the mind creates a situation in which the individual is in some way injured or at a disadvantage, in such a manner as to allow the person to evade responsibility. The result is that being injured or sick is actually advantageous. The effect of the deception can be more potent and effective than their own interpersonal skills (Snyder, Higgins, and Stucky, 1983). For example, the person who claims the inability to meet some obligation because of illness defers responsibility to a circumstance over which there is no control. To be effective, the handicap must, of course, appear to be beyond the control of the individual, but must eventually result in his or her favor. In a false claim of criminal victimization, it is automatically implied that the claimant is at a disadvantage by virtue of being harmed. Their innocence (lack of responsibility) is assumed because of the presumed actions of others who exploited them. In some cases, the mind may further defend itself by indicating that circumstances such as being lost, intoxicated, frightened, or confused further reduced the individual's normal ability to avoid victimization. By claiming to be the victim of a crime, the individual is thus able to derive support, care, and a degree of social control from a situation that was "beyond his or her control."

False Allegations and the Adaptation Continuum

The creation of a fictitious crime to avoid personal responsibility for some act or failure obviously represents an extreme departure from the way mature people normally deal with their problems. The extent to which false claims capitalize on actual events is unknown. However, there appears to be a rough continuum of inaccurate claims, ranging from a slightly distorted report of an actual event to the completely false report of an assault or rape. In its most extreme manifestation, the report can include bizarre scenarios supported by self-inflicted injuries and even self-mutilation. There have actually been incidents in which elaborate props, such as threatening letters or even messages written in blood, were used. Cases such as this at the far end of the continuum are extremely rare. Fictitious claims of criminal victimization at the more "normal" end of the continuum may be more frequent.

While the pathology involved in self-mutilation to support the false claim of rape is extremely rare, factitious claims of illness or injury on a much lower level are a well-recognized phenomenon in medical literature.

Severe cases of self-inflicted injuries or illnesses in which medical attention is sought have been termed *Munchausen's syndrome* (Asher, 1951). The name derives from the central figure in a book of tall tales and fabulous adventures who was named after Hieronymous Karl Friederich, Freiherr von Munchausen, a retired soldier known for his generosity and graphic conversations that took the form of the "serious narration of palpable absurdities." The key to understanding Munchausen's syndrome lies in awareness that the patient is trying to use hospitals and clinicians in the service of pathologic psychological needs under the guise of seeking medical treatment for an ostensibly legitimate illness.

Munchausen's syndrome is based on a preoccupation with manipulation. These patients appear to be compulsively driven to make their complaints. As Gawn (1955) has noted, "While he is aware he is acting an illness, . . . he cannot stop the act." Therefore, reports may capitalize on circumstances and occur only occasionally, or they may be a well-developed means of adapting and part of an extensive history (see Figure 1). The degree to which Munchausen's patients defend their claims is in direct proportion to their need to be seen as victims. Dramatic, extreme cases are not likely to confess to the hoax, and those who present such cases are prone to become enraged at the suggestion that their illnesses are anything but genuine (Nadelson, 1979; Pankratz, 1981).

In much the same way that Munchausen patients manipulate hospitals and doctors, a fraudulent claim of rape might be interpreted as a form of manipulation directed at the criminal justice system. This kind of manipulation is conceptually similar to other kinds of behavior (malingering, hysterical conversion reactions, and self-mutilation) that are well documented as medically achieved coping mechanisms (Ford, 1973). In Munchausen patients there is also a continuum, ranging from exaggerated claims of infirmity to actual self-induced illness (Grinker, 1961). At the extreme end of this continuum, life-threatening injuries are masqueraded as being legitimately contracted (Carney, 1980; Carney and Brown, 1983). Even child abuse, disguised as natural illness, is suspected of being an underrecognized means of gaining attention (Hodge et al., 1982; Kurlandsky et al., 1979; Meadow, 1982; Waller, 1983; Vaisrub, 1978).

Although police officers and investigators are used to seeing people who have been harmed or injured by others, they are less accustomed to seeing those who have harmed themselves. Most such instances involve a suicide or attempted suicide. However, since self-inflicted injuries used to support a claim of rape or assault are rare, it is "logical" for police to accept them at face value, at least initially. Where self-inflicted injuries are recognized as such and either are serious or appear to be very painful, it is understandable that police officers may look upon the victim as being mentally ill; yet, even those who reinforce their claims with severe self-inflicted injuries are seldom insane. Nevertheless, these individuals are psychiatrically impaired, and should be assisted in obtaining professional help. The following case is illustrative of this phenomenon:

Case 1

A 25-year-old housewife reported receiving obscene phone calls and threatening letters that were made out of words cut from magazines and newspapers and pasted on a blank sheet (see Figs. 1 and 2). A short while later, she reported being raped by an unidentified intruder who threatened to come back and kill her in a particularly brutal manner if she reported the rape to the authorities. She had numerous bruises and a bite mark on her left breast. During the course of a subsequent polygraph examination she admitted to fabricating the entire series of events. She also inflicted rope burns on her hands, bit her own breast, and ran face-first into a support

FIGURE 1

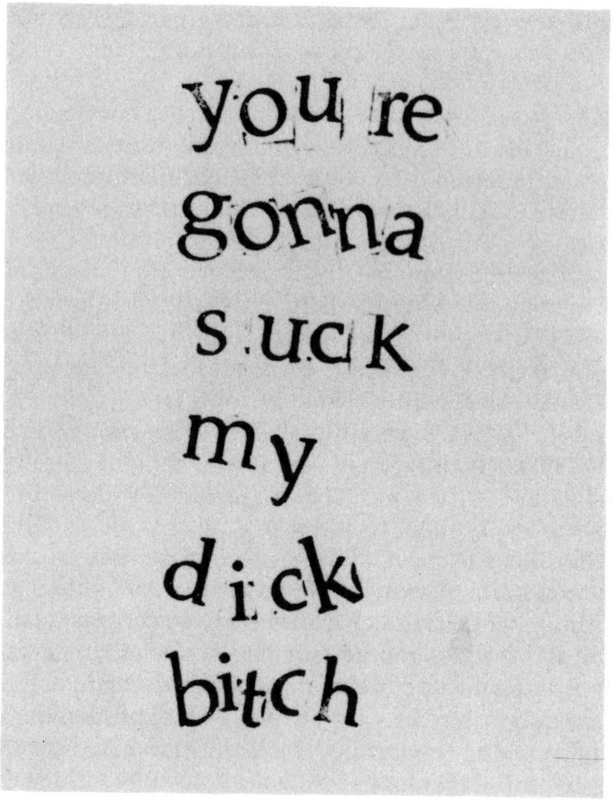

you re
gonna
suck
my
dick
bitch

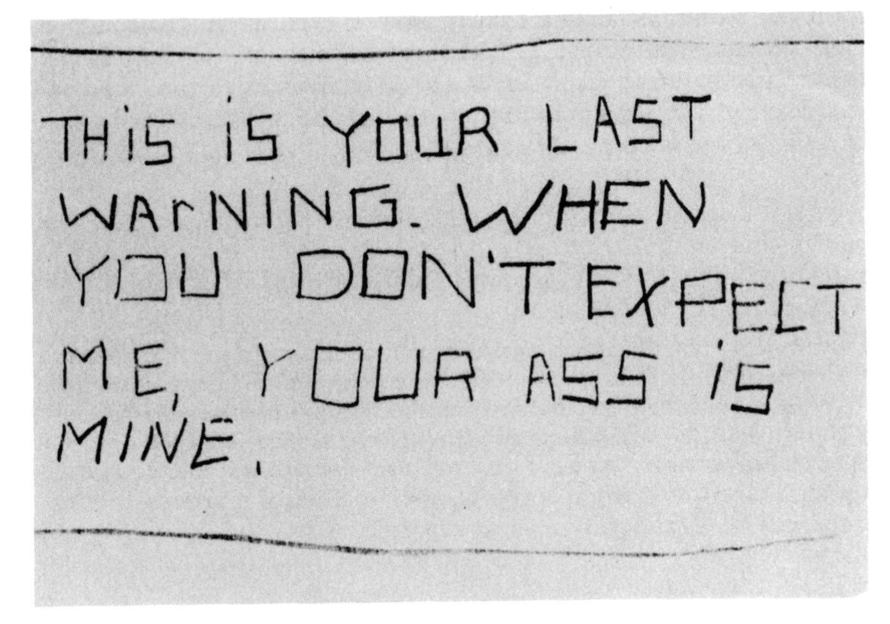

FIGURE 2

post in her basement in order to acquire the injuries she thought would support her claim of rape. She said her husband did not understand her or pay attention to her, and she wanted to "test his love."

As one proceeds along the continuum, the amount of violence the individual claims was used against her can reach fantastic levels, and the presenting dynamics of the case can become increasingly extraordinary. Keep in mind, however, that legitimate rapes may also incorporate varying levels of misperception. Because of this, every aspect must be scrutinized. For example, physical evidence and patterns of injury are always vital aspects in rape cases, and they require their own careful analysis. Appropriate support and assistance can only be given by a careful objective examination of both the information and the physical evidence available.

This woman's self-esteem had been eroded over time by her insensitive and uncaring husband. By claiming to be the recipient of obscene phone calls and letters, and by claiming to have been raped, she was effectively making a desperate statement of her worth, both as a person and as a sexually desirable partner. Her willingness to engage in self-injurious behavior to support her claim underscores the seriousness of her emotional problems.

Indicators of False Rape Allegations

There is, of course, no simple way to determine the legitimacy of any criminal complaint. This is true whether the report concerns the commission of a rape, a burglary, or any other offense. All complaints must, of necessity, be taken at face value and, unless there is some specific reason to believe otherwise, handled accordingly. False criminal reports are a relatively common reality in law enforcement. It is well known that victims frequently exaggerate the value of items taken in burglaries, and robberies are occasionally reported to explain the absence of money and other valuables to the victim's family. In most instances, it is impossible to determine whether the crime actually occurred unless the victim is moved to admit that the report was false. However, as in the false burglary or robbery complaint, certain characteristics are found with greater frequency in false rape reports than in actual rape cases. In and of themselves, none of these characteristics are significant, but taken together, they indicate a potential that the facts may be different from those reported.

The Victim–Offender Relationship

The literature suggests that a preponderance of rapes are committed by individuals who are known to the victim or with whom they have had some prior relationship. Many of these rapes are sexual assaults by friends, acquaintances, co-workers, associates, and even relatives. As a matter of fact, such affiliations often create additional problems for the victim because she must continue to face her assailant (as well as mutual friends) throughout the ordeal of the investigation and any subsequent legal proceedings. In false rape allegations there seems to be a somewhat higher probability that the assailant will be a stranger, a "slight acquaintance," or a "friend of a friend" whose name the victim has forgotten. The apparent reason for such a choice is that the victim removes the possibility of being confronted by a specific individual and, in addition, does not get anyone into trouble.

However, by creating an essentially anonymous rapist, the pseudovictim can effectively absolve herself of any responsibility for a relationship and thus affirm her basic innocence. In addition, by claiming to have been raped by an unidentifiable person, she makes it impossible for the police to "successfully" resolve the case, and the mind can freely shift responsibility from itself to the offender and ultimately to the police without fear of being contradicted.

Force and Resistance

One of the more obvious features of rape is that its victims typically report being overwhelmed by fear. Because of this, the actual level of physical resistance is frequently low and thus the actual force used by the rapist may not go beyond verbal threats. Even though the rapist may not employ physical methods or a visible weapon in his attack, the victim is convinced she is in mortal danger and reacts by doing whatever appears most likely to preserve her life. Often this involves a relatively nonviolent submission to her assailant. On the other hand, those making false complaints seem to claim more frequently to have fought with all their ability. They typically report punching, kicking, and scratching their assailants until they are themselves finally overpowered. Others bolster an inability to resist by claiming they were attacked and raped by more than one person. In other cases, the pseudovictim claims the assailant was exceptionally large or powerful and able to overcome her resistance with relative ease. The important point is that false victims more frequently include the face-saving element of either having resisted or having been confronted with a situation that made resistance impossible.

Nature of the Sexual Acts Performed

Although common law traditionally defines rape as an act involving sexual intercourse, the crime may also involve any number of other sexual acts. In a significant proportion of rape cases, women are subjected to acts other than or in addition to sexual intercourse. Such acts appear to be reported less frequently in the case of false complaints.

Apparently, the report of rape is not seen by false claimants as requiring collateral reports of oral or anal sex, unless such acts are included in the person's sexual repertoire. Thus, the false claim of rape is usually found to be more narrow in its construction and seldom includes much more than allegations of penile penetration and the manual manipulation of breasts or genitalia. This characteristic may arise from the reasoning that other acts are not required to support the claim, that the individual finds such acts personally repugnant and does not wish to debase herself, or that the mind does not require her to be more deceitful than is absolutely necessary. Just as important, under-describing of the attack may be another manifestation of the false claimant's naiveté as to what actually occurs in these crimes.

Recall of Details

Women who have been raped are generally able to provide a reasonably accurate description of the event, including the nature and sequence of the sexual acts performed. Women who make false allegations seem to more frequently report that they had their eyes closed at the time, that they "passed out" and do not recall the penetration, or that they cannot recall the specifics of the actual sex act itself. In the opposite extreme, they may also provide an emotionless, but exquisitely detailed, description of the event. It is important to note here that actual rape victims may also provide an emotionless description of what happened, a procedure that reflects their attempt to mentally disassociate themselves from the unacceptable experience. However, in the case of an actual rape, the description is seldom in the same exquisite detail.

Recounting the event may be embarrassing and emotionally unpleasant for the rape victim, but it is basically a recitation of what occurred. The woman making a false complaint is in a different situation. She must either "invent" the acts she alleges, or she must convert a consenting sexual experience into a "rape." In so doing, she finds herself in a culturally anomalous situation. Our society does not encourage women to discuss their sexual activities with others, especially with strangers (e.g., police officers). Reporting a false rape places the woman in just that circumstance. Unable to recount objectively something that was done to her, she tends either to become vague and evasive or to cross the cultural barrier and become overly descriptive.

Physical Injury

Based on our experience, approximately one-third of the legitimate rapes include some form of violence against the victim. In most instances this involves hitting or slapping the victim, choking her, knocking her to the ground, and/or forcibly tearing her clothes off. In a small percentage of the above cases, the level of violence is devastating. This is graphically illustrated in the following example.

Case 2

The victim was awakened at her residence by a co-worker and was told she was needed at her workplace, and that he had been sent to drive her there. She went with him and was abducted. He cursed and beat her and told her he was going to kill her. He attempted to strangle her with her skirt, burned her breasts with cigarettes, punched and slapped her. She was repeatedly raped and subjected to multiple forms of sexual abuse during which she was continuously beaten and threatened. The attack lasted several hours. He finally agreed not to kill her if she promised not to tell anyone what had happened.

Rape victims who are physically assaulted (beyond the rape itself) may sustain serious injuries, including broken bones, the loss of teeth, mutilation of the genitalia and breasts, and internal injuries. Indeed, some rape victims are murdered during the assault. False complainants do not usually present serious physical injuries. However, as one moves along the continuum of personal pathology, the extent of self-inflicted harm can increase.

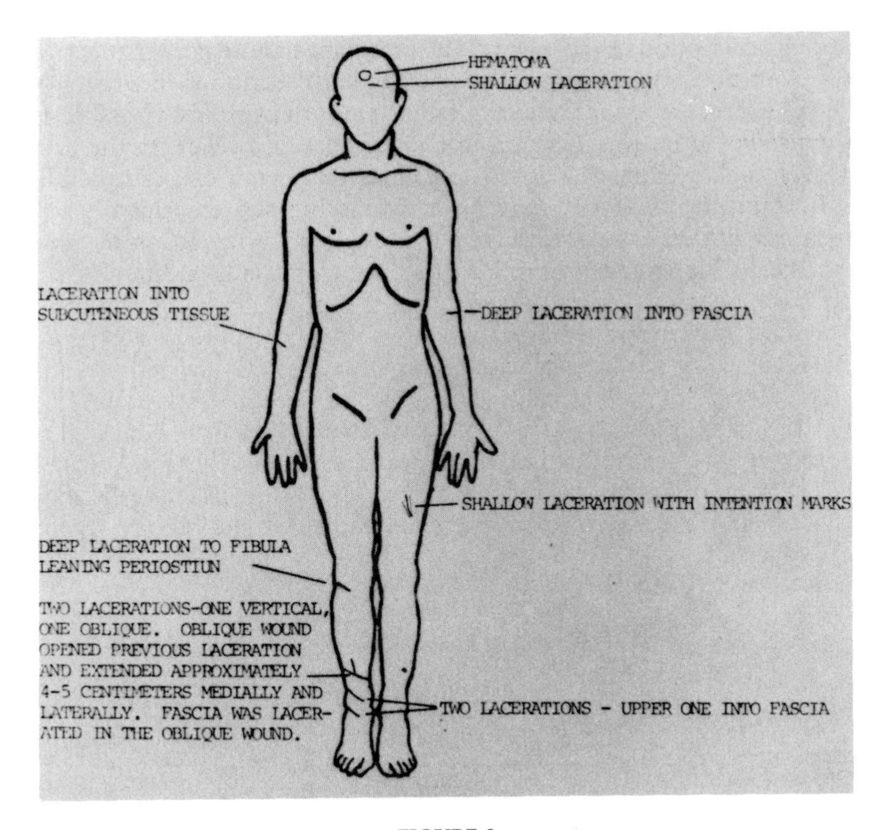

FIGURE 3

Case 3

A 27-year-old housewife was found, in a dazed state, lying on the ground in a wooded area near her house. A threatening letter was found tucked in her panties. She claimed to have been assaulted, but not raped. She sustained a number of scratches and bruises but was not seriously injured. About a week later, she claimed to have been assaulted in her basement, resulting in serious lacerations (see Figs. 3–9). A message written in blood informed her that she had been "warned."

This woman had been previously discharged from the armed forces for having made a false rape allegation, which was accompanied by self-mutilation. She had a long history of hospital admissions for suspicious injuries and illnesses. She was experiencing serious marital and financial problems and was having difficulty in evening college courses. Her claim of rape and serious assault was an effort to deny the many difficulties she faced. The allegation provided her with an

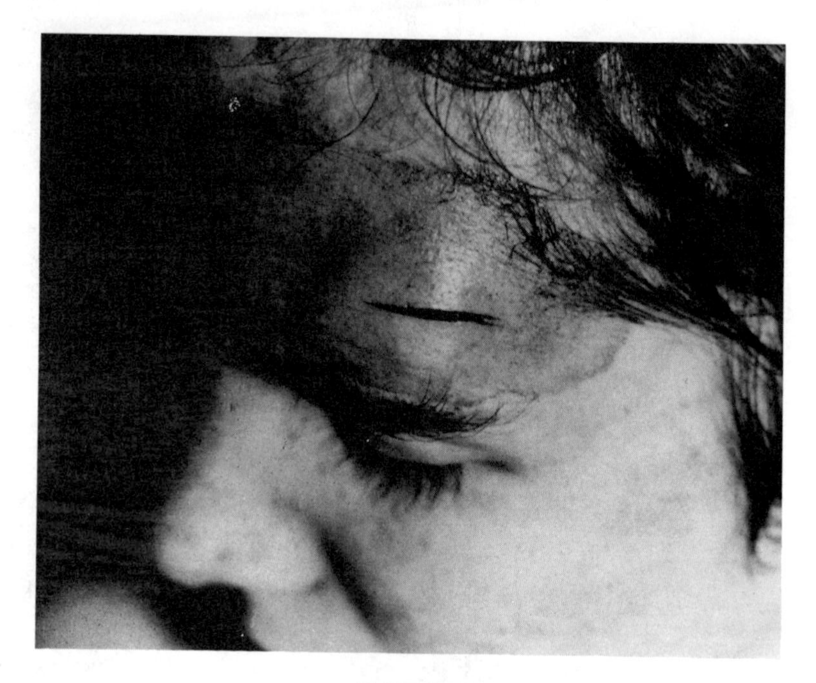

FIGURE 4

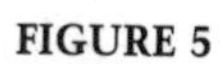

FIGURE 5

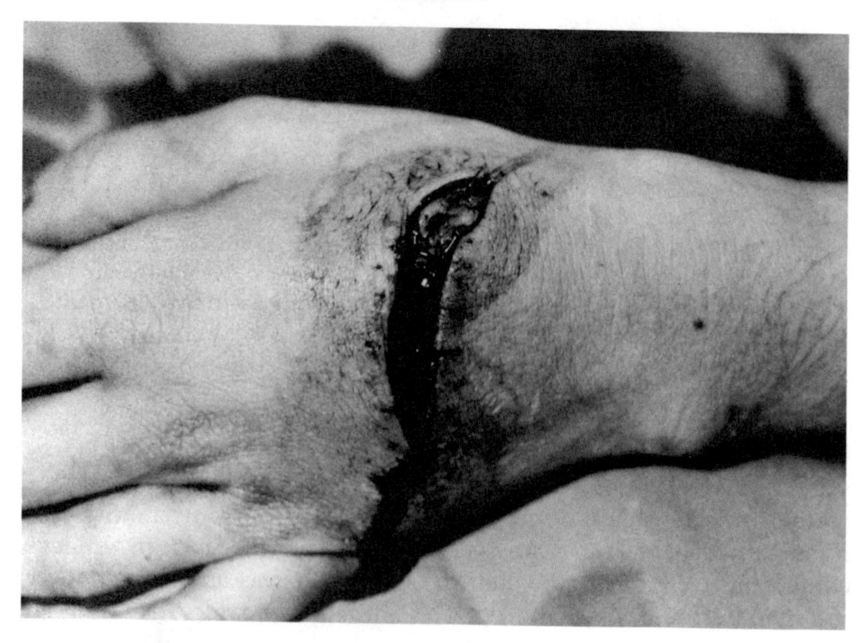

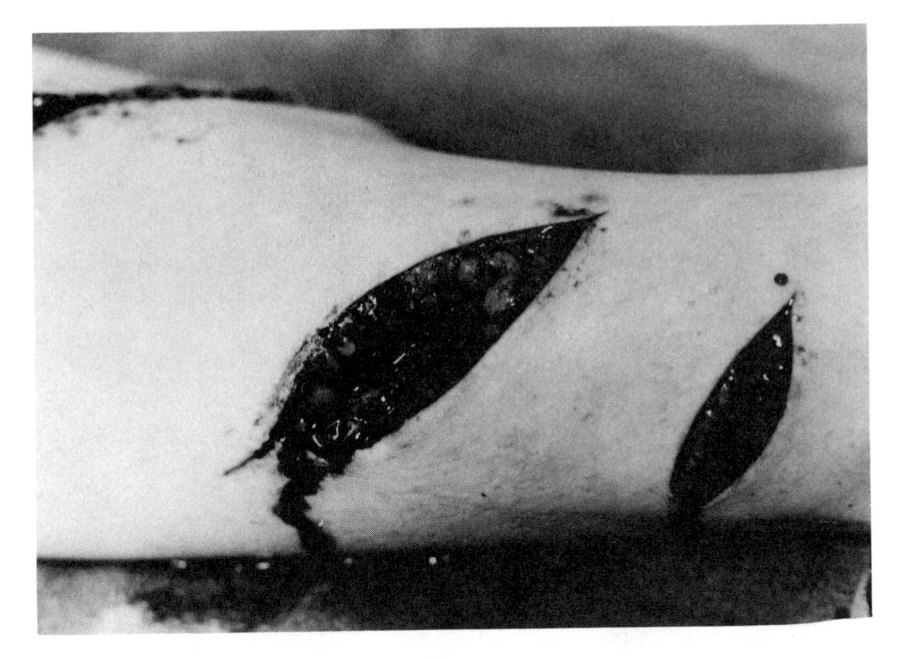

FIGURE 6

FIGURE 7

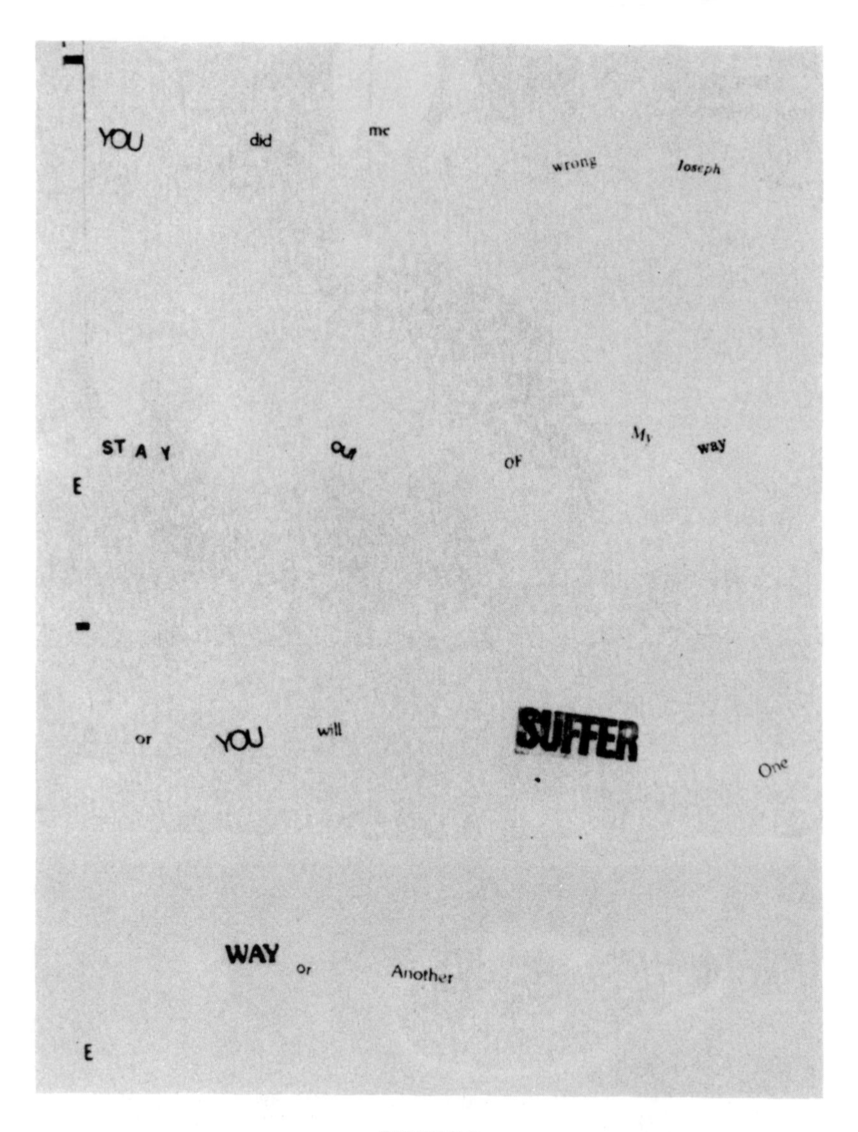

YOU did me wrong Joseph

STAY out OF My way

E

or YOU will SUFFER. One

WAY or Another

E

FIGURE 8

opportunity to become a "legitimate" victim and to receive care, sympathy, and support otherwise missing in her life.

These self-inflicted injuries are typically different from those that occur in actual sexual assaults. There are two characteristics about the injuries claimed in false rape allegations that should be of interest to the investigator. The first involves the wounds themselves, and the second concerns the victim's reaction to her injuries.

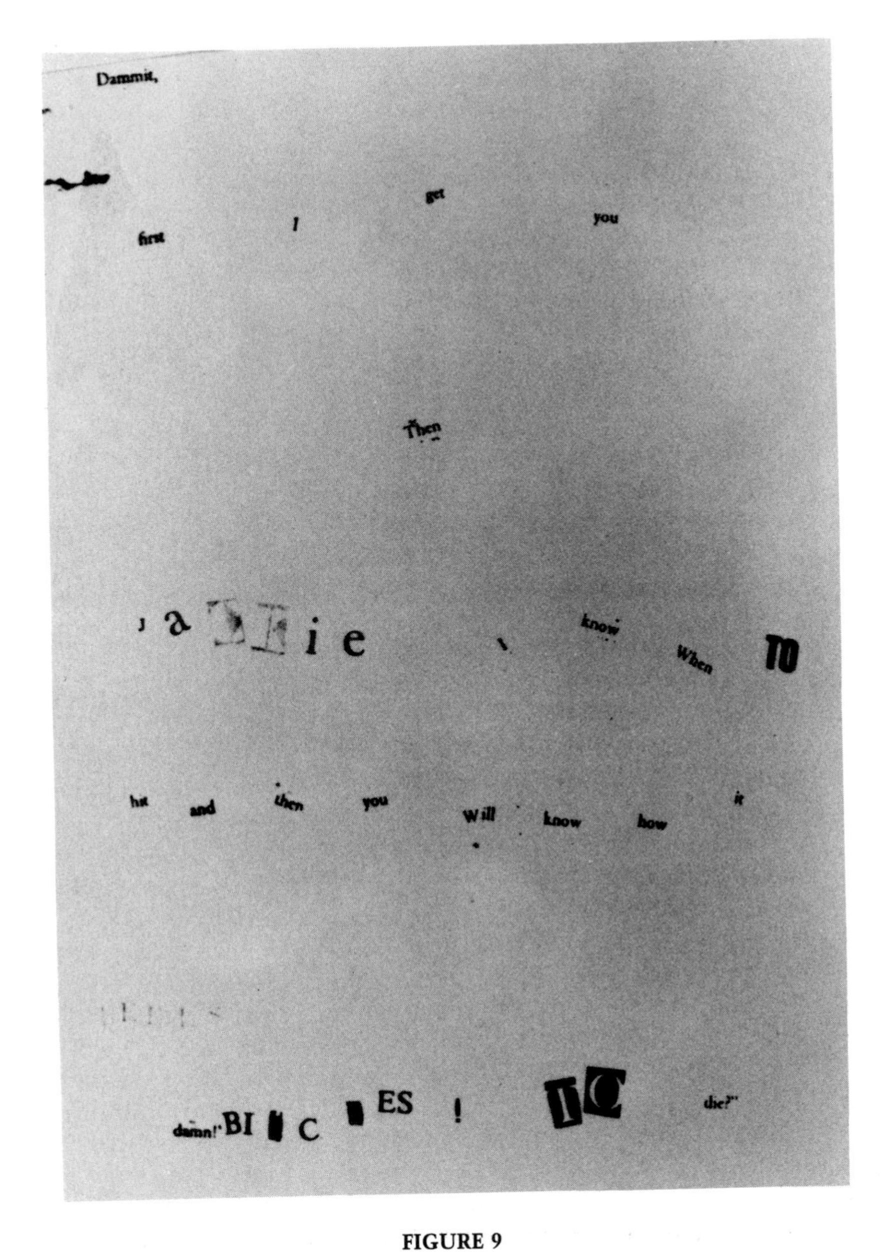

Dammit,

first I get you

Then

a ie know When TO

hit and then you Will know how it

damn!" BI C ES ! die?"

FIGURE 9

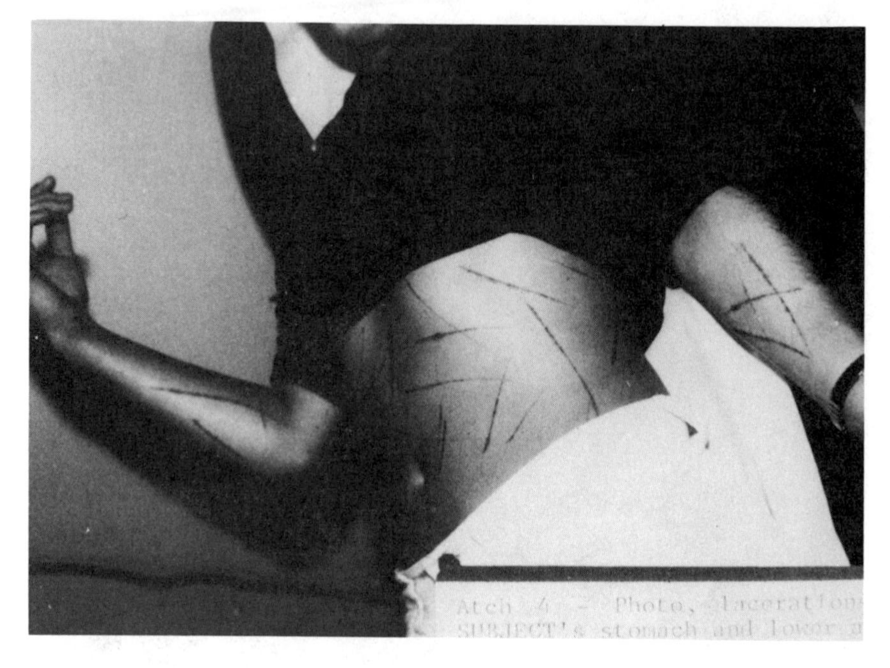

FIGURE 10

False victims who have injured themselves tend to exhibit an unusually wide array of wounds. In spite of this, extremely sensitive organs or tissues such as the eyes, nipples, lips, or genitalia are almost never injured. Self-inflicted injuries are usually caused by scratching with fingernails or by cutting with a razor or other sharp instruments. As such, the wounds tend to be located within reach and at unusual angles. Often they conform to the range of motion of the person's arm or hands. This is particularly noticeable in cuts or scratches on the sides, front, and lower back of the torso (see Figs. 10, 11, and 12). Although the wounds may range from minor scratches to life-threatening lacerations or punctures, they usually appear more severe than they really are. This is because they are inflicted for the purpose of supporting the individual's claim rather than to mutilate or kill. They also frequently reflect a sophisticated understanding of anatomy (i.e., major arteries or tendons are avoided and the likelihood of permanent disfigurement is minimal).

The second characteristic of pseudo-victims who injure themselves is their tendency to be strangely indifferent to their wounds. They appear to accept their injuries with a degree of nonchalance not found in people who sustain similar injuries at the hands of others (Marcus,

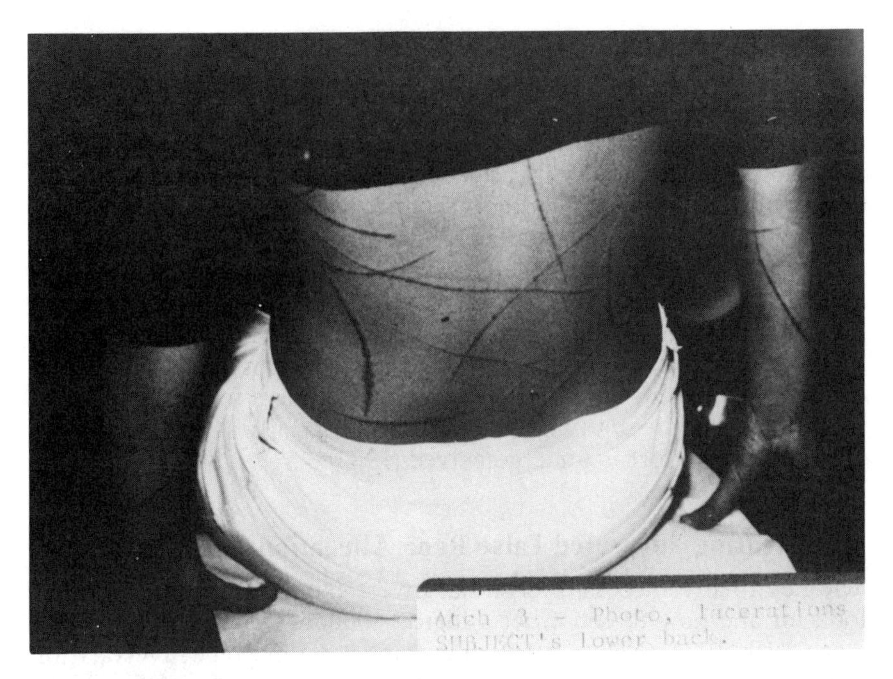

FIGURE 11

FIGURE 12

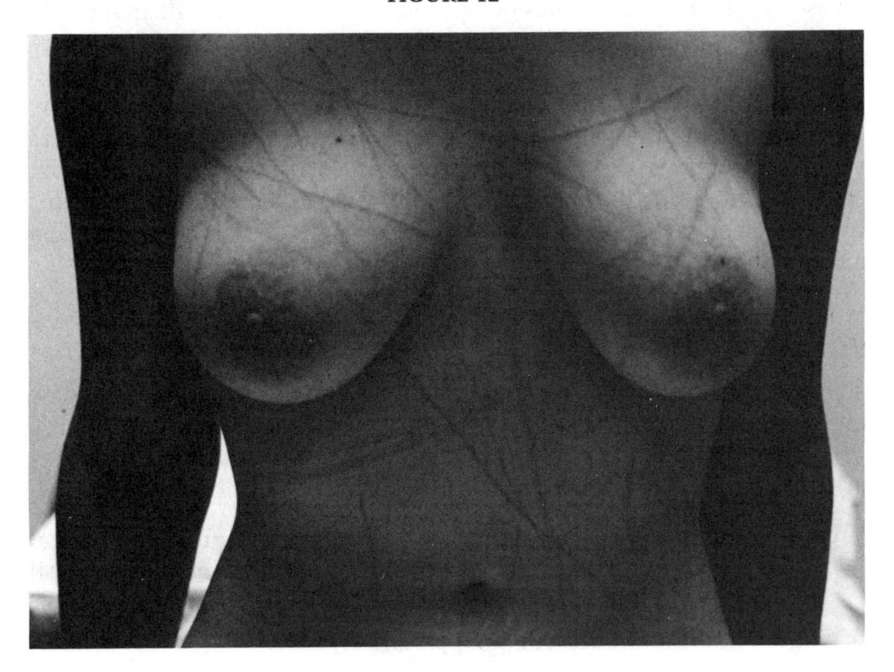

1981; Ross and McKay, 1979). Variations of this syndrome are often referred to as "la belle indifférence," and the feature is usually quite noticeable even though a general anxiety may be present. Panken hypothesizes that the lack of concern over their pain serves at least two purposes. First, the injury is the source of attention—a mechanism for obtaining the interest of others. Second, because the wound is self-inflicted, it is a form of punishment for guilt associated with being unable to persevere otherwise. In combination, these are masochistic acts that alleviate anxiety and serve as a form of self-directed retribution for the individual's perceived inadequacy. The result is a dramatic opportunity to further avoid responsibility by projecting blame onto an amorphous assailant and relying on others to resolve the difficulty. Hence, the injury may be so psychologically satisfying that its physical discomfort is underperceived (1983).

Investigating Suspected False Rape Allegations

The key to any successful criminal investigation is knowing what to look for and how to construct a logical sequence of the investigative steps (Kirk, 1974; O'Hara, 1977). If at some point in a rape investigation the allegation itself becomes suspect, immediate efforts should be made to resolve this question. Both the potential for false imprisonment and the need for objectivity demand this. To continue to work a case when the truthfulness of the victim is suspect will invariably result in a poor investigation and reduced cooperation, both then and in the future.

The information presented in the preceding sections discusses many of the key distinctions between actual and false rape allegations and suggests the investigative considerations set forth below. It is extremely important to remember that no single element is significant; it is only the combination of these factors that may suggest the possibility that an allegation may be exaggerated or false.

The Initial Complaint

The manner in which a rape allegation comes to the attention of law enforcement authorities is very significant. In our experience, the filing of a false report is usually somewhat delayed. Several other variables are also frequently associated with the filing of false complaints:

Complaint is usually first made to friends, associates, or medical authorities along with requests for tests for pregnancy or venereal disease.

Complainant is indifferent to apparent injuries.

Nature of Allegation

The concept of rape is deceptively simple, and women who make false allegations often structure their complaints in a fashion that seems to meet the "requirements" of rape but ignores its reality. False allegations, therefore, often contain less common elements, such as:

Complainant states she cannot describe her assailant because she kept her eyes closed.

Complainant alleges she was assaulted by more than one person, but cannot offer descriptions.

Complainant claims she offered vigorous resistance but was forcibly overcome.

Assailant was a total stranger or a person whom she can only describe in vague and nonspecific terms.

Complainant claims she received threatening notes or phone calls prior to or after the assault.

Complainant was unable to describe details and sequence of the sexual activities to which she was subjected.

Evidence

Law enforcement authorities correctly place a premium on the evidence supporting an allegation, because it often provides information needed for the prosecution of the case. Because of the nature of a rape case, evidence is particularly important. Moreover, the consistency or inconsistency of the evidence may suggest that a rape complaint has been exaggerated or is completely false. An absence of the kinds of evidence usually associated with rapes can sometimes be as revealing in identifying false allegations as its presence is in establishing that a rape has actually taken place. Some of the types of evidence that appear to suggest a false allegation are:

Complainant cannot recall where the crime took place even though she does not report being blindfolded, under influence of drugs or alcohol, or moved from location to location.

Crime scene does not support story (i.e., ground cover not disturbed; no footprints where there should be; no signs of struggle when they should logically be present).

Damage to her clothing is inconsistent with any injuries she reports (i.e., cuts or scratches inconsistent with tears or cuts in clothing).

Complainant presents cut-and-paste letters allegedly from the rapist in which death or rape threats are made.

Note or letter is identifiable with pseudovictim (via handwriting analysis, indented writing, typewriter comparison, paper stock, or fingerprint comparison).

Confirming laboratory findings are absent.

Injuries

The nature of the individual's injuries can provide a great deal of information about what did or did not happen. Women who make false rape allegations and attempt to support them with injuries tend to present a consistent picture in terms of the cues suggested below:

Injuries were made either by fingernails or by sharp instrument(s) usually not found at the scene.

Fingernail scrapings of victim reveal her own skin tissue.

Injuries are extensive, but do not involve sensitive tissues (i.e., lips, nipples, genitals, etc.).

Complainant reports seemingly painful injuries with an air of indifference.

Complainant's statement alleges wounds were incurred while she attempted to protect herself, yet the location and angle of injury are inconsistent with defense wounds.

Practice or hesitation marks are present (sometimes appear as older marks, indicating earlier attempt or rehearsals).

Personality and Lifestyle Considerations

In false rape allegations, extensive and important information on the complainant is often available. In general, this information suggests that the pseudo-victim has experienced numerous personal problems and that her ability to cope is seriously impaired. For example:

In temporal sequence, the "rape" follows one or more escalating incidents revealing difficulties in her personal relationships.

Complainant has history of mental or emotional problems (particularly referencing self-injurious behavior, with hysterical or borderline features).

Complainant has previous record of having been assaulted or raped under similar circumstances.

Allegation was made after a similar crime received publicity (suggesting modeling or "copycat" motive in which the similarity to the publicized crime offers credibility).

Complainant has extensive record of medical care for dramatic illnesses or injuries.

Friends or associates report that the complainant's postassaultive behavior and activities were inconsistent with her allegation.

Complainant becomes outraged when asked to corroborate her victimization.

Complainant tries to steer the interview into "safe" topics or those that tend to engender sympathy.

How to Deal with False Accusation Cases

Obviously, confronting the victim with "validity concerns" should take place only when there are serious questions concerning the truth of the report. Confronting a person suspected of making a false complaint is always a difficult matter. The critical issue is that if the doubts are incorrect, this would greatly compound the victim's trauma. Such a confrontation will also undoubtedly destroy any relationship that may have been developed between the victim and the investigator. One way to handle this challenge to the victim's credibility without sacrificing the investigator's rapport with the victim is to introduce a second party, a person who can act as a buffer. The principal investigator needs to be available to the person alleging rape and should maintain a nonjudgmental, supportive, and sympathetic relationship with her. It would be counterproductive for this person to voice any doubts as to the veracity of her report. Issues regarding unresolved inconsistencies, conflicts, or the lack of supporting data should be made by an investigative supervisor or co-worker. In this way, the vital relationship between the complainant and the principal investigator may be maintained and perhaps even improved.

The supervisor's style of confrontation should also be supportive, however, since false allegations are usually desperate attempts to protect self-esteem. Any harsh challenges to the person's credibility will increase her defensiveness. It is often effective to simply present doubts to the victim in a way that makes it clear they are based on the information she herself has provided. This decreases personal conflict while conveying an impression that investigators have been thorough and objective. It also allows for adjusting investigative hypotheses and gives the victim an opportunity to provide additional information without having to place herself in a psychologically threatening position.

The reaction of factitious victims to this approach varies. At the low end of the adaptation continuum there is usually an emotional confession, mixed with both despair and relief. The amount of energy required to maintain her story is exhausting, and this becomes a time for her to cooperate and to seek solace. Exaggerators and malingerers often provide great detail as to how and why they masqueraded as a rape victim. For those who adhere to their statements in the face of overwhelming contradictory evidence, it may be advantageous to request they take a polygraph examination.

At the extreme upper end of the adaptation continuum, the complainant's distortions will have been internalized and for her own well-being she will need to believe what she is saying because she is unconsciously terrified of losing control. Consequently, her denial will be intensified no matter how the confrontation is handled. Predictably, she will react with outrage. If the family is advised of the findings they may be of great assistance in her eventual recovery. Unfortunately, because of the disordered life of such individuals, they are often estranged from their families.

Summary

False allegations of rape occasionally are not recognized by investigators and are almost totally neglected in the literature. The reason for this is obvious. These are acts that are designed to appear plausible. The key to understanding false allegations lies in determining how a false allegation "helps" the complainant manipulate, control, or mentally recoup her self-esteem. Therefore, it is the context in which the allegation occurs that provides the framework for understanding the dynamics of the problem. It is also important to remember that many of the defense mechanisms employed in false allegations are also found in genuine rapes. A final word of caution: It must be remembered that even those who are emotionally prone to make a false allegation can be raped. Basic principles of police professionalism require that officers who investigate rapes remain objective and compassionate. If they do not, the veracity of the allegation may never be known, and the victim, for she is a victim in either case, may never receive the help and support she needs.

References

Aduan, R. P., Fauci, A. S., Dale, D. C., Herzberg, J. H., and Wolf, S. M. "Factitious Fever and Self-Induced Infection: A Report of 32 Cases and Review of the Literature." *Annals of Internal Medicine* 90 (2) (1979): 230–242.

Asher, R. "Munchausen's Syndrome." *Lancet* (1951/1): 339–341.

Bard, M. and Sangrey, D. *The Crime Victim's Book*. New York: Basic Books, Inc., 1979.

Carney, M. W. P. "Artifactual Illnesses to Attract Medical Attention." *British Journal of Psychiatry* 136 (1980): 542–547.

Carney, M. W. P. and Brown, J. P. "Clinical Features and Motives among 42 Artifactual Illness Patients." *British Journal of Medical Psychology* 56 (1983): 57–66.

Ford, C. V. "The Munchausen Syndrome: A Report of Four New Cases and a Review of Psychodynamic Considerations." *Psychiatry in Medicine* 4 (1) (1973): 31–45.

Freedman, A. M., Kaplan, H. I., and Sadock, B. J., eds. *Comprehensive Textbook of Psychiatry/II*. Baltimore, Md.: Williams and Wilkins, 1975.

Gawn, R. A. and Kauffmann, E. A. "Munchausen Syndrome." *British Medical Journal* 2 (1955): 1068.

Gorman, W. F. "Defining Malingering." *Journal of Forensic Sciences* 27 (2) (1982): 401–407.

Grinker, R. R. "Imposture as a Form of Mastery." *Archives of General Psychiatry*, 5 (1961): 53–56.

Haddy, R. I., Weber, R. M. and Joglekar, A. S. "Munchausen's Syndrome." *American Family Physician* 27 (2) (1983): 193–197.

Halpern, S. *Rape: Helping the Victim*. Oradell, N.J.: Medical Economics Co., 1978.

Hodge, D., Schwartz, W., Sargent, J., Bodurtha, J., and Starr, S. "The Bacteriologically Battered Body: Another Case of Munchausen by Proxy." *Annals of Emergency Medicine* 4 (1982): 205–207.

Kirk, P. O. *Crime Investigation*, 2nd ed. New York: Wiley, 1974.

Kurlandsky, L., Lukoff, J. Y., Zinkman, W. H. Brody, J. P., and Kessler, R. W. "Munchausen Syndrome by Proxy: Definitions of Factitious Bleeding in an Infant by Cr Labeling of Erythrocytes." *Pediatrics* 63 (2) (1979): 228–231.

MacDonald, J. M. *Rape: Offenders and Their Victims*. Springfield, Ill.: Charles C Thomas, 1971.

Marcus, M. *A Taste for Pain: On Masochism and Female Sexuality*. New York: St. Martin's Press, 1981.

McDowell, C. P. "The False Rape Allegation in the Military Community," unpublished paper, Washington, D.C.: U.S. Air Force Office of Special Investigations, March 1983.

Meadow, R. "Munchausen Syndrome by Proxy." *Lancet* 8033 (2) (1977):343–345.

Meadow, R. "Munchausen Syndrome by Proxy." *Archives of Disease in Childhood* 57 (1982): 92–98.

Nadelson, T. "The Munchausen Spectrum: Borderline Character Features." *General Hospital Psychiatry* 1 (1) (1979): 11–17.

O'Hara, C. E. *Fundamentals of Criminal Investigation*, 4th ed. Springfield, Ill.: Charles C Thomas, 1977.

Panken, S. *The Joy of Suffering*. New York: Jason Aronson, Inc., 1983.

Pankratz, L. "A Review of the Munchausen Syndrome," *Clinical Psychology Review* 1 (1981): 65–78.

Ross, R. R. and McKay, H. B. *Self-Mutilation*. Lexington, Mass.: Lexington Books, 1979.

Schlenker, B. R. *Impression Management: The Self-Concept, Social Identity, and Interpersonal Relations*. Monterey, Calif.: Brooks/Cole, 1980.

Snyder, C. R., Higgins, R. L., and Stucky, R. J. *Excuses: Masquerades in Search of Grace*. New York: John Wiley and Sons, 1983.

Vaisrub, S. "Baron Munchausen and the Abused Child." *Journal of the American Medical Association*." 239 (8) (1978) 752.

Waller, D. A. "Obstacles to the Treatment of Munchausen by Proxy Syndrome." *Journal of the American Academy of Child Psychiatry* 22 (1) (1983): 80–85.

12

Rape Investigators: Vicarious Victims

JAMES T. REESE, PH.D.

Rape investigators can and often do become vicarious victims—stressed, altered, and in some cases destroyed by the crimes they investigate. The job of the investigator pushes and pulls at him from many directions, forcing him to play the "hard nut" in one situation, then to move smoothly into the role of a sympathetic helper in the next. Often he will choose to ignore or repress the emotional concerns of role conflict, ambiguity, and stress caused by "shifting gears" into the various roles. When he does this, the conflicts within him can only intensify. He would do better to understand in broad terms *why* and *how* his job is stressful, and to bring sensible coping strategies to bear on his problems.

The rape investigator's life is usually taxing for many reasons. In the course of his work, he sees the worst manifestations of human behavior—and consequently feels compelled to hide his professional life from his family for its own protection. Moreover, his work with victims of rape on a daily basis emotionally drains him. And he is emotionally strained by dealing regularly with emergencies. All such variables add up to stress, and stress produces (1) family problems, (2) unsystematic and often counterproductive defense mechanisms, and ultimately (3) burnout. If the investigator looks for the early warning signs of stress in himself, however, and learns some effective stress management techniques, he will be able to maintain his physical and mental health in spite of the demands of his profession.

Professional Demands

Rape investigators routinely see the worst manifestations of human behavior. They deal with molested children, sexual assault of the elderly and defenseless, senseless beatings and murders, rape, and mutilated bodies. The sum total of these experiences can lead to depression, despair, and discouragement. At some point in time a sort of "hardening process" occurs, the method by which an officer can deal with all the human misery he sees. Dr. Martin Reiser (1974) has referred to this process as the "John Wayne Syndrome." This syndrome allows an officer to protect himself by becoming cynical, overly serious, cold, authoritarian, and emotionally withdrawn, especially from his family. Because he loves his family, he builds a protective "bubble" around them. He dares not tell them of the human suffering he has witnessed at work for fear they will become frightened. Yet his very attempt to protect his family often serves to alienate him from it and leads to lack of communication.

Another difficult pressure on investigators of rape stems from their constant exposure to victims of crime. The investigator must face the shocked relatives and friends, then deal with his own emotional response to the crime. If the victim is left alive, he must deal with her at the most traumatic time, the period immediately following the crime. Victims of rape and other violent crimes often are extremely emotional and draw on the officer's every resource to calm them. The investigator's own emotional reaction festers as he tries to comfort the victim of rape, knowing his words matter little in light of what the victim has just undergone. Then he must face seeing the rapist in court wearing a three-piece suit and accompanied by his entire family, all of whom avow his innocence, despite evidence to the contrary. When the sentence seems inadequate to the officer, as it often does (see Chapter 3), he must simply swallow his anger.

Although police officers are periodically killed in the line of duty, police psychologists say that the emotional dangers are far greater than the physical dangers. The fact is that police officers respond on a routine basis to situations that would be emergencies to others (Wilson, 1968). Although statistically the chances of being killed in the line of duty may be slight, the *threat* of being killed takes a huge emotional toll.

For rape investigators, dealing with terrible situations, traumatized victims, and possibly the threat of physical danger results in overwhelming stress. And it is this unusual amount of stress that explains the fact that police officers may have unusually high rates of problem drinking, suicide, and divorce (Somodevilla, 1978).

Stress

Stress has been defined as "the nonspecific response of the body to any demand placed upon it" (Selye, 1974, p. 14). More simply, it is described as the wear and tear on the body caused by living—which correctly implies that to eliminate all stress one must die. Stressors—those stimuli that place demands on the body—force individuals to readjust or readapt constantly to new situations. Alvin Toffler (1970) estimates that man, historically, has faced these readjustments for 800 lifetimes since the beginning of human existence. Toffler, in fact, credits man's unique ability to adapt to change as the reason for human survival. Yet, while man continues to adapt, his rate of adaptation may not be fast enough to keep pace with modern times. Man's traditional response to the events of life has been "fight or flight." Yet in the modern world, and particularly in the context of an investigator's profession, flight is not usually an option. With these reduced or frustrated options, a policeman's stress necessarily increases.

Police stress is universal. It has no geographical boundaries or political affiliations, and it is found whenever there are police officers functioning in their enforcement roles. In America, however, such stress may be heightened by the unusual violence found in some cities, which reputedly have more armed citizens than armed police officers.

The concern with police work is underlined in a recent survey conducted by the Training Division of the Federal Bureau of Investigation (FBI) on the training needs of state and local law enforcement agencies. The respondents represented by sample 90% of all sworn officers in the United States, and the majority of these rated the category "Handle Personal Stress" as the number one training priority (Phillips, 1984).

Stress and its consequent impact on the body and mind have long been explored in scientific and quasi-scientific studies. More work needs to be done, however, on the specific relationship between stress and the day-to-day job of the police officer. How exactly does stress cause attitude and behavior changes, impair family and social relationships, and develop cynicism, apathy, and an unwillingness to seek help? These concerns will be explored, together with the early warning signs of poor adaptation. Also, some techniques to combat poor adaptation will be outlined.

The Family

Rape investigators may hear from their spouses: "You're different." "You've changed." "You've become cold, callous, almost emotionless and unfeeling." "Whatever happened to the kind, considerate, patient, understanding person I used to know?" Experienced officers have almost certainly heard comments like these because their profession affects the way they live, impacts on their emotions, and consequently affects their relationships with others, especially family members.

Family members thus should be educated to identify the early warning signs of maladaptation to investigative stress, for they are in a position to see the changes in attitude as they occur. The hardened attitudes that officers will develop to get through the workday will stand out dramatically as inappropriate at home (Reese, 1982b). First, family members should be aware of being deliberately excluded from the investigator's life as, for example, when the officer identifies himself primarily as a member of a closed law enforcement community and adopts the attitude "silence is security, sex is survival, keep your cool, and stay on top" (Bennett, 1978). Second, the spouse should take note if the officer has increasing difficulty in relating to members of the family or is less able to respond emotionally or talk about feelings. Third, the spouse should be on the lookout for the defense mechanisms discussed in the next section.

At the same time, because the integrity of the family is affected by stress on the officer, the investigator and his department should be educated in ways to prevent damaging it. Above all, the family members, including the officer, must be regarded as a whole unit or support system. All members use the family unit as a resource pool for support and strengthening, and a change in the status of any of them will alter the balance of the whole unit. Thus, to keep the officer a vital and healthy member of the law enforcement community, he must be maintained as a vital and healthy member of his family.

Defense Mechanisms

Defense mechanisms arise as a response to stress, and they become habits through use. As the officer begins to succumb to the stress of his job, he begins to perceive that the offenders are winning, that everything that is meaningful to him is slipping out of his reach, that his family is upset, and that he doesn't seem to care about the public he serves. On the basis of these perceptions, he alters his behavior and attitudes to make them less threatening. In other words, he adopts defense mechanisms.

Defense mechanisms, in fact, may be thought of as mental functions that protect an individual from internal and/or external threats, conflicts, impulses, and hurts. They include isolation of affect, "sick" humor, displacement, substitution, repression, rationalization, and projection. While an individual can attack, compromise, or withdraw on a conscious level, on an unconscious level he will employ these defense mechanisms to protect the integrity of the self—that picture or image of self without which he cannot function.

The process by which defense mechanisms are developed hinges on the individual's perception. For an event to be stressful, it must be perceived as such in the mind. And *how* one perceives a situation will largely dictate one's response. The mind goes through three basic steps when confronted with a problem. First the problem is perceived; then an analysis is conducted; and, finally, a decision is made. The first step, perception, is a variable that can be manipulated and that, accordingly, can influence the remaining steps. One way to change perception is to adopt defense mechanisms.

Defense mechanisms were first identified by Sigmund Freud in 1894 in his study *The Neuro-psychosis of Defense.* Anna Freud later identified 10 defenses by name (1966), and by 1979 H. P. Laughlin had differentiated 22 major defenses, 26 minor defenses, and 3 special reactions and combinations. Of these, several are adopted most frequently by police officers.

Perhaps one of the most deceptive and, if uncontrolled, emotionally dangerous defenses used by officers is that of *isolation of affect.* Although extremely effective for the investigator while on the job, this defense is most responsible for domestic conflict, marital unhappiness, and divorce.

Isolation is in use when "an idea or object is divorced from its emotional connotation" (Laughlin, 1979, p. 476). Investigators see it in rapists who speak about their crimes expressionlessly. They see it in hospitals where medical and nursing professionals cope with rape victims with such detachment that they seem cold and indifferent. And they see it in themselves when they interview a victim and calmly order an investigation.

This altered perception of reality, this ability to view events less intensely, permits the officer to appear in control at all times, to live up to his image, and to deny any emotional stake in the situation. At the same time, however, it necessarily carries over into his social roles as father, husband, and neighbor. The emotional divorcement that allows him to perform well on the job cuts his ties at home. He will hear: "Why are you always so detached from what you're doing?" "I can't seem to get through to you any more," or "You have no feelings!"

An adjunct to emotional isolation is grotesque *humor*—the kind that is not funny and is not meant to be. "Sick" humor works. It maintains an investigator's sanity because it acts as a safety valve and lessens the emotional impact of the crime. The officer, in effect, reaches out to others instead of sitting on his emotions. By speaking the unspeakable and being understood, he can vent his wounded feelings and share his pain.

Using such humor as a release, however, is usually very controlled. It is expressed only within earshot of fellow investigators who are directly involved, and only veterans can get away with it—as if they have paid their dues through the years, have no more emotions to invest, and have all but dried up their coping resources. Richard Lazarus (1977) notes a similar defense mechanism among laboratory technicians at work on dissections.

So long as "sick" humor is tightly controlled by investigators, it performs a useful function. Once it finds its way out of the locker room, however, and into the public eye, it is a clear sign of maladaptation to stress.

Displacement is in operation when "an emotional feeling is transferred, deflected, and redirected from its internal object to a substitute external one. The emotional feeling is thus displaced to a new person, situation, or object" (Laughlin, 1979, p. 86). Investigators often see this phenomenon in the course of their work, as when a rape victim will revile the police for not arriving in time. But officers are often not aware of employing such a defense themselves—of taking their anger and job stress home and venting it on their spouses or children.

Displacement, in fact, is usually the defense most to blame for strife in the investigator's home. If the officer could recognize the symptoms, however, he could consciously employ a more acceptable defense. "Displacement frequently, if not universally, operates in conjunction with *substitution*, [a defense mechanism] through which an unacceptable or unobtainable goal, emotion, drive, attitude, impulse, interest, or need, which is consciously intolerable or repugnant, is replaced by a more acceptable one" (Laughlin, 1979, p. 402). In everyday life, substitution may be as simple as chopping wood to release hostility.

Repression has been referred to as the primary and most important ego (self) defense (Snyder, 1976, p. 186). Laughlin (1979) defines it as "the automatic, effortless, and involuntary assignment or relegation of consciously repugnant or intolerable ideas, impulses, and feelings to the unconscious" (p. 359). For example, a rape victim, when questioned by investigators, might not remember any details relating to the attack, even though the assailant was unmasked and the attack was in broad daylight. If the information is truly repressed, the victim will not be aware that she knows it, for her mind has protected itself by keeping this information out of her consciousness.

Although investigators may not use this defense themselves, they often see themselves victimized by it. Nothing is more trying to an investigator attempting to solve a crime than a victim (his best witness) who cannot recall a single thing.

Rationalization as defense is used when "the ego (self) justifies, or attempts to modify, otherwise unacceptable impulses, needs, feelings, behavior, and motives into ones that are consciously tolerable and acceptable" (Laughlin, 1979, p. 251). It is one of the most frequently used defense mechanisms. Officers rationalize why they became officers, why they work sex crimes, why rapes occur, and why they have become the type of individuals they are. On a daily basis investigators rationalize why they work long hours, spend long hours separated from their families, and even risk their lives. Too often these rationalizations are left unexamined and end by upsetting the lives of the very egos they are supposed to defend.

Finally, *projection* is a defense mechanism of major importance. Known as the defense of "blaming others," projection occurs when "consciously disowned aspects of self are rejected or disowned and thrown outward, to become imputed to others . . . a mirror-defense" (Laughlin, 1979, p. 221). Thus people who are never neat will accuse others of being messy, and individuals who swear often will be unduly offended when someone swears in their presence. In rape investigations, the investigators who can't seem to solve a crime will find it easier to blame their lack of success on someone or something than to face the fact that they may not be clever enough to sort out the evidence and conduct a proper and orderly investigation.

Defense mechanisms are used daily and productively by all people—so it's all right if readers have identified some of these defenses in their lives. But these defenses can become counterproductive if they are habitually used to excess, for the wrong reason, or in the wrong place, and they can lead to burnout.

Burnout

The complexities of the tasks and the many demands, responsibilities, and deadlines placed on rape investigators force them to be on alert throughout the workday. They are expected to be constantly energetic, self-motivated, independent, and task-oriented, as well as strong team members (Reese, 1982a). When the officer cannot meet these expectations, when he no longer has energy or interest in his work, chances are he suffers from *burnout*.

Burnout is a common affliction of those employed in human services and is easier to observe than to define. Cherniss (1980, p. 16) defines it as "to fail, wear out, or become exhausted by making excessive demands on energy, strength, or resources." Unfortunately, such a definition pays little attention to the emotional and attitudinal effects of burnout. Burnout often includes psychological withdrawal from work in response to excessive stress or dissatisfaction; loss of enthusiasm, excitement, and a sense of mission in one's work (Cherniss, 1980), and a change in attitude from empathy to apathy (Edelwich, 1980). Burnout has been called a disease of overcommitment, which, ironically, causes a lack of commitment. Above all it is a coping technique as regards occupational stress and, as such, it uses defense mechanisms of projection, withdrawal, detachment, avoidance-oriented behavior, and lowering of goals.

"What's it all for?" "Why am I doing this?" "I hate to go to work." "I have nothing to offer anymore." Statements such as these are frequently made by victims of burnout. They are not adjusting or coping well. They remain in a state of disequilibrium, and they strain to make it through each day. Studies have indicated that burnout correlates with other damaging indices of human stress, such as alcoholism, mental illness, marital conflict, and suicide (Maslach, 1976).

The 1980s have seen an increased interest in the concept of burnout and in the supportive role peer counseling can play in an officer's carreer. "Employees who experience short-term crises need to be heard, need to have the opportunity to feel understood, and need to receive peer recognition of the extent of the problems they face" (Capp, 1984). Such counseling formalizes the locker-room sessions that are in force in most police departments, but it improves those sessions by using time-tested professional skills.

Early Warning Signs

The numerous symptoms that may relate to stress disorders can be grouped in three categories: (1) emotional, (2) behavioral, and (3) physical. The number of symptoms a person may exhibit is not important, but rather the extent of changes noted from the person's normal condition. Furthermore, the combined presence of symptoms determines the potency of the problem. Indicators range from isolated reactions to combinations of symptoms from the three categories. Finally, the duration, the frequency, and the intensity of the symptoms indicate the extent to which the individual is suffering (Hibler, 1981).

In the *emotional* category, symptoms include apathy, anxiety, irritability, mental fatigue, and overcompensation or denial. Individuals afflicted with these symptoms are restless, agitated, overly sensitive, defensive, and preoccupied and have difficulty concentrating. These officers will overwork to exhaustion and may become groundlessly suspicious of others. They may be arrogant, argumentative, insubordinate, and hostile. Their feelings of insecurity and worthlessness lead to self-defeat. Depression is common and chronic.

Behavioral symptoms are often more easily detected than emotional ones, for its sufferers withdraw and seek social isolation. Such individuals are reluctant to accept responsibilities and/or tend to neglect current ones. They often act out their misery through alcohol abuse, gambling, promiscuity, and spending sprees. Much of their desperate behavior is a cry for help and should be recognized as such. Other indications could be tardiness, poor appearance, and poor personal hygiene, both at work and at home. These patterns can lead to domestic disputes and spouse/child abuse.

The *physical* effects of stress are extremely dangerous. The individual may become preoccupied with illness or may dwell on minor ailments, taking excessive sick leave and complaining of exhaustion during the workday. Among the many somatic indicators are headaches, insomnia, recurrent awakening, early morning rising, changes in appetite resulting in either weight loss or gain, indigestion, nausea, vomiting, and diarrhea. Such psychophysical maladies may be a direct result of excessive stress upon the officer.

Coping Strategies

Rape investigators could perform well under stress and reduce their chances of falling prey to stress-related disorders if they (1) monitored their own stress reactions and (2) learned skills that would help them cope with stress effectively. Unfortunately, many resist such procedures, believing that to admit the need for stress management is to admit they can't cope and thus appear weak to their friends.

The philosophy of stress management, however, emphasizes two reasonable techniques: exercise and relaxation, both normal means to good general health. Moreover, it recommends seriously and ruthlessly structuring one's life so time is systematically allotted for various important needs. Depue (1981) recommends a division into occupational time, family time, and the one most difficult to find, personal time.

Effective stress management practices include the following:

1. Eat three meals a day, including breakfast.
2. Avoid sugar, salt, animal fat, and processed white flour in your diet.
3. Pursue a regular program of physical exercise or other leisure activities.
4. Form new friendships and maintain old ones.
5. Get enough sleep each night (6–8 hours).
6. Practice abdominal breathing and relaxation.
7. Schedule time and activities for yourself, by yourself, and schedule the same to spend with others socially.
8. Stop smoking.
9. Limit your alcohol and caffeine intake.
10. Pace yourself and allow for an even flow of demands.
11. Identify and accept emotional needs.

12. Recognize early warning signs of stress.
13. Allocate time and energy to allow for outside interests and stimulation.
14. Take appropriate dietary supplements, if needed.
15. Avoid self-medication.
16. Take one thing at a time.
17. Give in once in a while.
18. Talk out your worries.
19. Make yourself available.
20. Learn to accept things you cannot change.

Summary

Law enforcement officers have long lived, and sometimes died, with the knowledge that their occupation seems to breed alcoholism, divorce, and suicide. Many, in fact, hold their job directly accountable for much of the misery in their lives, not reflecting that they might change the trends themselves. Today we know that, as a rule, personal problems stem not from the job itself, but from the failure of the officer to deal effectively with the stress created by the job. Thus, rape investigators must "self diagnose" their problems, measuring their level of happiness, job satisfaction, personal growth, family relationships, and other subjective concerns. Above all, they must assume responsibility for their own mental and physical health.

Rape investigators are involved in an important job and a rewarding one. Although the negative aspects of the job are often highlighted, no one should ever doubt its value to the individual and to society. One should, however, understand thoroughly and systematically how to cope with the negative aspects of the task.

Rape investigators must realize that they don't have to become vicarious victims. They must be willing to assume self-responsibility for their mental and physical health. And they must face the fact that there are no shortcuts to stress management. They must commit themselves strongly to understanding stress, its symptoms, and its causes, in order to achieve and maintain their personal and professional health.

References

Bennett, Barbara. "The Police Mystique." *The Police Chief*, April 1978, pp. 46–49.

Capp, F. L. "Peer Counseling: An Employee Assistance Program." *FBI Law Enforcement Bulletin*, November 1984, pp. 2–8.

Cherniss, Cary. *Staff Burnout*. Beverly Hills, Calif.: Sage Publications, 1980.

III

MEDICAL ASPECTS OF RAPE INVESTIGATION

13 Medical Exam in the Live Sexual Assault Victim

JOSEPH A. ZECCARDI, M.D.,
AND DIANE DICKERMAN, M.D.

Overview

The medical system becomes involved in the sexual assault investigation for two reasons: therapy involving the physical and emotional consequences of the assault, and evidence gathering to corroborate the initial charges or to be used in the adjudication of the complaint. Although these medical responsibilities have existed for years, it is only recently that sexual assault has been introduced into medical school curricula. Therefore, it is unusual that a physician is versed in the investigation of sexual assault without special training. Pediatricians, gynecologists, emergency physicians, and some family physicians are introduced to the subject of sexual assault during their training after medical school, but it is rare for them to have significant experience in sexual assault except as a member of a community response team. Medical personnel should have a procedure to follow in sexual assault cases so that victims receive the proper attention and evidence is preserved. Persons in all areas involved in the matter—medicine, prosecution, crime investigation, rape crisis, crime laboratory—need to proceed in a coordinated manner. They must educate each other as to the needs of the sexual assault victim from the various vantage points and agree on such particulars as the specific handling of historical and evidentiary matters within their jurisdiction.

The physician's role in sexual assault cases should be clearly defined before involving the patient in a medical evaluation. The physician's responsibilities, as mentioned above, are both medical and evidentiary. These medical responsibilities include treatment of any trauma involved, prevention and treatment of any possible venereal disease or pregnancy, and adequate follow-up for counseling to reduce emotional trauma.

Physicians and other medical staff members should be educated on common misconceptions and attitudes concerning sexual assault. They should also be advised of the definitions of sexual assault and rape in local jurisdictions. A medical definition of penetration, for example, usually assumes that there has been penetration into the vagina, whereas many legal jurisdictions consider penetration as between the labia.

The type of physician or facility used in sexual assault cases varies. Emergency departments, because of their 24-hour, 7-day-a-week availability, have a certain attractiveness that is counterbalanced by the realities of shifting priorities for medical crises; i.e., cardiac arrest must take priority over a sexual assault victim. Depending on the size and complexity of the emergency service, it may be possible to have some sections that deal with sexual assault and/or emotional emergencies. These special kinds of facilities usually will be able to arrange a more appropriate waiting space and the necessary personnel to deal with the victim. Large facilities may use physicians from the disciplines of emergency, gynecology, or pediatrics, or residents in training may handle these cases. Each of these groups has advantages and disadvantages that need to be considered. It is unlikely in a busy sexual assault program that a single physician can deal with all sexual assault cases. However, in a smaller jurisdiction where this is possible, a single physician would have the advantage of being able to coordinate information.

The medical personnel should be trained as to the scope of activity and responsibility of the district attorney's office, the law enforcement officers, the crime lab, the rape crisis workers, and the rape treatment facilities. The medical facility itself should be able to support a quick reception and registration process and a secure waiting space where information may be obtained from the patient and shared with the patient about the process that is about to occur. Rape crisis workers should be involved in this activity and thus will extend the ability of the medical facility to provide informed and caring support. The victim should be given visual and acoustical privacy and provided with printed material explaining the role of each of the members of the sexual assault team and the medical process. The victim's emotional state will make it difficult for her to absorb information being given to her. Thus, she will have the same information in print to refer to later.

It is not unusual to have a nurse, a physician, a social worker, police, and rape crisis workers all interviewing the patient. These interviews should be coordinated so that duplication of effort does not become another harassment and infringement on the patient's rights. It is not reasonable that the patient should be interviewed in various stages of undress in preparation for the medical evaluation. Preplanning can allow coordination of these various activities so that the patient is not made to feel vulnerable again.

Consent

Consent must be obtained for examination and treatment of the sexual assault victim, as well as for the release of information obtained during the medical examination to legal authorities so that prosecution may proceed.

Written permission for medical examination and treatment is obtained from all patients, and the staff is usually familiar with the process. In a true emergency, permission for medical examination and treatment is assumed and may proceed without written consent. In the area of sexual assault, however, special issues are raised, largely pertaining to the age of the victim. Many victims of sexual assault are adolescents and may, therefore, fall below the legal age of consent. Minors are variously defined by individual states as emancipated by marriage or if they have been pregnant or have graduated from high school. Some states permit medical treatment of venereal disease or pregnancy in a minor without parental permission. In most cases, it is advisable to obtain parental consent since successful long-range treatment of the minor depends on parental involvement and support. Moreover, parental consent is required for the dispensing of estrogen hormonal therapy as emergency treatment against pregnancy after informing the victim of possible side effects of such therapy (these side effects are discussed later in this chapter).

Rape is a crime, and the law in certain jurisdictions requires physicians to report any injury inflicted in violation of a penal code. Moreover, whether the patient claims sexual assault or not, if the physician has reason to believe it has occurred, reporting to local agencies may be not only advisable, but required. In addition, most municipalities have ordinances requiring reporting of sexual assault against children and adolescent victims to a multi-disciplinary group that reports to child welfare agencies, especially if the assault has occurred within the household.

Apart from written consent for examination and treatment, the sexual assault victim must provide authorization for the release of information gathered during the medical exam to law enforcement agencies. Should the patient refuse to press charges or share medical information with the legal system, the medical facility must retain the information, which may then only be released upon written consent of the parent or guardian or upon subpoena by the court. In the absence of consent or court order, the only information that may be released is a report of the injury to the police, the patient's name and address, and, in the case of a minor, a report to the child welfare agency.

Medical Examination

Prior to outlining the mechanics of the medical examination, several general factors regarding the approach to the sexual assault victim must be addressed. This is often the first interaction of the victim with society subsequent to the crime. While it is important that the medical evaluation be thorough, it must also be sensitive. Thus, medical personnel should respect the limits that the victim needs to set in order to maintain her integrity.

The mechanics of the evaluation should be reviewed with the patient prior to the examination by a nurse, crisis worker, or physician. The evaluation should, of course, take place in an acoustically and visually private area. A nurse should be present throughout the evaluation to provide emotional support and to assist the physician in the process. A friend or caseworker may also be present during the examination if the patient so desires. If pictures are to be utilized as evidentiary material, their purpose should be discussed with the patient and specific separate written consent should be obtained.

The medical examination includes history, physical examination, and collection of specimens for laboratory analysis.

History

The purpose of the history is to gather information that will aid in the medical and legal management of the case. Emphasis is placed on ascertaining a general medical history, a sexual history, and a history of the incident and postincident events.

General Medical History. A past medical history of injury or illness should be documented with emphasis on those disorders that may adversely affect the assault victim, e.g., bleeding tendencies. Any medications taken, as well as known allergies to medications, should be noted since medical therapy may be indicated, e.g., for the prevention of venereal disease. A history of past immunizations, especially tetanus, is important since booster shots may be required when injury has been sustained and immunizations are not up to date.

Sexual History. Inquiries must be made to determine whether the female assault victim is menarchal (has begun menstruating); if so, the date of the patient's last normal menstrual period should be documented. Also, a history of sterilization or the use of any type of birth control method should be noted. The number of pregnancies and the results of these pregnancies (live birth, stillbirth, miscarriage, abortion) should be recorded. In addition, the patient must be questioned about her most recent consensual sexual intercourse, as well as the existence and time of onset of any symptoms of pregnancy. Finally, it is necessary to assess the patient's attitude concerning pregnancy and its prevention or termination by hormonal or mechanical means. All of these questions will aid in evaluating the possibility of preassault or assault-related pregnancy, as well as any course of action that should be taken should pregnancy exist.

The patient's venereal disease history should also be ascertained. If the patient has been treated for syphilis, it is helpful to know whether her blood titers returned to normal. The facility at which the patient was treated should be recorded so that results of past blood tests may be compared with present laboratory analysis.

History of the Incident and Postincident Events. The history of the incident, for legal purposes, should include statements regarding several aspects of the assault that may be further corroborated by physical or laboratory examination. The time and location at which the assault took place should be recorded. Such information will lead the physician to look for the presence of grass stains, dirt, etc., during the physical examination. The specific nature of the physical/sexual assault should be noted. The physician must know if any body fluids (through ejaculation, urination, defecation) were left on the patient or if vaginal, oral, or anal penetration occurred during the incident, so that proper lab specimens may be obtained. It is helpful to know if any instruments, such as restraints, were used. By impeding blood return from the vein, restraints often lead to bruises and broken blood vessels (petechiae), which will be evident on physical examination.

Postincident events that should be noted include any activities that may interfere with the collection of evidentiary facts and specimens during the physical examination, such as bathing, douching, urinating, defecating, drinking, or changing clothes.

As a final word, it should be emphasized that the history should be conducted in a sensitive, caring manner, using terminology familiar to the patient. If the victim is a child, the interviewer should talk to other family members in order to determine what terminology is used for various body parts. Furthermore, it may be necessary to employ other techniques in order to obtain a history from a child, such as the use of anatomically correct dolls or the use of illustrations depicting the events as constructed by the child. It is noteworthy that children seldom lie about explicit sexual behavior. Accusation by a child of sexual abuse should, therefore, be taken at face value.

Physical Examination

The approach to the victim for the physical examination should be gentle and empathetic. Ideally, the mechanics of the examination should be previewed with the patient by a nurse, caseworker, or physician. Nevertheless, during the examination it is helpful for the physician to explain in a calm and mannerly voice, step by step, what he/she is doing. A young child may be examined on a mother's lap or, like the older patient, on the examining table. If supportive, the parent should be permitted to remain with the patient during the examination. An adolescent can be given the option of having anyone she wishes present. In all cases, the examination should be performed with a hospital employee, preferably a nurse, who can also assist the physician, as chaperone. Of course the examination should take place in an acoustically and visually private area. Finally, a gown and drapes should be used, as appropriate, to ensure modesty and decrease feelings of vulnerability.

The physical examination must be complete enough to note any abnormalities that have occurred as a result of the sexual assault. The physician should assess and record the patient's general appearance before she disrobes (e.g., patient appears disheveled, clothes torn). The physician should also note the patient's demeanor, emotional distress, or depression, which may manifest itself by inappropriate laughing, agitation, or withdrawal. Vital signs (blood pressure, pulse, temperature, respiration) should be taken and documented. Abnormalities such as elevated pulse may reflect emotional stress or major trauma. Foreign material such as blood or dried semen should be scraped and submitted for evidence as described in Chapter 5. Any sign of trauma should be documented on the medical record.

The patient's description of the assault may indicate parts of the physical exam requiring special consideration. For instance, the use of restraints may produce broken superficial vessels (petechiae). These may be especially notable on the inside of the eye when restraints about the neck were employed. When the assault included oral or rectal intercourse, these sites should be meticulously inspected. Bruises (ecchymoses) should be described in terms of location, size, shape, and color. Bruises evolve over a period of time, and their age may be estimated from their appearance. Thus, early on, a bruise appears as a reddened area, which, with time, evolves into the more traditional black and blue mark. Later, the bruise changes color again to various shades of green, reflecting the degradation and uptake of blood by the healing body. The physician's assessment of the age of a bruise by its appearance may be used in the courtroom to corroborate or dispute the victim's claim by comparing it to the historical timing of the alleged assault. Another physical finding of legal significance, soft tissue injury or contusion, is diagnosed by the physician by the ability to elicit pain on palpation of the traumatized body area.

Genital exam is required in order to assess the degree (if any) of trauma and to collect specimens for evidentiary purposes. Initially, the external genitalia and surrounding area are inspected. Signs of trauma such as a bruising on the inner thigh may result from attempts to pry or pull the legs apart. Combing the pubic hair for specimens of free foreign hair and clippings of a few of the patient's pubic hairs for comparison may be done at this point of the examination. While an integral part of the examination in the older female patient, internal (vaginal) examination may not be required of children. However, if blood is seen coming from the vagina in a child, a vaginal exam is indicated and is preferably performed under general anesthesia to permit adequate inspection and repair of physical trauma without further infliction of psychological trauma.

The internal examination begins with an inspection of the vaginal opening, the introitus. The presence of an intact hymen at this site should be documented but does not rule out vaginal penetration. Evidence of recent disruption of the hymenal ring, such as reddening, laceration, or bleeding, is rarely found but should nevertheless be sought. In practice, hymenal tissue is difficult to identify in the majority of patients, a fact that has been attributed to various activities during childhood and adolescence or to the active lifestyle of the modern-day woman, but not necessarily signifying previous intercourse. Thus, the status of the hymenal ring has minimal legal significance. In some centers, the findings of a relaxed vaginal opening in a child is used as evidence of sexual abuse; however, no objective data in the literature can be found to support this conclusion. Direct visualization of the vaginal vault and cervix is accomplished with the aid of a nonlubricated, water-moistened speculum of the smallest size to avoid further trauma of the tissue after the assault. Again, inspection for signs of trauma and collection of appropriate specimens from the cervix and from the deepest, most dependent portion of the vagina, the posterior fornix, is performed. In children, when a vaginal exam is not performed, a small catheter with a syringe on one end may be inserted into the vagina in order to withdraw a specimen for forensic testing.

The final portion of the physical examination is the bimanual examination. The physician performs the examination, after withdrawing the speculum, by inserting the first and second fingers of one hand into the vaginal vault and placing the other hand on the abdomen. The purpose of the examination is to assess by means of palpation (1) the size and consistency of the uterus and adjacent organs, the adnexa (ovaries and tubes), looking for signs of pre-existing pregnancy; and (2) the presence of tenderness resulting from trauma sustained during the assault.

Rectal examination is indicated if the assault included rectal intercourse and, similar to the genital examination, includes external examination for signs of trauma and foreign material and internal examination using an anoscope with inspection for signs of trauma and foreign material, collection of specimens for evidentiary and medical purposes, and palpation with a gloved finger for signs of tenderness and trauma.

Laboratory Evaluation

Evidentiary material should be collected and held for possible release to the law enforcement officer. As previously mentioned, release of this material requires the consent of the patient (or guardian in the case of a minor) or subpoena by the court. In the absence of such consent or court order, specimens should be set aside, preferably in a locked refrigerator or box.

Similar to the physician's report of the examination, specimens obtained from the assault victim have both medical and legal significance. It is, therefore, essential to label specimens properly (patient's name, date, time of collection, area from which the specimen is collected, collector's name) and to establish a written documentation of the custody of evidentiary material, a so-called written "chain of evidence" in which specimens are accounted for during every step from collection to possible introduction into courts. Failure to label specimens properly or to maintain written documentation when custody is transferred may render any evidence worthless from a legal point of view.

The type of evidence to be collected, as well as the method of collection and handling of evidence, will vary depending on the patient's history and the specific legal jurisdiction. If there is time for preplanning, medical facility staff should meet with crime laboratory personnel in order to discuss these issues. The law enforcement officers should also alert medical personnel to any specific evidence they have noted so that it will be collected with other specimens. Specimens collected routinely include any clothing that is torn, bloody, or soiled in the course of the assault; any foreign debris (e.g., hair or fibers) or dried secretions adhering to the patient's body; and fingernail scrapings. Routine studies performed on these specimens include analysis for the presence and concentrations of acid phosphatase. Acid phosphatase is an enzyme present in the ejaculation. The presence of this enzyme in a specimen serves as an indirect verification of the presence of semen. Specimens are also tested for the identification of blood group substances (ABO, Rh). Blood and saliva samples obtained from the victim are used to determine her blood type and whether she secretes her blood type in other body fluids. By comparing blood group substances found in various specimens to the patient's blood group, a secretion (e.g., semen) may be identified as foreign.

Other routine studies are performed for the detection of sperm, either live sperm in a wet mount, or dead sperm or sperm products on a dry slide. It is possible to estimate the length of time the sperm were present in their current state at the site of examination. Studies performed for the detection of venereal disease include Gram staining and culture of secretions for gonorrhea, and baseline serology for syphilis. It should be noted that it requires approximately one month from the time of infection before the blood test becomes positive for syphilis and that the blood test is not always negative after successful treatment of prior syphilis infection. The test thus serves only as a baseline in recent assaults. Pregnancy tests may be required in the postmenarchal female if the history (missed period, symptoms of pregnancy) or physical (increased size and softening of the uterus) indicates the possibility of a pre-existing pregnancy.

Additional specimens should be obtained from any orifice that, according to the assault report, was violated. Genital violation, therefore, would require the collection of any foreign material adherent to the external genitalia, free hairs, reference hair clippings, and swabbings from the vaginal pool.

Medical Therapy

As previously mentioned, medical therapy requires attention to life-threatening conditions first. In the absence of such conditions, prophylactic treatment for venereal disease and pregnancy should be addressed. It is a common practice in sexual assault centers to treat most adult victims for incubating gonorrhea and syphilis. This is due to several facts: a slightly increased incidence of venereal disease reported in victims of sexual assault, the poor medical follow-up of victims, and the frequency of asymptomatic gonorrheal infection in adult females who consequently serve as a reservoir for spreading the infection or develop significant complications before the infection is diagnosed. In contrast to the adult, however, the prepubertal female infected with gonorrhea is usually symptomatic, largely due to difference in anatomy and physiology that localize the infection and inflammation to the vagina with a resulting external discharge. For this reason, only symptomatic children are treated for gonorrhea in some facilities.

Treatment for the prevention of a potential pregnancy as a result of sexual assault should also be considered. An existing pregnancy, however, must first be ruled out, and the patient's attitude toward pregnancy and its prevention/termination should be assessed. Information on alternative methods of pregnancy prevention as well as the possible short- and/or long-term effects of such treatment should be offered. Diethylstilbestrol (DES), the "morning-after pill," has traditionally been employed as a medical prophylactic against pregnancy. When administered within the first 72 hours following unprotected intercourse, DES prevents implantation of the fertilized egg, and therefore pregnancy, in 99.9% of cases. Such therapy is not, however, without adverse effects. Significant nausea and vomiting are common following administration. Furthermore, there is a highly publicized risk of vaginal adenocarcinoma in the female offspring of mothers exposed to DES in the first trimester. It is wise, therefore, to obtain signed, informed consent prior to administration of DES and to follow up treated patients in order to detect the 0.1% in whom DES intervention failed. In such patients, abortion should be offered or advised.

As a result of the problems associated with DES, many facilities have switched to other forms of hormonal therapy for the prevention of pregnancy. It must be emphasized, however, that whereas they are reasonably effective, their long-term consequences will only be determined with time and may prove to be more devastating than those of DES. One such alternative is Premarin (conjugated estrogen). A single dose of 50 mg administered intravenously assures 100% compliance in spite of such adverse effects as nausea. Other nonhormonal options for pregnancy interruption that should be offered to the sexual assault victim include the insertion of an intrauterine device (IUD), elective abortions, or carrying potential pregnancy to term.

Medical Records

The medical facility staff should be advised of the medical record requirements in sexual assault cases. They must understand that their records should be nonjudgmental, use standard terms, and be legible. It is also important to notify the medical facility that the final diagnosis may be a sexual assault complaint and that society, in the form of a jury or its other agents, will decide whether sexual assault has occurred. The medical records should not reflect any conclusions as to whether or not a crime has occurred, and the final diagnosis should be "sexual assault complaint" rather than "sexual assault." The frequency of physician court appearance may be significantly reduced if the medical record is properly kept and legible.

Psychological Aspects

Rape trauma syndrome (described in Chapter 3) is of concern. The appropriate management of the patient in the facility may minimize additional stress. Victims are seeking from the facility assurance about their medical condition, emotional support, and external control. Patients should be prepared for events in the emergency department. This preparation need not be by physicians, and there may be some advantage to using female crisis workers. The patient should be assured she is in a secure environment and will not be left alone, and the crisis worker, if available, should accompany the patient through the entire process. It is important to be sensitive to the issue of repetitive interviews. Privacy after an assault is a sensitive issue, and questioning must be approached carefully. Assurances of safety are important, as patient fear of injury or death is common. Despite the need for sensitivity, it is important to ask about specific acts that the rapist performed, since the patient's embarrassment may lead to minimal responses.

Patient control during the examination is important, and the patient should be told of her physical condition immediately following the examination and reassured during such an examination. It is helpful, as mentioned earlier, to have written descriptions of the emotional reactions that accompany sexual assault, in addition to printed medical instructions and descriptions of what to expect of the process following the reporting of the sexual assault. This material then can be reviewed by the patient at a later time to refresh her memory. Some crisis workers provide outreach services the next day or so to talk with the victim and discuss her feelings. If a sexual assault treatment unit is available, the patient should be routinely referred there with reassurances that she is not required to go, but that these experts have been helpful to other victims.

The rape crisis workers who are organized for families of sexual assault victims are also helpful. There is a tendency to look for a negative cause for a negative result, and friends and family sometimes consider that the victim must have been at fault. Follow-up mental health consultation should be sought not only for the victim, but for significant others as well.

Any additional medical contact that is necessary for obtaining evidentiary material is accompanied by careful explanations of emotional sequelae, as well as written materials and referral to support therapeutic agencies, which can do much to optimize the outcome for the patient.

IV

PROSECUTION OF RAPE

14 Prosecuting Rape Cases: Trial Preparation and Trial Tactic Issues

WILLIAM HEIMAN

The focus of this chapter is the trial preparation and trial tactic issues arising in the prosecution of rape cases. However, before discussing those issues in any detail, it is important to briefly set forth general policies that should govern the prosecutor's handling of rape cases within his office.

In the category of policy issues external to the prosecutor's office, the prosecutor can have a direct impact in lobbying, primarily at the state level, for new statutes concerning issues ranging from admissibility of evidence of a victim's past sexual history to mandatory minimum prison sentences for repeat offenders. Other external policy issues include dealing with members of the press who publish rape victims' names and addresses; coordinating a sexual assault coalition in the local community made up of the treating hospitals, police departments, and rape crisis and victim counseling centers; and supporting in various ways the right of the rape crisis center to existence and financial viability.

In the category of internal office policies, the prosecutor should develop clearly defined standards for negotiating guilty pleas, nol-prossing (withdrawing from prosecution of cases), and administering polygraph tests to defendants or victims. There should also be a regularly scheduled series of training sessions for the staff, covering the legal, medical, and psychological issues in trying a rape case.

The prosecutor should be an advocate of victims' rights. As such, he should consult with the victim and seek her input and views concerning the terms of a proposed guilty plea or nol-pros.

Theory of the Trial

In approaching the trial of a rape case, indeed any criminal case, the prosecutor should look at it as a series of connected parts dependent on one another. A trial is a network of interrelated pieces, all making up one discernible pattern. Everything that is done in the preparation stage must serve a purpose in terms of setting up the closing argument. From the start—jury selection—90% of the closing statement should have already been prepared mentally and/or on paper. The remaining 10% is filled in based upon material that is unforeseen at the start and that is developed during the course of the trial.

Whether trying an identification issue case, consent defense case, or an unpopular victim case, the prosecutor should begin to educate the jury in his/her opening remarks to them, during the voir dire, and during the opening statement. In closing, he should tie together all of the pieces of the arguments that were threaded through in the preparation stage and that developed during the above-mentioned stages.

Preparation

The key to presenting a well-organized, logical, smooth-running case in court is careful and thorough preparation.

The first step in preparing a case is to gather all of the statements made by the witnesses. For a rape victim, this may mean gathering as many as eight different partial or full statements. They could include (1) the transcript of the telephone call to police emergency; (2) the brief interview by the first officer on the scene; (3) the nurse's interview at the hospital; (4) the examining physician's interview at the hospital; (5) the "formal" interview with the assigned investigator; (6) the notes of testimony from the preliminary hearing; (7) the notes of testimony from the pretrial motion to suppress; and (8) any statement given to a private investigator working on behalf of the defendant or on behalf of a third party who may have some civil liability to the victim.

After obtaining and reviewing all of these statements, a list of the differences should be compiled concerning such issues as the physical characteristics of the defendant's appearance, time of day, amount of alcohol or drugs consumed, etc. Reviewing these differences with the victim and attempting to reconcile them as much as possible is essential. In most cases these differences have a logical explanation if explored carefully.

Without exception, the actual trial attorney should interview all potential witnesses personally rather than rely on another investigator or another attorney to do so. It is helpful to have the investigator present at the preparation sessions. First, this validates a "team approach," which is often reassuring to the victim. Second, the investigator can make notes of work to be done prior to the start of the trial.

After the witnesses' statements are reviewed and the discrepancies are explored, the victim is prepared for direct and cross-examination. The victim should be informed about the areas of cross-examination that will undoubtedly come up. All of the sensitive, unpleasant, and indeed, embarrassing issues that will come out at trial must be sensitively but thoroughly reviewed. Sometimes it is appropriate to have a crisis counselor present during the preparation session for emotional support at this time. As discussed below, the identification issue or the key consent issues must be explored in minute detail.

It is important to review with the victim the areas of her testimony in which it is likely that she will become emotionally upset or angry. This helps to provide her with awareness of these issues and will prevent her from losing her self-control or dignity on the witness stand. However, if she feels as though she is going to break down and cry, explain that it is all right to do so and that she should move back from the microphone and take a moment to regain her composure.

Although it is not always possible or necessary to view the scene of the crime, if the scene has some confusing or unusual aspect to it, the prosecutor might wish to visit the location with the investigator. It is impossible to convince the jury of something that is not understood by the prosecutor. However, I do not recommend taking the victim back to the scene.

The key rule in the area of demonstrative evidence is to provide the jury with clear, visible exhibits. Pictures can be enlarged and mounted on cardboard so that they can be seen and handled easily by the jury.

Once the case has been dissected and analyzed, it is time to put it together for trial. Make a list of the order of witnesses to be called. Usually, the rape victim is the first witness, followed by additional witnesses. There are cases, however, when another witness is called first to "set the stage" for the victim. On the order of the witnesses sheet, list the major points the witness is expected to make. Review the bills of indictment and determine the bills upon which you will move to trial. Deleting minor bills will weed out those that are really enveloped by the major felony bills. This will assist the jury by simplifying the case. The testimony of the witnesses on your list should cover all of the elements of all of the crimes that are moving to trial.

At this point, the case should be thought through carefully to pinpoint the areas in which there will be a serious issue with respect to admissibility. Do the legal research, and obtain cases (with copies for the judge and your opponent) that will support the theory of admissibility. If necessary, prepare a short memorandum on the point. One of the reasons for doing this is that when the issue arises, the argument will already have been prepared, thereby permitting the judge to rule and move on rather than recess the trial for several hours while scurrying to the law library. Juries hate delays and will invariably blame the prosecutor for almost any delay, whether or not it is his fault.

There is no standard amount of time that a case preparation should take. It ranges from hours to weeks. The key is to be thorough and complete and not to have any surprises during the course of the trial, except those you have orchestrated.

After the preparation is completed and the trial is ready to begin, the rule of thumb is to have, in outline form, 90% of the closing argument prepared. Rape trials are not won by the prosecutor "winging it"; they are won by careful, meticulous preparation.

Jury Selection

Entire books have been written on jury selection. Purported experts and psychologists have designed and employed personality profiles and all types of analyses in an effort to pick the perfect jury for one side or the other. As a word of caution, most experienced trial lawyers can't agree on most issues in jury selection. For example, the two most experienced and successful trial lawyers in our office once gave a lecture on jury selection. The first attorney said that a prospective juror should be struck unless there is some specific positive reason why you want him. The second attorney said, if you are neutral about the person, take him. Obviously there are few rules in jury selection that apply in all cases.

However, in rape cases, there are some theories (not necessarily rules) that are certainly worth considering:

Some people think that women make better progovernment jurors than men. On the other hand, some argue that men are better jurors because they will want to act as the "protector" of the female victim. Without discussing specific fact patterns, this issue rates as a draw. Neither sex is inherently better for the prosecutor than the other.

In an interracial rape, the race issue is crucial; it is always there. All prospective jurors of the accused's race must be weighed very carefully before any of them are accepted. Recognizing that it is unusual to have a jury entirely of the same race as the victim's, the race issue can be minimized by picking people of the defendant's race who are of a different age and social bracket from the defendant.

Conventional wisdom also identifies certain occupational groups, ethnic groups, etc., as being more pro-prosecution than others. It is believed that people who have roots and a stake in the community, the "solid citizen" types, are good progovernment jurors. People on the fringes of society who are drifting through life, or who act or dress in a bizarre manner, or who answer questions inappropriately should not be selected. Look for the "mainstreamers" and achievers in the group.

Voir Dire Process

Because the voir dire process varies so greatly from judge to judge, it is impossible to recommend any one style. However, the following are some factors to keep in mind:

Voir dire is the first time that you have an opportunity to influence the jury. Speak to them as much as the judge will allow. This will permit you to educate them about crucial points of law in your case.

In the "unpopular victim" case, extract from the jurors a promise that they will follow the law, even if they don't agree with it.

At all costs, avoid embarrassing, humiliating, or insulting the jurors. They won't forgive you, and they certainly won't forget.

If the case depends heavily on police work, explore the juror's feelings about law enforcement. A person who believes he has been mistreated by the police will likely use your trial to "get even." This "get even" attitude will poison the jury or, at the least, will result in a hung jury.

If a juror is obviously not acceptable, thank him or her politely and abort the questioning. Don't provide a forum for the juror to espouse ideas and possibly influence the others on the panel.

Show utmost respect at all times for the judge, the defense attorney, the panel, and yes, the defendant. One's tone should be dignified and professional. Any attempts at sarcastic remarks or humor are inappropriate in a rape trial.

Avoid selecting a juror of the opposite sex from your own merely because the person is a smashing physical specimen. This may be a fatal distraction from the issues in the case.

Always keep in mind the number of peremptory strikes that are left and the type of people remaining on the panel. A person who did not initially appear to be a good selection might begin to look great when there is only one strike left and the remaining group is even less promising.

Try to avoid picking jurors who would be naturally antagonistic toward one another. The jury will have enough to discuss and argue about when they examine the case. Don't give them anything extra to disagree over.

Opening Statement

The following are some suggested guidelines for delivering an effective opening statement:

Be brief; avoid relating minute details or quoting specific conversations.

Promise the jury only what you know you will be able to deliver to them. If you are not sure that a certain witness will testify, don't tell the jury that the witness will definitely testify.

Don't tell the jury your entire case. Always leave a significant piece of your case for the jury to discover for themselves. If you tell them everything that you have, there will be nothing for them to look forward to. Encourage jurors to become involved in the unfolding of the case. Let them have the opportunity to hear some of your evidence for the first time as it comes from the witness stand.

Focus in on the key and crucial issue of the case. If it is an "ID" case, urge the jury to pay particularly close attention to the victim's opportunity to observe her assailant. If it is an "unpopular victim" case, remind the jury that they took an oath to be fair and impartial, that the lifestyle of the victim is not the issue.

Avoid law-school-esque catch phrases such as "I welcome the awesome burden of the Commonwealth" or "The government will prove to you beyond a shadow of a doubt that the defendant committed this heinous, dastardly act." They may sound good on a television show, but they're less persuasive in a real courtroom before real jurors. On the other hand, telling the jury that they are about to begin their "search for the truth" has a good ring to it and is effective.

Save the dramatics, the flamboyance, and the clever phrases for your closing. Be controlled and straightforward in your delivery of the opening statement.

Direct Examination

The goal of a good direct examination is to have the witness clearly and simply explain the facts to the jury. In guiding the rape victim through direct examination there must be a balance between short, choppy answers punctuated by frequent interruptions by the prosecutor, and a long, narrative, uninterrupted account by the victim.

The following are some guidelines in conducting direct examination:

In an identification issue case, as soon as the victim mentions the presence of the assailant, have her identify the defendant in the courtroom by pointing to him. From then on, he is to be referred to as the *defendant*.

In general, stay in the background during the victim's direct examination. She is the center of attention and the focus of the trial. Don't attempt to upstage her.

It is crucial that the jury hear what the victim is saying. Coach her to talk to the jury; involve them in her testimony. If necessary, stand at the far end of the jury box and cup your hand to your ear. Urge her to talk to the jury.

Utilize small but dramatic gestures to highlight a crucial part of the direct examination. Pausing, standing up, and hand gestures are good methods to highlight important testimony.

Your demeanor and voice tone should be controlled, mannerly, and mindful of the emotional trauma that the victim is suffering as she testifies.

Bring out the unfavorable facts from the victim on direct examination. Issues such as alcohol and drug use, hitchhiking, missing school, prostitution, prior relationship with the defendant, etc., should all be mentioned on direct examination.

The direct examination of the supporting witnesses should be short, succinct and to the point.

As the victim mentions items such as a gun, knife, her bloodied blouse, etc., show the item to her at that time, rather than waiting until the end of her testimony. The item should be marked, authenticated, and exhibited to the jury. Never proceed with your examination of a witness while any of the jurors are examining a piece of physical evidence. Of course, never pass a weapon or a piece of soiled clothing throughout the jury box.

Cross-Examination

Cross-examination of the defendant or any of his witnesses is obviously a crucial part of the truth-seeking and fact-finding process. It is also fraught with danger for the prosecutor. An excellent book on this subject is Francis Wellman's *The Art of Cross Examination*. It provides valuable background and a foundation. Another excellent resource is the writings (plus some video tapes) of Professor Irving Younger, particularly his famous piece, "Ten Commandments of Cross Examination."

Cross-examination should be discussed from a defensive posture. The following are some suggestions:

Avoid rehashing the witness's direct examination. Have specific areas of the direct examination in mind to challenge on cross. Repeating the direct examination is boring to the jury, and it allows the witness to emphasize the points a second time.

Try to ask as many leading questions as possible. Have in mind the answer you are looking for. Corner the witness into giving it to you by asking leading questions.

Two traditional rules of cross-examination are never to ask questions to which you don't know the answer, and never to ask a witness a question beginning with the word "why." There are exceptions to every rule, even the above. However, in general, these rules should be followed.

In cross-examining the defendant in the consent case, lock in the defendant to the physical conditions of the victim and/or her clothing just before the rape. For example, "Now, Mr. Jones, you didn't see any bruises on Miss Smith's left cheek when you and she went into the bedroom, did you?" "You didn't notice that her blouse was ripped down the front before she took it off, did you?" "She didn't complain of [fill in the nature of the injury to the victim] while she was with you, did she?" If you have a case where the victim has suffered injuries or torn clothing, this type of cross-examination will enable you to argue in your closing that even the defendant admits that the victim was not injured before the incident. Thus, her injuries/ripped clothing is consistent with her testimony that she was assaulted.

Any type of ripped clothing becomes crucial in corroborating the victim's testimony. Even popped buttons or stretched seams will support the victim's testimony of a struggle. The damaged article of clothing should be held up to the jury in your closing as the proof that the victim's version of what happened is a truthful one.

Rebuttal

The government's rebuttal to certain parts of the defense case is an explosive part of the prosecutor's package. Keep in mind the following points:

Rebuttal testimony or evidence should be very brief, pointed, direct, and specific. It should be aimed at challenging a specific point presented by the defense.

Rebuttal evidence is particularly persuasive to the jury because it is usually the last evidence they hear presented to them.

The jury already has a frame of reference in which they can evaluate the credibility of the evidence offered; that is, they know what defense evidence is being directly challenged by the rebuttal evidence.

Documents and records make particularly strong rebuttal evidence. By presenting records, the prosecutor doesn't have to worry about credibility factors, which are present when a live witness is being evaluated. The records are cold, unemotional facts that speak for themselves.

The way to present rebuttal evidence effectively is first to lock the defendant, or his witness, into his testimony regarding a particular fact. Make sure the fact to be challenged is on the record in a clear, unambiguous manner. Then put on your rebuttal witness in as short and succinct a manner as possible—get in and get out. Examples of documentation of records that are particularly effective include time cards from work records proving that the defendant, in fact, was not at work when he said he was; records from a television station showing that the program the defendant was supposed to have been watching that night, in fact, was preempted by a special news documentary, etc. The point is that when the jury has to evaluate a witness's testimony against a cold business record, they will invariably resolve any factual dispute in favor of the business record.

In rebutting an alibi defense, consider the alibi witnesses like links in a chain that is only as strong as the weakest link. You don't have to explode the entire testimony of every alibi witness. Search for the inconsistent part of one alibi witness's testimony. Rebut that witness's testimony, and then argue to the jury that when the weak link in the chain breaks, the entire alibi crumbles.

If the defendant testifies to materially different facts from those the victim has already testified to, you have to evaluate whether you want to call her in rebuttal. This may not be a wise move if she is an "unpopular" type of victim. However, if the defense raises a fact that the victim did not testify to (drug use, for example), it is incumbent on the prosecutor to bring back the victim on rebuttal to deny it. Be careful not to have the victim rehash her whole testimony on rebuttal. Raise the specific point and stop. This type of rebuttal is particularly effective in that it gives the jury one last opportunity to see, hear, and evaluate the victim.

Closing Argument

The closing argument is a crucial part of every criminal trial. Countless cases are won or lost based upon the quality of the closing argument.

The first point to keep in mind is preparation. As mentioned above, you should have about 90% of your closing argument already outlined in your head or on paper at the time you commence the trial. The remaining 10% of the content is based on material that came to light for the first time during the course of the trial.

The next point is to remember the importance of organizing your closing argument into a logical sequence of sections. A haphazard scatter-gun approach to a closing is ineffective. Break down the closing into different groups or sections. Finish one section and move on to the next.

The length of time of your closing will vary, of course, with the length and complexity of each case. In general, however, anything under 15 minutes is probably too short; 30 to 45 minutes is a good period of time; and anything over an hour in length may very well be too long.

Rather than reading your closing verbatim from your yellow tablet, it is advisable to refer to an outline as you proceed. This is entirely proper and is to be encouraged.

The following is a general outline of a closing argument in a rape trial:

Answer the most offensive or fallacious arguments made by the defense attorney in his closing. Mention to the jury that before you begin the merits of your argument, you feel obliged to respond to a few comments made by your opponent that you cannot let go by.

Cover the main thrust of your case. In an identification issue case, review those opportunities to observe, one by one. In a consent case, highlight issues such as the lack of a motive for the victim to lie, and other evidence in the case that supports her testimony. Review carefully the key portion of each witness's testimony, and point out how it adds to the government's overall case or how it supports the victim's testimony.

With respect to the victim's testimony, argue that the sole issue in the case is whether or not the jury believes her testimony, not whether they like her as a person or approve of her lifestyle. Emphasize that negative opinions regarding a victim's personality or lifestyle are never a valid excuse for the defendant to have raped her.

It is helpful to have the victim sitting in the front row of the courtroom so that you may gesture to her as you speak.

It is particularly important to stress the credibility of the testimony of the neutral or unbiased witness: the examining physician, the uniformed officer, the bystander stranger who obviously has "no axe to grind." These unbiased witnesses lead to the logical argument that they show conclusively the victim's testimony is indeed worthy of the jury's belief.

When the defense has offered evidence in the case, particularly by having the defendant testify, remind the jury that they must evaluate his testimony by the same yardstick as they did the victim's testimony. Mention the defendant's motive to lie, and pick apart logical inconsistencies in his testimony. Appealing to the jury's collective sense of logic and common sense is far more effective than appealing to their passion. Usually in the "he said versus she said" type of case, there is one witness or piece of evidence, possibly presented in rebuttal, that can be vigorously argued as indicative of which side is telling the truth.

After the facts have been analyzed and the jury has been urged to resolve the credibility issues in favor of the victim and the government witnesses, mention briefly the definition and elements of the crimes charged. Analyze carefully key issues, such as the sufficiency of a "substantial step" in an attempted rape or the lack of a requirement that the victim offer any physical resistance in the face of a substantial threat. Remind the jury again that they must obey and follow the law, even if they don't agree with it or approve of it.

It is often effective to reserve the last section of the closing argument for what I call the jury's "call to duty." I remind them that they represent the spirit and the conscience of the community, and that all of us have a right to expect that they will act fairly and impartially and will seek to do justice for all in this case. As always during the course of the trial, be proud to be a prosecutor, and be proud to represent the interests of the victim and the community at large.

Difficult Cases

Identification Issue Case

The identification issue case is the most straightforward type of rape case to try. The issue is not "Was she raped?" but, rather, "Is the defendant the one who did it?"

The identification case provides an excellent example of how the prosecutor should weave different parts of the trial into a coherent whole. Basically, the identification case breaks down into three distinct issues: (1) the victim's opportunity to observe the assailant, and, barring some unusual physical characteristic, specifically his face; (2) the accuracy of the physical description made by the victim to the authorities; and (3) the identification or "confrontation" of the defendant by the victim, whether by photograph, in person, in a lineup, or in a one-on-one confrontation.

The first key to successfully prosecuting this type of case is the preparation session with the victim. Having all of her prior statements in hand, review with her in minute detail each and every opportunity she had to see the defendant during the commission of the crime. Focus in on the victim's observation of the defendant's face. Write down each of the victim's observations of the defendant's face. For each opportunity ask her the following questions: How far from his face were you when you saw his face? What were the lighting conditions? What were you thinking of at the time? List each and every specific opportunity and the surrounding information separately. These small, isolated chips of information must be ascertained. Work with the victim carefully and help her to recall each and every opportunity.

Also at the preparation session, you must review with the victim why she is certain it was the defendant who assaulted her. If the victim merely says, "Yes, the defendant," when asked if she sees the person who attacked her in the courtroom, the jury won't know if "yes" means "I know that's him and I'll be positive until the day I die," or whether the "yes" means "I guess that must be he. After all, they arrested him, didn't they?" The prosecutor must review this issue with the victim very carefully. She must be prepared to tell you at the end of your direct examination, and stress during cross-examination, the basis or reason why she is able to swear under oath it was indeed the defendant, and no one else, who attacked her. By the conclusion of your preparation session you should have listed anywhere from 1 to 20 specific chips of facts, each constituting a separate and distinct opportunity to observe the defendant's face during the course of the incident.

The next step occurs during your opening statement to the jury. Remind them that while they must pay close attention to all of the testimony, they should listen very carefully to the victim as she describes each and every opportunity to see the defendant's face. They should also note carefully the accuracy of her description to the authorities and the identification confrontation that occurred.

The next important step occurs during direct examination of the victim. As soon as the victim mentions the presence of the assailant on the scene, immediately ask her if she sees the man she is describing physically in the courtroom. In other words, have the victim make her in-court identification as soon as she mentions him. Indicate that she identified Mr. Jones, the defendant. From then on, she should refer to him as "the defendant." This is preferable to waiting until the very end of her direct examination to ask her to make her in-court identification.

As mentioned, let the victim testify in a narrative, flowing form on her direct testimony. Interrupt her with specific questions only when necessary. You want the jury to hear her dramatic account of what happened in a narrative manner, without her constantly being interrupted with detailed "who cares"–type questions. After the victim has finished recounting the assault and has just testified to the defendant having left the scene, ask her to go back to the point at which she first saw the defendant and tell the jury about that and about the first time that she saw the defendant's face. Ask her the accompanying questions about how far away from the defendant she was when she saw his face, what the lighting conditions were (if that is an issue), and what she was thinking of when she saw the defendant's face. Take her through each and every opportunity to see the defendant's face, just as you worked it out in your preparation session. Have your "prep" notes in hand as she testifies so she does not omit any opportunities. The effect of letting the victim describe the incident in narrative form and then filling in with her the specific opportunities to observe the defendant's face is twofold. First, it organizes her opportunities to observe the defendant for the jury and makes it easy for you to argue the point in your closing. Second, it gives you two "bites at the apple," in that the jury will hear the violent aspects of the victim's testimony repeated again as she explains her opportunities to observe the defendant.

As the victim testifies, have her prepared, where relevant, to focus in on some distinctive aspect of the defendant's face in helping her to recognize the defendant in court. These features could be almond-shaped eyes, crooked eyeteeth, high arched eyebrows, round or oval face, evil-looking eyes, etc. Be sure that the victim also notes any changes in appearance between the time of the crime and the trial. End your direct examination by asking the victim why she is sure the defendant is the person who attacked her.

When you begin to discuss the identification issue in your closing argument, you might first point out to the jury that all faces on the earth are unique; no two faces are identical. Then point out that it was the trauma of the assault that has emblazened (pound your fist into your palm) that one face, that of the defendant, into the brain of the victim. It is this trauma that allowed the victim to *recognize* the defendant when she saw him again (the word *recognize* is a key word to be used often in an identification case).

At this point, review with the jury each and every opportunity the victim had to observe the defendant's face. Don't skip any. The cumulative effect of listing every single opportunity impacts quite significantly on the jury. Argue that it is these many opportunities that are the foundation of an accurate, reliable in-court identification.

Consent Issue Case

The "consent issue" case presents several difficult problems for the prosecutor. The issue in the case is not whether the sexual activity occurred. Most often the defendant will readily admit sexual contact with the victim. The issue is whether the act occurred by direct force or threats of force, or whether it happened with the victim's consent.

One of the problems presented by this type of case is that extraneous issues find their way onto the record about the prior relationship between the parties or the nature of the activities of the victim and the defendant prior to the assault. Obviously, the Rape Shield Law statutes do not preclude the introduction of prior sexual acts between the parties when the issue is consent. When you have this type of case, it is better to bring out the scope of the prior relationship on direct examination rather than wait for the defense attorney to "spring" it on the victim on cross-examination.

When your facts show that the victim and the defendant were engaged in an "unpopular" type of activity prior to the assault, such as drug or excessive alcohol use, follow the suggestions outlined in the unpopular victim section of this chapter.

The key to successfully prosecuting the consent defense case is to *corroborate* the testimony of the victim with as much supporting evidence as possible. The following are suggestions for handling the consent issue type of case:

If the victim claims she was slapped, choked, or in some manner physically abused by the defendant, introduce evidence of her physical injuries from the medical records custodian or from the examining physician. This documentation of her physical injuries, even minor scratches or bruises, becomes crucial in arguing to the jury in your closing that the victim's version of what happened can and should be believed. This is because it is supported by an objective, unbiased medical examination by a physician who did not know either of the parties and who clearly had no motive to fabricate anything. For this approach to be effective, you must have medical personnel who are aware of the importance of examining and noting all examples of nonpelvic trauma.

If the victim claims she was screaming during the incident, it is important to bring in the neighbor or the person who heard her scream. This corroborates the victim's testimony and supports her claim that the sexual contact was without her consent.

Any type of res-gestae or excited-utterance statement that is admissible is very valuable and should be introduced. Again, it supports the victim's testimony.

In a consent case where the victim has not suffered any trauma to her vaginal area, the defense attorney will make a major argument to the jury during his closing that the lack of vaginal injury is consistent with the defendant's version of consensual intercourse. After all, he will argue, if the victim had been forced, she would have naturally suffered some type of injury to her vagina. To a lay person, the argument is persuasive. However, it simply isn't valid. Therefore, in a consent case where there is no vaginal trauma, consider bringing in an expert medical witness, preferably the examining physician, to educate the jury on this issue. The doctor should explain the female pelvic anatomy and how rarely visible bruises are noted. The medical expert should conclude by offering his expert opinion that the lack of any vaginal trauma is entirely consistent with the victim having been forced to submit to the intercourse.

Unpopular Victim Case

The *unpopular victim* is a label used to describe a victim who, by virtue of her background or lifestyle in general or because of the particular activity in which she was engaged just prior to the rape, can be expected to elicit biased or negative feelings from the average juror. Examples of this include prostitutes, hitchhikers, drug and alcohol abusers, runaways, and truants.

Assuming that the judge will permit you to participate in voir dire, the key to winning this type of case is to extract a promise from the jurors before they are selected that, notwithstanding the fact that they might not approve of the victim's lifestyle or of what the victim was doing prior to the rape, nevertheless they will keep an open mind as they hear the testimony and not reach any conclusions until the appropriate time. Also, the jurors must promise that, like it or not, they will follow the law as it is stated by the judge in his charge to the jury.

One important benefit to bringing the unpopular facts out during voir dire is that you can judge whether or not the juror can be fair and impartial and give the government a fair trial, notwithstanding the unpopular aspects of the victim. If the juror indicates that he can't be fair or is hesitant in stating that he will be fair, it is obviously far better for the prosecutor to know that during voir dire, rather than to accept the juror and run the risk of poisoning the other jurors during deliberations.

The point is that you cannot make the jury think that the victim's lifestyle is other than it actually is. Since you can't disguise the unpopular aspect of the victim's lifestyle or activities, it is far better to bring the matter to the jury's attention as soon as possible during voir dire. It might then be argued that the defendant selected the victim as an "easy target" to rape.

During the opening address, don't be afraid to state again the negative aspects of the victim. Be sure to remind the jurors of the promise they made when they were selected, not to you individually, but on their oath, to keep an open mind and follow the law as the judge states it to them in his charge. As you present your case, at least the jury is not shocked when they actually hear the victim testify. Obviously, any type of corroboration at all will be crucial when you argue, in closing, that the victim's testimony was credible and worthy of the jury's belief.

Be sure to bring out on direct examination the nature and extent of the unpopular activity, assuming, of course, that it is admissible and would be brought out on cross-examination. The purpose of this approach is to be "up front" with the jury and not hide any biased aspects of the victim's activity or lifestyle. Take the "wind out of the sails" of your opponent by leaving no new material in these areas to develop on cross-examination. On the other hand, if the material is clearly inadmissible, file a motion *in limine*, and seek to have the judge rule that the defense attorney may not question the victim in that particular area.

In your closing argument, remind the jury of the promise they made to be fair and impartial. Tell them that the issue in the case is not whether they approve of the victim's lifestyle or of what she was doing before the rape occurred. Advise them that the only issue is whether the evidence proves, beyond a reasonable doubt, that the defendant assaulted her. Remind them they took an oath to follow the law, whether they like or approve of it or not. Explain that when the judge defines the law they must follow and obey, they will hear nothing that says a drug addict can't be raped or that it is a defense to the charge of rape that the victim had been hitchhiking, etc. You must have the jury focus on the true issues in the case and move them beyond the unpopular aspects of the victim.

It is also an effective approach in your closing to remind the jury that this type of victim is "easy prey" for the likes of the defendant and that she, as well as the defendant, is entitled to equal protection under the law.

Use of the Expert Witness to Establish the Presence of Rape Trauma Syndrome in the Victim

The use of the expert witness such as a psychiatrist, psychologist, or crisis counselor to establish that the victim's behavior is consistent with what has been labeled as "rape trauma syndrome" is a developing trial issue that has been addressed by courts in several states. As of this writing, the leading cases that permit the testimony of an expert witness to establish the presence of rape trauma syndrome are *State v. Marks*, 231 Kan 645, 647 P.2d 1292(1982); *State v. Saldana*, 324 N.W. 2d 227 (Minnesota 1982); and *State v. Taylor*, 663 S.W. 2d 235 (Missouri 1984); *People v. Reid*, 475 N.Y.S. 741 (New York 1984); *Comm. v. Baldwin*, 502 A.2d 253 (Penna. 1985); and *Comm. v. Gallagher*, 510 A.2d 735 (Penna. 1986).

Testimony in this area can be very important, indeed crucial, in cases involving small children, especially those who are too young to be qualified as witnesses. Also, it is important in certain "consent defense" type cases and those cases in which the victim's unusual or bizarre behavior has to be explained by the prosecutor.

If you are contemplating using this approach, research cases in your state to see if the courts have addressed the issue (see Chapter 15). If you wish to offer such testimony, check on the state of the law in your jurisdiction. Unless the appellate court has already ruled on the issue, it is recommended that a Memorandum of Law be prepared and submitted to the court before the expert is offered. Submit the Memorandum to the judge's law clerk two weeks before trial so he will have time to study the issue. You should obtain a ruling from the judge before trial so that you may consider referring to the expert's expected testimony in your opening statement.

In your Memorandum, you must argue in support of the court accepting the concept that *rape trauma syndrome* is an accepted, recognized term within the psychotherapeutic community and is used to describe the etiology and behavioral characteristics of stress and anxiety suffered by a victim following sexual assault. The author has found that referring to the widely recognized and accepted term *battered child syndrome* is a helpful, bridging-type argument in asking the court to accept rape trauma syndrome.

Several important factors the courts consider are the educational and professional background of the proffered expert, the length of time that elapsed between the sexual assault and when the victim and expert first met, and whether the expert is treating the victim in an ongoing psychotherapy program or simply examined the victim for the purpose of testifying.

Aside from nationally recognized experts in the field, psychiatric mental health professionals are acceptable and the highest-credentialed professional is preferable. A treating expert is preferable to one merely examining the victim for purposes of testifying. If you believe that you will need to call an expert, consider urging the victim to begin a counseling program with a qualified expert. By trial time, the expert will have accumulated a great amount of documentation to share with the jury.

When you frame the "ultimate question" to the expert, be careful not to ask if he believes that the victim was raped. Even if counsel's objection is overruled and the expert is permitted to opine (as in some of the leading cases) on the issue, it is a mistake to frame the question in that manner. You don't want to take away the jury's function of being the sole determinant of whether or not the victim was raped. You risk offending them by offering an expert's opinion. It is suggested that the question be framed as follows: "Doctor, based upon your examination/treatment of Miss Jones, do you have an opinion, within reasonable medical certainty, as to whether or not her behavior *is consistent with* her having suffered what you have defined and explained to the jury as rape trauma syndrome?" Then ask about the basis for this opinion. Having used the "consistent with" approach, you may tell the jury in your closing that the expert's testimony and opinion was offered to help the jury understand certain behavior of the victim and to indicate that the victim's testimony is, indeed, credible and worthy of their belief.

The tactic of using the expert witness to establish rape trauma syndrome is not one that can be used often. However, as other posttraumatic stress syndromes gain admissibility, rape trauma syndrome may well gain wider acceptance in the courts. Chapter 15 addresses this issue in more complete detail.

Cases Cited

Comm. v. Baldwin, 502 A.2d 253 (Penna. 1985)
Comm. v. Gallagher, 510 A.2d 735 (Penna. 1986)
People v. Reid, 475 N.Y.S. 741 (New York 1984)
State v. Marks, 231 Kan 645 P.2d 1292 (1982)
State v. Saldana, 324 N.W. 2d 227 (Minnesota 1982)
State v. Taylor, 663 S.W. 2d 235 (Missouri 1984)

Prosecuting Sexual Assault: The Use of Expert Testimony on Rape Trauma Syndrome

15

EUGENE BORGIDA, PATRICIA FRAZIER,
AND JANET SWIM

The use of expert psychological testimony on rape trauma syndrome in criminal sexual conduct trials is a relatively new phenomenon (Frazier and Borgida, 1985). Rape trauma syndrome consists of those behavioral, somatic, and psychological reactions that occur as a result of forcible rape or attempted forcible rape (Burgess and Holmstrom, 1974, 1985). These include nightmares, intrusive imagery, sleep disturbances, fears, and feelings of self-blame. As an acute stress reaction, rape trauma syndrome is generally regarded as a posttraumatic stress disorder (see Burgess, 1983) as defined in the *Diagnostic and Statistical Manual* (*DSM III*) of the American Psychiatric Association (3rd ed., 1980). Since publication of the original Burgess and Holmstrom study on rape trauma syndrome in 1974, other studies on the psychological aftereffects of rape have supported their basic findings (see Ellis, 1983).

The admission of rape trauma syndrome evidence typically involves the testimony of a qualified expert witness to the effect that the complainant's behavior following the alleged rape is consistent with, or similar to, that of other rape victims (Griffiths, 1985; Rowland, 1979, 1985). The rationale behind the introduction of expert testimony on rape trauma syndrome is twofold (Frazier and Borgida, 1985). First, this evidence is most often used in consent defense cases, where there is usually no corroborating evidence to support the complainant's claims regarding consent; it is the defendant's word against the complainant's. Thus, the testimony serves to corroborate the complainant's version of the facts. Second, it is assumed that jurors are not familiar with the typical reactions of rape victims and that their decision-making could be assisted by expert testimony. Research on juror misconceptions regarding rape victims is consistent with this assumption (Borgida and Brekke, 1985). It is not unusual, for example, for a victim to delay reporting a rape, although some jurors may believe that such a delay weakens the credibility of the victim's complaint (Frazier and Borgida, 1986). Therefore, rape trauma syndrome evidence also serves to educate the jury (Massaro, 1985).

Currently, appellate courts in the United States are divided regarding whether rape trauma syndrome evidence has been properly admitted at the trial court level. In this chapter, we first review a few of the more important decisions involving rape trauma syndrome evidence. These cases highlight the key arguments made for and against the admissibility of this type of expert testimony (see Lawrence, 1984, and Massaro, 1985, for further analyses of these arguments). Finally, we review and briefly discuss some of the common objections that have been raised about expert testimony on rape trauma syndrome.

Admissibility Rulings on Rape Trauma Syndrome

The case most often cited regarding rape trauma syndrome probably is *State v. Saldana* (1982). *State v. Saldana* and *State v. McGee* were companion cases, both decided by the Minnesota Supreme Court in August 1982. In *Saldana*, the primary case, a rape victim counselor testified about typical reactions of rape victims, stated that she believed the complainant had been raped, and testified that the rape had not been fantasized. Although the Court accepted the expert as qualified, it ruled that the testimony was scientifically unreliable, unhelpful, and unfairly prejudicial to the defendant. The Court ruled that testimony regarding how some, or most, people react to rape is not helpful to the jury in deciding a particular case and that the complainant need not display any typical symptoms in order to convince the jury she is telling the truth. Rape trauma syndrome was not deemed to be the type of evidence that accurately and reliably determines whether a rape occurred, and its level of scientific reliability was not seen as surpassing that of the common juror's understanding. Thus, although the concept may be useful in therapy, it does not assist the jury in its fact-finding function. The expert testimony in *McGee* was rejected for the reasons outlined in *Saldana*, although a dissenting opinion was filed. (See *State v. Taylor* (1984) and *Allewalt v. State* (1985) for further arguments against admissibility.)

The California Supreme Court (*People v. Bledsoe*, 1984) decided that rape trauma syndrome testimony was only admissible under certain circumstances. The *Bledsoe* decision stressed that expert testimony on rape trauma syndrome may be useful in educating juries about rape and rape victims, but that the evidence in *Bledsoe* had been admitted only to prove that a rape occurred and that the testimony was not admissible for this purpose. The Court explicitly noted that evidence of the emotional and psychological trauma of the complaining witness is not necessarily inadmissible. But the Court did decide that the evidence was prejudicial if it implied that a rape occurred because the complainant exhibited symptoms suggestive of trauma. Although the rape trauma syndrome evidence was deemed inadmissible, Bledsoe's conviction was nonetheless upheld.

In contrast, the Kansas Court in *State v. Marks* (1982) allowed the testimony of a psychiatrist that the complainant was suffering from rape trauma syndrome. The defendant argued that the testimony was inadmissible because it invaded the province of the jury and was based on "incompetent hearsay evidence" (i.e., the complainant's statements during the psychiatric examination). The Court concluded that if rape trauma syndrome is reliable and detectable as evidence that a rape occurred, then it is relevant to the issue of consent. It is offered as any other evidence, with the expert open to cross-examination and the jury left to determine its weight. Citing several scientific sources, the Court concluded that rape trauma syndrome is a concept generally accepted in the scientific community. (See *Delia S. v. Torres*, 1982; *People v. Reid*, 1984; *State v. Liddell*, 1984; *State v. McQuillen*, 1984; *State v. Ogle*, 1984; *State v. Whitman*, 1984; and *Terrio v. McDonough*, 1983, for other decisions upholding rape trauma syndrome testimony.)

The decisions in *Saldana, Marks*, and *Bledsoe* reflect the issues that have been discussed thus far in judicial decisions regarding rape trauma syndrome evidence. More detailed discussions of current case law can be found in Frazier and Borgida (1985), Lawrence (1984), and Massaro (1985). Table 15.1 presents most of the current decisions on the admissibility of rape trauma syndrome evidence in consent defense cases.[1] These cases are classified on the basis of the primary criteria used for the admission of expert testimony. Although the criteria vary somewhat, in general, the expert must be qualified, and the evidence must be scientifically reliable, helpful to the jury, and not unfairly prejudicial to the defendant.[2]

---

[1] Although the evidence has been used in other contexts, such as to establish the defense of diminished capacity in a homicide case (*People v. Matthews*, 1979) or to establish a basis for further compensation based on continuing disability (*White v. Violent Crimes Compensation Board*, 1978; *Alphonso v. Charity Hospital of Louisiana at New Orleans*, 1982; *Division of Corrections v. Wynn*, 1983), Table 15.1 only focuses on the use of the testimony in consent defense rape cases. Table 15.1 also does not include the few appellate decisions from the U.S. Court of Military Appeals.

[2] In determining reliability, courts often rely on *Frye v. United States* (1923), which outlines the standards for the admissibility of novel scientific techniques. The *Frye* test maintains that evidence must be based on techniques that are generally accepted by the relevant scientific community. However, according to the Federal Rules of Evidence (1984), expert psychological testimony need not be "generally accepted" in order to be admissible. Rather, all relevant evidence is admitted, with the jury left to determine its weight.

Table 15.1 Admissibility Criteria Applied in Appellate Decisions Involving Rape Trauma Syndrome Evidence

Qualification	Reliability	Helpfulness	Prejudice
Whitman (−)	Saldana (−)	Saldana (−)	Saldana (−)
	McGee (−)	McGee (−)	McGee (−)
	Marks (+)	Bledsoe (−)	Allewalt (−)
	Reid (+)	Taylor (−)	
	Whitman (+)	Marks (+)	
		Torres (+)	
		McDonough (+)	
		Ogle (+)	
		Reid (+)	
		McQuillen (+)	
		Liddell (+)	

An appellate decision was listed under a particular heading only if that criterion seemed to be a substantial consideration in the decision, with "−" or "+" indicating whether a judgment on that criterion was favorable or not.

In only one of the decisions (*State v. Whitman*, 1984) have the qualifications of the expert been at issue. The expert in *Whitman* was a social worker who had not previously made a diagnosis of rape trauma syndrome. Federal Rule 702 states that a witness is qualified as an expert "by knowledge, skill, experience, training or education . . ." Thus, there is no strict criterion by which to judge qualifications, and courts seem to grant fairly wide latitude in making this determination. Experts have been rape counselors (*Saldana, Torres, Bledsoe*), a psychiatric nurse (*McDonough*), physicians (*McGee, Ogle*), and psychiatrists (*Taylor, Marks*). The nature of the relationship between the complainant and the expert has also varied. An expert may be involved in an ongoing therapeutic relationship with a client (e.g., *Bledsoe*) or may never have met the complainant (e.g., *Ogle*).

Despite recent concerns about rape trauma evidence that focus in large part on its scientific reliability (Lawrence, 1984), this has been a less significant issue in the courts than the helpfulness of the evidence. The *Marks* decision, for example, concluded that rape trauma syndrome is "generally accepted" in the scientific community. *Bledsoe* and *Saldana* both concluded that rape trauma syndrome was generally accepted for counseling or therapy purposes, but that its use in court was improper because all victims do not respond to rape in the same way and because rape trauma syndrome cannot accurately and reliably determine whether a rape occurred.

As may be seen in Table 15.1, the helpfulness of the testimony has most often been at issue. The arguments against helpfulness usually take the form that the evidence invades the province of the jury, i.e., judgments regarding credibility should be made by the jury and not by the expert. It is also argued that expert testimony improperly bolsters the credibility of the complainant. In addition, the evidence is deemed not helpful if it is within the common knowledge of the jury, that is, if it is assumed that jurors are adequately knowledgeable about the psychological reactions of rape victims. The argument has also been raised that this kind of testimony might lead to a "battle of experts" that would only mislead and confuse the jury. Similar arguments have been made regarding expert psychological testimony on the accuracy of eyewitness identification (Loftus, 1983; McCloskey and Egeth, 1983; Wells, 1984).

Although it is difficult to distinguish arguments about helpfulness from those about prejudicial impact, the latter admissibility criterion has received less attention in judicial decisions to date. Some courts fear that jurors will give undue weight to expert testimony, which could make the testimony unfairly prejudicial to the defendant. This "bolstering" argument, therefore, relates to prejudice as well as to helpfulness. The court in *Taylor* argued that the term *rape trauma syndrome* itself was prejudicial because it implies that a rape occurred.

Whatever the exact nature of the testimony, rape trauma syndrome evidence is not likely to be admitted without objection. In the final five sections, therefore, we will consider some typical objections in greater detail. These objections will then be evaluated in light of empirical evidence and previous judicial decisions.

1. *Expert testimony regarding rape trauma syndrome is not beyond the common knowledge of the jury.*

Assumptions are often made in judicial decisions about the extent to which a certain body of knowledge is within the common understanding of the average layperson. Courts considering this question in regard to rape trauma syndrome have been divided. The decision in *Reid*, for example, asserted that since reactions to rape are sufficiently complex and unique to warrant scientific investigation, it follows that those reactions are not within the common knowledge of the jury. Other courts have assumed that most people are informed about the aftereffects of rape. However, these decisions need not be made on assumptions, but can also be viewed as empirical questions (Massaro, 1985; Penrod and Borgida, 1983). While only one study (Frazier and Borgida, 1986) has been conducted on the common understanding doctrine as it pertains to rape trauma syndrome, a few studies have tested this notion of "common understanding" in relation to eyewitness behavior. Studies by Deffenbacher and Loftus (1982) and Brigham and Bothwell (1983) both found that qualified jurors were not aware of the various factors that have been shown to affect the reliability of eyewitness identifications, and that expert testimony represented one way to educate the jury regarding those factors. Although one cannot conclude from these data that jurors do not share a common understanding regarding rape victim behavior, this evidence does argue against simply making assumptions about what constitutes "common knowledge."

Common understanding, it should be remembered, is not the only criterion for helpfulness. In *Saldana*, for example, it was argued that inclusion of expert psychological testimony on rape trauma syndrome would not be helpful in that it could lead to a time-consuming "battle of experts" that could distract the jury from its task. Some legal commentators have cogently taken issue with this argument (Massaro, 1985), and, in fact, no such battle of experts has taken place in any of the cases previously cited. Moreover, recent jury simulation research suggests that the presence of opposing experts does not create such confusion among jurors in a rape trial (Brekke, 1985).

2. *Rape trauma syndrome evidence invades the province of the jury because it is admitted only to bolster the credibility of the witness.*

There is a fine psychological line between evidence that corroborates the complainant's version of the facts and evidence that bolsters the credibility of the complainant. Corroborating evidence is admissible because it is relevant to the facts and only indirectly addresses credibility. Bolstering evidence invades the province of the jury because de facto the expert is testifying that he or she believes the complainant (Cade and Imwinkelreid, 1983). Rape trauma syndrome evidence has been construed as serving both corroborating and bolstering purposes. It is corroborating in that it supports the complainant's claim that intercourse was not consensual. It is seen by defense attorneys as bolstering because it is based solely on the complainant's self-report.

Because it is difficult to determine whether expert testimony corroborates or bolsters, experts should refrain from stating that they believe the complainant was raped. (This was specifically prohibited in the decision in *Reid*.) Some jurisdictions (see *Taylor*) have argued that even a statement that a complainant is suffering from rape trauma syndrome is too inflammatory because the term implies that a rape occurred. The expert may choose to state that the complainant shows symptoms of stress without relating these symptoms to the particular incident in question (see *Taylor*). There is even some precedent that the expert testimony is more likely to be admitted if the defendant first claims that the complainant acted in some way that is *atypical* of rape victims (see *Torres, McDonough, Bledsoe*).

3. *There is a danger that jurors will "overweigh" the expert testimony, causing prejudice to the defendant.*

This argument was first made by the court in *Saldana* and is based on the assumption that expert testimony creates an aura of special reliability and trustworthiness. However, whether jurors give special weight to expert testimony has only recently been evaluated empirically with respect to rape trauma syndrome evidence. Brekke (1985) found that when jurors were presented with expert testimony on rape trauma syndrome, they were more likely to find the defendant guilty than when no expert testimony was presented. However, if the defense also called an opposing expert, this effect was attenuated. The finding that there were more guilty verdicts with testimony from only one expert, however, did not seem to result from uncritical acceptance of the expert testimony or insufficient attention to other evidence. This is supported by the finding that the two groups did not differ in their recall of the details of the trial. Brekke also found that ratings of the defendant's credibility and honesty were not affected by the expert testimony, suggesting that the evidence did not result in unfair prejudice to the defendant.

The use of expert testimony has received more attention in studies on the reliability of eyewitness identifications (see Wells and Loftus, 1984). The results from these studies, however, have been inconsistent. In a typical study, simulated juries are presented with a trial transcript that either includes or does not include expert testimony on the accuracy of eyewitness identification, in order to determine the effect of such testimony on conviction rates. The results from a study by McKenna, Mellot, and Webb (1981), for example, demonstrated that expert testimony did not affect conviction rates. In this study, less than 10% of the juries found the defendant guilty whether or not they had heard expert testimony. However, other studies have demonstrated that expert testimony can affect conviction rates. For example, the inclusion of expert testimony decreased the percentage of jurors finding the defendant guilty by 12% in a nonviolent crime case and 25% in a violent crime case (Loftus, 1980).

Inconsistencies in the experimental studies conducted in the eyewitness area underscore the difficulty of determining exactly what weight jurors give to expert testimony. In the McKenna et al. (1981) study, the percentage of guilty verdicts was very low for all juries regardless of the inclusion of expert testimony. Thus it is possible that the evidence in these cases was so compelling that the expert testimony could not be shown to have a statistical effect on verdicts. The Loftus (1980) study, in which expert testimony did influence the final verdict, cannot determine whether the testimony was properly weighed. Indeed, there is no consensus on what standard to invoke to make this determination. An increase in conviction rates with expert testimony could mean that the testimony was given too much weight, but an equally plausible explanation would be that the expert testimony merely increased the amount of evidence against the defendant.

Similar issues arise in determining the proper weight to be given to expert testimony on rape trauma syndrome. That is, the impact of rape trauma syndrome testimony will be affected by the strength of the other evidence presented. Furthermore, the weight given the testimony cannot be determined by the jurors' final decision. An increase in conviction rates may reflect a decrease in juror skepticism about rape victim credibility, or may reflect an increase in the strength of the evidence against the defendant. Thus, the inconsistency in experimental evidence and the difficulty of determining (on the basis of conviction rates) the influence of expert testimony weaken the argument that the evidence is prejudicial because jurors tend to give it undue weight (see Massaro, 1985, on this issue).

4. *Rape trauma syndrome is not scientifically reliable and/or generally accepted in the scientific community.*

There are several different arguments that relate to the scientific reliability of rape trauma syndrome evidence. Before discussing these arguments against reliability, it might be helpful to describe briefly the psychological literature on which these criticisms are based (see Ellis, 1983, and Katz and Mazur, 1979, for more comprehensive reviews).

As mentioned earlier in this chapter, the term *rape trauma syndrome* was introduced by Burgess and Holmstrom (1974). Over a 1-year period, they interviewed every woman entering the emergency ward of a large metropolitan hospital whose complaint was that she had been raped. In this study, Burgess and Holmstrom described an acute phase immediately following the rape and a second phase that consists of a long-term process of reorganization in response to the rape. Although there were other rape victim studies conducted during the early 1970s (e.g., Notman and Nadelson, 1976; Sutherland and Scherl, 1970), the Burgess and Holmstrom study is by far the most widely cited in appellate decisions. Katz and Mazur (1979) reviewed these rape victim studies and found many of them to be methodologically deficient. For example, many studies included victims of different types of sexual assault, included only victims who were willing to participate in research, and failed to use adequate sample sizes, control groups of nonvictims, objective measures of symptoms, or long-term follow-ups. Nevertheless, these clinical studies were an important first step in describing the clinical profile of the aftereffects of rape, in raising public consciousness about sexual assault, and in the development of treatment centers for rape victims.

Current rape victim research is methodologically more sophisticated

(Frazier and Borgida, 1985). These studies have compensated for most of the deficiencies in the earlier clinical research (i.e., by including control groups, adequate samples, objective assessment measures, and long-term follow-ups). Ellis (1983) has reviewed the research on short-, intermediate-, and long-term reactions to rape and factors associated with different rates of recovery. For example, Kilpatrick, Veronen, and Resick (1979) examined reactions two to three hours postassault and found that victims recalled feeling depressed (80%), jumpy (88%), worried (96%), and withdrawn (76%). Two weeks postassault, 75% of the victims reported having physical symptoms such as nausea or vaginal irritation. Forty-four percent had nightmares, and 69% felt more fearful than they had prior to the assault. Using symptom checklists, fear surveys, and measures of mood and anxiety, Kilpatrick et al. (1979) found that victims scored higher than nonvictims on 25 of 28 subscales at one month postassault. Victims were significantly more depressed at two months postassault (Atkeson, Calhoun, Resick, and Ellis, 1982), and global ratings of their social adjustment were lower. Most victims returned to normal levels of functioning between three and four months postassault.

Ellis (1983) also reviewed studies of reactions up to a year postassault on measures of depression, social adjustment, sexual functioning, fear, and anxiety. Generally, there were no significant differences between groups from three months to one year postassault. However, the victim groups had higher mean scores on almost all measures, and a number of victims continued to have high levels of fearfulness, anxiety, and depression. At one year, many of the victims still reported feelings of intense rage. Higher levels of anger were still present at three years postassault, as were higher levels of depression, less enjoyment of pleasurable activities, hypervigilance to danger, and sexual dysfunction (Ellis, 1983).

Several studies have also examined various factors surrounding the rape experience that might relate to postrape recovery, such as whether the victim knew the attacker, whether she was threatened, and whether she had been raped previously (Frank, Turner, and Stewart, 1980; Norris and Feldman-Summers, 1981). Ellis concluded that factors surrounding the rape were not consistently related to recovery, although prerape psychological functioning has been found to be significantly related to postrape symptomatology (Frank, Turner, Stewart, Jacob, and West, 1981), as have prior levels of life change (Ruch and Leon, 1983; see Sales, Baum, and Shore, 1983, for a review).

Clearly, there is now a significant body of literature on rape victim behaviors, of which the preceding is only a sample. It is important to note that this more recent research has also been criticized on methodological and conceptual grounds. Methodologically, the studies have been criticized for including victims of all forms of sexual assault and not just rape victims (Lawrence, 1984). This criticism, initially made by Katz and Mazur (1979) in reference to the early rape studies, is less applicable to more recent research. Careful screening of victims along with confining one's sample to volunteers from rape crisis centers would appear to control adequately for the possibility that the study participants were really victims of other forms of sexual assault. Relatedly, it is true that the empirical studies are often limited to victims who are willing to participate, and who may, in fact, differ from those who are not so willing. Researchers are aware of this problem and are careful to compare the demographic characteristics of victims who choose to participate with the characteristics of those who refuse. While self-selection is an inherent problem in rape victim research, it does not render all rape victim studies unreliable.

Several of the judicial decisions, in deciding on scientific reliability, discuss the previously cited research and refer to rape trauma syndrome as an example of a posttraumatic stress disorder (American Psychiatric Association, 1980). While this classification may enhance the credibility of the diagnosis, some psychiatric and legal commentators have questioned this practice. Raifman (1983), for example, has criticized the notion that there is a causal connection between the traumatic event (e.g., rape) and the ensuing symptomatology. He argues that (1) the definition of the stressor as being outside the range of common human experience is fallacious because common stressors can produce the same symptoms; (2) the diagnosis of posttraumatic stress disorder is complicated by the fact that many of its symptoms occur in other disorders; (3) preexisting factors and indirect consequences of the event complicate the diagnosis; and (4) the diagnosis relies on self-report and assumes that the complainant is truthful. These concerns have led at least one critic to argue that the "classification of rape trauma syndrome as a Posttraumatic Stress Disorder does little to improve its probative value in rape trials" (Lawrence, 1984, p. 1698). Other commentators, however, have addressed these issues and defended the validity of posttraumatic stress disorder, particularly as it applies to rape trauma syndrome (Burgess, 1983; Burgess and Holmstrom, 1985; Massaro, 1985; Ross, 1983).

Lawrence (1984) has also argued that the scientific reliability of rape trauma syndrome is complicated by the fact that both rape and attempted-rape victims exhibit the same symptoms. While this claim has received some empirical support (Becker, Skinner, Abel, Howell, and Bruce, 1982), the distinction is not particularly relevant in consent defense cases. In such cases, there is no question as to whether the act of intercourse occurred (i.e., whether attempted or completed). Both parties admit to the act, and the central issue is consent. Thus, the fact that attempted rape victims show similar symptomatology does not undermine the diagnosis in this context.

Lawrence (1984), along with the Court in *Saldana*, also stressed the fact that not every victim responds to rape in the same fashion. He argued that the underlying principle of rape trauma syndrome is that all rape victims exhibit consistent, clinically observable symptoms etiologically related to the assault. The fact that individual and incident-specific factors affect responses then is claimed to undermine the validity of the "underlying principle." This reasoning leads to the conclusion (also reached in *Saldana* and *Bledsoe*) that, therefore, the requisite *causal* connection cannot be made between the incident in question and the ensuing symptomatology. Or, in other words, the diagnosis is not one that can accurately and reliably determine whether a rape occurred.

No clinical diagnosis, however, assumes that *all* persons in that category exhibit identical symptomatology or that all people will respond to a stressful experience in an identical fashion. Individual variability does not mean that rape trauma syndrome cannot accurately and reliably determine whether sexual intercourse has been consensual or forced, at reasonable levels of scientific certainty. Moreover, the existence of individual variability also does not suggest that evidence regarding common rape victim reactions, which at this time are well documented, is not helpful to jurors faced with making a determination regarding consent. When an expert testifies regarding the reactions of most rape victims, it is the jury's task to evaluate the weight of that evidence in relation to a particular complainant. Juries, we believe, should be allowed to decide how much weight to give to the evidence. Sound empirical research regarding postassault behavior and expert testimony based on that research may indeed be helpful to the jury in evaluating the evidence at hand. Evidence that a certain percentage of rape victims experience various symptoms, along with testimony regarding the complainant's postrape behaviors, is relevant to the jury.

5. *The admission of rape trauma syndrome evidence could have adverse implications for the complainant.*

So far we have examined several of the most common objections to rape trauma syndrome evidence. However, there is one further aspect of expert testimony on rape trauma syndrome that has not been raised in the case law but deserves comment. The admission of rape trauma syndrome evidence could have adverse discovery implications for the complainant (Lawrence, 1984; Massaro, 1985). Specifically, the admission of rape trauma syndrome evidence may "open the door" to the questioning of the complainant regarding the details of her emotional life. If the prosecution, for example, is allowed to enter testimony concerning the complainant's emotional state months after the rape, the defense could argue that it should be allowed to question the complainant regarding her emotional state months *prior* to the rape. If the complainant, for example, testifies to having fears and trouble sleeping in the aftermath of a rape, the defense might want access to her records to determine whether or not she had previously been bothered by these problems. Moreover, there has already been one appellate case (*State v. McQuillen*, 1984) in which the defendant attempted to present evidence that the complainant was *not* suffering from rape trauma syndrome. In *McQuillen*, however, the Court ruled that expert testimony on the *absence* of rape trauma syndrome is not relevant or admissible in a consent defense rape case. In addition, the *Liddell* court ruled that the defense could not order a complainant to undergo a psychiatric examination. Nevertheless, under certain circumstances, the admission of rape trauma syndrome evidence might expose the victim to a more difficult and intrusive experience in the courtroom, a possibility that runs counter to the thrust of rape shield laws (Borgida, 1981). This is certainly a possibility that prosecutors should consider carefully. However, we do not think the possibility of a more difficult cross-examination necessarily outweighs the benefits of introducing expert testimony on rape trauma syndrome.

References

American Psychiatric Association. *Diagnostic and Statistical Manual of Mental Disorders*, 3rd ed. Washington, D.C.: American Psychiatric Association, 1980.

Atkeson, B., Calhoun, K., Resick, P., and Ellis, E. "Victims of Rape: Repeated Assessment of Depressive Symptoms." *Journal of Consulting and Clinical Psychology* 50, No. 1 (1982): 96–102.

Becker, J., Skinner, L., Abel, G., Howell, J., and Bruce, K. "The Effects of Sexual Assault on Rape and Attempted Rape Victims." *Victimology: An International Journal* 7, Nos. 1–4 (1982): 106–113.

Borgida, E. "Legal Reform of Rape Laws," in L. Bickman, ed. *Applied Social Psychology Annual*. Beverly Hills, Calif.: Sage Publications, 1981.

Borgida, E. and Brekke, N. "Psycholegal Research on Rape Trials," in A. Burgess, ed. *Research Handbook on Rape and Sexual Assault*. New York: Garland, 1985.

Brekke, N. "Expert Scientific Testimony in Rape Trials," unpublished doctoral dissertation, University of Minnesota, 1985.

Brigham, J. and Bothwell, R. "The Ability of Prospective Jurors to Estimate the Accuracy of Eyewitness Identifications." *Law and Human Behavior* 7 (1983): 19–30.

Burgess, A. "Rape Trauma Syndrome." *Behavioral Sciences and the Law* 1, No. 3 (1983): 97–113.

Burgess, A. and Holmstrom, L. "Rape Trauma Syndrome." *American Journal of Psychiatry* 131 (1974): 980–986.

Burgess, A. and Holmstrom, L. "Rape Trauma Syndrome and Post-Traumatic Stress Response," in A. W. Burgess, ed. *Rape and Sexual Assault: A Research Handbook*. New York: Garland, 1985.

Cade, B. and Imwinkelreid, E. "Rape Trauma Syndrome Evidence." *The Champion* 3, No. 1 (1983): 2–4.

Deffenbacher, K. and Loftus, E. "Do Jurors Share a Common Understanding Concerning Eyewitness Behavior?" *Law and Human Behavior* 6, No. 1 (1982): 15–30.

Ellis, E. "A Review of Empirical Rape Research: Victim Reactions and Responses to Treatment." *Clinical Psychology Review* 3 (1983): 473–490.

Ellis, E., Atkeson, B., and Calhoun, K. "An Assessment of Long-Term Reaction to Rape." *Journal of Abnormal Psychology* 90 (1981): 263–266.

Federal Rules of Evidence. St. Paul, Minn.: West Publishing, 1984.

Feldman-Summers, S., Gordon, P., and Meagher, J. "The Impact of Rape on Sexual Satisfaction." *Journal of Abnormal Psychology* 88, No. 1 (1979): 101–105.

Frank, E., Turner, S., and Stewart, B. "Initial Response to Rape: The Impact of Factors within the Rape Situation." *Journal of Behavioral Assessment* 2 (1980): 39–53.

Frank, E., Turner, S., Stewart, B., Jacob, M., and West, D. "Past Psychiatric Symptoms and Response to Sexual Assault." *Comprehensive Psychiatry* 22 (1981): 479–487.

Frazier, P. and Borgida, E. "Rape Trauma Syndrome Evidence in Court." *American Psychologist* 40 (1985): 984–993.

Frazier, P. and Borgida, E. "Juror Common Understanding and the Admissibility of Rape Trauma Syndrome Evidence in Court," unpublished manuscript, University of Minnesota, 1986.

Griffiths, G. L. "Rape Trauma Syndrome: The Overlooked Evidence in Rape Investigations." *The Detective* 12, No. 1 (1985): 1–4.

Katz, S. and Mazur, M. *Understanding the Rape Victim*. New York: John Wiley and Sons, 1979.

Kilpatrick, D., Veronen, L., and Resick, P. "Assessment of the Aftermath of Rape: Changing Patterns of Fear." *Journal of Behavioral Assessment* 1 (1979): 133–148.

Lawrence, R. "Checking the Allure of Increased Conviction Rates: The Admissibility of Expert Testimony on Rape Trauma Syndrome in Criminal Proceedings." *University of Virginia Law Review* 70 (1984): 1657–1704.

Loftus, E. "Impact of Expert Psychological Testimony on the Unreliability of Eyewitness Identification." *Journal of Applied Psychology* 65, No. 1 (1980): 9–15.

Loftus, E. "Silence Is Not Golden." *American Psychologist* 38 (1983): 564–572.

Massaro, T. M. "Experts, Psychology, Credibility, and Rape: The Rape Trauma Syndrome Issue and Its Implications for Expert Psychological Testimony." *Minnesota Law Review* 69 (1985): 395–470.

McCloskey, M. and Egeth, H. "Eyewitness Identification: What Can a Psychologist Tell a Jury?" *American Psychologist* 38, No. 5 (1983): 550–564.

McKenna, J., Mellot, A., and Webb, E. "Juror Evaluation of Eyewitness Testimony," paper presented at the meeting of the Eastern Psychological Association, New York, 1981.

Norris, J. and Feldman-Summers, S. "Factors Related to the Psychological Impacts of Rape on the Victim." *Journal of Abnormal Psychology* 90 (1981): 562–567.

Notman, M. and Nadelson, C. "The Rape Victim: Psychodynamic Considerations." *American Journal of Orthopsychiatry* 40, No. 3 (1976): 503–511.

Penrod, S. and Borgida, E. "Legal Rules and Lay Inference," in L. Wheeler and P. Shaver, eds. *Review of Personality and Social Psychology*. Beverly Hills, Calif.: Sage Publications, 1983.

Raifman, L. "Problems of Diagnosis and Legal Causation in Courtroom Use of Posttraumatic Stress Disorder." *Behavioral Sciences and the Law* 1, No. 3 (1983): 115–130.

Ross, J. "The Overlooked Expert in Rape Prosecutions." *Toledo Law Review* 14 (1983): 707–734.

Rowland, J. "Rape Experts Dispell Jurors' Preconceptions." *Prosecutor's Brief* 5, No. 2 (1979): 21–25.

Rowland, J. *The Ultimate Violation*. New York: Doubleday, 1985.

Ruch, L. and Leon, J. "Sexual Assault Trauma and Trauma Change." *Women and Health* 8, No. 4 (1983): 5–21.

Sales, E., Baum, M., and Shore, B. "Victim Readjustment following Assault." *Journal of Social Issues* 40, No. 1 (1983): 117–136.

Sutherland, S. and Scherl, D. "Patterns of Response among Victims of Rape." *American Journal of Orthopsychiatry* 40, No. 3 (1970): 503–511.

Wells, G. L. "Reanalysis of the Expert Testimony Issue," in G. L. Wells and E. F. Loftus, eds. *Eyewitness Testimony: Psychological Perspectives*. New York: Cambridge University Press, 1984.

Wells, G. L. and Loftus, E. F., eds. *Eyewitness Testimony:* Psychological Perspectives. New York: Cambridge University Press, 1984.

Cases Cited

Allewalt v. State (1985) Md. 487 A.2d 664.
Alphonso v. Charity Hospital of Louisiana at New Orleans (1982) La. 413 So.2d 982.
Delia S. v. Torres (1982) 134 Cal. App. 3d 471.
Division of Corrections v. Wynn (1983) Fla. 438 So.2d 446.
Frye v. United States (1923) 293 F. 1013 (D.C. Cir.).
People v. Bledsoe (1984) 203 Cal. Rep. 461.
People v. Matthews (1979) 91 Cal. App. 3d 1018.
People v. Reid (1984) 475 N.Y.S.2d 741.
State v. Liddell (1984) Mont. 685 P.2d 302.
State v. Marks (1982) Kan. 647 P.2d 1292.
State v. McGee (1982) Minn. 324 N.W.2d 232.
State v. McQuillen (1984) Kan. 689 P.2d 822.
State v. Ogle (1984) 668 S.W.2d 138.
State v. Saldana (1982) Minn. 234 N.W.2d 227.
State v. Taylor (1984) Mo. S.W.2d 235.
State v. Whitman (1984) Ohio 475 N.E.2d 486.
Terrio v. McDonough (1983) 450 N.E.2d 190.
White v. Violent Crimes Compensation Board (1978) A.2d 206.

Index

D

E